MW01274453

The Morphosyntax of Reiteration in Creole
and Non-Creole Languages

Creole Language Library (CLL)

A book series presenting descriptive and theoretical studies designed to add significantly to the data available on pidgin and creole languages.
All CLL publications are anonymously and internationally refereed.

For an overview of all books published in this series, please see
http://benjamins.com/catalog/cll

Editors

Volume 43

The Morphosyntax of Reiteration in Creole and Non-Creole Languages
Edited by Enoch O. Aboh, Norval Smith and Anne Zribi-Hertz

The Morphosyntax of Reiteration in Creole and Non-Creole Languages

Edited by

Enoch O. Aboh
University of Amsterdam

Norval Smith
University of Amsterdam

Anne Zribi-Hertz
University of Paris 8

John Benjamins Publishing Company

Amsterdam / Philadelphia

The paper used in this publication meets the minimum requirements of the American National Standard for Information Sciences – Permanence of Paper for Printed Library Materials, ANSI z39.48-1984.

Library of Congress Cataloging-in-Publication Data

The morphosyntax of reiteration in Creole and non-Creole languages / edited by Enoch O.
        Aboh, Norval Smith, Anne Zribi-Hertz.
    p. cm. (Creole Language Library, ISSN 0920-9026 ; v. 43)
Includes bibliographical references and index.
1. Creole dialects--Morphosyntax. 2. Creole dialects--Morphology. 3. Creole dialects--
        Syntax. 4. Repetition (Rhetoric) I. Aboh, Enoch Oladé. II. Smith, Norval. III.
        Zribi-Hertz, Anne.

PM7831.M67   2012
417'.22--dc23   2012006326
ISBN 978 90 272 5266 1   (Hb ; alk. paper)
ISBN 978 90 272 7455 7   (Eb)

John Benjamins Publishing Co. · P.O. Box 36224 · 1020 ME Amsterdam · The Netherlands
John Benjamins North America · P.O. Box 27519 · Philadelphia PA 19118-0519 · USA

Table of contents

Acknowledgements

This volume grew out of collaboration between researchers of the University of Amsterdam and Université Paris 8 in the context of a Van Gogh project subsidised by The Netherlands Organisation for Scientific Research (NWO) on the Dutch side, and ÉGIDE on the French side. Enoch O. Aboh and Anne Zribi-Hertz coordinated this two-year collaboration, during which members of these research teams joined forces in order to gain a better understanding of the morphosyntax of reiteration in natural languages, with a special focus on creoles. The chapters presented in this volume report on the results of this interaction. The coordinators of this project, and the editors of this volume, would like to thank all of our colleagues for their valuable contributions made during these two years. A special mention needs to be made of our colleague and friend Hans den Besten, who took an active part in the first part of this project but sadly died on the 19th of July 2010, and to whose memory we wish to dedicate this volume. We are grateful to NWO and ÉGIDE for subsidizing this project and to the reviewers for their suggestions. Finally, we would like to thank the editors of the Creole Language Library for their supportive collaboration.

Reduplication beyond the word level

A cross-linguistic view

Enoch O. Aboh,[1] Norval Smith[1] & Anne Zribi-Hertz[2]
[1]University of Amsterdam / [2]UMR SFL, Université Paris-8

1. Introduction

This volume grew out of a two-year collaboration between scholars of the Universities of Amsterdam and Paris-8 in search of a better understanding of the morphosyntax of *reiteration* in natural languages, with a special focus on creoles. The chapters presented in this volume discuss some results of this interaction.

2. From *reduplication* to *reiteration*

Reiteration is meant here as a cover term denoting any situation where the same linguistic form X (segment, syllable, morpheme, word or phrase) occurs (at least) twice within the boundaries of some linguistic constituent or domain. Thus informally defined, reiteration immediately appears to subsume a set of heterogeneous cases commonly attested cross-linguistically and whose analysis may *a priori* involve syntactic emphasis (cf. (1)), or (derivational) morphology (cf. (2)). As these examples show, such reduplicated forms cannot be seen as a marginal phenomenon.

(1) a. [English] He screamed and screamed and screamed, but no one could hear him.

    b. [Gungbe] *Dó-wèzùn, dó-wèzùn, dó-wèzùn, dó-wèzùn bò*
                run-race,   run-race,   run-race,   run-race   and

                yrɔ̀-ɛ̀   *wá*
                call-3sg come

                'run, run, run, run and call him back.'

c.   [Haitian] *Li   kouri, kouri, kouri (,...), li   pa   te   vle   rate*
3SG   run   run   run   3SG NEG ANT want miss

avyon an.[1]
plane DET

'He ran, ran, ran (,...), he didn't want to miss the plane.'

(2) a. [Informal French]
fifille 'little girl, pejorative', *(ma) pupuce* '(my) little pet', *susucre* 'treat',

b. [Hebrew] *lavlav* 'puppy' (vs. *kelev* 'dog'); *shfanfan* 'bunny' (vs. *shafan* 'rabbit'); *zkankan* 'small beard' (vs. *zakan* 'beard'); *metak-tak* 'sweetish' (vs. *matok* 'sweet')

Available linguistic works on reiteration primarily focus on the subset of cases illustrated in (2), which fall under the label *reduplication*. Reduplication is a morphological process by which the root or stem of a word is repeated. This repetition may either be complete or partial.

Reduplication, thus restrictively defined (i.e. at the word level), is attested in an array of typologically diverse natural languages, in particular in creole languages, to which Kouwenberg (2003a) devotes an edited book, and which also occupy a central position in the present volume. The special relevance of reduplication for creole studies is motivated by the somewhat widespread though challenging assumption that this class of phenomena stands as a characteristic creole feature from a typological viewpoint. The reasoning leading to this assumption is sketched out below.

3. **Reduplication and iconicity**

Kouwenberg & LaCharité (2003) argue that two subtypes of reduplication may be distinguished on the basis of *iconicity*: in the wake of Lakoff & Johnson (1980: 128), Kouwenberg & LaCharité (2003: 7) assume that prototypically iconic reduplications are characterised by a form/meaning isomorphy whereby *XX* is construed semantically as 'more (of) X', and that this isomorphy follows from what Sapir (1921: 79) terms "the self-evident symbolism" of reduplication. Reduplications which do not exhibit this form/meaning isomorphy are, contrastively, non-iconic:

---

1. Abbreviations used in the Haitian glosses: ANT = anterior; DET = determiner; NEG = negation; PL = plural; SG = singular; 1, 2, 3 = first, second, third person. [Our thanks to Herby Glaude for the Haitian examples.]

(3) a. **Iconic reduplications (in Caribbean creoles)**
     inga 'thorn'   *inga-inga* 'many thorns'   (Berbice Dutch)
     pipita 'grain' *pipita-pipita* 'many grains'   (Papiamentu)
     saka 'sack'   *saka-saka* 'many sacks'   (Sranan)

     b. **Non-iconic reduplications (in Caribbean creoles)**
     pundi 'to squeeze' *pundi-pundi* 'sugarcane mill' (Berbice Dutch)
     chupa 'to suck'   *chupa-chupa* 'bloodsucker'   (Papiamentu)
     tai 'to tie'   *tai-tai* 'bundle'   (Sranan)
                                    [Kouwenberg & LaCharité 2003:9]

Kouwenberg & LaCharité (2003) argue that reduplications are primarily iconic, and that non-iconic cases are secondary developments of the basic iconic type. Iconic reduplications are assumed to exhibit properties characteristic of inflection: (i) no categorial change involved between X and XX; (ii) regular productivity of XX; (iii) semantic transparency of XX. Contrastively, non-iconic reduplications exhibit properties characteristic of lexical derivation: (i) possible change of category from X to XX; (ii) restricted productivity for XX; (iii) lexical irregularities and idiosyncrasies.

Following Dressler (1968: 56), Kouwenberg & LaCharité (2003) further assume that the basic iconic semantics of reduplication, viz. "more of the same", may result in two types of interpretation: continuous ("increase in magnitude"), or discontinuous ('increase in number'), this distinction accounting for the fact that regular (inflectional) reduplicative forms may trigger two intuitively opposite semantic effects: augmentative (4a), and diminutive (4b):

(4) a. *red-red* 'very red';   *luk-luk* 'keep on looking' (Jamaican)
     b. *redi-redi* 'red-spotted, reddish'; *bigi-bigi* 'biggish' (Jamaican)
                                    [Kouwenberg & LaCharité 2003: 13–14]

Kouwenberg & LaCharité (2003: 8) convincingly argue that from a semantic point of view, the diminutive, augmentative and plural readings associated with reduplication are all subsumed by the general principle: "more of the same form stands for more of the same content". Given this standpoint, the difference between intensifying reduplication (as in 4a) and diminutive reduplication (as in 4b) boils down to the continuous or discontinuous construal of "more of the same". The view that there is a straightforward relation between reduplication and the resulting meanings is further strengthened by the cross-linguistic observation that the same semantic effects – intensification and emphasis, augmentative and diminutive, frequentative, habitual, or progressive aspect, plurality and distributivity – arise crosslinguistically (e.g. Kouwenberg 2003a; Ghomeshi et al. 2004; Hurch 2005).

Due to the usual definition of reduplication, and to the iconicity approach summarised above, most studies on reiteration deal with morphology and argue that the iconic processes involved in word formation may help us understand the more general issue of the relation between form and meaning. Indeed, if we could show that such iconic linguistic mechanisms derive from a basic general human cognitive process operating at the conceptual level, we could also think of the evolution of language in terms of "primitive" structures modelled on iconicity. As the *Homo Sapiens* evolved into modern humans such "primitive" structures must have evolved into more opaque structures, thereby loosening the tight link between form and meaning, and leading to Saussure's 'arbitrariness of the sign'.[2]

4.   Iconicity and creole grammars

If we allow ourselves to entertain this scenario for a minute, we immediately realize that the study of reduplication and its relation to iconicity bears on two related issues:

(5)   i.   Cognitive properties underlying interpretation
       ii.   The roots of language

As regards (5ii), following Bickerton (1984), it has been long established that the study of creole grammars is a crucial source of information on the workings of the human mind, and of human language. On the assumption that human language is biologically determined, Bickerton (1984, 1988, 1999, 2008, 2009), argues that creoles could be regarded as the most transparent expression of the biological human faculty, due to the fact that they have emerged in exceptional situations where children were forced to create full languages on the basis of the "macaronic" pidgins of their parents, which previously served as auxiliary community languages.

Though this last view has been shown to be at best misleading on very many counts (Muysken 1988; Singler 1996; Mufwene 2001; 2003a, b, 2005, 2008; DeGraff 1999; 2001a, b, 2003), a long-standing tacit assumption in creolistics and typology is that creoles, being young languages, necessarily have something "primitive" about their structure. For instance, it is observed that these languages generally mark tense, mood and aspect (TMA) by means of free morphemes occurring in this fixed order (T, M, A) between the subject and the verb. The examples in (6) illustrate this pattern in two creoles having different lexifiers and substrates. Given that this pattern is found in creole after creole, regardless of the lexifier and

---

2.   As we show in the following sections, if this assumption was valid, one might not expect to find such a "primitive" feature still present and functional in so many languages of the world.

substrate languages, the usual conclusion is that the sequencing must stem from something deeper (e.g. the language bioprogram, Bickerton 1984):

(6) a. *Pol pa   ti   pu   pe   pans sa   lor li*   [Mauritian Creole]
         Paul NEG TNS MOD ASP think that on 3.SG
         'Paul would not have been thinking that about him/her.'
                                                    [Guillemin 2009: 46]

     b. *A   ɓi   o   sa   ta   wooko*   [Saramaccan]
         3SG TNS MOD MOD ASP work   [Veenstra 1996: 20]
         'He could have worked.' [lit. 'He could have been able to work.']

While this property is analysed by some scholars as a typical creole feature reveal-ing "transparency" (Bickerton 1984; Bakker and al. 2011), work by typologists such as Hengeveld (1989), and formal syntacticians such as Cinque (1999), has shown that the TMA sequences found in creole languages, are actually common to creoles and older languages, if we were to separate syntax (the respective structural positions of T, M, and A) from morphology (the spelling out of T, M and A as free morphemes or affixes). In other words, the T-M-A sequence represents a universal tendency which has nothing specifically 'creole' about it. The following example is taken from Turkish, an agglutinating language.

(7) *Oku-y-abil-ecek-ti-m*   [Turkish]
     read-y-MOD-FUT-PAST-1SG
     'I was going to be able to read/I would be able to read.'   [Cinque 1999:]

Though the affixes follow the verb in Turkish, they appear in the order V-Mood-Tense, which is just the mirror image of the Tense-Mood-V order found in creoles. Even more to the point, Cinque (1999) shows on the basis of the Mirror Prin-ciple as defined in Baker (1985) that other non-matching surface sequences found cross-linguistically can all be formally derived from a single underlying sequence that roughly follows the general format in (9).

(8) Speech Modality > Epistemic Modality > Tense > Deontic Modality > Aspect > Verb.

Given the findings in these studies, it is difficult to maintain that TMA sequencing in creoles tells us more about the properties of the human language faculty, than does any other linguistic phenomenon (e.g. focus structures and question forma-tion) in any given language (see Mufwene 2001 for discussion).

Another feature that has been long assumed to be particularly frequent in creoles happens to be: "reduplication". Bakker (2003a, b), for instance, argues that while pidgins show few or almost no reduplications, reduplications seem produc-tively attested in all creoles. This would indicate that reduplication is a typological property of creoles. The rationale here is that while pidgins can function with a limited stock of grammatical rules (if any) and lexical items, full languages cannot. In consequence, reduplication emerges in creoles as a simple and fast linguistic tool used by the creole creator to enlarge her vocabulary. As clearly phrased by Kouwenberg (2003b: 2) in her critical evaluation of theories of reduplication and their relation to creoles, the general assumption is that

(9)   Situations of communicative pressure are assumed to give rise to a
        prevalence of 'iconic' strategies of communication. In the situations
        from which Pidgin and Creole languages arose, communicative pressure
        undoubtedly operated. It is taken for granted that reduplication, which is
        often considered an iconic strategy, should therefore be present in these
        languages.

It is however easy to observe that reduplication, even as restrictively defined as above, is quite frequent and productive in non-creole languages, as already hinted at in (2) above. Compare, for example, the case of Philippine languages like Bikol (Mattes 2007). An equally productive and cross-linguistically attested class of cases involving reiterated *words* is illustrated in (10):

(10)   a.   [English] He was **very very** sick.
        b.   [English] I'll make the tuna salad and you make the SALAD salad.[3]

        c.   [Informal French]   *Il*   *a*   *vite*   *vite*   *changé*
                                  3MSG   AUX.PRS.3SG   quick   quick   change.PP

                                  de sujet.
                                  of topic
                                  'He quickly changed topics.'

        d.   [Informal French]   *C'est pas*   *joli*   *joli,*   *ce que*
                                  it-is NEG   pretty   pretty   what

                                  tu   *as*   *fait*   *là.*
                                  2SG   AUX.PRS.2SG   do.PP   LOC

                                  Lit. 'What you have done is not pretty pretty.'
                                  ('What you have done isn't very nice.')

        e.   [Hebrew] *yac'a*   *tmuna*   *yafa*   *yafa.*
                       come.PST.3FSG   picture   pretty   pretty
                       'The picture turned out really pretty.'

        f.   [Haitian] *Li* {*malad* MALAD/ *bèt*   BET/   *gran* GRAN/...}.
                        3SG sick   sick   stupid stupid big   big
                        '{(S)he/it} is really {sick/stupid/big/...}

---

3. (10b) is taken from Ghomeshi et al. (2004).

g.   [Gungbe] *Nú   ɖě   á   bàì má nyɔ́n **kpálí kpálí**
            thing REL 2SG do NEG good at.all at.all
            'What you've done is really, really not nice.'

Since the reiterated items in such examples may stand alone as full words, it is not immediately clear that the XX strings in (10) satisfy the morphological view of reduplication in (4). Should we analyse the XX strings in (10) as a kind of compound filling a single slot in syntactic structure (i.e. as instances of "reduplication"), or can it be argued that each X occupies a separate structural position, and hence calls for a syntactic rather than morphological, analysis, and if so, which one? Whichever way we answer the above question, there is no immediately obvious reason to analyse differently the two reiteration patterns in English (11a) (adapted from Ghomeshi et al. 2004) and in Haitian (11b) (from Harbour 2008):

(11)   a.   Are you LEAVING leaving (or planning to hang around for another hour)?

       b.   *Yo   touye TOUYE Janmari Vinsan.*
            3PL kill   kill   Janmari Vinsan
            'They REALLY KILLED Janmari Vinsan.'

Such data shed doubt both on the assumption that reduplication is a typical feature of creole languages, and on the assumption that linguistically relevant instances of reiteration pertain to morphonology. The term *reiteration* allows us to leave open the issue of whether or not the two identical items form a word in morphology at any stage of the derivation. In this wider perspective, patterns involving nonadjacent identical occurrences of a word or phrase within a syntactic domain – as illustrated in (3) above – may turn out to be significant for a theory of grammar.

5.   Is iconic reiteration iconic?

A relevant example is provided by Maori, an isolating Polynesian language of New Zealand (Bauer 1993). Maori is a predicate-first language where the verb and its TMA markers precede the subject and other arguments or adjuncts in the clause (17).[4]

---

4.   Abbreviations used in the Maori glosses: TMA: Tense, Mood, Aspect marker; DET.P: Personal Determiner; DET.APH: Anaphoric determiner; PROX.S: Near Speaker.

(12) *Ka   karanga atu   a   Hinemoa, ki taua   taurekareka nei*
      TMA   call   away DET.P Hinemoa, to DET.APH slave   PROX.S

      anoo he reo   tane
      as   a   voice man

      'Hinemoa called out to this slave in a man's voice.'

Like many isolating languages, Maori displays various instances of reiteration of lexical items (e.g. adjectives, adverbs, verbs), some of which are unpredictable both in terms of the words they target and the semantic effects they trigger. A case in point is iterative aspect. Bauer (1993: 452) indicates that there is no specialised marker of iterative aspect in Maori. Instead the language often resorts to reiteration; "however it cannot be predicted which verbs will have reduplicated forms in this context." The example in (13a), for instance, is introduced by the TMA maker *i*, which precedes the non-reiterated verb *tihewa* 'sneeze'. In (13b) on the other hand, the verb *mare* 'cough' is reiterated to encode iterative aspect.

(13) a. *I   tihewa ia   i   te   poo   roa nei*
          TMA sneeze 3SG at DET   night long PROX.S
          'She sneezed all night long.'

      b. *Ka   mare-mare   tonu ia*
          TMA   cough-cough still 3SG
          'He coughed many times.'

Interestingly, however, Bauer (1993: 452) reports that reiteration of the verb 'to sneeze' as in (14) "has the sense of periodic sneezes."

(14) *E   tihewa-hewa   ana ia   i   te   poo   roa nei*
      TMA sneeze-sneeze TMA 3SG at DET   night long PROX.S
      'She sneezed off and on all night.'

According to the translations provided, the sentence in (14) implies less sneezing than there is coughing in (13b). In other words, (14) triggers a diminutive distributive reading, while (13b) triggers an augmentative distributive reading. Assuming this characterization to be accurate, we obtain a paradox: Verb reiteration triggers two opposite semantic effects, both of which can be analysed individually as iconic. However, since these cases of reiteration are available in the same language, and with the same syntactic category, it seems to us unlikely that children would acquire these forms simply led by a general principle of iconicity whereby "more of the same form entails more of the same content." Instead, the semantic effects arising from these different reiterated verb roots must be determined by precise lexical, semantic or syntactic factors (whose nature still needs to be investigated).

In addition, in many languages for instance, functional or lexical categories come to be reiterated in certain contexts only, with often non-iconic resulting readings. (see Section 7).

Finally, if we consider reiteration beyond the word level, we immediately realise that the attested forms are very often NOT iconic. In addition, this type of reiteration has various motivations which obviouly have nothing to do with any human need to create new lexical items. Such non-iconic reiterations are found in creoles as well, but let us consider in Section 6 a small set of typologically unrelated languages which display similar patterns.

6.   Non-iconic reiteration

Kouwenberg & LaCharité (2003: 9) suggest that non-iconic

> "reduplication effects a change in the syntactic category, immediately affecting meaning in a way that is beyond the scope of the iconic principle that "more of the same form stands for more of the same content."

Mina, also referred to as Hina in the literature, is a Chadic language spoken in the Western and Northern Cameroon (Frajzyngier, Johnson, Edwards 2005). Mina can be considered an SVO language because the subject precedes the predicate in 'neutral' contexts as in (15).

(15) *íl   zék   yàw.*[5]   (Frajzyngier, Johnson & Edwards 2005: 194)
      3PL   make   competition
      'They had a competition.'

Mina displays various instances of reiterations that appear non-iconic. As Frajzyngier, Johnson & Edwards (2005: 74) indicate, the language also possesses constructions such as the examples in (16), where the reiterated verb occurs in a reduced relative clause to encode a (resultative) state (see Aboh & Smith this volume for discussion).

(16) a. *hídə̀   mə̀   gàr-gàr*   (Frajzyngier, Johnson, Edwards 2005: 74/75)
          man   REL   stand-stand
          'A standing man.'

      b. *ə̀   mə̀   fàt-fàt*
          cow   REL   slaughter-slaughter
          'A slaughtered cow.'

---

5.   Abbreviations used in the Mina glosses: assc: associative marker; INF: infinitive; PL: plural; PREP: preposition; PTCL: particle; REL: relative marker;

Aboh & Smith (this volume) present ample justification that similar strictly adjacent reiterations in the Gbe languages and the Surinam creoles spell out reduced relative clauses where reiteration is triggered by some syntactic constraints on the formation of past participles and adjectives. What Mina shows is that the phenomenon is attested beyond Kwa and related Atlantic creoles. In all these cases, there does not seem to be any iconic relation between form (reiteration) and the resulting meaning. Here, "more of the same form" in no way triggers "more of the same content". Indeed, the noun phrase pointing to a slaughtered cow equally denotes the same dead bovine by means of the reiterated lexeme in Mina and by the past participle in English.

Mina also displays another instance of non-iconic reiteration which serves to express past tense.[6] While this language licenses zero-TMA clauses, it also has various strategies for marking tense, mood, and aspect. More specifically, Mina displays two parallel patterns referred to as "dependent" and "independent" forms.[7] For instance, the example in (17a) instantiates the dependent future. Here, the sentence involves an infinitive marker which suggests that the verb belongs to a non-finite clause. On the other hand, sentence (17b) illustrates the independent future. The sentence requires the occurrence of a postverbal particle (Frajzyngier, Johnson & Edwards 2005: 180/181):

(17) a. *hí   n   kɔ́   nd-á   bɔ̀   tskòh*   [Dependent future]
         2PL   PREP INF   go-GO   ASSC   afternoon
         'You will come in the afternoon.'

      b. *dáwày nd-á   zɔ̀   bàká   bɔ̀   tskòh*   [Independent future]
         Daway   go-GO   PTCL   today   ASSC   afternoon
         'Daway will come this afternoon.'

A similar asymmetry is found in the past tense. The example in (18) illustrates the dependent past. We observe here that the pattern is similar to that in (17a), since the verb is preceded by the infinitive marker *kɔ́* (Frajzyngier, Johnson & Edwards 2005: 194/195):

(18) *háá nók   kɔ́   dzán-á   nók   ʝì   zá*   [Dependent past tense]
      yes 1PL   INF   find-GO   1PL   meat   PTCL
      'Yes we found the meat for ourselves.'

---

6. The language displays various tense and aspect paradigms, as well as verb forms that are not relevant for the ongoing discussion. The reader is referred to Frajzyngier, Johnson & Edwards (2005) for further details.

7. This corresponds to the well-known distinction drawn between *disjoint* and *conjoint* forms in the Bantu literature.

The following example of independent past is interesting because it requires that the verb root (ɟán) be reiterated, with one token preceding the subject and the other one following it:[8]

(19) ɟán   í   ɟán   zá   [Independent past tense]
      cross 3PL cross PTCL
      'They crossed [the river].'

Interestingly enough, while the verb root preceding the subject may support the goal marker á, the one following the subject may not:

(20) dá   dá   á   ɗɔ̀   ˌwane
      draw:go draw:go 3SG draw a lot
      'It rained a lot.'

What this last example further indicates is that the verb root occurring on the left of the subject can itself reiterate. As the translation also shows, this reiteration triggers an interpretive effect glossed by the authors as *past plural*, which signals the event as distributed over space and/or time.

The descriptive generalisation emerging from the data is that the expression of past eventualities in Mina requires reiteration of the verb root in terms of the pattern represented in (21a), and that this structure further allows reiteration of the leftmost verb root in an "iconic" fashion, as illustrated in (21b):

(21) a. V.........subject.....V → single event in the past
      b. V....V....subject.....V → reiterated event in the past

If this description is correct, we can see that the "iconic" reiteration in (21b) feeds on the non-iconic process expressing past tense in (21a). Given this finding, one wonders whether the same might be true of the following example from São Tomense which leads Parkvall (2003: 20) to assume that "the most iconic verb reduplication must certainly be one that indicates the repeated or continuous carrying out of an action":

(22) e   pɛga-pɛga   pifi   São Tomense, Parkvall (2003: 20)
      3SG catch-catch fish
      'He used to catch fish regularly.'

Assuming our description of (21) to be correct, this São Tomense example might not represent a prototypical case of "iconic reduplication". Could it be the case that reiteration primarily serves to formally license aspect (just as it licenses

---

8. The authors further show that the verbs occur with their underlying tones.

past tense in Mina)?[9] Under this line of thinking, the resulting meaning in (22) might be determined at the interface. This would mean that there is no direct (or "iconic") relation between reiteration and interpretation in (22), just as there is none between reiteration and interpretation in (16) and (17). The crucial point here is that from the learner's perspective the structure in (22) does not seem any more "transparent" than the ones in (17) or (16).[10]

I do not agree

Given this discussion, one wonders whether, apart from the examples in (2) where reiteration may be handled in morphology, many of the reiterated forms assumed to be iconic are not actually the result of certain syntactic operations. That this might be the right approach is further suggested by the reiteration of functional items.

7.   Reiteration of functional items

Parkvall (2003: 27) argues that "reduplication of grammatical morphemes is surprisingly rare, both in Creoles and Non-Creoles [...] The only Non-Creole language known to me which supports a similar phenomenon is Gorontalo (Austronesian), which reduplicates its imperative marker for emphatic purposes." This claim would support a restrictive view of "reduplication" as a word-formation process motivated by iconicity: Functional categories form closed classes by definition, therefore cannot be semantically scalar and should not be available for iconic reduplication triggering "more-of-the-same" effects. Under the broader perspective of reiteration explored here, it however turns out that reiteration of functional items is not that rare.

---

9.   Another language that has been reported in the literature to display verb reduplication as expression of tense-aspect is Kabye, a Gur language spoken in Togo (see Collins & Assizewa 2007).

10.   Emmanuel Schang (p.c. 16-06-2011) reported to us that none of his consultants accepted Parkvall's example in (22). Instead, they provide examples where the whole verb phrase seems to have been reduplicated:

(i)   e   *pixka   pixi-pixka   pixi*
       3SG   to.fish   fish-to.fish   fish
       'He used to catch fish regularly.'

This example, it seems to us, clearly points to the fact that iconicity cannot be the right explanation. Indeed, there appears to be no direct mapping between the reduplicated VP and the "used to perform X regularly" meaning that is assigned to the construction.

In Latin, there is a series of question words, whose most obvious feature is that they all begin with <u>qu</u> (or developments of this). Reduplication of this (i.e. reiteration within the word) will produce concessive pronouns or adverbs, e.g.

(23)

Question word		Concessive word	
quis	'who? (NOM.M)'	quisquis	'who(so)ever (NOM.M)'
quid	'what? (NOM/ACC.N)'	quidquid	'what(so)ever (NOM/ACC.N)'
quem	'who? (ACC.M)'	quemquem	'whom(so)ever (ACC.M)'
quantus	'how much? (NOM.M)'	quantusquantus[11]	'however much (NOM.M)'
quot	'how many?'	quotquot	'however many'
quam	'how?'	quamquam	'however'

Similarly, one finds reiteration of the auxiliary verbs in French. The French TMA paradigm regularly distinguishes so-called *temps simples* ("simple tenses"), where TMA and person-number agreement attach to the verb root in morphology, and *temps composés* ("composed tenses"), where TM-agr inflection attaches to a designated auxiliary verb (*avoir* 'have' standing as the unmarked auxiliary). This distinction obtains for every TM-agr specification, as illustrated by the sample in (23), and the primary interpretive effect of auxiliation may roughly be characterised as anteriority or completion: when the auxiliary occurs, the eventuality must be construed as completed before a certain Reference Time. The occurrence of the auxiliary is thus the French instantiation of the "A" (Aspect) category in the TMA acronym:

(24) Nonauxiliated and auxiliated verb forms in French

TM-agr specifications	nonauxiliated	auxiliated
(a) present, 3SG	Marie **dort**. 'Marie sleeps/is sleeping.'	Marie **a dormi**. 'Marie (has) slept.'
(b) imperfect, 3SG	Marie **dormait**. 'Marie used to sleep/was sleeping.'	Marie **avait dormi**. 'Marie had slept.'

(Continued)

---

11.   Note however that inflections do not normally occur in the middle of words, although the behaviour of reduplicated *functional items* has not been studied as far as we know.

(c) future, 3SG	Marie **dormira**. 'Marie will sleep.'	Marie **aura dormi**. 'Marie will have slept.'
(d) simple past, 3SG (literary)	Marie **dormit**. 'Marie slept.'	Quand Marie **eut dormi**,. 'Once Marie had slept,...'
(e) conditional, 3SG	(Si elle pouvait) Marie **dormirait**. '(If it were possible) Marie would sleep.'	(Si elle avait pu) Marie **aurait dormi**. '(If it had been possible) Marie would have slept.'
(f) subjunctive, 3SG	avant que Marie **dorme** 'before Marie sleeps'	avant que Marie **ait dormi** 'before Marie has finished sleeping'

The case in point for the present discussion is that the semantic effect of simplex auxiliation appears blurred in some contexts, in which case auxiliation may be reiterated to trigger the intended completion effect. Reiteration of auxiliation results in what French grammarians call the *temps surcomposés*. Three illustrative minimal pairs are given in (24), contrasting simplex auxiliation with reiterated auxiliation:

(25)   Simple vs. reiterated auxiliation in French

TM-agr specifications	simple auxiliation	reiterated auxiliation
(a) present, 3SG	Quand il m'**a quitté**, j'ai réfléchi que... 'When he left me, I told myself that...' (event completed at T0)	Quand il m'**a eu quitté**, j'ai réfléchi que... [J. Green quoted by Grevisse 1991: 1228] 'Once he had left me, I told myself that...' (event completed at RT anterior to T0)
(b) imperfect, 3SG	Si on lui **avait présenté** un autre prisonnier, il s'en serait aperçu. 'If they had shown him another prisoner, he would have noticed it.' (ambiguous: modality evaluation time at T0 or anterior to T0)	Si on lui **avait eu présenté** un autre prisonnier, il s'en serait aperçu. [M. Garçon quoted by Grevisse 1991: 1297] (nonambiguous: modality evaluation time anterior to T0)

(c) conditional, 3SG	En cas d'alerte, chacun **aurait** vite **fait** de retrouver son bien. 'In case of an alert, everyone would quickly figure out which is whose.' (modality evaluation time at T0)	En cas d'alerte, chacun **aurait eu** vite **fait** de retrouver son bien. [R. Bazin quoted by Grevisse 1991: 1229] 'In case of an alert, everyone would have quickly figured out which was whose.' (ambiguous: modality evaluation time anterior to T0; or modality evaluation time at T0 but event completed at ModT)

It is quite clear that reiterated auxiliaries (e.g. *a eu* in (24a)) cannot be analysed as sequences of lexical words, for the same reason that ⟨auxiliary+V⟩ strings (e.g. *a dormi* in (23a)) cannot be analysed as sequences of lexical words: Auxiliaries and lexical verb roots behave differently with respect to inflection (auxiliaries raise up to mood and tense while verb roots stay behind and are inflected for the past participle), they each contribute separately to interpretation, and the fact that auxiliaries can themselves be auxiliated is further evidence that they are identified as verbal entities of their own. When auxiliation is reiterated, the auxiliated auxiliary and the lexical verb are both inflected for the past participle:

(26) *quand   il   m'   a   eu   quitté...*   [= (24a)]
      when   3MSG.NOM 1SG.ACC AUX.PRS.3SG AUX.PP leave.PP
      Lit. 'When he had had left me...'
      ('Once he had left me...')

Another example of functional reiteration is that of the discourse marker *là* in Québécois French, as described by Dostie (2007). As in European French, this element may express various notions including spatial deixis (26a), anaphoric deixis (26b) (here *là* refers to a place that both the speaker and the hearer know about, and that the speaker is referring back to), and temporal deixis (26c):

(27) a. *Gare-toi   là.*
          park=2SG   there
          'Park (over) there.'

      b. *C'est   là   qu'on   va.*
          it.is   there   that-1PL go
          'That's where we are going.'

    c.   *Il*   *m'a*   *regardé,*
        3SG   1SG =AUX.PRS.3SG look-at.PP

        c'est ***là***   *que* *je* *me* *suis*   *fâché.*
        it.is then   that 1SG REFL AUX.PRS.1SG annoyed

        'He looked at me, that's when I got annoyed.'

                                                        [adapted from Dostie 2007]

However, Dostie (2007: 53, 54) shows that *là* can also function as a discourse marker where she claims it expresses "saliency". In the lack of a larger discourse context, its discourse motivation and precise semantic effect is pretty much untranslatable, so we merely gloss it as LA in our English translations. In such uses, *là* can occur either sentence-initially, as in (27a), or sentence-finally, as in (27b):

(28) a. *Les* *cousins,*   *les* *p'tits cousins*   *pis* *toute* *l'affaire.*
         the first.cousins, the second.cousins and all   the rest

         Là, *on*   *s'réunissait* *toute* *chez*   *celui*   *qui*
         LA   1PL gather.PST all   at-the-place-of the-one who

         s'était   *pas* *l'vé.*
         REFL.AUX.PST NEG rise.PP

         'The first cousins, the second cousins, and so on. LA we would all gather at the place of whoever hadn't got up.'

    b. *On* *allait* *se*   *faire* *des*   *espèces* *de camps*   *dans* *le*
         we go.IPF REFL make IND.PL sort.PL of camp.PL in   the

         champ ***là,*** *dans* *les* *arbres* *pis toute* *ça* ***là,*** *parce*   *qu'il y*
         field LA in   the trees and-all-that LA because there

         avait   *des*   *arbres, c'était le* *bois, plus* *loin.*
         have.IPF.3SG IND.PL trees it   was the   wood further

         'We used to go and build sorts of camps in the field LA, among the trees and all that LA, for there were trees, there was a wood out there.'

In this usage, *là* can be reiterated, as indicated by the following examples (Dostie 2007: 56, 57):

(29) a. *Je* *repasse*   *la*   *vadrouille, je* *secoue*   *les*   *tapis.*
         1SG use.again.PRS DF.FSG mop   1SG shake.PRS DF.PL rugs

         J'époussette *de nouveau* *et* *puis, c'est* *ça, ensuite* *là,*
         1SG-dust.PRS again   and then that's it   then   LA

         ben... ***Là là*** *des fois,* *j'ai*   *une chance*   *de tailler,*
         well LA LA sometimes 1SG have.PRS an opportunity of cutting

         de coudre, de prendre ma couture, pis *mon raccommodage*
         of sewing of taking my sewing and my   mending

> est   pas mal fait.
> BE.PRS.3SG NEG badly do.PP
>
> 'I mop the place a second time, I shake the rugs, I dust everything once over, that's it, then LA, well... LA LA sometimes I get a chance to cut, sew, take on my sewing, and my mending is pretty well done.'

  b. *J'aime   les   films   qui... divertissants, des   comédies*
      1SG like DF.PL movies that... amusing   IND.PL comedies

    par exemple. Pas   des   choses que ça se   bat   là...
    for instance NEG IND.PL things that it   REFL fight.PRS.3SG LA...

    tout le   temps des   canons... moi j'aime   pas ça. J'aime de
    all the time IND.PL cannons   1SG 1SG-like NEG that 1SG- like

    quoi de divertissant là là.
    stuff   amusing   LA LA

> 'I like movies which are....amusing movies, comedies for instance. Not things with a lot of fighting LA...cannons all the time... Me, I don't like that. I like amusing stuff LA LA.'

Dostie (2007:57) describes this reiterated discourse marker as fulfilling two pragmatic functions:

– On the one hand, it encodes a speech act modality of insistence (e.g. I insist that .....) that is to some extent comparable to deontic modality;
– On the other hand the use of the reiterated **là** seems to entail a stronger presupposition than its non-reiterated counterpart.[12]

Under this account, Dostie (2007) is led to admit that such reiteration of functional items cannot be fitted into the iconic theory whereby more of the same form entails more of the same content. Since functional items do not have gradable semantic contents, their reiteration cannot be accounted for in terms of iconicity. We may further add that it seems very doubtful that the reiterated *là là* strings in (29) should be analysable as lexical words. As hinted by the Québécois

---

12. Dostie (2007:57) – d'une part, le locuteur accomplirait un acte illocutoire d'insistance (cf. la paraphrase « j'insiste sur […] X » ; cf. aussi Vanderveken 1988 : 170 qui inclut *insister* parmi la liste des verbes illocutoires du français). Cet acte illocutoire serait comparable à une forme de surenchère verbale venant du fait que le mot X ne serait pas simplement dit, il serait *redit*;

– d'autre part, le locuteur exprimerait une implication plus marquée par rapport à son dire que s'il avait utilisé la forme non rédupliquée. C'est pourquoi ce type de réduplication pourrait être décrit comme servant à accomplir un acte illocutoire modal, axé sur l'engagement et l'implication.

French examples above, reiteration of the discourse marker LA does not affect the meaning of the discourse marker itself, but rather that of the entire clause which contains it. According to Dostie (2007) the reiteration of *là* is motivated by pragmatics. However, under an alternative approach deriving various pragmatic effects from the syntax of the clause periphery (Rizzi 1997), it would be possible to place là in a functional (e.g. 'modality') projection whose recursive occurrence within the complementizer system (CP) would account for là's which contains it.

One can think of various syntactic analyses to account for these cases, but what matters for our present discussion is that reiteration in these examples, as in various others discussed above, does not pertain to word-based morphology, and falls out of the range of iconicity.

A possible analysis of the examples in (29) would be to classify them as non-iconic, that is, as exceptional cases where the iconicity principle breaks down either because reiteration leads to non-transparent semantics or because it follows from some independent syntactic requirement.

Of course, we also encounter cases where functional morphemes can be reiterated within words, apparently with iconic effect, but indeed the effect may only be apparent. So, for instance in Latin it is possible to repeat the diminutive suffix, with a sense of further diminution. Cf. the forms in (30):

(30)   **The Latin diminutive**

kist-a		*cista*	'chest (NOM.F)'
kist-l-a	kist-ul-a[13]	*cistula*	'little chest (NOM.F)'
kist-l-l-a	kist-el-l-a	*cistella*	'casket (NOM.F)'
kist-l-l-l-a	kist-el-l-ul-a	*cistellula*	'little casket (NOM.F)'

One problem with this case is that the diminutive suffixes are definitely not in the same constituent as might be the case in supra-word iterations. So *cistellula* clearly has a nested structure:

(31)   *cistellula*   [[[[[kist]-DIM]-DIM]-DIM]-DECL1.NOM]

In other words, the first instance of *DIM* modifies *kist*. And the second instance of *DIM* modifies *kist]-dim*, while the third instance of *DIM* modifies *kist]-dim]-dim*. In fact, unlike the case of *quantusquantus* illustrated in (23), we have no reiteration as all, strictly speaking. Despite this fact, other languages allowing successive diminutive suffixes, like Ancient Greek, avoid phonologically identical sequences of diminutive suffixes by utilizing phonologically different allomorphs such as *-isk-*, *-i-*, and *-id-*, etc.

---

13.   The vowels marked in bold are the result of regular phonological processes in Latin.

One may wonder whether it would be inconceivable to take a radically different perspective assuming that so-called non-iconic or irregular reiterations are the rule, while the "iconic" ones are the exception. Indeed, the above discussion indicates that reiteration may apply to both lexical and functional categories, with no straightforward relation between the reiterated form and the resulting meaning. This suggests that reiteration, as a formal property, and iconicity, should be dissociated. This amounts to saying that there should be no tight relation between the formal operation of reiteration, and the iconic or non-iconic meaning that is assigned to the form it creates.

8. Reiteration and creole languages

As regards the alleged "creole-type", the view that creoles display *more* instances of reiteration than non-creole languages could be simply misguided, as hinted by the examples in (1)–(2) above, which show that reiteration is productively attested in non-creole languages. But even if it should turn out to be statistically true that reiterations were more *frequent* in all creole languages than in all non-creole languages, this result would need to be submitted to careful scrutiny. In the first place, supposing that an attested discourse in Gungbe (Kwa), Mandarin Chinese, Maori (Polynesian), Mina (Chadic), Saramaccan (Anglo-Portuguese-lexifier creole), Hebrew (semitic), Korean (unclassified), or Haitian (French-lexifier creole) could be shown to display a greater total number of reiterations than a similar attested discourse in English or French, we should first have to specify which types of reiteration are more frequent in each language, and in what kinds of stylistic contexts. For instance, statistical results comparing Haitian and Standard French are likely to reveal a greater frequency of reiteration in Haitian, but this result would be non-significant since it would ignore Colloquial French, where reiteration is quite common. We should also avoid cross-linguistic statistical comparisons bearing on completely different patterns. Should we compare Haitian and Colloquial French, for instance, we would find that morphological reduplication, as illustrated in (2), is equally productive in both languages for nicknames (cf. (32a,b)), and is otherwise productive in French (32c) but NOT in the creole; that the patterns illustrated in Haitian (33) are unattested in French; and that the pattern instantiated in Haitian (10f) (repeated under (34a)), is also productive in French (cf. (10d)/(34b)) :

(32)   a.   [Colloquial French]
             Dédé (André), *Loulou* (Louis), *Nini* (Nicole, Mélanie), *Popol* (Paul)...

       b.   [Haitian]
             Bibi (Herby), *Dodo* (Dorismond), *Dodonne* (Dieudonne), *Liline*
             (Wisline), *Nono* (Norès)...

c.   [Colloquial French]
     Nouns: *bobo* 'bourgeois bohême', *dada* 'hobby', *cocotte* 'chick(en)', *doudoune* 'feather-stuffed parka', *fifille* 'little girl, pejor.', *lolo* 'milk', *nounou* 'nanny'...
     Adjectives: *baba* 'amazed', *bébête* 'silly', *concon* 'silly', *cucul* 'silly', *fofolle* 'excentric', *fut-fut* 'smart', *jojo* 'pretty', *mimi* 'nice', *noeud-noeud, nunuche* 'silly', *zinzin* 'crazy'...

(33) a.   [Haitian]   *Pyè pote moun* BON *pote.*
                       Pyè carry people good carry
                       'Peter carried people for GOOD.'

      b.   [Haitian]   *Se* MALAD *Djo malad.*
                       it-is sick   Djo sick
                       'Djo is REALLY sick.'

(34) a.   [Haitian]   *Li {malad* MALAD/ *bèt* BET/ *gran* GRAN/...}.
                       3SG sick sick   stupid stupid/ big big
                       '{(S)he/it} is REALLY {sick/stupid/big/...}'

      b.   [Colloquial French]   *C'est pas joli, joli,   ce que*
                                  it-is NEG pretty pretty what

                                 tu   as   fait là.
                                 2SG AUX.PRS.2SG do.PP LOC

                                 Lit. 'What you have done is not pretty pretty.'
                                 ('What you have done isn't very nice.')

Cross-linguistic contrasts should further be correlated with other properties of the compared languages. For instance, we do not expect verb roots to be reiterable, as in Haitian (33a), in languages whose verb roots always support some kind of inflection (e.g. French); we expect available patterns of word-internal reiteration (cf. (2), (32)) to be crucially sensitive to such properties as word stress and morphological structure (templatic, inflectional, isolating, agglutinative); and we expect "syntactic" reiterations as illustrated in (33) and various other examples discussed above in Sections 5 and 6 to be sensitive to various general morphosyntactic properties including word order, Case, TMA, topic and focus marking – a nonexhaustive list.

We therefore conclude that further study of reiteration patterns beyond the word level and beyond creole languages is necessary to:

–   Understand the morphosyntactic properties underlying reiteration patterns and their status with respect to the human language capacity.
–   Understand how language contact may have led certain reiteration patterns to emerge or restructure in creole grammars.

9. The book

Several studies have already been conducted on *reduplication* in individual creoles, including the very comprehensive volume edited by Kouwenberg (2003a) on reduplication across creoles. Because reduplication is conceived as a morphological process whose main function is creating new lexical entries, these studies exclusively focus on the morphological, phonological and semantic properties involved in word-level reiteration (viz. reduplication). To the best of our knowledge, no comparative study has yet been conducted on reiteration from a cross-linguistic perspective encompassing creole and non-creole languages, and viewing reiteration beyond the word level, from the viewpoint of morphosyntax as a whole. This book offers both perspectives.

Enoch O. Aboh and Norval Smith discuss non-iconic reduplication in Eastern Gbe languages (viz., Fongbe and Gungbe) and Surinam creoles (viz., Sranan and Saramaccan). This chapter shows that in the Surinam creoles as well as in the Gbe languages, such non-iconic reduplication patterns relate to changes in meaning that often vary from process/event to state/result. While there does not seem to be any direct relation between such developments and iconicity, the authors demonstrate that reduplication in these contexts is conditioned syntactically to derive verbal nouns (or gerunds) and (verbal) adjectives. In addition, it is shown that the development of these non-iconic reduplications in the Surinam creoles derives partially from substrate influence from Eastern Gbe, while showing some properties of gerunds and past participles in English. Under this view therefore, reduplication, far from being a fast and cheap morphological operation available to an emergent creole deriving from a pidgin, represents a constrained morphosyntactic process that has consequences for issues of language contact and language transfer in general.

Herby Glaude and Anne Zribi-Hertz study a group of clausal constructions designated as *Verb Fronting with Doubling* (VFD), which exist in Haitian and other Caribbean French-lexifier creoles, have no counterparts in French, but do have counterparts in Gbe. VFD constructions are characterised in both Gbe and Haitian by the occurrence of a bare homonym of the verb root in the clause periphery, this resulting in a verb-reiteration pattern which regularly correlates with a verb-focus semantic effect. These constructions include in Haitian – but do not boil down to – the *Predicate Cleft* construction, to which a number of works have been devoted. The goal of Glaude & Zribi-Hertz's article is to present an updated description of VFD constructions in Haitian, to assess previous theories (most of which focus on Predicate Cleft), and to reach a satisfactory analysis that sheds light on the reiteration and verb-focus effects. On the basis of their synchronic description of Haitian, and of Haitian/Gbe/French comparison, the authors suggest that the development of Haitian VFD constructions may have arisen from a combination of contrastive verb reiteration (available in French and crosslinguistically), focus raising (a Gbe feature), and (in the subcase of Predicate Cleft) clefting (a French feature). They further show that the intensive (or emphatic) meaning that arises in such constructions results from restrictive modification rather than iconicity. As such this paper provides yet another argument that reduplication in creoles may have different sources, many of which involve very complex morphosyntactic processes.

Mélanie Jouitteau discusses verb doubling in Breton. In this language, tensed verbs display a synthetic versus analytic structure alternation, which appears to be regulated by syntactic conditions. One such constraint is that a tensed (verbal) element cannot occur in sentence-initial position. The language satisfies this constraint in various ways, including insertion of a pleonastic verbal element in a way comparable to expletive insertion. While in the most common cases, a non-finite verb is inserted in sentence-initial position, followed by a tensed auxiliary clause-internally, Breton also displays constructions where the non-finite verb reappears in its own inflected form clause-internally. This makes Breton similar to other languages (e.g. Gungbe, Haitian, Mina) where the predicate can repeat with various semantic effects. In accounting for this pattern in Breton, Jouitteau argues that it represents a last-resort strategy similar to expletive insertion. In this case, however, it is the verb root that is excorporated out of the complex tensed head and re-merged in the left periphery. The excorporated lexical verb appears fronted as an infinitive form by default, while the tensed part is either realised by a pleonastic auxiliary or, for an idiosyncratic list of verbs, by reiteration of the root. The proposed analysis is then extended to Gungbe where one also observes instances of verb doubling which appear to be strictly conditioned by syntax as discussed in Aboh and Smith (this volume). In a way similar to Glaude & Zribi-Hertz and Aboh & Smith, this paper concludes that the doubling or reiteration process in Breton cannot be understood in terms of iconicity given that the verb doubles once the sentence is fully computed. It is important, however, to emphasize that Jouitteau's conclusions call for future detailed work, because she argues that reduplication in Breton is a last resort post-syntactic phenomenon whose main function is to avoid ungrammaticality. As such the process does not come with any pre-identified meaning (e.g. emphasis, distributive), though such meanings may arise in certain contexts. According to this characterization, reduplication or reiteration can fall into three classes: Word-level reduplication (which may be iconic), morphosyntactic reduplication (which is typically not iconic), and post-syntactic reduplication which cannot be iconic, inasmuch as it only guarantees the well-formedness of sentences.

Dana Cohen studies noun reiteration (*noun-doubling*) patterns in Modern Hebrew. Two major uses can be distinguished: Contrastive and pluralising. Pluralising noun-doubling is shown to come in three distinct patterns. The paper examines the properties and function of these patterns, and their interaction with the number and mass/count distinctions. Singular noun-doubling is shown to modify dynamic events, and signal a plurality of sub-events; plural noun-doubling is shown to modify states, and signal the existence of multiple sub-components of a property; predicated noun-doubling (where the reduplicated noun is further modified or predicated) modifies a collective/mass participant of an event, and marks a distinguishing property among sub-components of this participant. With regard to the structure of such reiteration nominal constructions, Cohen shows that they all result from the insertion of the same lexical element twice in a given structure. As is often the case, such double merges may lead to various meanings, some of which might appear iconic. Still, Cohen shows that an analysis in terms of iconicity fails to capture all the interpretive properties of these forms.

Fabiola Henri discusses verb reiteration in Mauritian, focusing on one of its subtypes which she calls *attenuative reduplication* since it triggers an "attenuative" semantic effect and is shown to exhibit the characteristic features of derivational processes – and hence may be analysed as pertaining to morphology. While attenuative reduplication is found in various languages (e.g. Mandarin Chinese, Malagasy), this paper uses empirical evidence to demonstrate that verb reduplication, in Mauritian, is neither necessarily iconic nor necessarily pluractional. The author describes the various interpretations available for V-V strings and shows that the reading selected for each reduplicated V crucially depends on the aspectual properties of the predicate. She proposes an analysis couched within a constraint-based grammar, which may be extended to other types of reduplicated lexical roots in Mauritian and other languages.

Emmanuel Schang discusses lexical reiteration in São Tomense, a Portuguese-based creole spoken on the São Tomé, Island off the West-African coast in the Gulf of Guinea. Similarly to Cohen (this volume), this chapter shows that no specific morphosyntax is needed to account for the reiteration patterns attested in São Tomense. Instead, lexical reiteration results from the external merge of the same lexical item in two structural slots available in independently-motivated syntactic structures: The modification structure and the coordination structure.

Kofi Yakpo studies Pichi, an Afro-Caribbean English-lexifier creole spoken on the island of Bioko, Equatorial Guinea, also in the Gulf of Guinea, a language which features four distinct types of iteration. Amongst them, reduplication and repetition can be distinguished on formal and semantic grounds. Reduplication is a derivational process restricted to dynamic verbs that yields iterative, dispersive and attenuative meanings. Repetition occurs with members of all major word classes, renders more iconic meanings and is analysed as semi-morphological in nature. A comparison with verbal iteration in a cross-section of West African languages and two of its sister languages in the Caribbean allows for the preliminary conclusion that Pichi reduplication reflects an areally prominent pattern. By looking at reduplication from this areal perspective Yakpo demonstrates that the phenomenon is widely represented in West African languages, a fact that could have favoured the emergence of reduplicated patterns in the Atlantic creoles (see also Aboh & Smith this volume). Accordingly, the author concludes that reduplication in Pichi is neither "exceptionally iconic nor specifically 'creole' in nature."

We close with a short word on our friend and colleague, **Hans den Besten**, who died in the summer of 2010. Hans was a leading and widely-respected researcher in the field of theoretical linguistics. Among his most influential works were his contributions on Wh-movement, and word order in main and subordinate clauses in the Germanic languages. He also wrote extensively on contact linguistics, in particular on the formation of Afrikaans, as well as on Yiddish, Negerhollands and Bargoens. In the field of contact linguistics he studied reduplication in Afrikaans (Den Besten, Luijks & Roberge 2003), and thus participated in the series of workshops leading to this volume. He was a friendly and likeable man, who remained surprisingly cheerful under the Parkinson's Disease that made him progressively less mobile as time passed.

References

Baker, Mark. 1985. The mirror principle and morphosyntactic explanation. *Linguistic Inquiry* 16: 373–415.

Bakker, Peter. 2003a. The absence of reduplication in Pidgins. In *Twice as Meaningful. Reduplication in Pidgins, Creoles and Other Contact Languages* [Westminster Creolistic Series 8], Silvia Kouwenberg (ed.), 37–46. London: Battlebridge.

Bakker, Peter. 2003b. Pidgin inflectional morphology and its implications for creole morphology. In *The Morphology of Creole Languages*, Ingo Plag (ed.), 3–33. Dordrecht: Springer.

Bakker, Peter, Daval-Markussen, Aymeric, Parkvall, Mikeal & Plag, Ingo. 2011. Creoles are typologically distinct from non-creoles. *Journal of Pidgin and Creole Languages* 26: 5–42.

Bauer, Winifred. 1993. *Maori*. London: Routledge.

Bickerton, Derek. 1984. The Language Bioprogram hypothesis. *Behavioral and Brain Sciences* 7: 173–221.

Bickerton, Derek. 1988. Creole languages and the Bioprogram. In *Linguistics: The Cambridge Survey* 2, Frederick Newmeyer (ed.), 268–284. Cambridge: CUP.

Bickerton, Derek. 1999. How to acquire language without positive evidence: What acquisitionists can learn from creoles. In *Language Creation and Language Change* Michel DeGraff (ed.), 49–74. Cambridge MA: The MIT Press.

Bickerton, Derek. 2008. *Bastard Tongues*. New York NY: Hill & Wang.

Bickerton, Derek. 2009. *Adam's Tongue*. New York NY: Hill & Wang.

Cinque, Guglielmo, 1999. *Adverbs and Functional Heads: A Cross-linguistic Perspective*. Oxford: OUP.

DeGraff, Michel. 1999. *Language Creation and Language Change*. Cambridge MA: The MIT Press.

DeGraff, Michel. 2001a. Morphology in Creole genesis: Linguistics and ideology. In *Ken Hale: A Life in Language*, Michael Kenstowicz (ed.), Cambridge MA: The MIT Press.

DeGraff, Michel. 2001b. A Cartesian critique of Neo-Darwinian linguistics. *Linguistic Typology* 5: 213–310.

DeGraff, Michel. 2003. Against Creole exceptionalism. *Language* 79: 391–410.

den Besten, Hans, Luijks, Carla & Roberge, Paul T. 2003. Reduplication in Afrikaans. In *Twice as Meaningful. Reduplication in Pidgins, Creoles and Other Contact Languages* [Westminster Creolistic Series 8], Silvia Kouwenberg (ed.), 271–287. London: Battlebridge Press.

Dostie, Gaétane. 2007. La réduplication pragmatique des marqueurs discursifs. De là à là là. *Langue française* 154: 45–60.

Dostie, Gaétane & Pusch, Claus D. 2007. Les marqueurs discursif. Sens et variation. *Langue française* 154. Larousse: Paris.

Dressler, Wolfgang. 1968. *Studien zur verbalen Pluralität*. Vienna: Österreichische Akademie der Wissenschaften.

Frajzyngier, Zygmunt, Johnson, Eric & Edwards, Adrian. 2005. *A Grammar of Mina*. Berlin: Mouton de Gruyter.

Ghomeshi, Jila, Jackendoff, Ray, Rosen, Nicole & Russell, Kevin. 2004. Contrastive focus reduplication in English (the SALAD-salad paper). *Natural Language & Linguistic Theory* 22: 307–357.

Grevisse, Maurice. 1991. *Le bon usage*, 12th printing revised by André Goosse. Paris: Duculot.

Guillemin, Diana M. 2009. The Mauritian Creole Noun Phrase. Its Form and Function. PhD dissertation, The University of Queensland.

Harbour, Daniel. 2008. Klivaj Predika, or predicate clefts in Haitian. *Lingua* 118: 853–871.

Hengeveld, Kees. 1989. Layers and operators in Functional Grammar. *Journal of Linguistics* 25: 127–157.

Hurch, Bernhard. 2005. *Studies on Reduplication: Empirical Approaches to Language Typology*. Berlin: Mouton de Gruyter.

Kouwenberg, Silvia. 1994. Berbice Dutch. In *Pidgins and Creoles. An Introduction* [Creole Language Library 15], Jacques Arends, Pieter Muysken & Norval Smith (eds), 233–243. Amsterdam: John Benjamins.

Kouwenberg, Silvia (ed.). 2003a. *Twice as Meaningful. Reduplication in Pidgins, Creoles and Other Contact Languages* [Westminster Creolistic Series 8]. London: Battlebridge.

Kouwenberg, Silvia. 2003b. Introduction, In *Twice as Meaningful. Reduplication in Pidgins, Creoles and Other Contact Languages* [Westminster Creolistic Series 8], Silvia Kouwenberg (ed.), 1–6. London: Battlebridge.

Kouwenberg, Silvia & LaCharité. Darlene. 2003. The meanings of 'more of the same'. Iconicity in reduplication and the evidence for substrate transfer in the genesis of Caribbean Creole languages. In *Twice as Meaningful. Reduplication in Pidgins, Creoles and Other Contact Languages* [Westminster Creolistic Series 8], Silvia Kouwenberg (ed.), 7–18. London: Battlebridge.

Lakoff, George & Johnson, Mark. 1980. *Metaphors we Live by*. Chicago IL: University of Chicago Press.

Mattes, Veronika. 2007. *Types of Reduplication: A Case Study of Bikol*. Graz: University of Graz, Graz Database on Reduplication. ⟨http://reduplication.uni-graz.at/⟩

Mittwoch, Anita. 1998. Cognate objects as reflections of Davidsonian event arguments. In *Events and Grammar*, Susan Rothstein (ed.), 309–332. Dordrecht: Kluwer.

Mufwene, Salikoko. 2001. *The Ecology of Language Evolution*. Cambridge: CUP.

Mufwene, Salikoko. 2003a. *Créoles, écologie sociale, evolution linguistique*. Paris: L'Harmattan.

Mufwene, Salikoko. 2003b. Competition and selection in language evolution. *Selection* 3: 45–56.

Mufwene, Salikoko. 2005. Language evolution: The population genetics way. In *Gene, Sprachen, und ihre Evolution*, Guenther Hauska (ed.), 30–52. Regensburg: Universitaetsverlag Regensburg.

Muysken, Pieter. 1988. Are creoles a special type of language? In *Linguistics: the Cambridge Survey* Vol. 2: *Linguistic Theory: Extensions and Implications*, Frederic Newmeyer (ed.), 285–301. Cambridge: CUP.

Parkvall, Mikael. 2003. Reduplication in the Atlantic Creoles. In *Twice as Meaningful. Reduplication in Pidgins, Creoles and Other Contact Languages* [Westminster Creolistic Series 8], Silvia Kouwenberg (ed.), 19–36. London: Battlebridge.

Rizzi, Luigi. 1997. The fine structure of the left periphery. In *The New Comparative Syntax*, Liliane Haegeman (ed.), 281–337. Londen: Addison, Longman & Wesley.

Sapir, Edward. 1921. *Language. An Introduction to the Study of Speech*. New York NY: Harcourt & Brace.

Singler, John Victor. 1996. Theories of creole genesis, sociohistorical considerations, and the evaluation of evidence: The case of Haitian Creole and the Relexification Hypothesis. *Journal of Pidgin and Creole Languages* 11: 185–230.

Thun, Nils. 1963. *Reduplicative Words in English: A Study of Formations of the Types Tick-tock, Hurly-burly, and Shilly-shally*. Uppsala: Carl Bloms.

The morphosyntax of non-iconic reduplications

A case study in Eastern Gbe and the Surinam creoles*

Enoch O. Aboh & Norval Smith
Universiteit van Amsterdam

In this paper, we have studied non-iconic reduplication in Eastern Gbe languages (viz., Fongbe and Gungbe) and Surinam creoles (viz., Sranan and Saramaccan). We have shown that in the Surinam Creoles, as well as in the Gbe languages, such non-iconic reduplication is conditioned by a unique syntactic structure which derives both verbal nouns (or gerunds) and (verbal) adjectives. Put another way, we analyze reduplication as a morphological process (i.e. affixation) conditioned by structural properties. We further show that the resulting reduplicated items correlate with a change in meaning that often varies from process/event to state/result, and can therefore not be accounted for in terms of iconicity. With regard to the issue of the emergence of reduplication in creoles, we show that the development of these non-iconic reduplications in the Surinam creoles derive partially from substrate influence from Eastern Gbe, while showing some properties of gerunds and past participles in English. Under this view therefore, reduplication, far from being a fast and cheap morphological operation available to a creole emerging from a pidgin state, represents a constrained morphosyntactic process.

1. Introduction

This paper discusses non-iconic reduplication in Eastern Gbe languages (i.e. Fongbe and Gungbe) and Surinam creoles (i.e. Sranan and Saramaccan). Reduplication is common across languages and is often assumed to be especially

---

* A related article, with some positions we have revised here, was circulated under the title *Non-iconic reduplications in Eastern Gbe and Surinam* to appear in the Trans-Atlantic volume (Muysken and Smith eds). We would like to thank all our colleagues of the Trans-Atlantic project for their comments and suggestions on this earlier version. We are also very grateful to Anne Zribi-Hertz for her detailed comments which helped us significantly improve this version of the paper.

frequent among creole languages, where it is analysed by some as an economical, fast, and easy way of creating new words. For instance, Bakker (2003a) observes that reduplication appears to be generally absent in pidgins, though it seems to represent a universal feature of creoles. Under this view, reduplication operates more in creole languages due to the pressing need to create new vocabulary items.[1] Other authors, however, regard reduplication as a universal iconic process, which, in the context of creoles, may be boosted by substrate influence. The following tables, adapted from Kouwenberg & LaCharité (2003), illustrate certain common reduplication patterns found in some Surinam creoles.

Table 1. Iconic reduplication[2] (productive)

Creoles	Noun	Distributive Plural	Verb	Habitual/ Iterative Event	Adjective	Intensified Attributive
Sranan	saka bag	saka-saka bags	yepi help	yepi-yepi help habitually	bisi busy	bisi-bisi very busy
Ndyuka	soutu sort/type	soutou-soutou kinds	suku search	suku-suku search continuously	tuu true	tuu-tuu very true
Saramaccan	kamian place	kamian-kamian places	bia to turn	bia-bia windings (river)	langa long	langa-langa very long

Table 2. Non-iconic reduplication (productive)

Creoles	Verb	Derived adjective
Sranan	ferfi paint peindre	ferfi-ferfi in a painted state qui a été peint
Ndyuka	bai buy acheter	bai-bai bought qui a été acheté
Saramaccan	singi sink noyer	singi-singi sunken qui a été noyé

---

1.   See also Bakker 2003b on inflectional morphology in pidgins.

2.   Note that when quoting reduplicated forms in examples, we always include a morpheme boundary, irrespective of whether the source or the written form of the language does this or not. In the writing conventions of the Gbe languages reduplicated forms (and compounds) are written without hyphens, while in Saramaccan this has sometimes been done in the past (e.g. De Groot 1977).

The discussion on reduplication patterns in creoles often centres around examples such as those in Table 1, where reduplication allows the derivation of new words with varying meanings (e.g. augmentative, iterative, diminutive or (distributive) plural). As convincingly discussed by Kouwenberg & LaCharité (2003), there is a sense in which one can conceive of such reduplication patterns and their related meanings (e.g. distributive plural, emphasis, frequency) as being iconic. In this paper, we focus instead on instances of reduplications for which we cannot, by any stretch of imagination, establish an iconic link between the morphological process (i.e. reduplication) and the semantics. Table 2 presents items which we interpret as non-iconic. The following sentences further illustrate this type of reduplication in Saramaccan and Gbe.

The sentences under (1) instantiate a certain class of verbs in Saramaccan and in Gungbe. We refer to these verbs henceforth as "Adjectival" Verbs (AV) because they can be reduplicated to form *Verbal Adjectives*. The reason for choosing the term "Adjectival" is thus not because they all express adjectival (property) concepts, although many of them do, but because *adjectives* can be derived from the members of this class. In general what are simple adjectives in European languages are expressed then by Adjectival Verbs in Saramaccan and Gungbe.

(1) a. *dí   lío   dɛ́ɛ́*   (Saramaccan online dictionary[3])
          DET river dry
          'The river is low'

    b. *Tɔ̃   lɔ̃   xú*   (Gungbe)
          river DET dry
          'The river is dry/The river dried up.'

As we discuss in the following sections, these verbs form a special class in that they can reduplicate and enter constructions where they function as predicative or attributive adjectives, or as resultatives (see Jondoh 1980; Bole-Richard 1983; Aboh 2007a, for Gbe, and Aboh & Smith, forthcoming, for Surinam). The following Saramaccan examples taken from De Groot (1977), illustrate the case of a resultative as in (2a) and an attributive as in (2b).[4]

(2) a. *A   tá   nján gwamba **dɛ́ɛ́-dɛ́ɛ́***   *Saramaccan*
          3SG PROG eat   meat   dry-dry
          'He is eating the meat dried'

---

3. http://www.sil.org/americas/Surinam/Saramaccan/English/SaramEngDictIndex.html

4. According to Haabo (2002) the non-reduplicated verbs encode an event while the reduplicated equivalents relate to a state (or result).

    b.   *dí*   ***dɛ́ɛ-dɛ́ɛ***   *kɔkɔnɔ́tɔ-wáta*
        DET dry-dry   coconut-milk
        'The dried coconut milk' (= 'the coconut-flesh')

In Gungbe, a reduplicated verb can be used attributively as in (3).[5]

(3)   *É*   *ɖù* *lán* ***xú-xú***
     3SG eat meat dry-dry
     'He ate dried meat'

The following examples show that these verbs can also be used predicatively in copula constructions in Saramaccan and Gungbe. The example in (4a) illustrates the non-reduplicated verb functioning as main predicate. In such contexts, the interpretation is often that of a process. Example (4b) on the other hand features a reduplicated verb used as adjectival predicate.

(4)   a. *dí* *kúja*   *mandú*   Saramaccan
        DET calabash ripe
        'The calabash ripens'

    b. *dí* *kúja*   *dɛ́* *mandú-mandú*
        DET calabash COP ripe-ripe
        'The calabash is ripe'

A similar situation can be found in Gungbe and other Gbe languages, where however such copula constructions are only allowed with a sub-class of such verbs.[6]

(5)   a. *àvún lɔ́*   *kú* *tò*   *kɔ́-mɛ̀*
        Dog DET die COP ground-in
        'The dog died on the ground.'

    b. *àvún lɔ́* *tò* *kú-kú* *tò* *kɔ́-mɛ̀*
        Dog DET COP die-die COP ground-in
        'The dog was lying dead on the ground.'

Completely regular however are gerundial constructions such as those in (6):

---

5.   As is the case in Saramaccan, we have the intuition that the non-reduplicated verbs often denote an event or a property, while the reduplicated verbs are typically expression of a result or a state. It is not clear to us yet what the semantic principles underlying this derivation are, and we hope to come back to it in future work.

6.   Another puzzle that we hope to come back to is that the Gbe languages do not manifest these reduplicated verbs in a fully productive manner. In addition the languages differ as to the verbs which can undergo this process. For instance, it seems to us that such forms are more frequent in Fongbe and Gengbe (maybe also in Ewegbe) than they are in Gungbe.

(6) a. *àvún lɔ́   tò   kú-kú-ˋ*
         Dog DET PROG die-die-PRTL
         'The dog is dying'

     b. *àvún lɔ́   tò   kú-kú   tò   kɔ́-mὲ-ˋ*
         Dog DET PROG die-die COP ground-in-PRTL
         'The dog is dying on the ground'

We discuss these structures further in Section 2.3. At this point we want to draw the reader's attention to the fact that Gungbe element *tò* can introduce a progressive aspect as in (6a) or act as a *be-located* relator (or copula) as in the sequence *tò kɔ́-mὲ* 'lit. be.located ground-in' as in (5a–b) and (6b). As we will show in subsequent sections, the same relator can be used to introduce states or results (see for instance Example 10d). For the sake of exposition, we distinguish between these two functions (i.e. aspectual vs. relator/be-located copula) by glossing the former as PROG and the latter as COP (see Aboh 2004a, 2005a, b, 2009, 2010 for a detailed discussion on expression of aspect and adpositions in Gbe).

Finally, such gerunds may lexicalize[7] and be used as ordinary nouns. This process appears to be quite unproductive in both languages. (7a) (International Bible Society 2009) is an example of this in Saramaccan, and (7b) in Gungbe.[8]

(7) a. *Wan   musu tja   nja-njan*
         1PL.NEG must carry eat-eat
         'You must not take food.'

     b. *Àgbán lɔ́   hwὲn mù-mú*
         plate DET smell raw-raw
         'The plate smells like raw (or uncooked) food' (lit. 'rawness').

---

7. E.g. the gerund/verbal noun *kú-kú* 'dying' lexicalizes to *kú-kú* 'death'.

8. In Gbe communities, the expression *hwὲn mù-mú* refers to an unpleasant smell. As Anne Zribi-Hertz (p.c.) has brought to our attention the corresponding lexemes in French can easily nominalise, as in the following examples:

(i) *Inutile d'emporter son   manger*
     useless to take   one's eat
     'There is no need to bring one's own food'

(ii) *L'assiette sent le   cru.*
     The.plate smells the raw
     'This plate smells like raw (uncooked food)'

This sort of variation in languages leads to the question of whether some activity-denoting or property-denoting lexical verbs are more prone than others to denote results or states. We hope to come back to this issue in future work.

In the Surinam creoles as well as in the Gbe languages, such reduplication patterns relate to a change in meaning that often varies from process/event to state/result.[9] While there does not seem to be any direct relation between such development and iconicity, there are good reasons for believing that such reduplications are conditioned syntactically in order to derive verbal nouns (or gerunds) and (verbal) adjectives. In addition, we show that the development of these non-iconic reduplications in the Surinam creoles can be related to similar structures in the Eastern Gbe languages. In terms of this analysis, reduplication in the Surinam creoles derives partially from substrate influence. If our analysis is correct, we then have a case where reduplication, far from being a fast and cheap morphological operation available to a creole emerging from a pidgin, represents a constrained morphosyntactic process that has consequences for issues of language contact and language transfer in general. As the subject matter is fairly complex we will now discuss the phenomena in Gbe and Surinam in greater detail, respectively.

Sections 2 and 3 offer a description and an analysis of verbal reduplication in Gungbe. We show in these sections that verb reduplication is triggered by the need to license an expletive in an embedded subject position. Because the Gbe languages do not possess a "rich" morphology, reduplication in such cases is one means of modifying the form of the verb without employing any independent segmental processes of affixation. Syntactically, such reduplicated verbs can either be used as state adjectives, or as gerunds some of which may further be lexicalized. Given some striking similarities between the Surinam creoles and the Gbe languages, Section 4 extends the analysis to verbal reduplication in Saramaccan. We show there that the emergence of this type of reduplication in the creoles is mainly induced by Gbe morphosyntax but is reinforced by English in both its function and syntax. This conclusion is compatible with the data analysed in Section 5 where we suggest that lexicalised deverbal nouns in Saramaccan may have been modelled on Gbe reduplicated verbal patterns. Section 6 concludes the paper.

2.   Reduplication in Eastern Gbe

In most Eastern Gbe (e.g. Fongbe, Gungbe) non-iconic reduplications occur in two contexts: within the clause and within the noun phrase. For our purposes,

---

9.   Also instruments in Saramaccan.

we will discuss these two contexts using examples from Gungbe. We begin with reduplication within the noun phrase.[10]

2.1   Reduplication within the noun phrase

As mentioned in the previous section, Gungbe, like most Gbe languages, exhibits a class of verbs that appear to function like predicative adjectives in European languages, which we referred to as adjectival verbs (AV). In this regard, the sentence under (8a) shows that the AV follows the noun it predicates over in a way similar to a lexical verb in (8b).

(8)   a.   *Àvún lɔ́   kló*
           dog   DET   big
           'The dog is big.'

      b.   *Súrù zà   kɔ́-mὲ*
           Suru   sweep   ground-in
           'Suru swept the floor.'

The relation of AV's to other lexical verbs is further illustrated by the fact that the AV in (9a) and the transitive verb in (9b) can both combine with TMA particles. In the following examples, these verbal elements co-occur with the habitual marker (see Aboh 2004a for discussion). Finally, examples (9c–d) indicate that both elements can be fronted for focus in which case the predicate is repeated and the IP-domain contains the second verb token. In Gungbe only verbal predicates allow predicate focus with doubling. As a consequence, the predicative adjective in (9e) fails to front and reduplicate. (See Aboh 2006a, b; Aboh & Dyakonova 2009; Zribi-Hertz & Glaude this volume, for the analysis of such constructions)

(9)   a.   *Àvún lɔ́   nɔ̀   kló*
           dog   DET   HAB   big
           'The dog often becomes big.'

      b.   *Súrù nɔ̀   zà   kɔ́-mὲ*
           Suru   HAB   sweep   ground-IN
           'Suru habitually sweeps/swept the floor.'

      c.   *Kló àvún lɔ́   nɔ̀   kló*
           Big dog   DET   HAB   big
           'The dog often becomes BIG.'

---

10.   Though most of the data discussed here can be replicated for other Eastern Gbe languages as well, the reader should keep in mind that these languages are not isomorphic (see Aboh 2004a for some discussion).

    d.   *Zà   Súrù nɔ̀   zà   kɔ́-mὲ*
        sweep Suru HAB sweep ground-IN
        'Suru habitually SWEEPS/SWEPT the floor.'

    e.   **Kpὲví àvún lɔ́   nɔ̀   cí   kpὲví*
        small dog   DET HAB remain small
        'The dog often remains SMALL.'

We conclude, based on the facts in (8) and (9), that AVs function as verbal predicates. Accordingly, these examples respect the subject-predicate order of Gungbe. At this stage, one could conclude (as is sometimes done) that Gungbe (and Gbe languages in general) do not make any formal distinction between AVs and verbs. Instead, we assume that the class of verbs in the Gbe languages involves a subclass of elements which allow the derivation of reduplicated Verbal Adjectives. These reduplicated verbal adjectives may function as attributive adjectives, in which case they occur between the noun they modify and the determiner.

The contrast in (10a–b) shows that while the AV *klɔ́* 'big' in (8a) can be used attributively as the verbal adjective *kí-klɔ́* in (10a), the verb *zà* in (8b) cannot form a verbal adjective (and is therefore not an adjectival verb). In addition, the contrast between (10a) and (10c) shows that the attributive verbal adjective must precede the determiner, and therefore must be within the DP.[11] Finally, recall from the discussion in Section 1 that some of these reduplicated verbal adjectives can be used

---

11.   As we already mentioned in Footnote 5, the facts are not always the same across Gbe. In Benin Gengbe, for instance, Bole-Richard (1983) observes a distinction in tone between reduplicated verbal adjectives and Verbal Nouns (VNs). According to this author, the tone pattern used with H-tone reduplicated verbs is different from that used with reduplicated adjectives, whether attributive or predicative. Consider the meanings of the following two examples:

    (i)   [àmὲ   (bé)   kù-kú] wɔ̀-nà   ŋúzízí ná   mù   [VN]
        person (CON) dying make-HAB pity   give me
        'The death/dying of a person incites me to pity'

    (ii) [àmὲ   kú-kú ɖé]   mú téŋú pò-nùpo ò   [VA]
        person dead   DET NEG CAN chatter NEG
        'A dead person can't talk'

This would suggest that the derivation of adjectives is different from that of nouns. However, Jondoh (1980) who discusses Togo Gengbe does not seem to make any such difference, as *predicative* verbal adjectives have the same tone pattern as Gerunds, as do attributive ones in certain cases as illustrated by the following examples (function word glosses have been adapted).

    (i)   *kǔ-kú mú fá   ɔ̀*   [VN]
        die-die NEG be_easy PRTL
        'Dying is not easy'

predicatively in Gungbe. For convenience, we repeat example (5b) here as (10d), and add a Gengbe example (Jondoh 1980). We will return to the discussion of such examples in Section 2.3.

(10)   a.   *Súrù xɔ̀ àvún kí-kló lɔ́*
           Suru buy dog big-big DET
           'Suru bought the big dog'

    b.   **Súrù kpɔ́n kɔ́mɛ̀ zì-zà   lɔ́*
           Suru look floor sweep-sweep DET
           'Suru looked at the swept floor'

    c.   **Súrù xɔ̀ àvún lɔ́ kí-kló*
           Suru buy dog DET big-big
           'Suru bought the big dog'

    d.   *àvún lɔ́ tò kú-kú tò kɔ́-mɛ̀*
           Dog DET COP die-die COP ground-in
           'The dog was (lying) dead on the ground.'

    e.   *hèví á lè kŭ-kú lè fúnú*   [Gengbe]
           bird DET COP die-die COP there
           'The bird is lying dead over there'

Contrasting again example (10a) with that in (8a), it appears that the predicative constructions represent clauses where the AV heads the verb phrase and the noun phrase (i.e. a DP) functions as subject. This is partially schematized in (11).

(11)

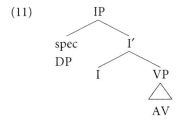

(ii)   *hèví á lè kŭ-kú*   [predicative VA]
        bird DET COP die-die
        'The bird is dead'

(iii)   *hèví kú-kú*   [attributive VA]
        bird die-die
        'dead bird'

(iv)   *kŭkú á dó vɔ̌vɔ́*   [attributive VA]
        die-die DET instill fright
        'The dead one is frightful'

On the other hand the attributive constructions instantiate contexts where the DP embeds the reduplicated verbal adjective, which therefore follows the noun it modifies. This order conforms to that of nominal modifiers (e.g. adjective, demonstrative, numeral, relative clause) which must follow the noun they modify in Gbe. An example is given in (12a) where we see that the reduplicated verbal adjective occurs bracketed with a sequence of modifiers including a color adjective, a numeral, a demonstrative and a relative clause. All these modifying expressions follow the noun and precede both the determiner *lɔ́* and the number marker *lɛ́* (see Aboh 2004a, b, 2005c and references cited therein for discussion). The brackets in example (12b) further indicate that the whole noun phrase in (12a) can function as argument of an adjectival verb like *kpèn* 'to be heavy'.

(12)   a.   *àvún [kí-kló   yù   àwè   éhè   ɖě   mí   xɔ̀]   lɔ́   lɛ́*
              dog   big-big black two   DEM   REL   1PL   buy   DET   PL
              'These two big black dogs that we bought'

      b.   *[àvùn kí-kló   yù   àwè   éhè   ɖě   mí   xɔ̀   lɔ́   lɛ́]*
              dog   big-big black two   DEM   REL   1PL   buy   DET   PL

              kpèn   gbáú
              heavy   too.much

              '[These two big black dogs that we bought] are too heavy'

With this description in place, we can now address the question of what triggers reduplication of the AV in (12a–b) to form a verbal adjective within the DP. This question further bears on the issues of (i) the semantic, and (ii) the syntactic properties, of the reduplicated verbal adjective. The latter question relates to the more general question of whether reduplicated verbal adjectives within the noun phrase have counterparts in the clausal domain. In an attempt to address these questions, we first discuss some semantic properties of the reduplicated verbal adjective.

2.1.1   *Some semantic aspects of reduplicated verbal adjectives*

The translation of the example in (10a) suggests that attributive reduplicated verbal adjectives denote a state. The following pairs of examples further support this point. For the sake of clarity, we present the predicative usage next to the attributive usage.

(13)   Predicative use
    a.   *Càzùn lɔ́   fá*
        pan   DET   cold
        'The pan is cold'

    b.   *Ján   lɔ́   kpèn*
        chair   DET   heavy
        'The chair is heavy'

Attributive use

    a′. *Càzùn   fí-fá   lɔ́*
          pan   cold-cold DET
          'The cold pan'

    b′. *Ján   kpì-kpèn   lɔ́*
          chair heavy-heavy DET
          'The heavy chair'

In these examples, the reduplicated verbal adjective is comparable to attributive adjectives in English or French (e.g. big/gros-se; heavy/lourd-e; difficult/difficile). However, certain reduplicated verbal adjectives describe the result of a process (i.e. post-processual state) and therefore convey a slightly different meaning. Some examples are given in (14).

(14)   a. *Kpòtín lɔ́   xú*
         stick   DET dry
         'The stick is in a dry state'

       b. *Àvɔ́   lɔ́   vún*
          cloth DET tear
          'The cloth is in a torn state'

       a′. *Kpòtín xú-xú   lɔ́*
          stick   dry-dry DET
          'The dried stick [that has been dried]'

       b′. *Àvɔ́   vún-vún   lɔ́*
          cloth tear-tear DET
          'The torn cloth [that has been torn]'

The translations of some of these examples remind us of past participles in French or in English in that the sequences in (14) allow a paraphrase with a processual relative clause unlike the cases under (13). Accordingly, example (14b′) can be interpreted or translated as 'the dried stick' (i.e. the stick that has been dried), unlike example (13b′) which can be read as 'the chair that is heavy'. Following Aboh (2007a) we argue that these postnominal reduplicated verbs derive from a reduced relative clause. This view is compatible with Cinque's (2010) recent analysis of certain prenominal adjectives in English which may involve a reduced relative clause as well. In this regard therefore, both Gungbe and English have access to the same syntactic tools for deriving adjectives. As the discussion shows, this view extends to Saramaccan as well.

    Indeed, it is important to observe that the reduplication patterns in (10), (13) and (14) are transparently similar to those found in the Surinam creoles and listed in Table 2. As we already mentioned in the previous section, this type of reduplication differs from that in table (1) because it does not trigger semantic effects such as intensification, plurality, or diminutive. Instead, the derived meaning is that of a state or a result. This fundamental difference suggests that reduplication in this case is more akin to a derivational process, which to some extent reminds us the use of what were originally past participles as adjectives in Germanic and Romance. Consider, for instance, the following examples from French and English.

(15)   a.   The plate has been broken
       b.   l' assiette a été cassée

       a'.   A broken plate
       b'.   Une assiette cassée

The contrast between the (a) and (a') examples shows that the participle form relates to a change in meaning from process/event to state/result. This recalls the observation we made about Gungbe and Saramaccan in Section 1, where the reduplicated forms could be used as adjectives with different functions. Keeping to the parallel between these examples and the reduplicated verbal adjectives in Gbe and Surinam, we can hypothesize that reduplicated verbal adjectives are to some extent comparable to participial forms in Romance and Germanic. Put differently, the reduplicated part of the AV is affixal (see also Farquharson 2007). Given this conclusion, the next question to ask is whether reduplication derives from a syntactic requirement to create an inflected verb. Put differently, the reduplicated part could be compared to an affix involved in two different processes: inflection in verbal sentences (e.g. progressive) and derivation in nominal contexts (e.g. reduplicated adjectives, formation of verbal nouns). In trying to answer this question, we first look at syntactic contexts in Gungbe which require verb reduplication.

2.1.2   *Reduplication in OV sequences*

The Gbe languages are commonly assumed to display an SVO order. However, these languages also exhibit contexts where the object precedes the verb. Aboh (2004a, 2005a, 2009) refers to such sentences as OV constructions. These typically occur in environments characterised by special aspectual properties such as those illustrated in (16).

(16)   [Prospective]
       a.   *Súrù tò   núsɔ́nú ná   ɖà   ná mì-`*
           Suru PROG soup   PROSP cook for me-PRTL
           'Suru is just about to cook soup for me'

       [Purpose clause]
       b.   *Súrù yì núsɔ́nú ná   ɖà   ná mì gbé*
           Suru go soup   PROSP cook for me PRTL
           'Suru has gone to cook soup for me [i.e. he is just about to do so]'

These examples indicate that certain *aspect verbs* (e.g. *tò, yì*) introduce OV structures which typically require a sentence-final particle. In example (16a), this particle is a floating tone attached to the pronoun *mì* 'me', while in (16b) it is the element *gbé*. These examples further show that the prospective aspect marker *ná* can intervene between the object and the verb. This is evidence that the sequence delimited to the left by the object and to the right by the sentence-final particle includes an inflectional projection (i.e. IP-related projection) which may host an aspect marker.

While transitive verbs require the object-verb order as shown in (16), intransitive verbs must reduplicate. This is illustrated by the example under (17b).

(17) a. *Jíkù jà*
          rain fall
          'It rained'

      b. *Jíkù tò   jì-jà-`*
          rain PROG fall-fall-PRTL
          'It is raining'

As discussed in Aboh (2004a; 2005a, 2009), the contrast in (16) and (17) should not lead one to conclude that reduplication is conditioned by argument structure. Indeed, transitive verbs must also reduplicate in some well-defined contexts. This happens when:

1. The internal argument is pronominalized (18).

    (18) *Súrù tò   ɖì-ɖà   ɛ̀   ná mì-`*
          Suru PROG cook-cook 3SG for me-PRTL
          'Suru is cooking it for me'

2. The internal argument is wh/focus-extracted (19a–b).

    (19) a. *Été   wɛ̀   Súrù tò   ɖì-ɖà   – ná mì-`?*
              what FOC Suru PROG cook-cook   for me-PRTL
              'What is Suru cooking for me?'

          b. *Núsɔ́nú wɛ̀   Súrù tò   ɖì-ɖà   – ná mì-`*
              soup   FOC Suru PROG cook-cook   for me-PRTL
              'Suru is cooking SOUP for me'

An interim conclusion that we now reach is that in OV contexts, verb reduplication is triggered by the absence of a phrase (e.g. the object) in the preverbal position. This would actually mean that the preverbal object counts as a 'blocker' of verb reduplication. In other words a pre-verbal object is not compatible with a reduplicated verb. The fact that a syntactic category (e.g. a DP-object) can block reduplication is, of course, evidence that reduplication in OV contexts is a syntactic and not a semantically motivated phenomenon that results from anything lexical. Put differently, the reduplicated verb in (17), (18), and (19) satisfies some syntactic requirement. Given this description, one naturally wonders what other element can block reduplication. The following examples show that the prospective aspect marker *ná* is a 'blocker' too. In (20a), the object is pronominalized but the verb cannot reduplicate because it is preceded by the prospective marker *ná*. We observe a similar fact in (20b) and (20c) where the object is wh-extracted but the verb cannot reduplicate because of the intervening prospective marker.

(20) a. *Súrù tò ná (*ɖì-)ɖà ὲ ná mì-ˋ*
    Suru PROG PROSP cook 3SG for me-PRTL
    'Suru is just about to cook for me'

  b. *Été wὲ Súrù tò ná (*ɖì-)ɖà – ná mì-ˋ?*
    what FOC Suru PROG PROSP cook for me-PRTL
    'What is Suru just about to cook for me?'

  c. *Núsɔ́nú wὲ Súrù tò ná (*ɖì-)ɖà – ná mì-ˋ?*
    soup FOC Suru PROG PROSP cook for me-PRTL
    'Suru is just about to cook SOUP for me?'

These facts indicate that the fronted DP-object (i.e. a phrase) and the prospective marker (i.e. a functional head) block reduplication. Yet, these two elements are not in complementary distribution. Recall from example (16a), repeated here as (21a) for convenience, that a transitive verb in prospective aspect, must still have its internal argument preposed to the left of the prospective marker *ná*. As the ungrammatical (21b) shows, the object cannot remain post-verbal in this context.[12]

(21) a. *Súrù tò núsɔ́nú ná ɖà ná mì-ˋ* [Prospective]
    Suru PROG soup PROSP cook for me-PRTL
    'Suru is just about to cook soup for me'

  b. **Súrù tò ná ɖà núsɔ́nú ná mì-ˋ*
    Suru PROG PROSP cook soup for me-PRTL
    'Suru is just about to cook soup for me'

These facts indicate that there are at least two independent positions in front of the verb where both the preposed object and the prospective marker can be inserted.

---

12. As reported in Aboh (2004a), however, members of the first author's family (including himself) do have OV constructions where the object can follow the verb and for whom (13b) is grammatical (or at worst marginal). I do not discuss these cases, as most people in our community would reject them.

Because these elements represent different categories, that is, a phrase and a head, respectively, we conclude from the fact that they must be adjacent to each other when co-occuring that they express the same syntactic projection and (presumably) stand in a specifier-head relation. This view is supported by the fact that, though Gungbe allows double object constructions as in (22a), the two objects cannot occur in a preverbal position (22b). Instead, only one object can be fronted to the left of the verb (22c) or the prospective marker (22d). These data indicate that there is only one position available to the left of the prospective that can host the fronted DP.

(22)   a.   *Súrù kplɔ́n glénsì   Sàgbó*
            Suru teach English Sagbo
            'Suru taught Sagbo English'

       b.   **Súrù tò   glénsì   Sàgbó kplɔ́n-`*
            Suru PROG English Sagbo teach-PRTL
            'Suru is teaching Sagbo English'

       c.   *Súrù tò   glénsì   kplɔ́n Sàgbó-`*
            Suru PROG English teach Sagbo-PRTL
            'Suru is teaching Sagbo English'

       d.   *Súrù tò   glénsì   ná   kplɔ́n Sàgbó-`*
            Suru PROG English PROSP teach Sagbo-PRTL
            'Suru is about to teach Sagbo English'

In accounting for this phenomenon in Gungbe, Aboh (2004a, 2005a, 2009) proposes that verb reduplication is a syntactic requirement. This would make such a reduplication process non-iconic, as it is not related to any transparent semantic feature that could be predicted from the reduplicated form. We will not enter the details of Aboh's analysis here and the reader is referred to the references cited. For the purpose of this paper, we assume without further discussion that OV sequences have the structure (23): An aspect verb in Asp selects for a small clause (or predicate phrase) FP that involves both an edge and an inflectional domain which we refer to here as IP (for simplicity). [Spec IP] functions as an embedded subject position and is therefore sensitive to the EPP as originally defined in Chomsky (1986), and subsequently in Chomsky (1995). I^0 is realised by the prospective marker *ná* or the verb that may raise to that position. F^0 hosts the sentence-final particle (e.g. the floating tone in (16a), or *gbé* in (16b)).[13]

---

13.   In this work, we adopt a more traditional approach to the EPP (Extended Projection Principle) which basically states that every predicate must have a subject. Our view here is that FP is a reduced proposition with a subject position that must be licensed in syntax overtly or covertly (see Aboh 2004a, 2009) for discussion.

(23)

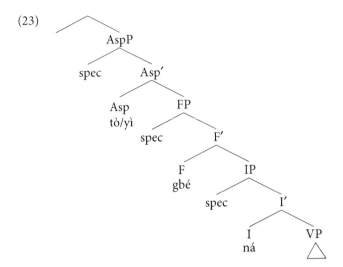

Under this representation, OV sequences are derived by object fronting to [spec IP] due to the EPP. When the prospective aspect marker is present, as in (23), verb movement is blocked and the verb remains VP-internal, (24a). When the prospective marker is absent, however, the verb raises to I^0 as indicated in (24b). Finally, the whole IP raises to [spec FP] as shown in the representations below.

(24)   a.

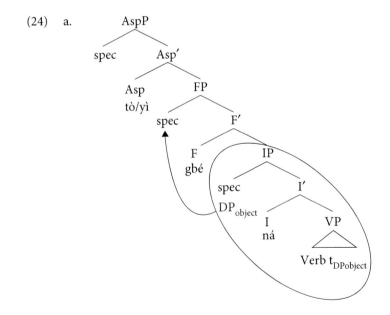

b.

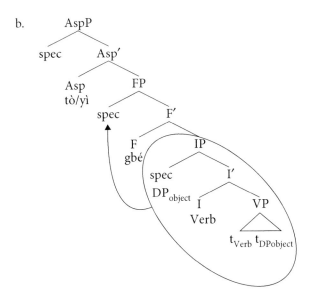

No reduplication ever arises in the cases described under (24). Reduplication occurs when both the object and the prospective marker are missing. Aboh (2004a, 2005a, 2009) proposes that in such contexts, a null expletive merges in [spec IP]. This element, he claims, is licensed under a spec-head configuration by the prospective marker under I, or else by a reduplicated form of the verb that has moved there (25a–b). Finally, IP raises to [spec FP].

(25)   a.

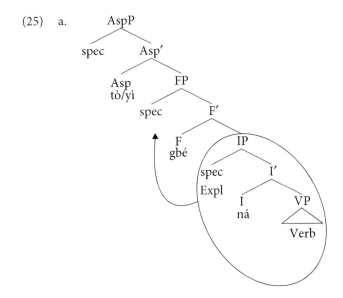

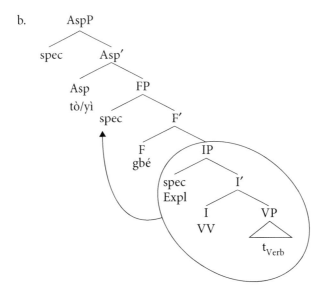

A seemingly simpler solution would be to assume that in structures such as (24), the doublet (i.e. a copy of the verb) is inserted in [spec IP]. Under such an analysis, there would be no need of a null expletive. This view however makes several wrong predictions. First it suggests that the reduplicated verb represents a phrase whereby the doublet is in [spec IP] and the root sits in I. This is counterintuitive because certain phonological processes affecting reduplicated verbs in Gungbe seem to operate at the word level. For instance, stem vowels are reduced in reduplication such that the reduplicated equivalent of the verb *kò* 'to laugh' is *kì-kò* and not **kòkò*, as is the case when the verb reduplicates and fronts in sentence-initial position for focus (see Aboh 2006a; Aboh & Dyakonova 2009; Jouitteau (this volume), and Zribi-Hertz & Glaude (this volume). Similarly, the copy analysis cannot explain why in the context of bisyllabic words in Gungbe, reduplication targets the first syllable only. Accordingly, a verb like *sísé* 'to push' is reduplicated as *sísísé* but not **sísésísé*.

Second, an analysis in terms of copying in [spec IP] predicts that the doublet is separate from the verb root and could therefore be fronted to the left periphery for the purpose of focus (Zribi-Hertz & Glaude this volume). Again this is impossible in Gungbe OV constructions where the OV sequence as a whole has to front in the context of focus (see Aboh & Dyakonova 2009). Finally, this hypothesis is compatible with the idea that Gungbe could have sequences such as V-*ná*-V, where the doublet in [spec IP] would precede the prospective marker in a similar fashion to what happens with an object, or else sequences like *ná-ná*-V where the prospective marker reduplicates to fill in [spec IP]. No such sequences are found in Gungbe. In consequence, we assume that the analysis briefly presented here and further discussed in Aboh (2004a, 2005a, 2009) is on the right track. As we said earlier, we will not discuss the details of this analysis as they do not bear directly on the conclusion that verb reduplication in OV contexts is driven by syntactic requirements. As an interim conclusion, we can observe that object fronting, verb reduplication, and prospective aspect marking satisfy the same requirement: license [spec IP] within the small clause as an EPP requirement (but see Jouitteau this volume, for an alternative).

2.1.3   *Reduplication in OVV sequences*

This view is further supported by the so-called OVV gerundial constructions, referred to above, where an object precedes a reduplicated transitive verb. Of course, intransitive verbs only have VV-structures in such contexts. These (O)VV sequences have the same distribution as normal DPs, and could be regarded as nominalized verb phrases. In (26a) the OVV sequence functions as the subject of the clause while in (26b) it functions as the direct object. The example in (26c) indicates that the OVV complex can be fronted to the focus position, where it gets marked by the focus marker. Finally, the nominal character of these sequences is further indicated by example (26d), which shows that the OVV complex may be embedded under a determiner.

(26)   a.   [Àzɔ́n wì-wà]   nɔ̀   dó   àwútù   mɛ̀
             work do-do   HAB   plant   illness   person
             'Working too much/too much work makes one sick'

        b.   Súrù gbɛ́   [àzɔ́n   wì-wà]
             Suru refuse   work   do-do
             'Suru refused to work/working'

        c.   [Àzɔ́n wì-wà]   wɛ̀   nɔ́   jró   Súrù
             work do-do   FOC   HAB   please   Suru
             'Suru likes WORKING/TO WORK'

        d.   [Pípàn dí-dó   lɔ́]   nɔ̀   kpé   àgbɔ́   ná   mì
             train take-take   DET   HAB   cause   fatigue   PREP   1SG
             'Taking the train [all the time] makes me feel tired'

These examples show that the verb reduplicates even though it is preceded by the object. We claim that this is possible because the object in such constructions is not in [spec IP]. Put differently, the object is not in a position where it can block reduplication. Instead, we suggest that the object has moved to [spec FP] where it expresses the topic-comment articulation typical of such OVV structures. As a consequence of object movement to [spec FP], a null Expl is merged in [spec IP] that is licensed under spec-head configuration due to the reduplicated verb under I^0. [spec FP] being filled, no IP pied-piping occurs in consequence. OVV constructions lack the sentence-final particle found in OV sequences (see Aboh 2005a and references cited there for discussion).[14]

(27)

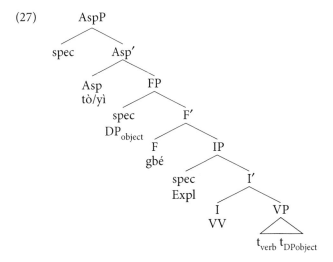

Because there is no extra position for the prospective marker to move to (unlike the object), this analysis predicts that reduplication will never occur in the context of *ná*. This analysis is borne out, as shown in (28).

(28) a. [Àzɔ́n ná   wà dìn] má jró   mì
          work PROSP do now NEG please me
          'Working now does not please me'

      b. *[Àzɔ́n ná   wì-wà dìn] má jró   mì
          work PROSP do-do now NEG please me
          'Working now does not please me'

With the analysis of OV as well as OVV sequences in mind, let us now turn to verbal adjectives.

3.   Extending the analysis to reduplicated verbal adjectives in Gungbe

Given our analysis of verb reduplication in OV and OVV contexts, we may now ask the question of whether the proposed analysis can be extended to cases of verb reduplication for attributive modification. Aboh (2007a) actually extends this

---

14.   Interestingly, these OVV constructions do not allow VV-clitic sequences such as in (18) where the verb reduplicates because the object fails to front as it is a clitic. The impossibility of having such VV-CL constructions here can be taken as further evidence that object fronting to [spec FP] is mandatory in order to indicate the topic-theme articulation that these sequences express.

analysis to reduplicated verbal adjectives, an example of which is given again in (29) for state adjectives and in (30) for eventive adjectives.

(29)   a.   *Núsɔ́nú lɔ́   fá*
            soup   DET cold
            'The soup is cold'

       b.   *Núsɔ́nú fí-fá   lɔ́*
            soup   cold-cold DET
            'The cold soup'
            'The soup that became cold'

These examples describe a state, just as English or French attributive adjectives do. On the other hand, the examples in (30) have a slightly different meaning in that they express a resultative state, and these examples can be paraphrased with a relative clause.

(30)   a.   *Àgbán lɔ́   gbà*
            plate DET break
            'The plate broke'

       b.   *Àgbán gbì-gbà   lɔ́*
            plate break-break DET
            'The broken plate'

Finally, as already mentioned in Section 2, the determiner occurs to the right of the noun modified by the reduplicated verb, so that attributive sequences can be schematized as in (31a). The ungrammatical example in (31b), as opposed to (31c), indicates that the reduplicated verb cannot be outside the determiner phrase.

(31)   a.   NP-[Modifier]-[VV]-Determiner

       b.   *Kpòtín gà   lɔ́   xú-xú*
            stick   long DET dry-dry
            'The long dried stick'

       c.   *Kpòtín gà   xú-xú   lɔ́*
            stick   long dry-dry DET
            'The long dried stick'

We conclude from these facts that the reduplicated verbal adjective is embedded within the determiner phrase (DP) headed by the determiner *lɔ́*, which occurs at the right edge of its phrase. In order to account for these data, we hypothesize that (29a) involves the underlying structure (32). Here, the determiner D takes FP (the sequence embedding OV in verbal domain) as complement. However, we propose that these constructions differ from the contexts of OV constructions because the embedded verb (i.e. an AV) is a one-place predicate whose sole argument is introduced in [spec AV] by hypothesis. In this representation, and subsequently, we label AVs as V_A and such reduplicated verbs as VV_A.

(32)

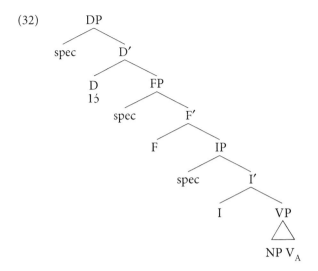

What this analysis suggests is that FP is comparable to a (small) clause, which can be headed by different types of predicates (i.e. verbs or adjectival verbs). FP in turn can be selected by an auxiliary verb as in OV contexts, or by a determiner leading to structures involving reduced relative clauses (Kayne 1994; Aboh 2005c, 2007a). Under this analysis, NP moves to [spec FP] (in a way comparable to OVV constructions. A null expletive merges in [spec IP], where it is licensed under a spec-head relation by the reduplicated verb in I^0. Finally, FP raises to [spec DP].

(33)   a.

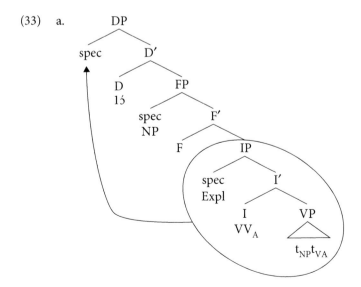

b.
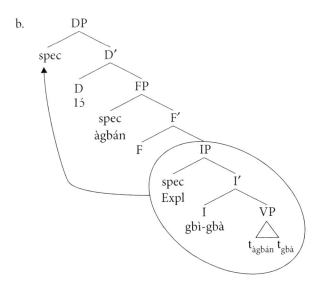

The bracketed sequence in the following example illustrates a case where FP headed by a verbal adjective is selected by an auxiliary verb (or a copula).

(34) [Xɔ̀   lɔ́   mɛ̀   ní   nyín zì-zà]   whécó   má   gɔ̀
      Room DET INSIDE INJ COP sweep-sweep before 1SG.FUT return
      'The room should be swept before I come back'

Such examples are analyzed as types of passive sentences in that the sole internal argument moves out to [spec TP] for case reasons, as partially represented in (35).

(35) [_FinP xɔ̀ lɔ́ mɛ̀ [_Fin ní [_TP [_AspP nyín [_FP [_F [_IP Expl [_I zì-zà [_VP t_zà

      t_[xɔ̀ lɔ́ mɛ́]]]]]]]]]]… [_AspP whéco ma gɔ̀]

As is clear from the proposed structure, (32) is akin to relativised DPs. This is further indicated by the fact that these structures are parallel to relative clauses in Gungbe. The only difference between these structures is that full relative clauses involve an overt relative complementizer ɖé as illustrated by the representation in (36b) (see Aboh 2005c).

(36) a. [Kpòtín   ɖé   mí   xɔ̀]   lɔ́
          Stick   REL 1PL buy DET
          'The stick that we bought'
      b. [_DP [_D lɔ́ [_CP kpòtín [_C ɖé [_IP mí [_I xɔ̀ [_VP t_xɔ̀ t_kpòtín]]]]]]]

We propose that this difference correlates with the fact that a full relative CP (36b) has an overt relativizer, which is why it can include various tense, mood, negation, and aspect markers. The embedded small clause represented by FP in (32) lacks all these properties. It represents what we may refer to as a *reduced relative clause* (see also Kayne 1994; Aboh 2007a; Cinque 2010).[15]

4.   Reduplicated verbal adjectives in Saramaccan

Saramaccan (Surinam) allows two contexts for reduplicated verbal adjectives: predicative and attributive. In their predicative usage, reduplicated verbal adjectives may be linked to the noun phrase they predicate over by a copula, giving rise to the order DP-copula-VV. In some cases however, the copula is absent and the reduplicated verb acts as a secondary predicate. These two sequences are schematized as in (37).

(37) a.   [Subject]>Copula>Reduplicated verbal adjective
       b.   [Subject]>Reduplicated verbal adjective

We will come back to these two patterns in Sections 4.1 and 4.2 respectively. In the attributive usage however, the reduplicated AV is embedded within a noun phrase where it occurs pre-nominally as indicated in (38).

(38)   Determiner>reduplicated verbal adjective>Noun

4.1   Predicative reduplicated verbal adjectives

The following examples illustrate predicative reduplicated verbal adjectives in Saramaccan. In these examples, the predicative reduplicated verbal adjectives follow the noun and are introduced by a copula *dɛ́*.

(39)   *dí   físi   dɛ́   kúa-kúa*[16]   [Bakker 1987:25]
        DET fish COP fresh-fresh
        'The fish is fresh'

---

15.   Cinque (2010) shows quite convincingly that some prenominal adjectives in English (usually analysed as "attributive") are actually reduced relatives; so that it becomes impossible to claim that only postnominal adjectives (e.g. a man proud of his son) are or may be reduced relatives. This view is compatible with the analysis proposed in this paper, on the basis of Gungbe and Saramaccan.

16.   We depart from some analyses of Saramaccan which do not clearly represent the bimorphemic status of these reduplicated forms.

The Saramaccan example (39) is parallel to the Gungbe example in (40): *tò* (Gungbe) and *dɛ́* (Saramaccan) occur in locative (and progressive) constructions.

(40) *Àwù lɔ́ tò bì-bɔ̀ tò távò jí*
Shirt DET COP fold-fold COP table on
'The shirt is/was folded on the table' [only in the state reading]

Similarly to Gungbe, these predicative expressions can receive tense and aspect markers as illustrated in (41).

(41) *A bi dɛ́ tái-tái ku búi*   [Bakker 1987:29]
3SG TNS COP bind-bind PREP string
'He was tied with a string' [only in the state reading]

In such predicative reduplicated verbal adjectives the reduplicated predicate can front for the purpose of emphasis yielding a structure like that in (42).

(42) *Wípi-wípi dí wómi dɛ́*
Whip-whip DET man COP
'The man is WHIPPED [i.e. he is in a whipped state].'

Though focusing of the verbal adjective does not result in predicate doubling, as is normally the case in Saramaccan (see Bakker 1987, 2003b; Veenstra 1996; Aboh 2006b, 2007b) the fact that the reduplicated sequence can be fronted, stranding the copula, indicates that the two do not head one and the same constituent. Instead, what seems to be the case here is that the copula introduces a constituent which contains (or is headed) by the reduplicated verb. Accordingly, we take this example to mean that the copula represents a functional position (e.g. Asp) which selects the phrase containing the verbal adjective as complement. Keeping the parallel with Gungbe, this would mean that the copula selects for FP as represented in (43). By analogy to Gungbe, we further propose that reduplication arises because the sole argument of the verbal adjective moves to [spec TP] for case reasons. As a consequence, a null expletive is inserted in [spec IP] which is licensed by reduplication.

(43) [$_{TP}$ dí fisi [$_{AspP}$ dɛ́ [$_{FP}$ [$_F$ [$_{IP}$ Expl [$_I$ kúa-kúa [$_{VP}$ t$_{di fisi}$ t$_{kua}$]]]]]]]

Put in the context of example (42), where the predicate has fronted to the left periphery, this analysis leads us to conclude that Saramaccan constructions such as those in (39) represent full clauses headed by a one-place predicate.

4.2   Predicative reduplicated verbal adjectives as secondary predicates

As mentioned earlier, Saramaccan also displays predicative constructions where the reduplicated verbal adjective is adjacent to the noun it predicates over as indicated in (44).

(44)   a.   *dá   mi   [dí   páu   latjá-latjá]*   [Bakker 1987:30]
            Give   1SG   DET   wood   split-split
            'Give me the wood split'[17]

       b.   *A   njan   [dí   bakúba   lépi-lépi]*
            3SG   eat   DET   banana   ripe-ripe
            'He ate the banana (in a) ripe (state)'

Because the bracketed sequences in these examples show a similar word order to the examples in (37), one could conclude at first sight that the sentences under (41) are just variants of (37) where the copula is missing. This is the view presented in Aboh and Smith (forthcoming), but which now appears to us to be misleading. Indeed the bracketed sequence seems to occur in object position only. We haven't found any instance of such reduplicated verbal adjectives in subject position. The same condition is applicable to Bakker's (1987:31) cases where reduplicated predicative verbal adjectives can be fronted for focusing as in (45), from a position directly following an object only.

(45)   *Síki-síki   mi   kó   féni   hén*
       sick-sick   1SG   come   find   3SG
       'I found him sick.'

In accounting for the pattern in (44), therefore, we hypothesize that such examples are instances of secondary predicates where the bracketed sequence contains both the subject of a predicate and a reduplicated verbal adjective functioning as the predicate, as partially represented in (46a). Put differently, these examples are similar to English secondary predicates such as "He ate the banana ripe" or "I found the plate broken". Assuming this characterization is the right one, we propose to derive such constructions as represented in (46b), for sentence (44b): The rationale here is the same as in the case of Gungbe, with the only difference that FP is being selected by a lexical verb.

---

17.   Translation modified.

(46) a.

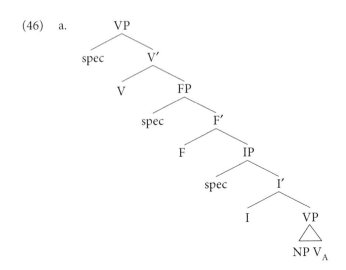

b.

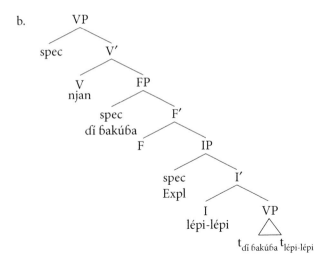

Given our previous observation that similar structures in Gungbe are reduced relative clauses that can be selected by a determiner, the question now arises whether Saramaccan displays such reduced relative clauses as well. An aspect of the constructions in (44) which suggests that this might indeed be the case is that these sentences can be paraphrased by full relative clauses where, for instance, (44b) would mean something like "He ate the banana that has ripened", or "He ate the banana that has become ripe". In the next section, we show that Saramaccan exhibits reduced relative clauses where the sequence FP is embedded under a determiner phrase.

4.3 Prenominal reduplicated verbal adjectives

While both Gungbe and Saramaccan display reduced relative clauses that involve a noun and a reduplicated adjective that functions as an attributive adjective, Saramaccan is unlike Gungbe, in that the attributive reduplicated verbal adjectives precede the modified noun. Compare the Saramaccan examples in (47b–c) to the Gungbe example (29b) repeated here as (47a) for convenience.

(47) a. *Núsɔ́nú fí-fá   lɔ́*
       soup   cold-cold DET
       'The cold soup'
   b. *dí   lái-lái   góni*   (Bakker 1987: 25)
       DET load-load gun
       'The loaded gun'
   c. *dí   dɛ́ɛ-dɛ́ɛ   koósu*
       DET dry-dry   cloth
       'The dry/dried cloth'

[handwritten marginal annotations: "exact copies", "repetition", "why not just ... to work", "formation"]

As is clear from these examples, the attributive reduplicated verbal adjective follows the noun and precedes the determiner in Gungbe, while it follows the determiner and precedes the noun in Saramaccan. Aside from word order differences, these reduplicated verbal adjectives, and their Gungbe equivalents, discussed in previous sections, have a state meaning and allow for a paraphrase with a relative clause.

In accounting for these examples, we hypothesize that reduplicated verbal adjectives derive from a structure where FP is embedded under a DP. Compared to the representations in (46), this would mean that the sequence *dí bakúba lépi-lépi* is embedded under a determiner phrase. This brings us back to the Gungbe structure in (32), repeated as (48a) for convenience. This description suggests that Gungbe and Saramaccan attributive reduplicated verbal adjectives display the same underlying structure. The derivation goes as follows: Starting with (48a), NP moves to [spec FP] of the reduced relative clause. Expl is inserted in [spec IP], licensed by the verbal adjective that raises to I and reduplicates there. This produces the order NP>VV, that is, *dí góni lái-lái* (lit. "the gun load-load") which is grammatical in Gungbe DP's but not in Saramaccan.[18]

---

18. The usual objection to this analysis (see e.g. Jouitteau this volume) is that having null expletives is counter-intuitive. Setting aside the case of traditional null subject languages which are assumed to involve expletive pro (e.g. Burzio 1986; Chomsky 1981, 1982; Rizzi 1982) one sometimes comes across examples like the following taken from Albiou (2007: 5) where it seems to us reasonable to postulate a null expletive.

(48) a.   [_DP [_D [_FP [_FP [_IP [_I [_AV NP V]]]]]]

b.

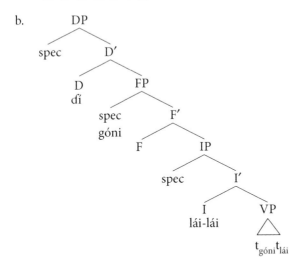

Indeed, Saramaccan differs from Gungbe in that the attributive reduplicated verbal adjective must precede the noun it modifies. We argue that in this context, the reduplicated VP must front to a position higher than the noun which occurs in [spec FP]. For the time being it is not clear to us what motivates this movement, but because we saw in examples (42) and (45) that the reduplicated predicate can front for the purpose of focus, we tentatively propose that the predicate fronts for the same reasons but inside the DP. This view is compatible with recent developments with regard to the morphosyntax of the DP (Aboh (2004a, b, 2005c, 2006c) that assume that the DP involves a left periphery including topic and focus projections. Under this view, the final stage of the derivation can be represented as in (49) below, where the reduplicated verb (presumably the whole IP) fronts to [spec FocP] inside the DP. This analysis therefore assumes that pre-nominal reduplicated verbal adjectives in Saramaccan represent an instance of predicate (or IP) inversion as shown in (49b). This representation stands for the Saramaccan example in (47b), repeated here as (49a).

(i)   Ø Was old chaps called Toutes use to do it.

(ii)   You could hardly see 'cause Ø was so much dust around

Indeed, unless we can prove that these constructions are subjectless predicates, it seems to us that a reasonable working hypothesis is to assume that they involve a null expletive that is syntactically constrained.

(49)   a.   *dí lái-lái góni*

   b.

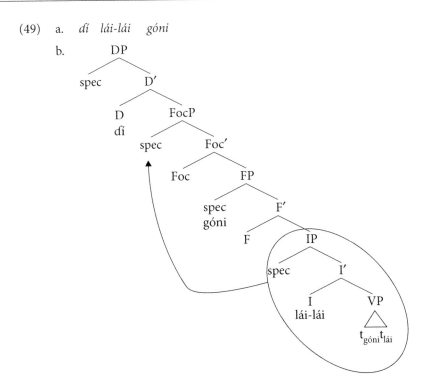

The analysis presented here to account for the Saramaccan reduplicated AV is comparable to the distribution of participles in English which can occur post-nominally or prenominally as in (50). Notice from these examples that the position of the participial adjective affects the meaning of the DP.

(50)   a.   I already had my egg boiled   [process > result]
             (= I already saw to it that my egg was boiled)

   b.   I already had my boiled egg   [process > state]
             (= I already ate my boiled egg)

In these cases too, we can hypothesize that (50b) derives from (50a) by predicate inversion just as in Saramaccan. Given this, we can further conclude that though reduplication serves to create "participle"-like forms which enter adjectival and resultative constructions in Saramaccan and Gungbe, the two languages differ as to the distribution of these reduplicated elements. While the reduplicated element always follows the noun in Gungbe, it follows the noun in resultative constructions in Saramaccan, but must precede it in attributive constructions. Given this analysis, we conclude that Saramaccan is similar to English. Put differently, while the Gbe languages might have influenced the development of the reduplicated forms in Saramaccan, the latter display structures that remind us of English.

In the following section, we show that while the Gbe languages sometimes use reduplication to derive nouns from verbs, some of which are completely lexicalized in the language, Saramaccan seems to have gone a step further in deriving such nouns.

5. Lexicalized nominal forms

This section will deal with possible lexicalizations of the Gbe reduplicated patterns in Saramaccan, and the Surinam creoles more generally.

We will examine possible cases in all three creole languages of Surinam, as Sranan, Ndyuka, and Saramaccan all illustrate the same feature of nonproductive deverbal reduplicative nominalizations. Some individual cases occur in all three languages, suggesting that this is an old feature, and sometimes we have to assume the replacement of an English-based case by a Portuguese-based case in Saramaccan.

First, however, we have to attempt to filter out cases of reduplicated iterative, diminutive or augmentative verb forms, which have undergone conversion to nouns. Take for example the reduplicated noun *tak(i)-taki* 'chatter' in Sranan. This is clearly derived from the verb *tak(i)-taki* 'to chatter'. How do we know this? *Taki* itself is a verb meaning 'to talk, say, speak'. The verb *tak(i)-taki* has an iterative meaning in relation to the non-reduplicated form. The noun *tak(i)-taki* cannot have the meaning 'talking' in Sranan. Similarly in Saramaccan we find *papiá* 'to chat(ter)', *papiá-papiá* 'to chatter', and *papiá-papiá* 'twaddle', which series we can probably derive in a similar fashion.

The remaining cases are probable genuine cases of Verbal Nouns in Saramaccan. Most cases are specialized in meaning, reinforcing our belief that this Gbe pattern was more or less stifled at birth, and probably never became productive in the Surinam creole languages.

There are various types of Verbal Nouns that we find in the various dictionaries,[19] or that these are based on: Action nouns, Result nouns, Gerunds, States, and Instruments.

---

19. De Groot 1977; SIL online dictionary; Haabo 2002; Glock 1996; Donicie & Voorhoeve 1963.

Language	Verb	Gloss	Derived Noun	Gloss	Oldest Form	Effect
Sranan	bari	shout	babari	tumult	balibali ca. 1765	Result
Ndyuka	bali (1)	shout	babali	noise		Result
Ndyuka	bali (2)	shout	balibali	noise		Result
Saramaccan	bɛ	red	bɛbɛ	yolk		State noun
Sranan	redi[20]	red	rediredi[21]	bloody flux		State noun
Sranan	bron	burn	bronbron	burnt rice in pan	id. 1856	Result
Ndyuka	boon	burn	boonboon	burnt rice in pan		Result
Sranan	doro	sieve	dorodoro	sieve	id. 1856	Instrument
Sranan	djompo	jump	djompodjompo	grasshopper	djompo djompo	Gerund > Patient
Sranan	fon	beat	fonfon	blow, beating	fomfom 1770	Action
Saramaccan	fon	beat up	fonfon	beating	fummfumm 1778	Action
Ndyuka	fon	spank	fonfon	severe beating		Action
Sranan	frey	fly	freyfrey	fly		Gerund > Patient
Ndyuka	fee	fly	feefee	fly		Gerund > Patient
Saramaccan	ɓuwá	fly	ɓuwaɓuwa	fly (sp.)		Gerund > Patient
Sranan	griti	grate	gritgriti	grater	gritigriti 1856	Instrument
Ndyuka	hei	be high	heihei	hill		State noun

(Continued)

Language	Verb	Gloss	Derived Noun	Gloss	Oldest Form	Effect
Sranan	kan	comb	kankan	comb	kankamm 1783	Instrument
Ndyuka	kan	comb	kankan	comb		Instrument
Saramaccan	kan	comb	kankan	bird's comb		Instrument
Sranan	kapu	chop	kap'kapoe 1856	machete	id. 1856	Instrument
Sranan	kofu	cuff	kofoe kofoe 1856	cuff	id. 1856	Action
Sranan	koti	cut	kottikotti 1856	slice	id. 1856	Result
Sranan	krabu (1)	scratch, scrape	krabbo-krabbo	rake	id. 1783	Instrument
Sranan	krabu (2)	scratch, scrape	krabkrabu	boot-scraper		Instrument
Sranan	krasi	scratch	kraskrasi	rash	krassikrassi 1778	Result
Saramaccan	kaási	itch	kasikaasi	wound		Result
Ndyuka	koolu	curl hair	koolukoolu	wood-curls		Result
Ndyuka	kuutu	complain, argue	kuutkuutu	court of justice		Gerund
Ndyuka	kuutu	complain, argue	kuutkuutu	arbitration meeting		Gerund
Saramaccan	(Fongbe: mὲ)	roast	maemae	barbecue	id. 1778	Instrument
Sranan	moy	(be) beautiful	mo'mooi	finery	id. 1856	State noun
Sranan	moy	complain, argue	moymoy	finery		State noun
Ndyuka	moi(n)	be beautiful	moi(n)moi(n)	present		State noun
Sranan	nai	sew	nanai	needle	nainai 1783	Instrument
Ndyuka	nai(n)	sew	nanai(n)	needle		Instrument

(Continued)

Language	Verb	Gloss	Derived Noun	Gloss	Oldest Form	Effect
Sarramaccan	nái	sew	nainai	needle	id. 1778	Instrument
Sranan	njan	eat	nja(n)njan	food	jam jam ca. 1765	Gerund?
Ndyuka	nyan	eat	nyanyan	food		Gerund?
Ndyuka	obo, opo	open	oboobo, opoopo	opener		Instrument
Saramaccan	peká	stick, fasten	pekápeká	rod		Instrument
Saramaccan	pindya	pinch	pindyapindya	clothes peg		Instrument
Sranan	saka	let down	sakasaka	dregs	sakkasakka 1783	Result
Sranan	seki	shake	sekseki	rattle		Instrument
Ndyuka	seke	shake	sekeseke	rattle		Instrument
Saramaccan	séki	shake	shekisheki	Canna Indica[22]	id. 1778	
Sranan	sibi	sweep	sisibi	broom	zibi zibi ca. 1765	Instrument
Ndyuka	sibi	sweep	sisibi	broom		Instrument
Sranan	tai (1)	tie	ta(i)tai	bundle		Result
Saramaccan	tái	tie	táitái	bundle		Result
Sranan	tai (2)	tie	titei	rope	tyty ca. 1765	Instrument
Ndyuka	tei	tie	tetei	rope		Instrument
Saramaccan	tái	tie	tatái	rope, creeper	taitai 1778	Instrument
Saramaccan	tapá	cover	tapátapá	ceiling		Gerund

(Continued)

Language	Verb	Gloss	Derived Noun	Gloss	Oldest Form	Effect
Sranan	tja(ri)	carry	tjatjari	headpad	tgerre tgerre 1761	Instrument
Saramaccan	tuwɛɛ	throw away	tuweituwei	fleamarket		Gerund?
Sranan	wai	fan	wawai	fan	waiwai 1783	Instrument
Ndyuka	wai	blow, wave	wawai	fan		Instrument
Saramaccan	wái	wave	wáiwái	fan		Instrument
Saramaccan	wái	wave	waiwai	whisk	id. 1778	Instrument
Sranan	weti	white	wetweti	dandruff		State noun
Saramaccan	(dɛ) (w)ógi	angry, evil, mean	wógi-wógi	anger		State noun
Saramaccan	(dɛ) (w)ógi	angry, evil, mean	ógi-ógi	naughtiness, tricks		Result

This seems to constitute a fairly complete list of reduplicated deverbal nouns for which only non-reduplicated verbs appear to provide the basis. We cannot of course know with complete certainty whether there is not a reduplicated iterative, diminutive or augmentative verb form that is just not listed, but does provide the basis for one of the cases in the table. However, we would then expect to observe a difference in meaning as between the verb and the noun. Although there are cases of deverbal nouns with a more specialized meaning than the corresponding verb, these do not seem to fall into the three categories just mentioned.

Some of the base verbs listed have either an iterative meaning, or the possibility of an iterative reading. So the Sranan *doro* 'to sieve', like its English counterpart, describes a repetitive action. The deverbal noun, however, does not, referring as it does, like its English counterpart again, to the instrument used for 'sieving'. In fact an instrumental meaning is a frequent meaning for a deverbal noun derived from a base verb with an iterative aktionsart. Let us now turn to a consideration of Fongbe/Gungbe Verbal Nouns.

5.1 The derivation of verbal nouns in Eastern Gbe

These Verbal Nouns appear to come in various flavours involving gerunds/action nouns, or result/state nouns. In addition, it is not clear how productive these forms are and what lexical rule (if any) underlies them. For instance, while the two reduplicated intransitive verbs in (51a–b) can be used as gerunds in Gungbe, the transitive verb in (51c) appears less adequate.

(51) a. *hì-hɔ̀n*
         Flee-flee
         'fleeing, flight'

      b. *kú-kú*
         die-die
         'death

      c. ??/*kì-kàn
         write-write
         'writing'

At first, one could think that there might be a transitivity restriction on reduplicated forms such that only intransitive verbs can double to derive nouns. Things do not seem so clear-cut though. Indeed, (52b) shows that the verb *ɖù* 'eat' which under other circumstances requires an object or must be followed by the dummy object *nú* 'thing', can reduplicate to form a verbal noun (52b). In such cases, the noun can have a completely different meaning. In the case at hand, *ɖù-ɖù* is taken to mean 'backsheesh' and not 'thing to eat' or 'food'. The latter is rendered as *nú-ɖù-ɖù* (lit. "thing-eat-eat").

(52) a. *Ùn jró   ná   ḍù   *(àklà/nú)*
          1SG want PREP eat biscuit/thing
          'I want to eat a biscuit/I want to eat'

      b. *À   kɛ̀   nù   bló   ḍù-ḍù   dín   wɛ̀   é   tɛ̀*
          2SG open mouth NEG eat-eat look FOC 3SG ASP
          'Don't mind him, he is looking for baksheesh'

With this caveat in mind, we propose that such reduplicated forms are actually phrases that are comparable to other instances of reduplications that we discussed in previous sections. This view is confirmed by certain distributive properties of these reduplicated verbs. In Gungbe (and in Fongbe) they can be embedded under a possessive determiner phrase functioning as nominal arguments.

(53) a. *hì-hɔ̀n   é-tɔ̀n   lɔ́   kpácá   mì   Gungbe*
          Flee-flee 3SG-GEN DET surprise 1SG
          'His flight/fleeing surprised me'

      b. *kú-kú   é-tɔ̀n   lɔ́   kpácá   mì*
          die-die 3SG-GEN DET surprise 1SG
          'His death/dying surprised me.'

When other transitive verbs are involved (different from the *ḍù*-type), an object, even if only a dummy object noun like *nù* 'thing', is obligatory. In the following example this role is taken by *wé*, which in this context means 'written letter'.

(54) *Dàwè énè sín   wé   kì-kàn   lɔ́   nɔ̀   jɛ̀   cé   jí   tàùn*
       man DEM GEN letter write-write DET HAB fall 1SG.GEN on very
       'This man's writing pleases me a lot.'

In Fongbe, the process seems more productive. Compare the following quote from Anonymous (1983: VII, 4):

(55) "1. Si c'est un verbe d'état, on obtient le substantif indiquant la qualité.
           /kló/= être gros →/klókló/= (le fait d'être gros) = la grosseur
       2. Si c'est un verbe d'action, on obtient le substantif indiquant le fait de
           faire cette action
           /sí/= respecter →/sísí/= (le fait d'être poli) = le respect"

This certainly seems to be the likely starting-point as far as the interpretation of these deverbal formations by non-Gbe speakers is concerned. However, to refer to these forms in an across-the-board fashion as substantives represents a simplification of the facts. Like English gerunds these forms are more than mere nouns. We will return to this point later.

5.2   The structure of (O)VV "Gerunds" again

This type of structure was briefly discussed in Section 2.3 in connection with the
so-called OVV structures for which Aboh (2005a) assumes the following structure
(56) repeated from (27).

(56)

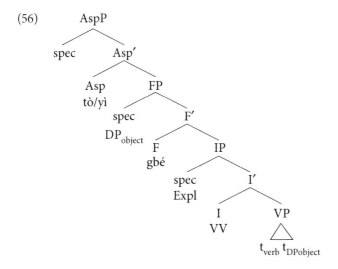

Recall that the reason for the verb remaining reduplicated here despite the presence of an object was that the object in such constructions was not in [spec IP]
but had moved to [spec FP]. This is comparable to the situation described in
Section 2.2 on reduplication in OV sequences whereby verb reduplications occur
if the object fails to occur in the preverbal position either because it is missing
(e.g. in the case of intransitives), has been pronominalized, or wh-extracted for
questions and focus. In these types of constructions we concluded that the verb
reduplicates because of the need to create an inflected form that licenses the expletive in [spec IP]. We therefore reach the generalization that instances of reduplication involve phrases. Above in (26), see also (57) below, we showed that this
is indeed the case because the phrases involving reduplicated verbs can occur in
argument positions.[20]

(57)   a.   [Wè   ɖú-ɖú]   nɔ̀   nyɔ́n   tàùn   (Gungbe)
            Dance dance-dance   HAB   good   very
            'Dancing is very pleasant'

---

20.   It is important to keep in mind that in these OVV contexts, the fronted object cannot be
omitted nor can it be pronominalized.

    b.   *Súrù gbὲ*   [*wὲ*   *ɖú-ɖú*]
            Suru refuse   dance dance-dance
            'Suru refused to dance'

    c.   [*Wὲ*   *ɖú-ɖú*]   *wὲ*   *nɔ*   *jró*   *Súrù*
            dance dance-dance   FOC HAB please Suru
            'Suru likes DANCING/TO DANCE'

Under certain circumstances, for example the occurrence of a Prospective in the gerundial phrase, reduplication is blocked as illustrated again in (58).[21]

(58) a.   [*Xó*   *ná*   *ɖò*   *dìn*]   *má*   *jró*   *mì*
           word PROSP say now NEG please me
           'Speaking (a word) now does not please me'

      b.   *[Xó*   *ná*   *ɖì-ɖò*   *dìn*]   *má*   *jró*   *mì*
           work PROSP say-say now NEG please me
           'Working now does not please me'

In Fongbe, where similar examples are easy to find (Lefebvre & Brousseau 2002:208), such reduplicated verbs preceded by the object may occur with a determiner:

(59) a.   *làn*   *ɖì-ɖà*   (*ɔ*)
           meat prepare-prepare (DET)
           '(the) preparing of meat'

      b.   *làn*   *ɖì-ɖà*   *bàyí*   *tɔn*   (*ɔ*)
           meat prepare-prepare Bayi GEN (DET)
           'Bayi('s) preparing (of) the meat'

Lefebvre and Brousseau's translations, although they reflect the meaning pretty accurately, do not reflect the Fongbe structures properly. Actually *làn ɖì-ɖà* ought rather to be regarded as an incorporated structure *làn-ɖì-ɖà* 'meat-preparing, meat-preparation'.

Similarly to parallel English structures such as *wood-cutting* or *tree-climbing* where we also find what we will call here *de-incorporated* or *externalized* structures such as *cutting of (the) wood* and *climbing of (the) tree*, such structures also exist in Fongbe.[22] Lefebvre and Brousseau exemplify this with examples where the former object has a postposed genitive marker. There are in fact two such markers,

---

sín, misleadingly translated by Lefebvre and Brousseau as OBJ, and *tɔ̀n*, given the translation GEN. We gloss these both as GEN here.

(60) a. *kɔ̀kú* **sín** *ɖì-ɖé*   *ɖàgbè élɔ́ ɔ́ lɛ́ bí Fongbe*
           Koku GEN draw-draw good DEM DET PL all
           'all these good drawings of Koku' [in question]

      b. *ɖì-ɖé*   *ɖàgbè kɔ̀kú* **tɔ̀n** *élɔ́ ɔ́ lɛ́ bí*
           draw-draw good Koku GEN DEM DET PL all
           'all these good drawings of Koku' [in question]

In fact, also just like English, Fongbe appears to have the option of preposed and postposed genitive structures. So *kɔ̀kú* **sín** could be compared with *John's*, and *kɔ̀kú* **tɔ̀n** with *of John('s)* (see Aboh 2002, 2005c for discussion). Note also that similarly to English genitive structures we find a wide range of meanings associated with these genitive constructions. So, to take the above Fongbe examples, the meaning can apparently involve all the relationships expressible by *of*, in this case:

(61) 'all these good drawings made by Koku'   [agent]
      'all these good drawings made of Koku'   [theme]
      'all these good drawings possessed by Koku' [possessor]

Note then that the de-incorporation of the incorporated object involves a disassociation of the object and its reduplicated verb. The verb remains reduplicated, since the nominalized verbal structure remains what it was prior to extraction. However, there is also an important difference between *tɔ̀n*-phrases and *sín*-phrases. The above patterns seem at first sight to be the same (apart from their positions), but this is not the case. For a start only one co-dependent *tɔ̀n*-phrase is possible, not a sequence, just like genitive-marked cases in English (Brousseau & Lumsden 1992:8):

(62) a. **ɖì-ɖé*   [*Aristote* **tɔ̀n**] [*kɔ̀kú* **tɔ̀n**] *lɛ̀*
           Draw-draw Aristotle GEN Koku GEN PL
           'Koku's sketches of Aristotle'

      b. *Koku's [Aristotle's sketches]

In contrast a sequence of co-dependent *sín*-phrases is possible, following a strict thematic hierarchy (Brousseau & Lumsden 1992:8) as described in (63).

(63) <u>*sín*-phrase thematic hierarchy</u>
      Possessor – Agent – Goal – Source – Theme

This is illustrated by the following example:

(64) [*kɔ̀kú* **sín**] [*Rembrandt* **sín**] [*aristote* **sín**] *ɖì-ɖé*   *lɛ̀*
      Koku GEN Rembrandt GEN Aristotle GEN draw-draw PL
      'the sketches **of** Koku's **by** Rembrandt **of** Aristotle'

The fact of the existence of de-incorporated nominalized reduplicated structures like the three types illustrated would ease the "free" interpretation of such
structures by non-Gbe speakers. We do not have to assume that the Saramaccan
reduplicated deverbal noun pattern occurred first with intransitive verbs, spreading later to transitives. Much more likely is that de-incorporated structures also
formed the basis of the pattern directly. So the Saramaccan phrase as in (65),

why is it much more likely?

(65) bigúngú bi   púu   a   dí   tapá-tapá   (f)u dí   wósu
      bedbug PST remove LOC DET cover-cover GEN DET house
      'The bedbug fell from the ceiling of the hut'

contains a reduplicated de-verbal noun *tapá-tapá*, literally 'covering', from the
verb *tapá* 'to cover'. The reduplicated verbal nouns in Fongbe and Gungbe give us
gerunds and result nouns (see above), and this example can indeed be interpreted
as deriving from a result noun meaning 'covering'.

At the same time intransitives presumably also contributed to the pattern.
Consider the following sentence from De Groot (1977):

(66) dí   wógi-wógi   u   sɛmbɛ
      DET angry-angry GEN person
      'the anger of the people'   De Groot (1977:44)

This is clearly a nominal expression with a state meaning, as can be seen from the
definite article. In the next section we will compare the two English possibilities,
of Gerund (*describing*) and Verbal Noun (*describing (of)*).

5.3   English verbal nominalizations

This account, and the parallels drawn therein with Saramaccan and Gbe language
structures are very preliminary. We distinguish here between Gerunds and Verbal
Noun-formations in English. In truth, both types in *-ing* are frequently referred
to as gerunds. The difference is somewhat parallel to the distinction we have
drawn above between incorporated and de-incorporated structures in the Gbe
languages, although none of the examples in (67a) involves incorporation. So the
difference between Gerunds (in the narrower sense in which we are employing it
here) and Verbal Nouns in English is basically that illustrated between the (a) and
(b) sentences here.

(67) **Gerunds**
      a.   [Reading a book] will be good for you
      a'.   [Reading the book] will be good for you
      a''.   [Reading books] will be good for you
      a'''.   [Reading the books] will be good for you
      a''''.   *[The reading the book] will be good for you
      a'''''. *[A reading the book] will be good for you

Verbal nouns

b.   *[Reading of a book] took five hours
b′.   *[Reading of the book] took five hours
b″.   [The reading of a book] took five hours
b‴.   [The reading of the book] took five hours   *Count nominals*
b⁗.   [A reading of the book] took five hours
b‴‴.   [Readings of the book] went on for days
b‴‴‴. [Some readings of the book] went on for days

These examples show that there is a fundamental difference between type-a and type-b cases. The plain gerund with a direct object must be unmarked for number and cannot be accompanied by a definite article. Type-b "verbal nouns" bear no direct internal arguments, and display the normal distribution of articles. Nouns bearing semantic relationships to verbal noun predicates have to have these expressed with the help of prepositions. Furthermore the verbal noun must either be marked for plurality, or else be accompanied by an article, determiner, or a quantifier. This means that type-a "Gerunds" cannot be count nominals, whereas type-b "Verbal Nouns" have to be count nominals.

It should be mentioned that the use of incorporated forms is also possible in English. We appear to have two types also here. A gerund type version which is non-countable:

(68)   Book-reading is good for you   *eg An oven-cleaning is not something to look forward to.*

And a verbal noun type countable version: *I disagree*

(69)   a.   A book-reading is something to look forward to
        b.   Book-readings are something to look forward to.

The difference in meaning between (68) and (69) emphasizes the distinctions noted above between gerunds and verbal nouns. (69) has been lexicalized, while (68) has not. *So it should only work with lexicalized compounds !*

The conclusion so far must be that English and Gbe verbal nouns and gerunds show partial parallels. Indeed we observe a difference when it comes to the expression of external arguments of the verbal action. A verbal noun in English may only indicate an external argument by a genitive-marked subject preceding the verbal noun. Also any modification of the verbal action must be expressed by an adjective and not by an adverb. Both these two facts indicate the more nominal nature of the expression.

(70)   a.   He didn't like my slapping of his donkey
        b.   He didn't like my (frequent) slapping of his donkey (*frequently)

The use of an adverb in final position in (70b) is interpreted as an awkward equivalent of:

(70)   b'.   He frequently didn't like my slapping of his donkey   *!o*

where the adverb *frequent(ly)* modifies the verb *like* and not *slap*.

The gerund, on the other hand, despite its possibility to function as an argument retains certain verbal characteristics in English, in particular the fact that modification of the verbal action has to be expressed by an adverb.

(71)   He didn't like my (*frequent) slapping his donkey (frequently)

Another possibility is that of using the object form of the pronoun or the non-genitive-marked form of the noun preceding the verb. In object position this has been described in terms of Raising:

(72)   a.   He didn't like me (*frequent) slapping his donkey (frequently)
       b.   He was annoyed by me (*frequent) slapping his donkey (frequently)

In some forms of Standard English however, e.g. in Scottish Standard English, a similar set of forms occurs in subject positions.

(73)   a.   [Me slapping his donkey] annoyed him.   [subject position]
       b.   [Me slapping his donkey], it annoyed him   [topic position]

Clefts and pseudo-clefts illustrate a similar pattern:

(74)   a.   It was [me slapping his donkey] that annoyed him   [cleft position]
       b.   What annoyed him was [me slapping his donkey]   [pseudo-cleft position]

To speakers who use both the "me"-gerund forms in (72–73) and the corresponding "my"-gerund forms in different social/situational contexts, the "me"-gerund forms feel more verby (cf. Aarts 2003: 32, examples (95–7)).

The possible structures of Fongbe and English seem to be roughly comparable as illustrated in Table 3. The full range of possibilities in Saramaccan has still to be investigated.

Verbal nouns that are or are based on State nouns, Gerunds, Action nouns and Result nouns are the expected types. An unexpected type that occurs frequently is the Instrumental type. This cannot be a direct reflection of Gbe structures as instrumental nouns always involve the final element -*nú* 'thing' in these languages.

We quote a few examples from Lefebvre & Brousseau (2002):

(75)   àzɔ̀-wá-nú   work-do-thing   'tool'
       nù-tɔ́-nú   thing-sew-thing   'needle'
       sìn-glɔ́-nú   water-protect-thing   'raincoat/umbrella'

Lefebvre & Brousseau regard the final -*nú* 'thing' as a nominal element in a compound. We are of the opinion that it could just as well be regarded as a (semantically bleached) suffix.

Table 3. Fongbe and English verbal nominalization

	Fongbe			English
incorporated	<u>làn</u>-**dì-dà** meat-**prepare-prepare**			<u>meat</u>-**preparing**
1 dependent	**dì-dé** draw-draw	[kòkú tòn] of Koku('s)		[<u>Koku</u> 's] **drawing**
>1 co-dependents	[<u>kòkú</u> sín] of Koku's	[<u>aristote</u> sín] of Aristotle	**dì-dé** draw-draw	**drawings** [of <u>Koku('s)</u>] [of Aristotle]
mixed	[<u>báyí</u> sín] **dì-dé** [kòkú tòn]			[<u>Koku</u> 's] **drawing** [of <u>Bayi</u>]

6.   Conclusion

In this article we have attempted to show that in particular the non-iconic reduplications occurring in Eastern Gbe languages share structural affinities with similar structures occurring in the Surinamese creole languages, in particular, Saramaccan.

All such non-iconic reduplications can be categorized as falling into either "Adjectival" or "Gerundial" categories. The gerundial type falls in the Gbe languages into two types which can be characterized as more verbal like English true gerunds, and more nominal like English *ing*-verbal nouns. In both languages we also encounter lexicalized deverbal nouns, and this is the only type found in Saramaccan and the other Surinamese creoles.

We refer back to examples in the text, keeping their numbers for ease of reference.

A productive category of adjectival reduplications in Saramaccan and Gungbe are derived from what we have called Adjectival Verbs (AVs). These correspond to concepts expressed by adjectives in European languages. Typical examples of Adjectival Verbs were found in (1):

Adjectival Verbs

(1) a. *dí*   *lío*   *dɛɛ́*   Saramaccan online dictionary
         DET river dry
         'The river is low'

     b. *Tɔ̀*   *lɔ́*   *xú*   Gungbe
         river DET dry
         'The river is dry/dried up'

These AVs can be reduplicated to form resultative adjectives in Saramaccan:

(2) a. *A   tá   nján gwamba **dɛɛ́-dɛɛ́***   Saramaccan
         3SG PROG eat   meat   dry-dry.
         'He is eating the meat dried'

and attributive adjectives in both Saramaccan and Gungbe.

     b. *dí   **dɛɛ́-dɛɛ́** kɔkɔnɔ́tɔ-wáta*   Saramaccan
         DET   dry-dry   coconut-milk
         'The dried coconut milk'(= 'the coconut-flesh')

(3) *É   dù   lán   **xú-xú***   Gungbe
     3SG eat   meat dry-dry
     'He ate dried meat'

Note the difference between the Progressive Aspect in the two languages. In Saramaccan no reduplication takes place, whereas in Gungbe it is required if no pre-verbal object is present. In the examples in question the verb *die* is intransitive. Aboh (2005a, 2009) would regard the Gungbe form as a gerund, similarly to the (origin of the) Progressive form in English in *-ing*.

(76) *A   tá   **dɛ̌dɛ̀***[23]   Saramaccan online dictionary
      3SG PROG die
      'He's on his deathbed, is dying'

(77) *dí   wáta tá   **dɛɛ́***   Saramaccan online dictionary
      DET water PROG dry
      'The river is getting low'

(6) a. *àvún lɔ́   tò   **kú-kú-**`*   Gungbe
         Dog   DET   PROG die-die-PRTL
         'The dog is dying'

Note the presence of a (tonal) particle following the reduplication in Gungbe. Fongbe has a particle with segmental make-up *-wɛ̀* in the same context.

Corresponding to the Adjectival Verb (AV) in (1a, b) above, which Vinije (2002) characterizes as an *action verb* ('actieve handeling'), we find reduplicated predicative adjectives expressing *static situations*. The contrast can be seen for

---

23. This is not a reduplicated form. It is the Saramaccan word derived from English *dead*. The reduplicated form would be *dɛ̌dɛ-dɛ̌dɛ*.

Saramaccan in (4a, b), where (4a) is yet another example of an AV, while the reduplicated adjective is found in (4b):

(4)   a.   *dí   kúja   mandú*   Saramaccan
          DET   calabash ripe
          'The calabash ripens'

      b.   *dí   kúja   dɛ̌   mandú-mandú*
          DET   calabash COP ripe-ripe
          'The calabash is ripe'

In Gbe, reduplicated adjectives, are restricted in their occurrence:

(5)   b.   *àvún lɔ́   tò   kú-kú   tò   kɔ́-mὲ*   Gungbe
          Dog   DET COP   die-die COP ground-in
          'The dog was (lying) dead on the ground'

Note that this form only differs from the Gungbe progressive in the absence versus presence of the final (tonal) particle.

(6)   b.   *àvún lɔ́   tò   kú-kú   tò   kɔ́-mὲ-ˋ*
          Dog   DET PROG die-die COP ground-in-PRTL
          'The dog is dying on the ground'

Gerunds of a more nominal character are typified by the (O)VV constructions of Gbe languages. An O(bject) present in such a construction can be regarded as an incorporated object-noun, rather like an incorporated form *tree-climbing* in English.

(26) d.   [*Pípàn dí-dó   lɔ́*]
          train   take-take. DET
          'Taking the train'

In the type of construction represented by (26d) the internal argument structure associated with the predicate *dó* 'take' is retained. It is possible also however to de-incorporate the object. Any DPs used with the gerund must the be used with postpositions *sín, tɔ̀n*, equivalent to English *of*, Saramaccan *(f)u* 'of', where the relationship of the DP to the noun can be quite varied, including agent, theme, possession, and so on.

Some of these "stripped" gerunds are then lexicalized, developing specialized meanings. It is at this point that we see a parallel with the reduplicated verbal nouns of Saramaccan and the other Surinamese creoles. So Gungbe *kú-kú* has the meaning 'death' as a lexicalized verbal noun. This is somewhat different in its semantics from the meaning of the same form as a gerund, i.e. 'dying', in the sense that it refers specifically to the *result* and not the *process*.

Similarly, we see that an English lexicalized verbal noun can retain the same form as a gerund, but still differ in meaning. Cf. (67), where the gerund *reading* retains the semantics of the verb *read*, as against the homophonous verbal noun typically refers to an individuated act of 'reading out loud'.

Saramaccan, on the other hand, only has lexicalized verbal nouns. So *buwa-buwa* 'species of fly' is a lexicalization of an original gerund 'flying', derived from *buwá* 'to fly'. There is no present gerund form *buwa-buwa* with the meaning 'flying', however.

The differences in productivity are striking. In the Gbe languages reduplication of verbs to form OVV gerundial structures occurs regularly under strictly defined syntactic conditions. Sometimes these conditions are not met (cf. 28), and then no reduplication takes place. In Saramaccan there is no productive formation of reduplicated deverbal nominal structures. Only a relatively small number of reduplicated deverbal nouns occur (see Section 5).

When we turn to adjective-formation, it is Saramaccan that has a completely productive process, while the Gbe languages tend to restrict this process to quality verbs.

We do not fully understand this difference. It may be possible to relate it to the fact that English has a more productive relation between verbal forms (participles) and adjectives derived from participles. This is a subject requiring further attention.

References

Aarts, Bas. 2004. Modelling linguistic gradience. *Studies in Language* 28: 1–49.

Aboh, Enoch O. 2002. Morphosyntaxe de la périphérie gauche nominale. In *La syntaxe de la définitude*, Anne Zribi-Hertz & Anne Daladier (eds), *Recherches linguistiques de Vincennes* 31: 9–26.

Aboh, Enoch O. 2004a. *The Morphosyntax of Complement-head Sequences: Clause Structure and Word Order Patterns in Kwa*. Oxford: OUP.

Aboh, Enoch O. 2004b. Topic and Focus within D. *Linguistics in The Netherlands* 21: 1–12.

Aboh, Enoch O. 2005a. Object shift, verb movement and verb reduplication. In *The Oxford Handbook of Comparative Syntax*, Guglielmo Cinque & Richard Kayne (eds), 138–177. Oxford: OUP.

Aboh, Enoch O. 2005b. The category P: The Kwa paradox. *Linguistic Analysis* 32: 615–646.

Aboh, Enoch O. 2005c. Deriving relative and factive constructions in Kwa. In *Contributions to the Thirtieth Incontro di Grammatica Generativa*, Laura Brugè, Giuliana Guisti, Nicola Munaro, Walter Schweikert & Giuseppina Turano (eds), 265–285. Venezia: Cafoscarina.

Aboh, Enoch O. 2006a. When predicates go fronting. *ZAS Working Papers in Linguistics* 46: 21–48.

Aboh, Enoch O. 2006b. Complementation in Saramaccan and Gungbe: The case of c-type modal particles. *Natural Language and Linguistic Theory* 24(1): 1–55.

Aboh, Enoch O. 2006c. The role of the syntax-semantics interface in language transfer. In *L2 Acquisition and Creole Genesis: Dialogues* [Language Acquisition and Language Disorders 42], Claire Lefebvre, Lydia White & Christine Jourdan (eds), 221–252. Amsterdam: John Benjamins.

Aboh, Enoch O. 2007a. A 'mini' relative clause analysis for reduplicated attributive adjectives. *Linguistics in The Netherlands* 24: 1–13.

Aboh, Enoch O. 2007b. La genèse de la périphérie gauche du saramaka: Un cas d'influence du substrat? In *Grammaires Créoles et Grammaire Comparative*, Karl Gadelii & Anne Zribi-Hertz (eds), 73–97. Paris: L'Harmattan.

Aboh, Enoch O. 2009. Clause structure and verb series. *Linguistic Inquiry* 40: 1–33.

Aboh, Enoch O. 2010. The P-route. In *Mapping Spatial PPs. The Cartography of Syntactic Structures*, Vol. 6, Guglielmo Cinque & Luigi Rizzi (eds), 225–260. Oxford: OUP.

Aboh, Enoch O. & Dyakonova, Marina. 2009. Predicate doubling and parallel chains. *Lingua* 119: 1035–1065.

Aboh, Enoch O & Smith, Norval. Forthcoming. Non-iconic reduplications in Eastern Gbe and Surinam. To appear in *The Trans-Atlantic Sprachbund: Benin and Surinam*, Pieter C. Muysken & Norval Smith (eds), Berlin: Mouton de Gruyter.

Alboiu, Gabriela. 2007. Null expletives and case: The view from Romance. Paper presented at the 37th Linguistic Symposium on Romance Languages March 15–18, 2007, University of Pittsburgh.

Anonymous. 1983. *Éléments de recherche sur la langue fon*. Cotonou: n.p.

Bakker, Peter. 1987. Reduplications in Saramaccan. In *Studies in Saramaccan Language Structure* [Caribbean Culture Studies 2], Mervyn C. Alleyne (ed.), Amsterdam: ATW, Universiteit van Amsterdam.

Bakker, Peter. 2003a. The absence of reduplication in pidgins. In *Twice as Meaningful. Reduplication in Pidgins, Creoles and Other Contact Languages* [Westminster Creolistic Series 8], Silvia Kouwenberg (ed.), 37–46. London: Battlebridge.

Bakker, Peter. 2003b. Reduplication in Saramaccan. In *Twice as Meaningful. Reduplication in Pidgins, Creoles and Other Contact Languages* [Westminster Creolistic Series 8], Silvia Kouwenberg (ed.), 73–82. London: Battlebridge.

Bakker, Peter. 2003c. Pidgin inflectional morphology and its implications for creole morphology. In *Yearbook of Morphology 2002*, Geert Booij & Jaap van Marle (eds), 3–33. Dordrecht: Kluwer.

Bole-Richard, Remy. 1983. *Systématique phonologique et grammaticale d'un parler ewe: le genmina du Sud-Togo et Sud-Bénin*. Paris: L'Harmattan.

Brousseau, Anne-Marie, & John S. Lumsden. 1992. Nominal Structure in Fongbe. *The Journal of West African Languages* 22: 5–25.

Burzio, Luigi. 1986. *Italian Syntax: A Government-binding Approach*. Dordrecht: Kluwer.

Chomsky, Noam. 1986. *Lectures on Government and Binding*. Dordrecht: Foris.

Chomsky, Noam. 1995. *The Minimalist Program*. Cambridge MA: The MIT Press.

Cinque, Guglielmo. 2010. The syntax of adjectives: A comparative study. Cambridge MA: The MIT Press.

de Groot, Adrianus H.P. 1977. *Woordregister Nederlands-Saramakaans*. Paramaribo: VACO.

Donicie, Anton & Voorhoeve, Jan. 1963. *De Saramakaanse Woordenschat*. Amsterdam: Bureau voor Taalonderzoek in Surinam van de Universiteit van Amsterdam.

Farquharson, Joseph T. 2007. Creole morphology revisited. In *Deconstructing Creole* [Typological Studies in Language 73], Umberto Ansaldo, Stephen Matthews & Lisa Lim (eds), 21–37. Amsterdam: John Benjamins.

Glock, Naomi. 1996. *Holansi-Saamaka wöutubuku*. Paramaribo: Evangelische Broedergemeente.

Haabo, Vinje. 2002. Grammatica en fonetiek van het Saramaccaans. Ms, Wageningen.

International Bible Society. 2009. *Gadu Buku: Nieuwe Testament in Het Saramaccaans*, 2nd edn.

Jondoh, E.E. 1980. Some Aspects of the Predicate Phrase in Gengbe. UMI Dissertation Series.

Kayne, Richard. 1994. *The Antisymmetry of Syntax*. Cambridge MA: The MIT Press.

Kouwenberg, Silvia & LaCharité, Darlene. 2003. The meanings of 'more of the same'. Iconicity in reduplication and the evidence for substrate transfer in the genesis of Caribbean Creole languages. In Twice as Meaningful. Reduplication in Pidgins, Creoles and Other Contact Languages [Westminster Creolistic Series 8], Silvia Kouwenberg (ed.), London: Battlebridge.

Lefebvre, Claire & Brousseau, Anne-Marie. 2002. *A Grammar of Fongbe*. Berlin: Mouton de Gruyter.

McWhorter, John. 2001. The world's simplest grammars are Creole grammars. *Linguistic Typology* 5: 125–166.

Rizzi, Luigi. 1982. *Issues in Italian Syntax*. Dordrecht: Foris.

Rizzi, Luigi & Shlonsky, Ur. 2007. Strategies of subject extraction. In *Interfaces+Recursion=Language?*, Hans-Martin Gärtner & Uli Sauerland (eds), 115–160. Berlin: Mouton de Gruyter.

Saramaccan online dictionary. ⟨http://www.sil.org/americas/Surinam/Saramaccan/English/SaramEngDictIndex.html⟩

Sebba, Mark. 1981. Derivational regularities in Surinam. *Linguistics* 19: 101–117.

Simpson, A. 2001. Definiteness agreement and the Chinese DP. *Language and Linguistics* 2(1): 125–156.

Smith, Norval. 1990. Deverbal nominalization in Sranan: A search for regularities. In *Unity in Diversity: Papers Presented to Simon C. Dik on his 50th Birthday*, Harm Pinkster & Inge Genee (eds), 265–277. Dordrecht: Foris.

Veenstra, Tonjes. 1996. *Serial Verbs in Saramaccan: Predication and Creole Genesis* [HIL Dissertation 17]. The Hague: HAG.

Verb focus in Haitian

From lexical reiteration to Predicate Cleft*

Herby Glaude & Anne Zribi-Hertz
SFL/Université Paris-8-CNRS and ACLC/Amsterdam /
Université Paris-8/SFL, CNRS

This article bears on *VFD* (Verb Fronting with Doubling) constructions in Haitian, whose left periphery contains a bare homonym of the lexical verb and which trigger a Verb-Focus effect. We seek to update the description of VFD and to reach a satisfactory analysis providing empirical support for addressing the theoretical issues central to the present volume. Our study leads us to conclude that: (i) The syntactic operations involved in the derivation of VFD are available independently of reiteration; (ii) The semantic effect of VFD is not 'intensive' but contrastive, and arises from restrictive modification, a form-meaning relation hardly analysable as 'iconic'; (iii) Haitian VFD may have arisen from a regular recombination of features partaking in focus effects in French, Gbe, and Universal Grammar.

1. Introduction

The constructions under study here, which we call *Verb Fronting with Doubling* (VFD)[1], are attested in Haitian and some other French-Caribbean Creoles. In Haitian, VFD may occur as a bare complete sentence, as in (1a), or be part of larger

---

* We owe a serious debt of gratitude to the various fellow linguists and native speakers of Haitian who provided precious feedback during the several years we spent over this research, among whom Enoch Aboh, Muhsina Alleesaib, Edelyn Dorismond, Stephanie Durrelman, Duvelson Emilien, Dieudonne Exius, Dominique Fattier, Karl Gadelii, Fabiola Henri, Alain Kihm, Mélanie Jouitteau, Roberson Pierre, Emmanuel Schang, Norval Smith.

1. This is an adaptation of the term *Predicate Fronting with Doubling* used by Aboh & Dyakonova (2009). The term *Predicate Fronting with Doubling* emcompasses another type of construction involving the fronting of a reiterated Verb Phrase, rather than that of a verb root. VP fronting with doubling is attested in other languages including, e.g. Polish (Bondaruk n.d.), Russian (Aboh & Dyakonova 2009), Yiddish (Cable 2004), and French (see below example (3)), a.o.

syntactic structures, as illustrated in (1b–d). Some of the labels used to designate the contexts licensing VFD are borrowed from Lefebvre (1998). However previous studies all fail to distinguish the case illustrated in (1a), which we call *Bare VFD*, from the Predicate Cleft pattern in (1d), and they generally leave aside the ALA and ATA cases illustrated in (1b,c):

				VFD subtype
(1a)	*Malad m te malad.*[2]			Bare VFD

(1a)   *Malad   m   te   malad.*[2]   Bare VFD
      sick   1SG   ANT   sick
      'I was SICK (not LAZY).'

(b)   *Ala   bèl   li   te   bèl!*[3]   *ala*-VFD
     ala   pretty   3SG   ANT   pretty
     'She was SOOO pretty!'

(c)   *Ata   malad   m   te   malad*   *ata*-VFD
     ata   sick   1SG   ANT   sick

     lè   Brezil   pèdi.
     when   Brazil   lose

     'I was even SICK when Brazil lost.'

---

2.   Abbreviations and labels used in the glosses: ACC = accomplished marker (Haitian); ANT = anteriority marker (Haitian); AUX = auxiliary (French); DET = determiner (LA in Haitian); EXCL = exclamation marker; F = feminine gender (French); FUT = future (French); GND = gerund; INF = infinitive (French); IPF = imperfect (French); LocP = Locative Phrase (e.g. Haitian *lakay*); M = masculine gender (French); NEG = negation; NONP = nonpunctual (Matinikè *ka*); PL = plural; P= preposition; PP = past participle (French); PRS = present tense (French); REFL = reflexive; SBJ = subjunctive (French); SG = singular; UNAC = unaccomplished (Haitian *ap*); 1, 2, 3 = first, second, third person; SE = Haitian *se* (expletive subject in identificational and cleft clauses).

The acceptability judgements borne on our Haitian examples are primarily those of Herby Glaude, who was born in 1977 in L'Estère, in the Northern department of Artibonite, but later lived for ten years in Port-au-Prince, before moving on to Paris, where he has been speaking creole daily amongst the Haitian community.

We assume throughout that such lexemes as *malad* 'sick', *bèl* 'pretty', in predicate position, fill the same structural slot as, e.g. *vini* 'come' or *pati* 'go, leave' – the V head. As previously argued by DeGraff (1992) (see Section 2.1.1. below) the VFD construction may actually provide the main diagnostic test for identifying the Verb category (or rather, position), in Haitian.

3.   *Ala* (example (1b) and *ata* (example 1c) are two clause-initial functional morphemes whose properties are left undescribed in the present study – they clearly call for further research: at this point we don't even have a satisfactory gloss to propose for them. Both seem to readily combine with the VFD structure discussed in this study.

(d) *Se* **malad** *m* *te* **malad**!   Predicate-Cleft
SE sick 1SG ANT sick

  i. 'I was actually SICK (e.g. not LAZY).'   ⟨contrastive⟩
  ii. 'I was REALLY SICK.'   ⟨intensive⟩

(e) [**Malad** *m* *te* **malad** *la*]   Factive
  sick 1SG ANT sick DET

  te *fè* *manman* *m* *tris.*
  ANT make mum 1SG sad

  'The fact that I was SICK made my mum sad.'

(f) [**Malad** *m* *te* **malad** *la*],   Causative
  sick 1SG ANT sick DET

  manman *m* *te* *tris.*
  mum 1SG ANT sad

  'Because I was SICK, my mum was sad.'

(g) [**Rive** *m* *te* **rive**],   Temporal
  arrive 1SG ANT arrive

  (*epi*) *Pòl* *te* *pati.*
  and-then Paul ANT leave

  (Lit. 'I had ARRIVED, so-then Paul (had) left.')
  'Once I had ARRIVED, Paul (had) left.'

VFD constructions are mentioned and discussed in a number of linguistic works bearing on Haitian (Sylvain 1936; Piou 1982a, b; Hutchison 1989; Lefebvre 1989, 1990, 1991, 1998; Lefebvre & Ritter 1993; Lumsden 1990; Lumsden & Lefebvre 1990; DeGraff 1992; Manfredi 1993; Harbour 2008), other Caribbean (Bernabé 1983; Méry 1988) and Non-Caribbean (Mufwene 1987) French-lexifier creoles, and some African languages (Koopman 1984, 1997; Mufwene 1987, 1994; Aboh 2003, 2004; Aboh & Dyakonova 2009). Available analyses of VFD are however not consensual, and with one major exception (Lefebvre 1998), they either focus on Kwa languages rather than Haitian (cf. Aboh 2003, 2004 and Aboh & Dyakonova 2009), or on Haitian and/or other French-Caribbean creoles but only on one subcase – generally[4] the one labelled *Predicate Cleft* (Piou 1982a; Lumsden 1990; Lumsden & Lefebvre 1990; Larson & Lefebvre 1991; Manfredi 1993; Harbour 2008), a term indiscriminately used in reference to (1a) and (1d). Lefebvre (1998) proposes a comprehensive analysis of VFD in Haitian, but her assumptions raise

---

4. Piou (1982b) however focuses on the temporal subcase illustrated in (1e) and is therefore an exception to this generalisation.

some problems discussed below in Section 3.3. Harbour (2008) focuses on Haitian Predicate-Cleft (e.g. (1d)) but leaves to future research the possible generalisation of his analysis to the other instances of VFD exemplified in (1).

The properties of VFD constructions raise challenging problems for theories of natural-language syntax and of creole genesis. Although Mufwene (1987, 1994) points out some parallelisms between cleft constructions in Haitian and French, it is quite clear that the grammars of French do not generate VFD constructions similar to those in (1):

(2a)   *Déprime   je   déprime !
        be-depressed 1SG   be-depressed.PRS

  (b)   *C'est malade que je   suis   malade.
        it-is sick   that 1SG be.PRS.1SG sick

  (c)   *Arrivé   je   suis   arrivé,   et   puis Paul
        arrive.PP 1SG AUX.PRS.1SG arrive.PP and   then Paul

        est   parti.
        AUX.PRS.3SG   leave.PP

French only allows such constructions as those illustrated in (3), which involve the fronting of a nonfinite null-subject intransitive clause introduced by a preposition – *à* (3a), *pour* (3b) or *en* (3c) – and construed as topical, rather than focal:

Standard French:
(3a)   A *dormir*   comme il   *dort,*   il   doit   être
        P sleep.INF as   3MSG sleep.PRS.3SG   3MSG must   be

        en pleine forme.
        in full   shape
        Lit. 'Sleeping the way he sleeps, he must be in top shape.'

  (b)   (*Ah*) pour *dormir,*   il   [*dort*   bien/a
        ah   as-for sleep.INF 3MSG sleep.PRS.3SG   well/AUX.PRS.3SG

        bien *dormi*].
        well sleep.PP
        Lit. 'Ah, as for sleep(ing), he sleeps well/has slept well.'

  (c)   En *dormant*   comme il   *dort,*   il   doit   être
        in sleep.GND as   3MSG sleep.PRS.3SG   3MSG must   be

        en pleine forme.
        in full   shape
        Lit. '(By) sleeping the way he sleeps, he must be in top shape.'

Previous studies on VFD therefore explore similarities between Haitian and Kwa (Koopman 1984; Piou 1982a, Lefebvre *passim*), or Bantu (Mufwene 1987, 1994).

In what follows we first present (Section 2) an updated description of VFD in Modern Haitian, encompassing the various types of contexts in which it is licensed. We then devote Section 3 to the syntactic analysis of VFD. Reviewing the available literature on this topic, we aim at working out an analysis which should both account for the surface diversity and underlying unity of the data in (1), and shed light on the apparent paradox that VFD seems to involve A'-movement applying to a V-head. The analysis we select is a revised formalisation of Harbour's (2008) intuition that VFD is fed by 'low contrastive V reiteration'. On the basis of the descriptive results achieved in Section 3, we conclude by addressing (Section 4) the main theoretical issues raised in the introduction of this volume.

2. VFD in Haitian: A descriptive update

In this section, we survey the properties shared by all instances of VFD in Haitian, and bring out the properties specific to the different contexts where VFD is licensed.

2.1 Properties shared by all VFD constructions in Haitian

2.1.1 *Lexical doubling and extraction: (X) L1 + [$_{TP}$ ...... [$_{V0}$ L2].......]*
In Haitian, all instances of VFD linearly surface as (X) L1 + TP strings, where the fronted lexeme labelled L1 is phonologically identical to the lexeme (L2) filling the V head inside the following tensed clause. In the constructions under study here, L1 (the verb's homonym) crucially does NOT support any modifier which fails to occur on L2 (the verb), as is the case in, e.g. (4b) below, a clefted variant of (4a), where L1 is modified by *bon*:

  (4a) *Elsi malad **bon** malad.*
        Elsi sick   real sick
        'Elsi is REAL sick.'

  (b)   *Se   **bon** malad Elsi malad.*
        it-is real sick   Elsi sick
        Lit. 'It is REAL sick Elsi is.' ('Elsi is REAL sick.')

Sentences of the type exemplified in (4) share important syntactic properties with those exemplified in (1), but we leave them out of this study for reasons of space, and focus on constructions involving a fronted *bare* homonym of the verb, correlating with a verb-focus effect.

The fact that the reiterated lexeme is the one filling the V head in the TP domain has been convincingly shown by DeGraff (1992). Such predications as those in (5a) and (6a), crucially do not allow the reiteration-and-fronting of any lexeme within their predicate:

(5a)   [$_{DP}$ Jan] [$_{PP}$ sou tab   la].
          John   on table DET
          'John is on the table.'

(b)   *Sou Jan sou tab la.

(6a)   [$_{DP}$ Jan] [$_{LocP}$ lakay].
          John   at-home
          'John is (at) home.'

(b)   *Lakay Jan lakay.

In (7), where la may ambiguously be construed either as a property-denoting predicate meaning 'to be around' or a deictic locative meaning 'there', VFD only correlates with the property-denoting reading:

(7a)   Jan la.
          i.   'John is around.'
          ii. 'John is there.'

(b)   La Jan la.
          i.   'John is (indeed) AROUND
               (e.g. though he doesn't DO anything).'
          ii. *'John is THERE$_1$ (not THERE$_2$).'

These facts support DeGraff's (1992) assumption that VFD exclusively applies to verbal predications and involves the reiteration-and-fronting of the lexeme filling the V head. That is, VFD is unavailable if the predicate is nonverbal (contains no (V), as in (5) and (6), and it only applies to (7a) if la is identified as a V. VFD thus provides a diagnostic test for identifying verbs, in Haitian.

VFD is associated with a single argument grid: L1 cannot have an overt subject of its own, as witnessed by (8), and L1 cannot be assumed to have a covert (PRO) subject, since a bound subject would be likely to be overtly realised, as witnessed by the 'control' contexts in (9):

(8)   Se   (*m) malad m   te   malad.   [= (1a/d)]
          SE   1SG sick   1SG ANT sick
          'I was SICK (not LAZY).'

(b)   [(*M) malad m   te   malad la]   [= (1e)]
              1SG sick   1SG ANT sick   DET

te   fè   manman   m   tris.
ANT make   mum   1SG sad
'The fact that I was SICK made my mum sad.'

(9a)   *M   pwòmèt   Mari$_k$ *(m)   ap   pati.*
1SG promise Mary   1SG UNAC leave
'I promised Mary I would leave.'

(b)   **M   pwòmèt   pati.*
1SG   promise   leave

(c)   *Jan   mande   m   pou   *(m)   pati.*
John ask   1SG for-to   1SG leave
Lit. 'John asked me that I leave.'

If the verb governs an object, the object may only be realised on L2. This well-acknowledged restriction is exemplified in (9b–c) with the Predicate-Cleft construction, but it obtains across all the VFD subtypes illustrated above in (1):

(10a)   *Pòl   achte   machin   sa   a.*
Paul buy   car   DM DET
'Paul bought this car.'

(b)   *Eske   se   **achte**   Pòl   achte   machin   sa   a?*
Q   SE buy   Paul buy   car   DM DET
'Did Paul BUY this car?'

(c)   **Eske   se   **achte machin sa   a**   Pòl   achte   (machin   sa   a)?*
Q   SE buy   car   DM LA Paul buy   car   DM DET

The relation between L1 and L2 in VFD further exhibits the unbounded-dependency effects taken as characteristic of A'-movement (Chomsky 1977). Harbour (2008: 855) recalls Piou's (1982a: 130–133) original evidence revealing successive-cyclicity effects in the Predicate-Cleft subtype:

(11a)   *Li   di   li   vle   se   **ale** pou   Jan   **ale**   avè   li.*
3SG say 3SG want SE go   COMP John go   with 3SG
'He said she wants John to GO with her.'

(b)   *Li   di   se   **ale**   li   vle   pou   Jan   **ale**   avè   li.*
3SG say SE go   3SG want COMP John go   with 3SG
'He said she wants John to GO with her.'

(c)   *Se   **ale**   li   di   li   vle   pou   Jan   **ale**   avè   li.*
SE go   3SG say 3SG want COMP John go   with 3SG
'He said she wants John to GO with her.'

[Piou's (1982a) examples, quoted by Harbour (2008)]

Piou (1982a) further notes that when a long-distance dependency obtains between L1 and L2, as in (11b, c), the intervening context may only contain 'bridge' verbs – a restriction generally associated with A'-movement under Chomsky's (1977) theory:

(12a) *Se renmen Mari ap   **di** ou renmen l.*
       SE love   Mary UNAC say 2SG love   3SG
       Lit. 'It-is love Mary is saying you love her.'
       'Mary is saying you LOVE her.'

(b)   **Se renmen Mari ap   **chichote** ou   renmen l.*
       SE love   Mary UNAC whisper   2SG love   3SG
       Lit. 'It-is love Mary is whispering you love her.'

                                              [examples from Piou (1982a)]

According to Piou (1982a, b), Lefebvre & Ritter (1993) and Lefebvre (1998), only the Predicate-Cleft subtype of VFD illustrated in (1b) allows for an unbounded dependency between L1 and L2. We (Herby Glaude and our Haitian consultants) however find the examples in (13b) through (15b) acceptable alongside (11a), which shows that an unbounded dependency may also obtain in VFD in the Bare (13), factive (14), causative (15) and temporal (16) subtypes.[5] In other words, an unbounded dependency between L1 and L2 is a general characteristic of VFD in Haitian:

Bare VFD

(13a) Yo di/soufle   [*plase*[6] Pòl **plase**   Pòtoprens].
       3PL say/whisper live.wsc   Paul live.wsc Port-au-Prince
       'They say/whisper (that) Paul IS LIVING WITH SOMEBODY in Port-au-Prince.'

(b)   ***Plase** yo   di/*soufle [Pòl **plase**   Pòtoprens].*
       live.wsc 3PL say/whisper Paul live-wsc Port-au-Prince
       'Paul is said/whispered to BE LIVING WITH SOMEBODY in Port-au-Prince.'

Factive VFD

(14a) Yo di/soufle   [**pati** Pòl **pati** a] fè   Elsi tris.
       3PL say/whisper leave Paul leave DET make Elsi sad
       'They say/whisper that the fact that Paul LEFT makes Elsi sad.'

---

5. We must leave the ALA and ATA cases aside here for reasons of space, but the unbounded-dependency effect may be shown to obtain in such examples as well. The syntax and semantics of ALA and ATA call for a completely separate study.

6. *Plase* means 'to live with somebody as a couple'. We gloss it by 'live.wsc'. In (13) through (16) we substitute *soufle* to Piou's *chichote* (example (12)). Both lexemes translate as 'whisper' but *chichote* sounds so acrolectal it hinders our consultants' intuitive judgments.

(b) *Pati* *yo* *di/*soufle* [*Pòl* *pati* *a*] *fè* *Elsi* *tris.*
leave 3PL say/whisper Paul leave DET make Elsi sad
'[The fact that Paul is said/whispered to have LEFT] makes Elsi sad.'

Causative VFD
(15a) *Yo* *di/soufle* [*pati* *Pòl* *pati* *a*], *Elsi* *tris.*
3PL say/whisper leave Paul leave DET Elsi sad
'They say/whisper (that) because Paul LEFT, Elsi is sad.'

(b) *Pati* *yo* *di/*soufle* [*Pòl* *pati* *a*], *Elsi* *tris.*
leave 3PL say/whisper Paul leave DET Elsi sad
'Because Paul is said/whispered to have LEFT, Elsi is sad.'

Temporal VFD
(16a) *Yo* *di/soufle* [*soti* *volè* *a* *soti*], *lapolis* *tire.*
3PL say/whisper come-out thief DET come-out the-police fire
'They say/whisper (that) as soon as the thief CAME OUT, the police fired.'

(b) *Soti* *yo* *di/*soufle* [*volè* *a* *soti*],
come-out 3PL say/whisper thief DET come-out

(*epi*) *lapolis tire.*
(and-then) the-police fire

'As soon as the thief is said/whispered to have COME OUT, the police fired.'[7]

2.1.2 *Primary stress*
In all the VFD examples in (1), the extracted lexeme (L1) bears primary stress. This property is transcribed in (17), and in further Haitian examples, as well as in our English translations, by means of small capitals:

(17a) *MALAD m te malad.*   [= (1a)]
'I was SICK (not LAZY).'

(b) *Ala BÈL li te bèl!*   [= (1b)]
'She was SOOO pretty!'

---

7. An alternative structural analysis (and correlated interpretation) is available for (16b), but left out in the text since it should be derived from (i) below, rather than from (16a):

(ia) *Yo* *di/chichote* [*soti* *vole* *a* *soti*].
3PL tell/whisper come.out thief LA come.out.
'They told/whispered (to) the thief to COME OUT.'

(ib) *Soti* [*yo* *di/*chichote* *volè* *a* *soti*], *lapolis* *tire.*
come-out 3PL tell/whisper thief DET come.out the.police fire
'As soon as the thief was told/*whispered to COME OUT, the police fired.'

(c)   *Ata MALAD m te malad lè (...)*   [= (1c)]
      'I was even SICK when...'

(d)   *Se MALAD m te malad.*   [= (1d)]
      i.   'I was actually SICK (not LAZY).'
      ii. 'I was REALLY SICK!'

(e)   *MALAD m te malad la te fè manman m tris.* [= (1e)]
      'The fact that I was SICK made my mum sad.'

(f)   *MALAD m te malad la, manman m te tris.*   [= (1f)]
      'Because I was SICK, my mum was sad.'

(g)   *RIVE Pòl rive, (epi) Elsi te pati.*   [= (1g)]
      'Once Paul had ARRIVED, Elsi (had) left.'

2.1.3   *Focus*

In all instances of VFD, the reiterated lexeme is construed under focus.[8] In the Verb-Focus, *ala, ata* and Predicate-Cleft subtypes illustrated in (1a–c)/(17a–c), this property is quite straigthforward. But in the factive, causative and temporal subtypes, the same property may also be shown to obtain. The contextualised examples in (18)–(20) show that VFD is infelicitous if focus is intended on an argument rather than on the predicate. In (18), factive VFD is felicitous in a discourse context licensing predicate focus (18a), not in a context licensing argument focus as in (18bi)): if the focused constituent must be an argument, another construction is called for, e.g. (18bii)):

---

8.   In Lumsden & Lefebvre (1990), emphasis is placed on the ambiguity of focus, which may have wide scope on the VP (ia) or narrow scope on the V head (ib):

   (i)   *Se*   **manje** *Jan*   *ap*   **manje** *pen*   *an.*
         it.is eat   John   UNAC   eat   bread   DET
         (ia) 'John is actually EATING THE BREAD
               (not LAYING THE TABLE).'
         (ib) 'John is actually EATING (not BAKING) the bread.'
                                  [adapted from Lumsden & Lefebvre 1990:773]

However, this ambiguity arises from a general discrepancy between the prosodic and syntactic scope of focus (cf. Büring 1997). Thus, the single sentence in (iii), with primary stress on *Mary* (the right edge of the predicate), may provide a felicitous answer to (iia) (all-focus reading), (iib) (wide focus on the predicate) or (iic) (narrow focus on the object):

   (iia) *What happened?* >   (iii) — *John invited MAry.*
   (iib) *What did John do?* >   (iii) — *John invited MAry.*
   (iic) *Who did John invite?* > (iii) — *John invited MAry.*

Factive VFD

(18a) [CONTEXT: *Elsi p-ap   travay, men Pòl pa   enkyete.*]
       Elsi NEG-UNAC work   but Paul NEG worried
       'Elsi is out of work, but Paul is not worried.'

       Malad li   malad la   enkyete l.
       sick   3SG sick   DET worry   3SG
       'The fact that she is SICK worries him.'
       ('What worries him is the fact that she is SICK.')

(b) [CONTEXT: *Tout moun gen   grip, men sa   pa   di Jan anyen.*]
      everyone   have flu   but this NEG tell John nothing
      'Everyone is down with the flu, but John doesn't give a hoot.'

(i) **Malad ELSI malad la   enkyete Pòl.*
    sick   Elsi sick   DET worry Paul
    Intended reading: 'Only the fact that ELSI is sick worries Paul.'

(ii) *Se paske   ELSI malad ki   fè   l   enkyete.*
    SE because Elsi sick   that make 3SG worried
    Lit. 'It is because ELSI is sick that makes him worried.'

Similarly in (19), causative VFD is felicitous in a discourse context licensing predicate focus (19a), not in a context calling for argument focus (19bi). Under such pragmatic conditions, focus is signaled by means of another construction (19bii):

Causative VFD

(19a) [CONTEXT: *Elsi p-ap   travay, men sa   pa   enkyete Pòl.*]
       Elsi NEG-UNAC work   but DM   NEG worry   Paul
       'Elsi is out of work, but this does not worry Paul.'

       Malad li   malad la,   li   tris.
       sick   3SG sick   DET 3SG sad
       Lit. 'Because she is SICK, he is sad.'
       ('The reason he's sad is that she is SICK.')

(b) [CONTEXT: *Tout moun gen   grip, men sa   pa   di Jan anyen.*]
      everyone   have flu   but this NEG tell John nothing
      'Everyone is down with the flu, but John doesn't give a hoot.'

(i) **Sèlman malad ELSI malad la, Pòl tris.*
    only   sick   Elsi sick   DET Paul sad
    Intended reading: 'Paul is sad only because ELSI is sick.'

(ii) *Sèlman paske   ELSI malad, Pòl   tris.*
    only   because Elsi sick   Paul sad
    Lit. 'Only because ELSI is sick, Paul is sad.'
    ('Paul is sad only because ELSI is sick.')

Temporal VFD is similarly felicitous in a discourse context calling for predicate focus, as in (20a), but not in a context calling for argument focus, as in (20bi) vs. (ii)):

Temporal VFD

(20a) [CONTEXT: *Eske Elsi te   manje yè?*]
                  Q   Elsi ANT eat   yesterday
                  'Did Elsi eat yesterday?'

                  Wi: RIVE *Pòl   rive,   li   manje.*
                  yes arrive Paul arrive 3SG eat
                  'Yes: as soon as Paul ARRIVED, she ate.'

(b) [CONTEXT: *Elsi pa   t(e) vle   manje depi yè,   men..*]
                Elsi NEG ANT want eat   since yesterday but
                'Elsi had been refusing to eat since yesterday, but..'

(i) **Rive   POL rive,   li   manje.*
       arrive Paul arrive 3SG eat
       Intended reading: 'As soon as PAUL arrived, she ate.'

(ii) *Lè   POL rive,   li   manje.*
       When Paul arrive, 3SG eat
       'When PAUL arrived, she ate.'

These data are evidence that a verb-focus effect characterises VFD constructions independently of clefting. The fact that the reiterated V is construed under focus regardless of the external syntax of VFD is confirmed by the minimal pairs in (21)–(23). When a clause contains two or several combined Vs available for VFD (e.g. a modal V and a lexical V, a matrix V and an embedded V, a serial-verb string[9]), reiteration always indicates which V must be construed under focus:

---

9. The ambiguity of focus in a serial-verb construction is illustrated by (i) below (with VFD occurring in the Predicate-Cleft subtype):

(ia) *Pòl   pote liv   la   montre Elsi.*
      Paul take book DET show Elsi
      'Paul took the book to Elsi to show it to her.'

(ib) *Se* POTE *Pòl pote liv   la   montre Elsi*
      se take Paul take book DET show   Elsi

      (*se pa   BAY li   bay Elsi liv   la*).
      SE NEG give 3SG give Elsi book DET

      'Paul (just) TOOK the book to Elsi to show it to her
      (he didn't GIVE Elsi the book).'

Factive VFD

(21a) [VLE Pòl vle vini an] fè manman li kontan.
 want Paul want come DET make mum 3SG happy
 'The fact that Paul WANTS to come pleases his mum.'

 (b) [VINI Pòl vle vini an] fè manman li kontan.
 come Paul want come DET make mum 3SG happy
 'The fact that Paul wants to COME pleases his mum.'

Causative VFD

(22a) [VLE Pòl vle vini an], manman li kontan.
 want Paul want come DET mum 3SG happy
 'Because Paul WANTS to come, his mum is happy.'

 (b) [VINI Pòl vle vini an], manman li kontan.
 come Paul want come DET mum 3SG happy
 'Because Paul wants to COME, his mum is happy.'

(ic) Se MONTRE Pòl pote liv la montre Elsi
 se show Paul take book DET show Elsi
 (se pa BAY li bay Elsi liv la).
 SE NEG give 3SG give Elsi book DET
 'Paul (just) took the book to Elsi to SHOW it to her (he didn't GIVE Elsi the book).'

Verb series made up of intransitive verbs are analysed by Bernabé (1983) as verb compounds. As regards the ambiguity of focus, the available structural options and correlated interpretive effects are the same as in (i) above:

(iia) Pòl kouri desann.
 Paul run come.down
 'Paul came down quickly.'

(iib) Se KOURI Pòl kouri desann
 SE run Paul run come.down
 (li pa MIZE nan wout).
 3SG NEG dawdle on way
 'Paul came down RUNNING (he didn't DAWDLE on the way).'

(iic) Se DESANN Pòl kouri desann
 SE come.down Paul run come.down
 (li pa MONTE).
 3SG NEG go.up
 'Paul CAME DOWN running (he didn't run UP).'
 ('What Paul did at full speed was COME DOWN (not GO UP).')

Temporal VFD

(23a)   [*Di yo di volè a sòti*],   *lapolis   tire.*
            say 3PL say thief DET come.out the.police fire
            'As soon as they SAID the thief came out, the police fired.'

(b)   [*Sòti   yo di volè a   sòti*],   *lapolis   tire.*
            come.out 3PL say thief DET come.out the.police fire
      i.   'As soon as the thief is said to have COME OUT, the police fired.'
      ii.   'As soon as they told the thief to COME OUT, the police fired.'

2.2   Distinguishing VFD subtypes

We propose to describe VFD as a single syntactic structure which forms a root sentence in the Bare subtype exemplified in (1a), and whose embedding in larger syntactic contexts gives rise to the other cases distinguished in (1) – *ala, ata*, factive, causative, temporal, and Predicate Cleft. In this section we survey the empirical properties of five of these subtypes, starting with the Bare subtype, and leaving Predicate Cleft to the last, due to the greater intricacies of this construction.

2.2.1   *The Bare-VFD subtype*

The Bare-VFD construction is exemplified above in (1a) and below in (24) in an appropriate pragmatic context calling for contrastive focus on the lexical V:

(24)   *MALAD Elsi te   malad (li pa te   PATI).*
            Sick   Elsi ANT sick   3SG NEG ANT leave
            'Elsi was SICK (she hadn't LEFT).'

Unlike the Predicate-Cleft construction in (25a) (further discussed below, Section 2.2.5), the Bare VFD construction may only host one Tense specification, as witnessed by the minimal pair in (25):

(25a)   *Se te   MALAD Elsi te   malad (li pa te   PATI).*
            SE ANT sick   Elsi ANT sick   3SG NEG ANT leave
            'Elsi was SICK (she hadn't LEFT).'

(b)   **Te   MALAD Elsi te   malad (li pa te   PATI).*
            ANT sick   Elsi ANT sick   3SG NEG ANT leave

Bare VFD may only host sentence negation within its inflectional domain:

(26a)   [CONTEXT: Although Elsi is supposed to be on sick leave, I just learned that
                she organised a huge party last night]
                A, MALAD Elsi pa te   malad!
                ah sick   Elsi NEG ANT sick
                'Ah, so Elsi wasn't SICK!'

(b)   *Pa MALAD Elsi (pa) te   malad.
      NEG sick   Elsi NEG ANT sick

If properly contextualised, Bare VFD may host what Lefebvre (1998) calls the
clausal determiner, LA (spelt out as *a* in (27b)):[10]

(27a)   [CONTEXT: As I get up I can see Paul does not believe I am about to leave –
        maybe he thinks I'm just going to get myself a drink]
        ALE m   ale.
        go   1SG go
        'I'm LEAVING.'

(b)   [CONTEXT: Paul was expecting me to leave, but as I get up I can see he rather
        believes I intend to get myself a drink and return to my seat]
        ALE m   ale a.
        go   1SG go   DET
        'I'm LEAVING (as you know I was planning to do).'

---

10. This morpheme is labelled *determiner* by Lefebvre (1998) on account of its morphology
(allomorphic variation LA: -LA/-A/-AN, cf. (i) and (iib) below; compare (iii), where locative LA
exhibits no allomorphy), its syntax (right-edge position), and its semantics (presuppositional
effect), three properties shared by the nominal determiner LA. Used as a 'clausal determiner',
this element occurs mainly in intransitive clauses, where it signals the reported state of affairs
as *expected*, as exemplified in (ii):

(ia)   Pòl   travay **la.**
       Paul work   LA
       'Paul works (as expected).'

(ib)   Pòl   fini/tounen   **an.**
       Paul finish/return LA
       'Paul has finished/returned (as expected).'

(ic)   Pòl   soti/ale   **a.**
       Paul go.out/leave LA
       'Paul has gone out/left (as expected).'

       [CONTEXT: *Poukisa ou leve*? 'Why are you getting up?'
(iia) M   ale.
       1SG go
       'I'm going.'

(iib) M   ale **a.**
       1SG go   DET
       'I'm going, as you knew I would.'

(iii) Pòl   achte liv   la   *(l)a.
       Paul buy   book DET   LOC
       'Paul bought the book there.'

In the *ala, ata*, Factive, Causative, Temporal and Predicate-Cleft subtypes distinguished in (1), the Bare VFD pattern described above may be argued to occur as a substructure, embedded in several types of broader syntactic contexts. For lack of space, we must leave aside here the details of *ala* and *ata*-VFDs. They share the main distributional characteristics of Bare VFD. *Ala*-VFD however gives rise to an intensive reading requiring a scalar predicate, while *ata*-VFD gives rise to a narrow restrictive-focus reading. In the next subsections we further explore the Factive, Causative, Temporal and Predicate-Cleft subtypes.

2.2.2   *Factive VFD*

In the factive subtype, VFD occurs in Haitian (H) where English (E) or French (F) would license nominalised clauses of the form *the fact that+TP/le fait que+TP*. Just like their English analogues, factive VFDs may occur in Haitian as subject-binding dislocated topics (28a), in subject position (28b), or in object position, as in (28c).

(28a)   H   [*PATI Duvalier pati a*],   *sa   bon.*
             go   Duvalier go   DET, DM good

(a′)   E   [*The fact that Duvalier is* GONE] *that is a good thing.*

(a″)   F   [*Le   fait   que   Duvalier   soit   PARTI*], *c'est   bien*
             DET fact   that   Duvalier   be.SUBJ.3SG   gone   it is   good

(b)   H   [*PATI Duvalier pati a*]   *bon.*
             go   Duvalier go   DET good

(b′)   E   [*The fact that Duvalier is* GONE] *is a good thing.*

(b″)   F   [*Le   fait   que   Duvalier   soit   PARTI*] *est   une*
             DET fact   that   Duvalier   be.SBJ.3SG   gone   is   a

           bonne   chose.
           good   thing

(c)   H   *Elsi kontan/regret*   [*PATI Duvalier pati a*].
           Elsi pleased/regret   go   Duvalier go   DET

(c′)   E   *Elsi {is pleased with/regrets}* [*the fact that Duvalier is* GONE].

(c″)   F   *Elsi {est   contente   de/regrette}*   [*le   fait   que   Duvalier*
           Elsi is   pleased   with/regrets   DET   fact   that   Duvalier

           soit   PARTI].
           be.SBJ.3SG go.PP

(d)   H   *Elsi pa   asepte*   [*TOUYE   yo   touye   Masiyon*].
           Elsi NEG accept   kill   3PL   kill   Masiyon

(d′)   H   *Eli does not accept* [*the fact that they* KILLED *Masiyon*].

(d″)   F   *Elsi n'   accepte pas   [le   fait qu' on   ait*
           Elsi NEG accept   NEG DET fact that one AUX.SBJ.3SG

           TUÉ   Massillon].
           kill.PP Masiyon

Importantly, in contexts which fail to license a nominalised clause of the form
the fact that TP (English) or *le fait que*+TP (French), VFD fails to be licensed
in Haitian, regardless of the presuppositional properties of the matrix predicate.
VFD is thus unacceptable throughout (29), although under Kiparsky & Kiparsky's
(1979) semantic definition of factivity, the verb meaning 'know' licenses a factive
complement clause, unlike 'think' and '(be) possible':

(29a)   H   *[PATI Duvalier pati a]   (, sa) pòsib.
            go   Duvalier go   DET   DM   possible

  (a′)   E   *The fact that Duvalier is GONE (, it's) possible.

  (a″)   F   *Le   fait que Duvalier soit   PARTI (, c') est possible.
             DET fact that Duvalier be.SBJ.3SG go.PP   it   is   possible

  (b)   H   *Elsi konnen [PATI Duvalier pati a].
             Elsi know   go   Duvalier go   DET

  (b′)   E   *Elsi knows the fact that Duvalier is GONE.

  (b″)   F   *Elsi sait   le   fait que Duvalier est PARTI.
             Elsi knows DET fact that Duvalier is   gone

  (c)   H   *Elsi panse [PATI Duvalier pati a].
             Elsi thinks go   Duvalier go   DET

  (c′)   E   *Elsi thinks the fact that Duvalier is GONE.

  (c″)   F   *Elsi pense le   fait que Duvalier est PARTI.
             Elsi thinks DET fact that Duvalier is   gone

Under our own use of the term *factive*, the subject or object argument clause is
nonfactive in (29a, b, c) since it may not be realised as *the fact that* TP in English,
le fait que TP in French, or VFD in Haitian.

   Like nominalised argument clauses of the form *the fact that* + TP/*le fait que* +
TP in English or French (cf. (30c, d), factive VFDs in Haitian may be clefted, as
witnessed by (30b):

(30a)   H   [PATI Duvalier pati a]   bon.
            go   Duvalier go   DET   good
            'The fact that Duvalier is GONE is a good thing.'

(b)   H   *Se* [PATI *Duvalier pati a*]   *ki   bon.*
           SE   go   Duvalier go   DET that good
           'It is the fact that Duvalier is GONE that is a good thing.'

(c)   E   *It is* [*the fact that Duvalier is* GONE] *that is a good thing.*

(d)   F   *C'est* [*le   fait   que   Duvalier   soit   PARTI*]
           It is   DET   fact   that   Duvalier   BE.SBJ.3SG   gone

           qui   est   une   bonne   chose.
           That is   a   good   thing

           'It is the fact that Duvalier is gone that is a good thing.'

In Haitian, however, the clefting of factive clauses seems restricted to subjects. Thus, clefting the object VFD in (31a) gives an unacceptable result in (31b), contrasting both with the acceptable clefted nominal object in Haitian (31c), and the acceptable clefted clausal object in English (31d) and French (31e).

(31a)   H   *Elsi   pa   asepte* [TOUYE *yo   touye   Masiyon   an*].
             Elsi   NEG   accept   kill   3PL   kill   Masiyon   DET
             'Elsi does not accept the fact that they KILLED Masiyon.'

(b)   H   **Se* [TOUYE *yo   touye   Masiyon   an*] *Elsi   pa   asepte.*
           SE   kill   3PL   kill   Masiyon   DET   Elsi   NEG   accept
           Intended reading: 'It is the fact that they KILLED Masiyon that Elsi doesn't accept.'

(c)   H   *Se* [FLÈ] *Elsi   pa   asepte.*
           SE   flower   Elsi   NEG   accept
           'It is FLOWERS that Elsi doesn't accept.'

(d)   E   *It is* [*the fact that they* KILLED *Masiyon*] *that Elsi doesn't accept.*

(e)   F   *C'est* [*le   fait   qu'   on   ait   TUÉ   Massillon*]
           it   is   DET   fact   that   one   AUX.SBJ.3SG   kill.PP   Masiyon

           qu'   Elsi   n'   accepte   pas.
           that   Elsi   NEG   accept   NEG

           'It is the fact that they KILLED Masiyon that Elsi does not accept.'

In order to turn (31b) into an acceptable cleft in Haitian, we need to make the clefted VFD a subject, as in (32):

(32)   *Se* [TOUYE *yo   touye   Masiyon   an*]
         SE   kill   3PL   kill   Masiyon   DET

         ki   fè   Elsi   pa   dakò.
         that   make   Elsi   NEG   agree

         Lit. 'It is the fact that they KILLED Masiyon, that makes Elsi disagree.'
         ('It's [the fact that they KILLED Masiyon], which upsets Elsi.')

These Haitian data are in keeping with Keenan & Comrie's (1977) Noun Phrase Accessibility Hierarchy,[11] which states that from a crosslinguistic viewpoint, 'subjects are easier to relativise (or cleft) than any of the other major constituents of a sentence'. In Haitian it appears that nonsubjects may be relativised or clefted when they are noun phrases (cf. (31c)), but not when they are clausal.

The factive VFDs in (28) through (32) contain the allomorphic[12] morpheme LA in phrase-final position, which correlates with an aspectual effect: in the presence of LA, the factive VFD is construed as denoting an actualised and completed event, while in its absence it is construed as generic or habitual. This aspectual effect of allomorphic LA, illustrated by the contrast between (33a) and (33b), is crucially distinct from the presuppositional effect triggered by the so-called clausal determiner (see Footnote 10), as witnessed by the unavailability of the reading glossed in (33b–ii):[13]

(33a)   [GENYEN   Pòl   genyen]   fè   li   enteresan.
          earn/win   Paul   earn/win   make   3SG   interesting
          'The fact that Paul WINS/EARNS (GOOD MONEY) makes him interesting.'

(b)   [GENYEN Pòl   genyen   an]   fè   li   enteresan.
          win   Paul   win   DET   make   3SG   interesting
     i.   'The fact that Paul has WON/EARNED (GOOD MONEY) makes him interesting.'
     ii.   *'The fact that Paul WINS/EARNS (GOOD MONEY) as expected makes him interesting.

The semantic effect of LA in (33b), contrasting with (33a), is similar to the one it has in relativised DPs, as in (34b), contrasting with (33a) (cf. Zribi-Hertz & Glaude 2007):

(34a)   [mori   Pòl   achte]   chè.
          codfish   Paul   buy   expensive
          'The codfish which Paul buys is expensive.'

(b)   [mori   Pòl   achte   a]   chè.
          codfish   Paul   buy   DET   expensive
          'The codfish (which) Paul (has) bought is expensive.'

---

11.   Thanks to Luigi Rizzi (p.c.), who reminded us of this generalisation.

12.   The determiner LA exhibits allomorphy but the homonymous locative lexeme *la* (cf. example (7)) does not.

13.   Like its French lexifier *gagner*, Haitian *genyen* ambiguously means 'to earn' or 'to win'. If translated as 'to earn' it is transitive and its object only seems ellipsable under a generic or habitual reading – as in (32a). In (32b), the determiner triggers a completion effect, thus blocking the 'to earn' option.

With predicates a priori open to a stage-level (temporary) or individual-level (permanent) reading, phrase-final LA in factive VFD selects a temporary or telic interpretation. The more the predicate resists this type of interpretation, the less LA-insertion seems felicitous. Thus LA in (35c) would have to involve temporary ugliness, e.g. due to some hideous mask worn for the carnaval. With inherently stative predicates such as *renmen* 'like, love', LA is on the other hand obligatory in factive VFD (35d):

(35a)   *MALAD Pòl malad fè   manman li   tris.*
        sick   Paul sick   make mum   3SG sad
        'The fact that John is ill makes his mum sad.'

   (b) *MALAD Pòl malad la   fè   manman li   tris.*
        sick   Paul sick   DET make mum   3SG sad
        'The fact that John has fallen ill makes his mum sad.'

   (c) *LÈD Pòl lèd   (?la) fè   li   enteresan.*
        ugly Paul ugly   DET make 3SG interesting
        'The fact that Paul is ugly makes him interesting.'

   (d) *RENMEN Pòl renmen Elsi *(a) fè   li   kontan.*
        Love   Paul love   Elsi DET make 3SG happy
        'The fact that John LOVES Elsi makes him/her happy.'

The data presented in this section are consistent with the assumption that factive VFDs are nominalised clauses, viz. DPs. As is expected of DPs, they are available in argument positions; also, as expected of DPs, they may be headed by the specific determiner (LA). Similarly to relativised DPs, the LA determiner in factive VFDs is crucially sensitive to Aktionsart.

2.2.3   *Causative VFD*
Causative VFD differs from factive VFD only with respect to external syntax. While factive VFD fills or binds an argument slot in the thematic grid of some predicate, causative VFD is left-adjoined to a matrix clause and construed as a causative adverbial. In (36) and (37) we see that with a dynamic predicate such as *kouri* 'run', the non-occurrence (36) or occurrence (37) of the specific determiner LA has the same aspectual effect in causative VFDs ((36b)/(37b)) as it has in factive VFDs (33):

(a) Factive and (b) causative VFD without LA
(36a)   H   [*KOURI   Pòl kouri anpil*], (*sa*) *fè   manman li   kontan.*
            run   Paul run   alot   DM make mum   3SG happy
            Lit. 'The fact that Paul runs a lot (, it) makes his mum happy.'

(a')   E   [*The fact that John* RUNS *a lot*] (*, it*) *makes his mum happy.*

(a")   F   [*Le   fait   que   Jean* COURE   *beaucoup*]
             DET   fact   that   Jean   run.SBJ.3SG a.lot

             (*, ça*) *fait   plaisir   à   sa   mère.*
             it   make   pleasure   to   his   mum

             'The fact that John runs a lot (, it) pleases his mum.'

(b)   H   [KOURI *Pòl   kouri   anpil*], *li   bouke.*
             run   Paul   run   a.lot   3SG   knackered
             Lit. 'The fact that Paul RUNS a lot, he is knackered.'

(b')   E   [*Because John* RUNS *a lot*], *he is knackered.*

(b")   F   [*Du   fait   que   Jean* COURT *beaucoup*], *il   est   crevé*
             of.the fact   that   John   runs   a.lot   he   is   knackered
             'Due to the fact that John RUNS a lot, he is knackered.'

(a) Factive and (b) causative VFD with LA

(37)   H   [KOURI *Pòl   kouri   anpil   la*] (*, sa*) *fè   manman*
             run   Paul   run   a.lot   DET   DM make   mum

             li   kontan.
             3SG   happy

             'The fact that Paul has RUN a lot (, it) makes his mum happy.'

(a')   E   [*The fact that John has* RUN *a lot*] (*, it*) *makes his mum happy.*

(a")   F   [*Le   fait   que   Jean   ait*   *beaucoup* COURU]
             DET   fact   that   Jean   AUX.SBJ.3SG a.lot   run.PP

             (*, ça*) *fait   plaisir   à   sa   mère.*
             it   make   pleasure   to   his   mum

             'The fact that John has RUN a lot makes his mum happy.'

(b)   H   [KOURI *Pòl   kouri   anpil   la*], *li   bouke.*
             run   Paul   run   a.lot   DET   3SG   knackered
             Lit. 'The fact that Paul has RUN a lot, he is knackered.'

(b')   E   [*Because Paul has* RUN *a lot*], *he is knackered.*

(b")   F   [*Du   fait   que   Jean   a*   *beaucoup* COURU],
             of.the fact   that   John   has   a.lot   run

             il   est   crevé.
             he   is   knackered

Note that argument clauses of the form *the fact that*+TP (Fr. *le fait que*+TP) are typically (though not necessarily, cf. (1a)) theta-marked by their predicate as CAUSE, viz. [+c, −m] under Reinhart & Siloni's (2005) Theta System, both in subject

position (cf. *The fact that John is ugly makes him interesting*) and in the object position of some psychological predicates (cf. *John regrets the fact that Duvalier is gone*).
Conversely, the causal connection between the adjunct and matrix clauses in, e.g.
(37b), requires that the adjunct VFD be construed as reporting a *fact* whose truth
value needs to be checked as positive for the matrix assertion to obtain. Further
note that in French, a factive clause of the form *the fait que+TP* may occur as a
causative adverbial when introduced by the functional preposition *de* – etymo-
logically a Source marker (cf. (37b″)). In Haitian, factive VFDs are licensed as sentence adverbials and construed as causative without any overt causal theta-marker.

Basing ourselves on their similar internal morphosyntax, we assume that the
factive and causative subtypes are two instances of nominalised VFDs, sketchily
represented in (38), which may be merged in a larger clause either as arguments
or as dislocated topics:[14]

The factive and causative subtypes

(38) $[_{DP} [VFD] D^0]$[15]

Factive and causative VFDs differ with respect to clefting, since clefting, in Haitian,
only seems available for clauses if they occur as subjects (see Section 2.2.2). In
this respect, causative VFD is more restricted than causal adverbials in English or
French:

(39a)   E   *It is [because (of the fact that) Paul is* SICK] *that Mary is sad.*

(b)   F   *C'est [(à   cause)   du   fait que Paul est* MALADE] *que*
             It   is because of.the fact that Paul is sick   that

             Marie est   triste.
             Mary is   sad

             'It is because Paul is SICK that Mary is sad.'

(c)   H   **Se [MALAD Pòl   qmalad la]   Elsi   tris.*
             SE   sick   Paul sick   DET Elsi sad
             Lit. 'It is the fact that Paul is SICK (that) Elsi is sad.'

(d)   H   *Se [MALAD Pòl   malad la] ki   fè   Elsi tris.*
             SE   sick   Paul sick   DET that make Elsi sad
             'It is the fact that Paul is SICK that makes Elsi sad.'

---

14.   The causative connection may be viewed as a special effect of topicality, with the topic
introducing a 'fact' – a proposition whose own truth value conditions that of the eventuality
denoted by the matrix clause.

15.   On the internal structure of Haitian DPs, cf. Zribi-Hertz & Glaude (2007), a.o., and
references therein.

2.2.4   *Temporal VFD*

Temporal VFD occurs in sentence-initial position and precedes a tensed clause optionally introduced by *epi* '(and/so) then', expressing temporal succession. In such cases the initial VFD sets a time-reference background for the onset of the following event. Construed as salient, the predicate of the second clause is in the matrix focus. Depending on lexical and functional aspect within the sentence-initial VFD, the onset of the matrix event is located at the reference time-point of the VFD event, if the VFD event is punctual (40a) – or at the endpoint of the VFD event, if the VFD event is nonpunctual (40b). Similar temporal connections may be conveyed in English by, e.g. *when, as soon as, once*, introducing a temporal topic clause:

(40a)   [*RIVE   Pòl   rive*],   (*epi*)   *Elsi* PATI.
       arrive   Paul   arrive   then   Elsi   leave
       Lit. 'Paul ARRIVED, so then Elsi left.'
       'As soon as Paul ARRIVED, Elsi left.'
       ('Once John had ARRIVED, Mary left.')

  (b)   [*MANJE Pòl   te   fin   manje diri a*],   (*epi*)   *Elsi soti*.
       eat   Paul   ANT   finish eat   rice LA   THEN   Elsi go.out
       Lit. 'Paul had finished EATING the rice, so then Elsi went out.'
       ('As soon as Paul had finished EATING the rice, Elsi went out.')
       ('Once Paul had finished EATING the rice, Elsi went out.')

The temporal-succession effect characteristic of this subtype requires VFD to be construed as event-denoting and telic. Hence, the VFD predicate cannot denote a state (41a/(b), and its TMA specification must allow the successive connection to obtain (cf. (42)):

(41a)   *[*GRAN Pòl   gran*],   (*epi*)   *Elsi pati*.
       big   Paul   big   then   Elsi   leave
       Lit. 'Once Paul is BIG, Elsi left.'

  (b)   [*GRAN Pòl   fin   gran*],   *Elsi pati*.
       big   Paul   ACC   big   Elsi   leave
       Lit. 'Once Paul had become BIG, Elsi left.'
       ('Once Paul had GROWN UP, Elsi left.')

(42)   [*MANJE Pòl   t-ap   manje*],   *Elsi t-ap   pale*.
       eat   Paul   ANT-UNAC eat   Elsi   ANT-UNAC talk
       i.   *'While Paul was/had been EATING, (so-then) Elsi was/had been talking.'
       ii.   'Due to the fact that Paul was EATING, Elsi was talking.'

In (41a), with zero TMA specification, the predicate in the VFD component is construed as stative, and the result is rejected as ill-formed. In (41b), the temporal

VFD is made acceptable by the aspectual marker *fin* which triggers an inchoative, hence dynamic, effect. In (42), where VFD is specified as unaccomplished by the *ap* particle, it may be construed as causative (42ii), but excludes the temporal reading glossed in (42i).

If the temporal VFD hosts the determiner LA, LA must be construed as the clausal determiner, not as the DP-determiner. Conversely, if LA is construed as the DP-determiner, the dislocated VFD is interpreted as causative, not as temporal. Thus, if the semantic connection between the sentence-initial VFD and the following clause is left morphologically unspecified, the LA determiner is a priori ambiguous (DP- or clausal determiner), whereas if the temporal connection is overtly specified by *epi*, as in (43b), the LA determiner may only be construed as clausal:

(43a)   [*RIVE   Pòl   rive   a*],   *Elsi pati.*
        arrive   Paul   arrive   DET   Elsi   leave
        i.   'As soon as Paul ARRIVED (as we thought he would), Elsi left.'
        ii.   'Due to the fact that Paul had ARRIVED, Elsi left.'

  (b)   [*RIVE   Pòl   rive   a*],   *epi*   *Elsi pati.*
        arrive   Paul   arrive   DET   and.then   Elsi   leave
        'As soon as Paul ARRIVED (as we thought he would), Elsi left.'

With predicates denoting permanent properties, LA-less VFDs dislocated in sentence-initial position are straightforwardly ungrammatical (cf. (41a)), since their properties satisfy no requirement for VFD licensing. The paratactic context calls for some inter-clausal connection to be construed, but the absence of the DP determiner precludes the causative connection, while the stative predicate precludes the temporal connection.

Temporal VFD cannot undergo clefting, as witnessed by (44):

(44)   **Se* [*RIVE   Pòl   rive*],   (*epi*)   *Elsi pati.*
        SE   arrive   Paul   arrive   and.then   Elsi   leave
        Lit. 'It's Paul had arrived, so-then Elsi left.'

Lefebvre (1998:366) proposes to derive this restriction from Ross's (1967) assumption that extraction is universally banned out of a conjoined constituent.

2.2.5   *Predicate Cleft*
2.2.5.1   *Argument-Cleft and Predicate-Cleft.*   In Haitian as in English or French, arguments may be clefted, i.e. placed in the predicate of a matrix identificational clause hosting an expletive subject pronoun (cf. Piou 1982a; Lumsden 1990;

DeGraff 1992; Lefebvre 1998; Veenstra 2007; Harbour 2008).[16] Haitian clefts only contrast with their English or French homologues as to the (c)overt realisation of the copula and complementiser:

(45a) E   *It is books$_z$ that Paul hates t$_z$.*

(b) F   *C' est les   livres$_z$ que Paul déteste t$_z$.*
         it is DET books that Paul hates
         'It's books that Paul hates.'

(c) H   *Se liv$_z$ Pòl   rayi t$_z$.*
         SE book Paul hate
         'It's books (that) Paul hates.'

The biclausality of clefts is witnessed by the availability of TMA markers in both the upstairs and downstairs domains: [17]

---

16.   Alternative analyses of Haitian *se* treat it as a copula verb (Mufwene 1994), or as ambiguous between a pronoun and a copula verb (Déprez 2003; Gadelii 2007). In cleft constructions, however, it unambiguously exhibits the behaviour of a subject pronoun, since, like the subject pronoun or DP in (ia–b), and unlike the V in (ia), it sits on the left-hand side of sentence negation and TMA in (ic) (compare (id)):

  (ia)   *Li/Pòl pa te   soti.*   [subject-NEG-TMA-VP]
       3SG/Paul NEG ANT go.out
       '(S)he/Paul did not go out/has not gone out.'

  (ib)   *Li/Pòl pa te   yon chyen.*   [subject-NEG-TMA-DP]
       3SG/Paul NEG ANT a   dog
       '(S)he/Paul was not a dog.'

  (ic)   *Se pa te   yon flè.*   [se-NEG-TMA-DP]
       SE NEG ANT a   flower
       'It was not a flower.'

  (id)   **Pa* te   se yon flè.*   *[NEG-TMA-*se*-DP]
       NEG ANT SE a   flower

17.   In such examples as (46), if T is overtly specified upstairs, the embedded T must agree with it. A full paradigm for Constituent-Cleft is given in (i):

  (ia)   *Se liv Pòl   rayi.*
       SE book Paul hate
       'It's BOOKS that Paul hates.'

  (ib)   *Se liv Pòl te   rayi.*
       SE book Paul ANT hate
       'It's BOOKS that Paul used to hate.'

(46)   *Se te   liv   Pòl te   rayi.*
        SE ANT book Paul ANT hate
        'It was BOOKS that Paul used to hate.'

As regards interpretation, clefting – in Haitian, as in English and French – signals contrast, viz. the selection of an option (or subset of options) from a preidentified (topical) set. Thus, the clefted sentence *Se ELSI Pòl renmen* ('It is ELSI that Paul loves.') provides a felicitous response to (47b) rather than to (47a):

(47a)   *Kisa Pòl   renmen? — #Se [ELSI] li   renmen.*
        who Paul love   it   Elsi 3SG love
        'Who does Paul love?'   'It's ELSI he loves.'

  (b)   *Pòl renmen Mari? — Non: se [ELSI] li   renmen.*
        Paul love   Mary   no it Elsi 3SG love
        'Does Paul love Mary?' 'No: it's ELSI he loves.'

A remarkable property of Haitian, which has no counterpart in English or French, is that clefting may affect the fronted homonym of the verb in the VFD structure, giving rise to the construction known as Predicate Cleft:

(48)   *Se [MALAD] tifi a   malad.*
        SE sick   girl DET sick
        'The girl is SICK.'   [adapted from Piou 1982a:123]

Like the argument-cleft construction exemplified in (46), the Predicate-Cleft construction is biclausal, as witnessed by (49):

  (ic)   *Se te   liv   Pòl te   rayi*
        SE ANT book Paul ANT hate
        'It was BOOKS that Paul used to hate.'

  (id)   **Se te   liv   Pòl rayi.*
        SE ANT book Paul hate

The distribution of Tense across (i) in Haitian echoes the distribution of Tense in French clefts:

  (iia) *C'est [les livres] que Paul déteste.* [= (ia)]
        it-is   the books that Paul hates

  (iib) *C'est [les livres] que Paul détestait.* [= (ib)]
        it-is   the books that Paul hated

  (iic) *C'était [les livres] que Paul détestait.* [= (ic)]
        it-was   the books that Paul hated

  (iid) **C'était [les livres] que Paul déteste.*   [= (id)]

(49)   *Se* **te**   [*malad*] *tifi* *a*   **te**   *malad*
    SE ANT   sick   girl DET ANT sick

    (*se* **te** *pa* MOURI *l*   **te**   *mouri*).
    SE ANT NEG die   3SG ANT die

    'The girl was SICK (she did not DIE/was not DEAD).'

Predicate Cleft crucially contrasts with Argument Cleft in that the clefted predicate is a lexical root and seems to leave no trace, since it also overtly occurs in
what looks like the V head within the TP domain. We return to this paradox in
Section 3.

2.2.5.2 *Bare VFD and Predicate-Cleft.*   The biclausal Predicate-Cleft construction must be compared to the monoclausal Bare VFD construction discussed in
Section 2.2.1. From a formal viewpoint, reiteration-with-fronting and clefting
both and independently signal the verb as focused. The contrastive-focus reading
of the verb is common to Bare VFD and Predicate-Cleft, but Predicate-Cleft further allows an *intensive* reading of the focused verb, glossed in (50bii), which goes
unlicensed in the Bare VFD in (50aii). Under the intensive reading, Predicate-
Cleft is semantically similar to *ala*-VFD, but further work needs to be done on the
precise semantics of *ala*:

(50a)   MALAD *li*   *malad.*
    sick   3SG sick
    i.   '(S)he is actually SICK (e.g. not DEAD).'
    ii. * '(S)he is REALLY SICK.'

(b)   *Se* MALAD *li*   *malad.*
    SE sick   3SG sick
    i.   '(S)he is actually SICK (e.g. not DEAD).'
    ii. '(S)he is REALLY SICK.'

(c)   *Ala* MALAD *li*   *malad!*
    ALA sick   3SG sick
    '(S)he is SOOO SICK!'.

Under the intensive reading, the Predicate-Cleft construction occurring as a
complete utterance is – like the *ala*-VFD construction – perceived as having
exclamatory force.

    Among the pragmatic contexts which a priori license both Bare VFD and
Predicate-Cleft, we may mention the type exemplified in (51), where VFD (with
or without clefting) occurs sentence-initially, followed by a clause optionally conjoined by *men* ('but') – or some other opposition connector (e.g. *poutan* 'however',
etc.) – whose predicate is also under focus. The resulting interpretive effect may be

conveyed in English or French either by oppositive conjunction – as translated in (i), or by concessive subordination – as translated in (ii):

(51a) ENTELIJAN *Pòl   entelijan,   (men/poutan)   li   PA*
      intelligent   Paul   intelligent   but/however   3SG   NEG

      RENMEN   LEKOL.
      like   school

    i.   'Paul is CLEVER, {but/however} he DOESN'T LIKE SCHOOL.'
    ii. 'Although John is CLEVER, he DOESN'T LIKE SCHOOL.'

(b) *Se* ENTELIJAN *Pòl   entelijan,   (men/poutan)   li   PA*
     SE   intelligent   Paul   intelligent   but/however   3SG   NEG

     RENMEN   LEKOL.
     like   school

    i.   'Paul is CLEVER, (but/however) he DOESN'T LIKE SCHOOL.'
    ii. 'Although Paul is CLEVER, he DOESN'T LIKE SCHOOL.'

In such cases, Bare VFD and Predicate-Cleft are intuitively perceived as synonymous.

2.2.5.3 *Predicate Cleft and sentence negation.*   As emphasised in previous works on clefting, sentence negation may freely occur upstairs and/or downstairs in argument-clefts:

(52a) *Se* [LIV] *Elsi* **pa** *renmen.*
      SE   book   Elsi   NEG   like
      'It's BOOKS that Elsi does not like.'

(b) *Se* **pa** [LIV] *Elsi renmen.*
     SE   NEG   book   Elsi   like
     'It's not BOOKS that Elsi likes.'

(c) *Se* **pa** [LIV] *Elsi* **pa** *renmen.*
     SE   NEG   book   Elsi   NEG   like
     'It's not BOOKS that Elsi does not like.'

In the Predicate-Cleft construction, however, sentence negation appears to be blocked:

(53a) *Se* MALAD *tifi   a   pa   malad* *(*ki   fè   l   ap*
      SE   sick   girl   DET   NEG   sick   that   make   3SG   UNAC

      kouri konsa).
      run   thus

    i.   *'The girl is not SICK (e.g. she's BUSY).'
    ii. 'It is [the fact that the girl is not SICK] (which makes her run the way she does).'

(b) *Se pa* MALAD *tifi a malad* *(*ki fè l*
SE NEG sick girl DET sick that make 3SG

bouke konsa).
tired thus

   i. *'The girl is not SICK (e.g. she's BUSY)'.

   ii. 'It is not [the fact that the girl is SICK] which makes her so tired.'

(c) *Se pa malad tifi a pa malad* *(*ki fè l ap*
SE NEG sick girl DET NEG sick that make 3SG UNAC

kouri konsa).
run like-this

   i. *'The girl is not (NOT) SICK.'

   ii. 'It is not [the fact that the girl is NOT SICK] which makes her run the way she does.'

Unlike the affirmative sentence in (50b), which is licensed as an independent clause involving a focused V, the negated examples in (53) are not construed as *Predicate* Clefts. The only available readings involve the clefting of a factive VFD – hence of a DP – whether negation occurs downstairs (as in (53a)), upstairs (as in (53b)), or both upstairs and downstairs (as in (53c)). In other words, the sentences in (53a, b, c) only allow the structural and logical representations in (54), where focus and negation crucially do not scope together over the same predicate:

(54a) *Se*   [MALAD *tifi a pa malad*] *ki fè l ap kouri konsa.*   [= (53a)]

  (b) *Se pa* [MALAD *tifi a malad*] *ki fè l bouke konsa.*   [= (53b)]

  (c) *Se pa* [MALAD *tifi a pa malad*] *ki fè l ap kouri konsa.*   [= (53c)]

Correlatively, an example such as (55) can only be licensed with the indicated structure involving a clefted factive VFD providing the subject of an elliptical predicate: in other words, as an incomplete sentence, an elliptical variant of, e.g. (54a):

(55) *Se* [$_{DP}$ MALAD *tifi a pa malad*] (...)
     SE   sick girl DET NEG sick
     'It's the fact that the girl is NOT SICK (which...)'

These data therefore support the assumption that the Predicate-Cleft construction cannot be placed under sentence negation. This constraint crucially distinguishes Predicate Cleft from Bare VFD: Bare VFD allows sentence negation to occur within its Inflectional Domain, as witnessed by (26a) above, whereas – according to all our consultants – Predicate Cleft does not, as shown by (53a).

    Piou (1982a) already observes that sentence negation is constrained with Predicate-Clefts, leaving the issue open for future research. She notes

(1982a: 135–136) that in the paradigm of examples reproduced below in (56), only (56b) may be construed as an instance of Predicate-Cleft:

(56a) *Se pa   renmen Mari   renmen Nouyòk.*
       SE NEG   like   Mary   like   New York

    i. *'Mary DOESNT LIKE New York.'
    ii. *'Mary doesn't LIKE New York (e.g. she LOVES it).'
    iii. 'It is not [that Mary LIKES New York].' [Piou's adapted translation]
       'It is not [the fact that Mary LIKES NY] (which causes this situation).'
       [our own translation]

  (b) *Se travay Mari   pa   vle   travay.*
      SE work   Mary   NEG want work

    i. 'Mary doesn't want to WORK.' [Piou's translation]
    ii. 'What Mary doesn't want to do is WORK.' [our own translation]

  (c) *Se pa   etidye Mari   pa   etidye leson   an.*
      SE NEG study Mary   NEG study lesson DET

    i. *'Mary hasn't STUDIED the lesson.'
    ii. 'It is not [that Mary hasn't STUDIED the lesson].' [Piou's adapted translation]
    ii'. 'It is not [the fact that Mary hasn't STUDIED the lesson] (which causes this situation).' [our own translation]

Piou's intuitions as regards the previous examples converge with Herby Glaude's, and our other consultants', suggesting that the same predicate cannot be at once clefted and negated: (56b) is thus well-formed because its negated V is *vle* while its clefted V is *travay*. But this restriction seems to bear specifically on the Predicate-Cleft subtype, hence on clefting, since negation seems to freely combine with verb focus in all other VFD subtypes (cf. (26a) for Bare VFD). An open issue at this point.[18]

---

18.   We are leaving out such examples as the one in (i) below, which involve verb reiteration, sentence negation and clefting, but fall outside the range of the present study since the clefted homonym of the verb is not bare – but crucially modified by *ti* '(a) little':

  (i) *Se pa   TI   MALAD Elsi (pa)   malad!*
      SE NEG little sick   Elsi NEG sick
    Lit. 'It is not LITTLE that Elsi is SICK!'
    'Elsi is REAL sick!'

Cf. Section 3.2 below for further comments.

2.2.5.4   *The clausal determiner* LA.   What Lefebvre (1998) calls the 'clausal deter-miner' LA may occur in Haitian Predicate Clefts, with its usual presuppositional effect. The example in (57b) is intuitively synonymous with its bare-VFD counter-part in (57a) (repeated from (27b)):

[CONTEXT: Paul was expecting me to leave; but as I get up I can see he now believes I intend to get myself a drink and return to my seat]

(57a)   ALE   m   ale   a.
 go   1SG   go   DET
 'I'm GOING (as you know I was planning to do).'

(b)   *Se* ALE   m   ale   a.
 SE   go   1SG   go   DET
 'I'm GOING (as you know I was planning to do).'

Although these two elements are identical as to their morphology (base form LA, same allomorphic variation) and (phrase-final) linear position, the clausal determiner (hereunder: *clausal* LA) which occurs in Bare and Predicate-Cleft VFD differs as to its distribution and interpretation from the nominal deter-miner (hereunder: *DP*-LA) which occurs in factive VFD: (i) unlike DP-LA, clausal LA is always syntactically optional, including with stative predicates; (ii) unlike DP-LA, clausal LA does not trigger a completion effect with dynamic predicates (cf. (57)); (iii) unlike clausal LA, DP-LA does not trigger the presuppositional effect glossed in our examples by 'as expected' or 'as you know I was planning to do' (cf. (57)).

2.2.6   *Descriptive summary*

Our descriptive survey leads us to revise our initial subclassification of VFD based on the examples in (1). VFD in Haitian first and foremost comes out as a Verb-Focus construction. Verb Focus signaled by VFD may (among other options) combine with clefting, giving rise to the Predicate-Cleft structure. Noncleft VFD may be placed under the scope of the exclamative-intensive marker *ala*, or of the restrictive-focus marker *ata;* VFD may also be nominalised, viz. embedded in a DP phrase revealed by the availability of the DP-determiner LA – distinct from the homonymous clausal determiner. In the variety of Haitian under consideration (see Footnote 2), the clausal determiner seems available in a subset of cases where the homonymous DP-determiner is not – an issue we leave open for future research. Nominalised VFD is a factive nominalization contain-ing a focused V.

3.   In search of a syntactic analysis

3.1   Laying out the issues

We now turn to the syntactic analysis of VFD in Haitian. An optimal analysis should be consistent with all the descriptive results presented above: it should account both for the central unity of VFD as a Verb-Focus strategy and for the crucial contrast between nominalised and non-nominalised VFD. It should bring a solution to the Extraction Paradox identified by Harbour (2008). On the one hand, the properties surveyed above (single argument grid for the iterated lexeme, unbounded dependency between the two identical instantiations, with sensitivity to bridge verbs) is evidence that the fronted lexeme in VFD has undergone A'-movement, hence landed in a specifier in the clause periphery. On the other hand, the fronted constituent appears to be a lexical root rather than a phrase, it cannot govern an argument the way a 'fully verbal' head can, and its extraction *seems* to leave no gap since the same lexeme is overtly spelt out in the V position within the TP domain. An optimal analysis should shed light on these apparently mysterious properties, and also provide empirical grounds for a theory of reiteration phenomena in natural languages, e.g.: Why is VFD attested in some natural-language grammars (e.g. Haitian) while it goes unlicensed in others (e.g. French)? Do the VFD constructions of Haitian indicate an 'iconic' relation between reiteration and 'intensive' semantic effects? Does the lexical reiteration characteristic of VFD constructions arise from a 'Copy' mechanism at any level of representation?

The available linguistic literature contains various analyses of VFD. We shall straightforwardly discard those proposals which crucially hinge on the presence of *se*, hence only account for the Predicate-Cleft subcase: Piou (1982a), Mufwene (1987), Lefebvre (1989, 1990, 1991), Lumsden (1990), Lumsden & Lefebvre (1990), DeGraff (1992). This leaves us with four major lines of analysis, discussed below.

3.2   The Cognate Object assumption (Bernabé 1983)

Bernabé (1983) discusses a number of Matinikè examples which are akin to the VFD constructions considered in this study but not strictly identical to them. His VFD-like examples are either cleft constructions whose cleft component is quantised and placed under negation, as in (58), or left-dislocated strings quantified by *tout*, as in (59):

Matinikè

(58a)   *Sé pa   ti   dòmi Pyè dòmi.*
         SE NEG little sleep Pyè sleep
         'It is not little sleep that Peter slept.'
         ('Peter slept a lot.')   [adapted from Bernabé 1983: 1183–84]

   (b)   *Sé **pa** **an sèl**   chayé Pyè chayé dlo.*
          SE NEG a   single carry Pyè carry water
          Lit. 'It is not a single carry Peter carried water.
          ('Peter did a lot of water-carrying.')   [adapted from Bernabé 1983: 1114]

(59a) ***Tout dòmi** i   ka   dòmi a,   i   toujou las.*
       all   sleep 3SG NONP sleep DET, 3SG always tired
       Lit. '(For) all the sleeping he sleeps, he's always tired.'
       ('Although he sleeps a lot, he's always tired.')
                                  [adapted from Bernabé 1983: 1090]

   (b)   ***Tout alé** ou   alé lékòl   la,   ou   pa   apwann ayen.*
          all   go 2SG go school DET 2SG NEG learn   nothing
          Lit. '(For) all the going you went to school, you didn't learn anything.'
          ('Although you went to school a lot, you didn't learn anything.')

Such examples have analogues in Haitian, e.g.:

(60a) *Se **pa ti**   dòmi Elsi dòmi.*
       SE NEG little sleep Elsi sleep
       Lit. 'It's not little sleep Elsi slept.'
       ('Elsi REALLY slept.')

   (b)   ***Tout lèd** li   lèd la,   (men) tout   moun   renmen li.*
          all   ugly 3SG ugly DET but   every person like   3SG
          Lit. 'However ugly she is ugly, everyone likes her.'
          ('UGLY (as) she may be, (but) everyone likes her.')

Bernabé doesn't propose any structural representations for such examples, but he clearly relates them to sentences involving non-extracted occurrences of what he informally labels *homonymous complements* of the verb, exemplified in (61) for Matinikè, and in (62) for Haitian:

Matinikè
(61a) *Pyè dòmi **an bon   dòmi**.*
       Pyè sleep a   good sleep
       'Peter had a pleasant sleep.'   [adapted from Bernabé 1983: 1083]

   (b)   *Pyè ka   chayé moun {bon/gwo} chayé.*
          Pyè NONP carry people good/big carry
          'As for carrying people, Peter does a lot of that.'
                                [adapted from Bernabé 1983: 1111]

Haitian
(62a) *Pyè dòmi **bon   dòmi**.*
       Pyè sleep good sleep
       Lit. 'Peter slept good sleep.'
       ('Peter slept real good.')

(b) *Pyè pote moun* **bon pote.**
Pyè carry people good carry
Lit. 'Peter carried people good carry.'
('Peter carried people for good.')

Since such 'homonymous complements' of V may cooccur with direct objects, as witnessed by (60b)/(62b), Bernabé concludes (1983:1118) that they themselves cannot be identified as direct objects. He proposes to analyse them as *secondary cognate objects* (French: *compléments d'objet internes seconds*), and assumes that the Matinikè constructions exemplified in (58) and (59) involve the clefting or raising of such secondary cognate objects to the clause periphery. He further emphasises that secondary cognate objects are *complements of* the verb, unlike 'NON-complement copies' of the verb, illustrated in (63):

Matinikè

(63a) *Pyè ka dòmi dòmi é(pi) i ka kité*
Pyè NONP sleep sleep and 3SG NONP leave

tout travay la ban mwen.
all work DET to 1SG

'Peter is sleeping sleeping and he's leaving all the work to me.'
[adapted from Bernabé 1983:1080]

(b) *Sa Pyè ni ka dòmi dòmi konsa?*
What Pyè have NONP sleep sleep like that?
Lit. 'What does Peter have (to) be sleeping sleeping like that?'
('What's the matter with Peter sleeping on and on like that?')
[adapted from Bernabé 1983:1080]

Bernabé draws a syntactic parallel between 'homonymous complements' of the verb, as in (61) above (repeated in (64a)), and the nonhomonymous complement of *fè* 'do' in (64b):[19]

Matinikè

(64a) *Pyè dòmi an bon dòmi* [= (61a)]
Pyè sleep a good sleep
'Peter had a pleasant sleep.'

(b) *Nou fè an ti dòmi.*
1PL do a little sleep
'We took a little nap.'
[adapted from Bernabé 1983:1086]

---

19. Bernabé's assumption that (64a) and (64b) are structurally parallel is disputable on empirical grounds, but this issue is orthogonal to our central issue. We leave the matter open here and intend to take it up in a separate work.

To summarise, Bernabé discusses Matinikè constructions which are similar to the VFD constructions considered in this study, in that they involve a homonym of the verb, but are also distinct from the VFD contructions under consideration in two crucial respects: (i) the homonym of the verb which they contain is crucially quantified and/or modified; (ii) the interpretative effect they trigger is distinct from contrastive verb focus. In the constructions he discusses, Bernabé analyses the 'copy phrase' (the phrase containing the verb's homonym) as a 'secondary cognate object' of the verb, therefore as nominal. The assumption that 'homonymous complements' are nominal in nature, also emphasised by Mufwene (1987), is consistent with the cognate-object analysis. However, in the absence of any modifier or determiner on the verb's homonym in the VFD constructions under study here, the claim that the V-homonymous extracted expression is nominal needs to be supported by independent evidence. However, such supportive evidence is lacking. Thus, although many lexical roots in creole may alternatively occur as nouns or verbs in syntax (e.g. Haitian *manje* = 'to eat' or 'food', cf. Filipovich 1987, a.o.), some lexical roots are restricted to one type of position. Haitian examples of such V/N pairs are given in (65) and (66):

bay 'give' vs. *don* 'gift'

(65a)   *Elsi {bay/*don}   LaCroixRouge rad   sa   yo.*
        Elsi   give gift   the.Red.Cross clothes DM PL
        'Elsi gave (*gift) the Red Cross those clothes.'

(b)   *Elsi fè   LaCroixRouge {*bay/ don} sa   a.*
     Elsi make the.Red.Cross give gift DM DET
     'Elsi made the Red Cross this gift (*give).'

opere 'operate on' vs. *operasyon* 'surgery'

(66a)   *Doktè a   {opere/*operasyon} yon malad.*
        doctor DET operate/surgery   a   patient
        Lit. 'The doctor {operated/*surgeried} a patient.'

(b)   *Doktè a   fè   {*opere/operasyon} sa   a.*
     doctor DET did   operate/surgery   DM DET
     'The doctor performed this {*operate/surgery}.'

It turns out that of the two members of such lexical pairs, only the one available for the V head may fill the extracted position in VFD constructions:

(67a)   *(Se) {BAY/*DON} Elsi bay LaCroixRouge rad   sa   yo.*
       SE   give/*gift   Elsi give the.Red.Cross clothes DM PL
       'Elsi actually GAVE the Red Cross those clothes.'

(b)   *(Se) {OPERE/*OPERASYON} dòktè a   opere   malad la.*
     SE   operate/*surgery   doctor DET operate patient DET
     'The doctor actually OPERATED on the patient.'

These examples challenge the claim that the extracted expression in VFD constructions is a (bare) nominal instantiating a (secondary) cognate object.

3.3   The Event-Argument assumption (Manfredi 1993; Lefebvre 1998)

Unlike the previous theory, this one aims at accounting for VFD constructions of the types described in Section 2, viz. involving extraction of a lexical root. Like the previous theory, this one treats the extracted expression as nominal. It however departs from the previous approach in assuming that this raised nominal instantiates an *event argument* of the verb, phonologically spelt out as a copy of V. Although categorially nominal, it may cooccur with a thematic argument (a direct object) because it instantiates an event feature. The fact that the fronted L1 in VFD may not project is derived from its inherent feature content. Lefebvre (1998) further assumes that the availability of the type of event feature which gives rise to VFD crucially correlates with the existence of an *event clausal determiner* in the grammar of the language. The two minimal pairs in (68) and (69), adapted from Lefebvre (1998), are meant to illustrate the clausal determiner LA in Haitian, distinguishing two uses of this element: as an assertion marker (68b), and as an event determiner (69b):

The clausal determiner LA as an assertion marker (Lefebvre 1998)

(68a)   *Jan   rive   Pòtoprens.*
John   arrive   Port-au-Prince
'John arrived in Port-au-Prince.'

(b)   *Jan   rive   Pòtoprens   la.*
John   arrive   Port-au-Prince   DET
'Actually, John arrived in Port-au-Prince.'

[example (68b) from Lefebvre 1998:224]

The clausal determiner LA as an event determiner (Lefebvre 1998)

(69a)   *Moun   nan   kraze   yon   manchinn.*
man   DET   destroy   a   car
'The man has destroyed a car.'

(b)   *Moun   nan   kraze   yon   manchinn   nan.*[20]
man   DET   destroy   a   car   DET
'The man has destroyed a car (as we knew/as expected).'

[example (69b) from Lefebvre 1998:229]

---

20.   This example is ill-formed in Herby Glaude's dialect and rejected by our Haitian consultants. When it is adjacent to an N, LA is automatically construed as the nominal determiner. Since LA and YON cannot occur together on the same N, (69b) is discarded as ungrammatical.

Lefebvre thus predicts that VFD should arise in Haitian and Fongbe, whose grammars are both claimed to license an event clausal determiner, but not in, e.g. French or English, assumed to have no such determiner.

Lefebvre's theory of VFD however faces at least three problems. First, in at least one variety of informal French (Modern Parisian French), we find a very widespread use of the functional locative morpheme LA (the lexifier of Haitian LA) exemplified in (70b), which is very reminiscent of Haitian LA used as a 'clausal event determiner':

(Parisian) French

(70a) *Le   type (il)   a   bousillé   une   voiture.*
DF.MSG guy   3MSG AUX.PRS.3SG destroy.PP a.FSG car
'The guy (he) (has) destroyed a car.'

(b) *Le type (il) a bousillé une voiture, là.*
'There you see, the guy destroyed a car.'

The occurrence of unstressed LA in clause-final position in informal French triggers a range of interpretations, one of which (glossed by 'there you see' in (70b) and below) an expectation effect very similar to the one Lefebvre glosses by 'as expected' and associates with 'clausal LA' in Haitian. Furthermore, like Haitian LA in (71), the clause-peripheral unstressed LÀ in French (72) seems incompatible with a predicate denoting a permanent property:

Haitian

(71a) *Li   mouri (a).*
3SG die   LA
'(There you see/this time) she's dead.'

(b) *Li   entelijan   (*an).*
3SG intelligent   LA
'(*There you see/this time) she's intelligent.'

French

(72a) *Elle   est   morte   (, là).*
3FSG AUX.PRS.3SG dead.FSG   LA
'(There you see/this time) she's dead.'

(b) *Elle   est   intelligente   (*, là).*
3FSG AUX.PRS.3SG intelligent.FSG   LÀ
'(*There you see/this time) she's intelligent.'

Second, the event-argument theory predicts that VFD in Haitian should be globally incompatible with noneventive predicates, viz. stative predicates denoting permanent properties. This prediction, however, is not empirically borne out, as witnessed by the acceptability of (73):

(73)   ENTELIJAN li   entelijan   (li   pa   konn   KOPYE).
       intelligent 3SG intelligent 3SG NEG know   crib
       '(S)he's INTELLIGENT ((s)he wouldn't CRIB).'

Only the temporal use of VFD excludes predicates denoting permanent properties: this follows from an external factor – the successivity connection which, in this subcase, must link the VFD string to the following clause.

Third, in claiming that the fronted expression in VFD is an event argument of the V raised by A'-movement, the event-argument theory predicts that the same event argument should be able to be spelt out, prior to raising, in some position within the inflectional domain. As pointed out by Harbour (2008), low V reiteration *does* occur in Haitian, as exemplified in (74b). However, the semantic effect of low V reiteration is contrastive focus (as glossed in (74bi)), rather than any effect we would be entitled to expect from an 'event argument' – e.g. those glossed in (74bii), (74biii), (74biv):

(74a)   Li   malad.
        3SG sick
        '(S)he's sick.'

  (b)   Li   malad MALAD.
        3SG sick sick
        i.   '(S)he's actually SICK (e.g. not DEAD).'
        ii.   *'There you see, (s)he's SICK (as expected).'
        iii. *'This time (s)he's SICK.'
        iv.   *'She has become SICK.'

This is evidence that the event argument assumed to occur in VFD could not be spelt out in its base position, hence should undergo obligatory raising to the clause periphery. But the event-argument theory explains neither why event arguments should be obligatorily focused, nor why focus marking should obligatorily trigger movement for this type of arguments.

We conclude that the event-argument theory of VFD cannot be upheld for Haitian.

3.4   The Parallel-Chain Theory (Koopman 1997; Aboh & Dyakonova 2009)

Under these two theories the derivation of VFD in Gbe crucially involves two independently-motivated movements of the V, one to Tense/Aspect, the other to a Focus projection in the clause periphery. Under Koopman's analysis, these two movements are respectively Head Movement (V-to-Tense), and Phrasal

Movement (VP to spec,FocP): the object (should there be one) moves out of VP to some functional projection within the inflectional domain, and what raises up to the periphery is the remnant VP (now reduced to V). The V ends up being spelt out both in Tense and in a Focus head in the clause-periphery, with reiteration explained by the fact that focus requires overt spell out. Under Aboh & Dyakonova's theory, both movements instantiate Head Movement, and they respectively target the Aspect and Focus heads, analysed as different types of heads.

Each one of these two theories brings its own solution to the Extraction Paradox and sheds light on other properties: Koopman makes use of the 'remnant movement' idea to account for the paradoxical status of the fronted expression in VFD – it must be phrasal (a VP) in order to undergo A'-movement; but it is reduced to a lexical root, since the object has left the VP prior to extraction. Under this analysis, we expect long-distance dependencies to obtain across VFDs, a correct prediction as regards Haitian, but not as regards Gungbe, according to Aboh & Dyakonova (2009). Under these authors' theory, the analysis of Focus Movement as Head Movement predicts that long-distance dependencies in VFD should exhibit Minimality effects, an assumption supported by the fact that VFD cannot host sentence negation in Gbe: since Focus and Negation are two heads of the same (quantificational) type – Aboh and Dyakonova argue – V cannot move past Negation on its way up to Focus. The fronted V in VFD generally cannot undergo long-distance extraction in Gbe: Aboh & Dyakonova (2009) (following Aboh 2003, 2004) derive this constraint from the overt spell-out of the C head. This idea may account for the fact that unlike Gbe, Haitian (where C is null), allows long-distance extraction of the fronted V:

(75a)   Gbe   *__Xò__   ùn   sé   __dò__   Súrù   __xò__   wémá.
                 buy   1SG   hear   that   Suru   buy   book
              Intended reading: 'I heard that Suru BOUGHT a book.'
                                           [adapted from Aboh & Dyakonova 2009]

(b)   H   (*se*)   ACHTE   yo   di   m   Elsi   __achte__   yon   liv.
              SE   buy   3PL   tell   1SG   Elsi   buy   a   book
           'I'm told Elsi BOUGHT a book.'

Unlike the other theories discussed above, the Parallel-Chain theory does not treat the raised expression in VFD as a nominal argument. Nevertheless, the transference to Haitian of this theory proposed for Gbe runs into a few problems.

First, the claim (put forward by Aboh & Dyakonova, but not by Koopman) that the fronted expression targets the Focus *head* conflicts with the assumption that cleft constructions in Haitian are structured – as are clefts in e.g. English or French – as identificational predications whose subject is filled by an expletive pronoun (*se* in Haitian, cf. DeGraff 1992) and whose predicate is instantiated by the clefted constituent (cf. (45) above). If the clefted expression stands as a predicate with respect to the expletive pronominal subject *se*, the clefted expression should occupy a phrasal position, not a head position, whatever its categorial status.

Second, the Parallel-Chain theory crucially hinges on the availability of V-to-Asp in languages licensing VFD (this remark applies to both Koopman's and Aboh & Dyakonova's theories). In Haitian, however, unlike in Gbe, there is no sign of V raising to Tense, Mood or Aspect – no such examples as (76b) below, showing affixation of a TMA marker to the verb root:

(76a)   Gbe   *Elom dù-na   mónlu.*
              Elom eat-HAB rice
              'Elom habitually eats rice.'

[Aboh & Dyakonova 2009, example (18a)]

(b)   H   **Pòl   manj-ap   diri.*
              Paul eat UNAC rice

(c)   H   *Pòl   ap   manje diri.*
              Paul UNAC eat   rice
              'Paul will eat/is eating rice.'

Third, the Parallel-Chain theory proposed by Aboh & Dyakonova is claimed to be supported by the unavailability of sentence negation in VFD, in Gbe. But as shown above by (26a) and other examples (cf. Section 2.2.5.2), VFD is compatible with sentence negation in Haitian, In this language, what seems to block sentence negation in VFD is not VFD itself but Predicate Clefting, which does not appear to have an exact equivalent in Gbe.

We conclude that the Parallel-Chain theory, as formulated either by Koopman or by Aboh & Dyakonova to account for the Gbe data, does not provide a satisfactory account of VFD in Haitian.

3.5   The Contrastive-Doubler theory

3.5.1   *Deriving VFD from low contrastive V-reiteration*
Basing his analysis on the Predicate-Cleft construction of Haitian (*Klivaj Predika*), which he does not distinguish from the Bare VFD, Harbour (2008) proposes to derive, via A′-movement, the Predicate-Cleft construction in (77b) from the low V-reiteration structure in (77a) (so-called *Contrastive Reduplication* (CR)), which also triggers a verb-focus effect. Harbour observes that the CR pattern exemplified in (77a) is productive in Haitian and may trigger either an intensive reading (as in, e.g. 'FRIGHTFULLY sick') or a contrastive reading (as in 'actually SICK'). The same ambiguity arises from the English translation '*really*+ Predicate':

(77a)   *Yo **touye** touye Janmari Vinsan.*
       3PL kill   kill   Janmari Vinsan
       Lit. 'They KILLED-killed Janmari Vinsan.'
       ('They REALLY KILLED Janmari Vinsan.')

(b)   *Se **touye** yo   **touye** Janmari Vinsan.*
       SE kill   3PL kill   Janmari Vinsan
       'They REALLY KILLED Janmari Vinsan.'

The CR pattern illustrated in (77a) for Haitian verbs is the same as the one illustrated by the English examples in (78), taken from Ghomeshi & al. (2004), who show that CR may a priori apply to any lexical category:

(78a)   *I'll make the tuna salad and you make the SALAD-salad.*

(b)   *They are rich, of course, but not RICH-rich, not NEW YORK CITY rich.*

(c)   *Are you LEAVING-leaving?*

The CR examples in (77a) and (78) must crucially be distinguished from the Haitian constructions illustrated in (79), already mentioned above, where the verb's homonym supports a modifier and no verb-focus effect obtains:

(79a)   *Pòl **dòmi** [yon ti   **dòmi**].*
       Paul sleep a   little sleep
       'Paul slept a little.'

(b)   *Kite m   **ekri** [**ekri**   m].*
       let 1SG write write 1SG
       'Let me write as I please.'

Harbour's major assumption is that the verb-focus effect observed in the Predicate-Cleft construction – but we showed above (Sections 2.1.2 and 2.1.3) that verb focus is a property of all VFD subtypes – primarily arises from a low V-reiteration (CR) structure, and thus obtains prior to both V-fronting and clefting. In other words, a Predicate-Cleft VFD construction such as (80a) is derived from (77a) above. This analysis straightforwardly predicts that VFD and CR are in complementary distribution in Haitian. This prediction is borne out regardless of the VFD subtype. (80) illustrates this restriction for the Bare VFD:

(80a)   *TOUYE yo touye Janmari Vinsan.*
       'They REALLY KILLED Janmari Vinsan.'

(b)   **TOUYE yo touye touye Janmari Vinsan.*

Further evidence supporting Harbour's assumption that Haitian VFD is fed by low contrastive V reiteration is the fact that the same small set of monosyllabic degree adverbs (mainly *trè* 'very' and *byen* 'well, very, much') may optionally be included in the reiterated material both in the low contrastive V-reiteration construction (cf. (81a), (82a)) and in the VFD construction (cf. (81b), (82b)):

(81a) *Li*   TRE   FO   *trè*   *fò*   (*oubyen*   *li*   *jis*   PASAB)?
       3SG very strong very strong (or   SG just so-so)
       'Is (s)he REALLY VERY STRONG (or is (s)he just so-so)?'

   (b) *Se*   TRE   FO   *li*   *trè*   *fò*   (*li*   *pa*   *jis*   PASAB).
        SE very strong 3SG very strong 3SG NEG just so-so
        '(S)he's REALLY VERY STRONG ((s)he's not just so-so).'

(82a) *Li*   BYEN   MANJE   *byen*   *manje*   (*oubyen*   *li*   *jis*   GOUTE)?
       3SG well   eat   well   eat   or   3SG just pick
       'Did (s)he REALLY EAT WELL (or did she just PICK AT HER FOOD)?'

   (b) *Se*   BYEN   MANJE   *li*   *byen*   *manje*   (*li*   *pa*   *jis*   GOUTE).
        SE well   eat   3SG well   eat   3SG NEG just pick
        '(S)he REALLY ATE WELL ((s)he didn't just PICK AT HER FOOD).'

We assume that the degree adverbs under consideration are in such cases construed as forming with the V head a complex lexeme (e.g. *trè-fò*, *byen-manje*), which regularly undergoes low contrastive V reiteration and Focus Raising.

3.5.2   *In search of a formal analysis*

Harbour's analysis however raises two problems for Haitian. First, he analyses the reiterated string (e.g. *touye touye* in (77a)) as a complex lexeme, therefore assumes that A′-movement applies from within a word. However this option does not seem a priori available. Thus in such English examples as in (83), the verb-internal modifier cannot be extracted:

(83)   John **double**-locked the door.

   (a)   How did John lock the door? – #**Double**.

   (b)   *It was [**double**] that John locked the door.

(84)   John was **clean**-shaven

   (a)   How was John shaven? – #**Clean**.

   (b)   *It was [**clean**] that John was shaven.

(85)   They **dry**-cleaned my coat.

   (a)   How did they clean your coat? – #**Dry**.

   (b)   *It was [**dry**] that they cleaned my coat.

In order to smooth out this problem, the expression undergoing A′-movement in the derivation of VFD should be as a syntactic phrase, rather than as a word-internal constituent.[21]

Another problem lies in the assumption that both the intensive (which Harbour calls 'augmentative') and the 'contrastive' readings available for low contrastive V-reiteration are triggered by a single structure, from which VFD is derived. While it is true that Predicate-Clefts may trigger intensive effects (cf. (1dii), this property neither obtains across all Predicate-Clefts, nor extends to all other VFD subtypes. Harbour further notes that the intensive reading of Predicate-Clefts is only available with scalar predicates. With nonscalar predicates, Predicate-Clefts only allow a contrastive-focus reading:[22]

(86a) *Se MALAD Pòl   malad!*
       SE sick   Paul sick
       'Paul is REALLY SICK.'

  i.   'literally SICK, as opposed to sick-ISH' or DEAD.' [contrastive]
  ii. 'FRIGHTFULLY sick' [intensive]

(b)   *Se BILENG   Pòl   bileng!*
       SE bilingual Paul bilingual
       'Paul is REALLY BILINGUAL.'

  i.   'literally BILINGUAL, as opposed to KINDA-bilingual' or 'MONOLINGUAL'
       [contrastive]
  ii. *'FRIGHTFULLY bilingual' [intensive]

---

21. Though phrased differently, a similar objection to a morphological analysis of VFD is made by Aboh & Dyakonova (2009).

22. The *bilingual* example in (86b) is borrowed from Harbour (2008: 865), but our glosses and comment are a free adaptation of Harbour's description. *Bileng* is an obvious borrowing from French – basilectal Haitian would have, e.g. *li pale de lang* '(s)he speaks two languages', rather than *li bileng* '(s)he is bilingual'. Harbour suggests that with non-scalar predicates such as *bileng*, 'bilingual', or with some other predicates such as *konnen* 'know', Predicate-Cleft is available while low contrastive V-reiteration is not – a potential problem for his central assumption. Herby Glaude and our other consultants however find low contrastive V-reiteration quite acceptable with all such predicates, under the proper prosody and pragmatic context. The resulting reading involves the contrastive-focus effect described by Ghomeshi & al. (2004) as characteristic of contrastive reiteration (CR) in English.

(i)   *Yo   konnen- KONNEN l   (oubyen yo   jis RABACHE l)?*
      3PL know   know   3SG   or   3PL just parrot   3SG
      Lit. 'Do they KNOW-know it (or are they just PARROTING it)?'
      ('Do they actually KNOW it or are they just PARROTING it?')

Similarly, in bare VFDs, as well as in the factive, causative and temporal subtypes, only the contrastive reading arises:

(87a)   [MALAD *Pòl malad la] fè manman li tris.*
      'The fact that John is SICK makes his mum sad.'

      i.   'SICK, as opposed to, e.g. UNEMPLOYED'   [contrastive]
      ii. *'FRIGHTFULLY sick'   [intensive]

(b)   *RIVE Pòl rive, Elsi SOTI.*
      'Once Paul had ARRIVED, Elsi WENT OUT.'

      i.   'ARRIVED, as opposed to NOT-ARRIVED'   [contrastive]
      ii. *'FRIGHTFULLY arrived'   [intensive]

This indicates that intensiveness is only a side-effect of VFD with a subclass of scalar predicates, and in a subclass of external contexts (Predicate Clefts, or *ala*-exclamatives, cf. (1b)). The semantic effect of Bare VFD is *contrastive focus*, which also characterises one subtype of low lexical reiteration – the one described by Ghomeshi & al. (2004) under the label *contrastive reduplication* (CR), and illustrated above by the English examples in (78). This type of reiteration, whose effect may be roughly paraphrased by 'actually X (not (Y)', is shown by Ghomeshi & al. to apply to items having lexical features, whose denotation they describe as 'restricted to [their] prototype' (Ghomeshi & al. 2004: 316). We may note that unlike intensive reiteration, as in Haitian (88a), or English (88b), CR does not allow more than two occurrences of the reiterated lexeme:

(88a)   H   *Li   ekri   ekri   (ekri) (...), jiskaske men   li   fè   l   mal*
            3SG write write write   until   hand 3SG make 3SG pain
            '(S)he wrote wrote (wrote) (...), until his/her hand hurt.'

(b)   E   *He wrote (and) wrote (and) wrote (until his wrist hurt).*

(c)   H   *Li   bileng   BILENG   (*BILENG), oubyen li   jis*
            3SG bilingual bilingual   or   3SG just

            debrouye   l[23]   *annanglè?*
            handle.the.basics REFL   in.English

            'Is she actually BILINGUAL, or can she just handle the English basics?'

---

23. *debrouye l(i)* ('manage', 'get along') is an intrinsically reflexive verb similar to French *se débrouiller*. The postverbal weak pronoun must be coindexed with the local subject, viz. *mwen debrouye m* ('I manage'), *ou debrouye-w* ('you manage'), etc.

(d)   E   *Is (s)he (*bilingual) BILINGUAL bilingual, or can (s)he just handle the basics?*

Since, as noted by Harbour, VFD cannot involve more than two occurrences of the reiterated item, as further witnessed below by (89), the contrast between (88a, b) and (88c, d) brings empirical support to our claim that CR (NOT intensive reiteration) must be singled out as the low contrastive reiteration structure which feeds VFD:

(89a)   *Se TOUYE (*TOUYE) yo   touye Janmari Vinsan.*
      SE kill   kill   3PL kill   Janmari Vinsan
      'They actually KILLED Janmari Vinsan.'

(b)   *[Touye (*TOUYE) yo   touye Janmari Vinsan]*
      kill   kill   3PL kill   Janmari Vinsan

      fè   Elsi pa   dakò.
      make Elsi NEG agree
      'The fact that they actually KILLED Janmari Vinsan seriously upsets Elsi.'

(c)   *[Rive (*RIVE) Jan rive],   (epi)   Elsi SOTI.*
      arrive   arrive Jan arrive   and.then Elsi go.out
      'Once John had ARRIVED, Elsi WENT OUT.'

This discussion leads us to conclude that although Harbour's leading idea – that VFD in Haitian is fed by low contrastive V-reiteration – is correct, the derivation he proposes needs to be amended for at least two reasons: (i) the extracted expression should be a syntactic constituent filling a phrasal position; (ii) the low contrastive V-reiteration configuration should only trigger contrastive focus, with the intensive effect triggered by independent properties (e.g. clefting, *ala*, exclamative force).

Ghomeshi & al. (2004) propose to derive Contrastive Reduplication (CR) via a copy rule analysed as an instance of Head Movement, as represented in (90):

(90)   Deriving CR   [Ghomeshi & al. 2004: 347]

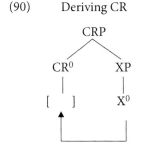

These authors analyse CR^0 as a functional head which hosts a strong contrastive feature, hence attracts the head of its lexical complement (XP). Reiteration results from the tail of the chain failing to be deleted. This property distinguishes CR (91a) from contrast without reiteration (91b):

(91a)   *It's* YELLOW-*yellow.*

(b)   *It's* YELLOW.

Exported to Haitian, this analysis however does not allow us to derive VFD from CR, if VFD should – as shown above – be derived via A'-movement: if CR is derived by Head Movement, as in (88), and VFD by A'-movement, we are led back to the paradox which Harbour's analysis was attempting to solve.

The Morphological Doubling Theory proposed by Inkelas & Zoll (2005), followed by Ghaniabadi & al. (2006), could lead us to a solution. Under this theory, the low contrastive reiteration structure crucially does not involve any copying rule (hence, no Head Movement operation as in (90)). It simply involves the external merging of the same lexeme in two different structural positions, which in this case triggers a contrastive-focus effect. Following Jackendoff (1997, 2002), the authors assume that the reiterated string (e.g. *yellow yellow*) forms a lexical entry. However, if we consider the Persian example in (92) from Ghaniabadi & al. (2006), which exhibits the typical CR semantics, we note that its two lexical constituents are syntactically articulated by the *ezafe* morpheme:

Persian
(92a)   *âbi*
        'blue'

(b)   *âbi-e   âbi*
        'completely/pure blue' [Ghaniabadi & al.'s translation]
        'BLUE blue' (our own translation)

The *ezafe* morpheme[24] may be identified as a functional head linking together a lexeme and its modifier/specifier. We may therefore assume for (92b) the structure in (93):

---

24. 'An indispensable element inside any noun phrase comprising a head modified by at least one non-clausal modifier and/or complement' [Parsafar 2008].

(93)

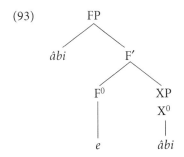

Since *ezafe* only links the modifier and the phrasal head, and does not in itself trigger any contrastive effect, and since lexical reiteration does not *as such* trigger a contrastive-focus effect (as witnessed by, e.g. (79)), we assume that the contrastive effect in (92b), as well as in the English CR examples discussed by Ghomeshi & al. arises from the fact that the same lexical item is merged in (93), both in the X^0 head, and in the modifier scoping over this head.

We further propose to analyse CR in English (94b) as a special instance of the restrictive-modification pattern otherwise exemplified by (94a):

[*What kind of blue shirt was he wearing*?]
(94a)   *He was wearing a* PALE-*blue shirt* (*not a* DARK-*blue one*).

   (b)   *He was wearing a* BLUE-*blue shirt* (*not a blue-*ISH *one*).

In (94a), where the head adjective and its restrictive modifier are lexically distinct, contrastive focus on the modifier comes as a free option, as witnessed by the acceptability of (95a) below, where focus scopes over the entire object DP, rather than on the adjective modifier; in (94b), on the other hand, the lexical identity of the head adjective and its modifier automatically forces narrow contrastive focus on the modifier, as witnessed by the infelicity of (95b), which shows that unlike the non-reiterated modifier in (95a), the reiterated modifier is only licensed under primary stress:

[*What was he wearing?*]
(95a)   *He was wearing a pale-blue shírt.*

   (b)   **He was wearing a blue-blue shírt.*

We now return to low contrastive V-reiteration in Haitian, as in (96):

(96a)   *Pòl   malad* MALAD.
        Paul sick   sick
        Lit. 'Paul is SICK sick.'
        ('Paul is REALLY SICK.')

(b) *Duvalier pati* PATI.
     Duvalier go   go
     Lit. 'Duvalier is GONE gone.'
     ('Duvalier is REALLY GONE.')

(c) *Yo   touye* TOUYE *Janmari Vinsan.*
     3PL kill kill   Janmari Vinsan
     'They KILLED killed Janmari Vinsan.'
     ('They REALLY KILLED Janmari Vinsan.')[25]

We propose in (97) to analyse low contrastive V-reiteration as a special instance of the restrictive-modifier structure assumed above in (93):

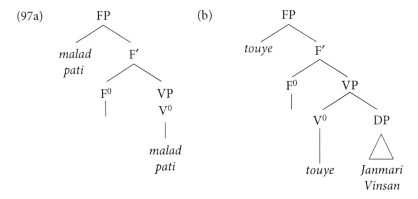

In such structures, the same lexeme is merged in the lexical (V) head, and in the specifier of a Modifier phrase (FP) dominating VP.[26] The contrastive effect, as

---

25. In Haitian, as in French, and unlike in English, the modifier linearly follows the modified element at spell-out (e.g. adnominal modifiers follow the noun). We assume that the Modifier is universally merged above the modified element in syntactic structure, and that the Modified expression moves up past the Modifier in some languages and constructions (cf. Knittel 2005; Cinque 2010).

26. A reviewer of an earlier draft of this text reacts to (97) in the following way: 'If two verbs are merged, what about the Theta-Criterion?' This objection however fails to be relevant under the assumption that lexical roots have no categorial features until they are merged in syntax (cf. Halle & Marantz 1993; Kayne 2009). Thus *malad* and *touye*, in (97) 'are verbs' only if they are inserted in the V head; if inserted in spec,FP, they are construed as restrictive modifiers scoping over the V head, viz. as adverbial modifiers – 'adverbs'.
     Schang (this volume) argues that a modifier structure similar to the one assumed in (97) is consistent with a subtype of reiteration constructions in São Tomense.

described by Ghomeshi & al. (2004), arises from the lexical identity of the phrasal head and its restrictive modifier.

VFD may now be regularly derived from the CR structure via A'-movement, as shown in (98):

(98)   Deriving the core VFD construction: *pati Duvalier pati*

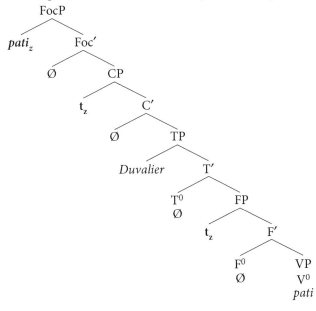

The derivation proposed in (98) allows us to clarify the status of the raised constituent in VFD. As a restrictive modifier, it originates in a specifier position, and is therefore available for A'-movement. The special contrastive effect triggered by CR crucially arises from the strict lexical identity of the (V) *head* and its *bare modifier*. The expression merged in the spec of FP is thus a lexeme – a replica of the item merged in the V head.

The restrictive-modifier syntactic structure proposed in (98) for CR should be distinguished from the morphological structure of verbal compounds such as those mentioned in Footnote 9 (example (ii)), since (99d) below is ill-formed, contrasting with (99b). (99f) may be derived from (99e) via syntactic movement from the specifier of FP in diagram (98), while in (99d), movement is blocked from within a lexical entry.

(99a)   *Pòl kouri   kouri.*
       Paul run   run
       'Paul REALLY RAN.'

(b) $Kouri_k$ Pòl t_k kouri.
     run   Paul run
     'Paul REALLY RAN.'

(c) Pòl   kouri-desann.
     Paul run-come.down
     'Paul came down running (= came down fast).'

(d) *$Kouri_k$ Pòl t_k desann.

(e) Pòl   kouri kouri-desann.
     Paul run   run-come.down
     'Paul came down REALLY FAST.'

(f) $Kouri_k$ Pòl t_k kouri-desann.
     run   Paul   run-come.down
     'Paul came down REALLY FAST.'

The contrast between (99d) and (99f) thus supports our assumption that the source of VFD is the syntactic structure represented in (98), rather than the morphological structure proposed by Harbour (2008).

As shown in Section 2, the Bare VFD may occur as an independent clause indicating Verb Focus, or as the protasis of a structure overtly or covertly conjoined by *epi*, as in (100):

(100) PATI   Duvalier pati, (epi)   Elsi vini.
       leave Duvalier leave so-then Elsi come.back
       Lit. 'Duvalier LEFT, so-then Elsi came back.'
       = 'Once/as soon as Duvalier (had) LEFT, Elsi came back.'

If the VFD structure in (98) is nominalised, viz. embedded within a DP, as in (101), we derive the factive subtype, which fills an argument or dislocated-topic position within a larger clause:

(101) Nominalised VFD (the factive subtype)
       pati Duvalier pati (a)[27]

---

27. We assume DP to be head-initial in Haitian, with the complement of D raising up to the specifier, and the D head filled by LA when specified as specific (+locative), cf. Zribi-Hertz & Glaude (2007). Similar configurations are found in Gbe, cf. Aboh (2002, 2005).

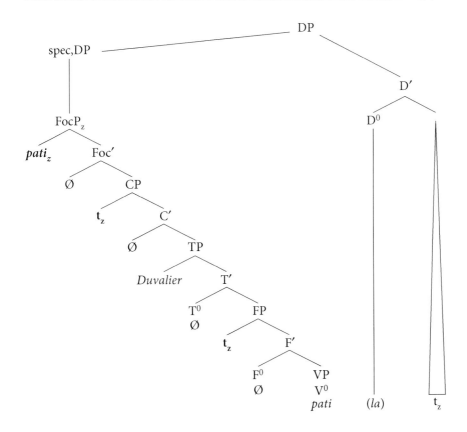

(102a) [PATI Duvalier pati a] fè   Pòl   kontan.
        go   Duvalier go DET make Paul happy
        'The fact that Duvalier is GONE makes Paul happy.'

(b) [KOURI Pòl kouri], Elsi KONTAN.
     run   Paul run   Elsi happy
     '(Due to) the fact that Paul RUNS, Elsi is HAPPY.'

In the Bare VFD structure in (98), the Verb Focus effect arises from two steps in
the derivation: the CR structure represented in (97), and Focus Raising. In the
Predicate-Cleft construction illustrated in (103bi) below, the Verb Focus effect
is further enhanced by clefting, which places the focused expression in a predicate position with respect to the expletive subject pronoun *se*. As shown above
(Section 2.2.5), however, a sentence such as (103b) is a priori ambiguous between
the Predicate-Cleft reading in (103bi) and the VFD-cleft reading in (103bii) – an
instance of Argument Cleft:

(103a)   *Pati   Duvalier   pati!*
         go   Duvalier   go
         'Duvalier is REALLY GONE.'

(b)   *Se Pati Duvalier pati*
      SE go   Duvalier go

   i.   'Duvalier is REALLY GONE.' [Predicate-Cleft]
   ii. 'It is [the fact that Duvalier is GONE] (which...)' [Argument-Cleft]

The structural representations in (104) are intended to distinguish the two analyses of (103b):[28]

(104a)   Predicate Cleft: *se [pati] Duvalier pati*

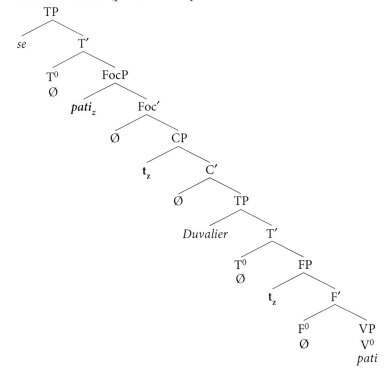

_____

28.   For lack of space, we must leave out here the ALA and ATA VFD subtypes. We assume that like all other VFD constructions, they contain the core substructure represented in (98). But we leave further structural details open for future research.

(b) VFD-cleft: *se [pati Duvalier pati (a)] (ki fè Pòl kontan)*

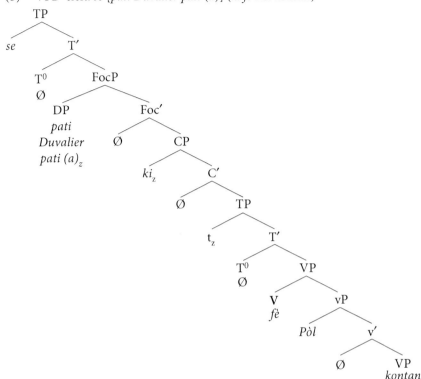

4. Concluding assumptions

Our descriptive update of Haitian VFD departs from all previous descriptions on three counts:

i.   It reduces VFD to a single core structure represented in (98), whose derivation crucially involves Focus Movement, an instance of A′-movement;
ii. It distinguishes the Bare VFD structure from the Predicate-Cleft construction represented in (104a), which involves a further matrix level of predication;
iii. It treats the factive and causative subtypes as nominalised instances of VFD, and the temporal subtype as containing Bare VFD in the protasis of a conjoined structure whose constituents are linked by temporal succession.

We have been led to discard, on empirical grounds, the assumption that VFD is a form of relativisation involving a cognate object or 'event argument' raising up to the clause periphery. We have further argued that the 'Parallel-Chain theory' proposed by Koopman (1997) and Aboh & Dyakonova (2009) to account for VFD in Gbe must be revised for Haitian, since some of the empirical properties it hinges on (Verb-to-Aspect raising, head-movement properties) are not shared by Gbe and Haitian.

The data of Haitian lead us to adopt – and generalise to all subtypes of VFD in this language – Harbour's (2008) assumption that VFD is derived from low contrastive verb reiteration. This analysis sheds light on the apparently paradoxical fact that VFD, in Haitian, seems to involve *A′-movement* applying to a V-*head*. Under our own analysis, VFD is regularly derived by raising to the clause periphery a VP modifier (an adverbial phrase) containing but a bare lexeme identical to the V head. We assume that the contrastive effect triggered by low contrastive reiteration makes the restrictive modifier a natural candidate for Focus Movement, and (optionally) for further layers of focus or intensive marking (clefting, *ala, ata*). Under the derivation proposed in (98), an example such as (103a) is crucially not analysed as an elliptical variant of its Predicate-Cleft counterpart in (103b). The V-focus effect obtains prior to Focus Movement, and Focus Movement occurs prior to clefting or further focus or intensive marking. Contrastive reiteration (CR), Focus Movement, Clefting, and intensive or contrastive markers such as *ala* and *ata*, appear as independent though combinable strategies which trigger or highlight a contrastive focus effect.

As regards reiteration, the above descriptive results do not support the iconic theory of reiteration stipulating that 'more form stands for more meaning'. Under the analysis proposed here, the semantic effect of reiteration in VFD constructions is contrastive focus, which primarily arises from a special instance of *restrictive* modification – in effect quite the opposite of 'more-of'.

As regards the respective roles of syntax and morphology in reiterated strings, the derivation proposed above for VFD in Haitian entirely pertains to syntax. It involves the external merge of a V-identical VP modifier, followed by Focus Movement and (optionally) Clefting or nominalization (embedding under DP). The reiterated XX(Y) string which feeds VFD constructions does not form a word in morphology, but a VP modified by an adverbial.

A brief final word about the diachronic issue. Among the focus-marking strategies which may combine in the derivation of VFD constructions in Haitian, low contrastive reiteration, clefting, and adverbial focus markers are all available in French (both Standard and dialectal). However, contrastive *verb* reiteration in French seems restricted to non-finite forms, as illustrated in (105):

(105a) *Tu   vas   les   manger-* MANGER *(ou   seulement*
       2SG FUT.2SG 3PL eat.INF   eat.INF   or   only

       les   LECHOUILLER)?
       3PL kind.of.lick-INF

       'Are you planning on actually EATING them (or just on kinda LICKING them)?'

(b) *Tu   les   as   mang-és-* MANG-ÉS
     2SG 3PL have.PRS.2SG eat-PP   eat-PP

     (ou   seulement   LECHOUILLES)?
     or   just   kind.of.lick-PP

     Lit. 'Have you actually EATEN them (or just kinda LICKED them)?'

(c) **Tu   les   manges   -MANGES*
     2SG 3PL eat.PRS.2SG -eat.PRS.2SG
     (ou tu te contentes de les LECHOUILLER)?
     Lit. 'Do you actually EAT them (or do you just kinda LICK them))?'

If this generalisation is correct, it is reasonable to assume that the uninflected morphology of verbs in Haitian contributed to allow the expansion of low reiteration as a Verb Focus strategy, hence the development of VFD. Focus Raising (i.e.. the raising of a focused constituent to the clause periphery, without clefting) is *not*, on the other hand, a natural focus-marking strategy in French, where focus is generally phrase-final, especially for verbs (compare Haitian VFD with the French examples in (3)). This suggests that the one non-French property involved in the diachronic development of Haitian VFD was *Focus Raising*, a property characteristically attested in Gbe (Koopman 1984, 1997; Aboh 2003, 2004; Aboh & Dyakonova 2009), a plausible substrate for this creole. The descriptive results of the present study are thus consistent with the assumption that the grammars of French and Gbe each contributed to the emergence of VFD constructions as observed in Modern Haitian. This hypothesis should however be refined on the basis of further empirical work on other 'VFD-like' constructions in Caribbean French-lexifier creoles, as well as in dialectal French[29] and Indian-Ocean creoles, where a Gbe influence is less likely.

---

29. Wittman (1998) thus quotes the following examples from Magoua, a Canadian variety of French still spoken in the 1970s by senior citizens of Trois-Rivieres, on the Northern bank of the Saint-Lawrence river, South of Quebec City:

(ia) *Malad   yé   te   malad, yon pa   té   kapab l   -sové.*
      Sick   3SG/SUBJ ANT sick   3PL NEG ANT can   3SG/OBJ -save
      Lit. 'Sick (as) he was sick, they couldn't save him.'

References

Aboh, Enoch. 2002. La morphosyntaxe de la périphérie gauche nominale. *Recherches Linguistiques de Vincennes* 31: 9–26.

Aboh, Enoch. 2003. Focus constructions across Kwa. In *Kinyira njira!—Step Firmly on the Pathway!* [Trends in African Linguistics 6], Chege Githiora, Heather Littlefield & Victor Manfredi (eds), 7–22. Trenton NJ: Africa World Press.

Aboh, Enoch. 2004. *The Morphosyntax of Complement-head Sequences. Clause Structure and Word Order Patterns in Kwa.* Oxford: OUP.

Aboh, Enoch. 2005. Deriving relative and factive clauses. In *Contributions to the Thirtieth Incontro di Grammatica Generativa, Venice, February 26–28,* 2004, Laura Brugè, Giuliana Giusti, Nicola Munaro, Walter Schweikert & Giuseppina Turano (eds), 265–285. Venice: Università Ca' Foscari.

Aboh, Enoch & Dyakonova, Marina. 2009. Predicate doubling and parallel chains. *Lingua* 119(7): 1035–1065.

Bernabé, Jean. 1983. *Fondal-natal.* Paris: L'Harmattan.

Bondaruk, Anna. n.d. Constraints on predicate clefting in Polish. Ms, John Paul II University of Lublin. ⟨http://www.unileipzig.de/~jungslav/fdsl/fdsl7/abstracts/Bondaruk_FA.pdf⟩

'Il était malade au point qu'ils n'ont pas pu le sauver.'   (Wittman's F. translation)
('He was so sick they couldn't save him.')

(ib) *Se   manje   i   -manj.*
      SE   eat   3SG/SUBJ -eat
      Lit. 'It-is eat he eats.'
      'Il ne mange pas, il bouffe.'   (Wittman's F. translation)
      ('He doesn't EAT, he STUFFS HIMSELF.')

These sentences are at first glance similar to some VFD examples in Haitian. However (ia) could a priori result from a continuous development from French (iia), where the expression in clause-initial position is topical (as in (3) above) rather than focal; and due to its initial *se*, (ib) could a priori result from a continuous development from French clefting, where focus is primarily clause-final rather than clause-initial, cf. (iib):

(ia) *Malade   comme   il   était,   on   n'a   pas   pu   le   sauver.*
      sick   as   he   was   they   couldn't   save him

(ib) *(Il   mange)   CA   c'est   MANGER* !
      he   eats   that is   eat(ing)
      '(He's eating) THAT is (what you may call) EATING!'

It also seems (Muhsina Alleesaib & Fabiola Henri, p.c.) that the VFD constructions found in Caribbean French-lexifier creoles – as illustrated above in Haitian – have no exact equivalents in Indian-Ocean French lexifier creoles, e.g. in Mauritian. Further empirical and detailed comparative work, covering morphology, syntax and contextualised interpretation revealing information structure, clearly needs to be done to allow finer diachronic assumptions to be drawn.

Büring, Daniel. 1997. *The Meaning of Topic and Focus–The 59th St. Bridge Accent*. London: Routledge.

Cable, Seth. 2004. The Yiddish predicate cleft: A base-generation analysis. Talk presented at the EC05 Syntax Workshop, University of Maryland, College Park. ⟨http://www.ling.umd.edu/Events/SyntaxConf/⟩

Chomsky, Noam. 1977. On Wh-movement. In *Formal Syntax*, Peter Culicover, Thomas Wasow & Adrian Akmajian (eds), 71–132. New York NY: Academic Press.

Cinque, Guglielmo. 2010. *The Syntax of Adjectives*. Cambridge MA: The MIT Press.

DeGraff, Michel. 1992. Creole Grammars and the Acquisition of Syntax: The Case of Haitian. Ph.D. dissertation, Pennsylvania State University.

Déprez, Viviane. 2003. Haitian Creole *se*: A copula, a pronoun, both or neither? On the double life of a functional head. In *Recent Development in Creole Studies*, Dany Adone (ed.), 135–173. Tübingen: Max Niemeyer.

Filipovich, Sandra. 1987. La morphologie de l'haïtien. MA thesis, UQAM.

Gadelii, Karl. 2007. Les phrases copulatives dans les créoles français. In *Grammaires créoles et grammaire comparative,* Karl Gadelii & Anne Zribi-Hertz (eds), 209–236. Saint-Denis: Presses Universitaires de Vincennes.

Ghaniabadi, Saeed, Ghomeshi, Jila & Sadat-Tehrani, Nima. 2006. Reduplication in Persian: A morphological doubling approach. In *Proceedings of the 2006 Annual Conference of the Canadian Linguistic Association*. ⟨ling.uwo.ca/publications/CLA2006/Ghaniabadi_etal.pdf⟩.

Ghomeshi, Jila, Jackendoff, Ray, Rosen, Nicole & Russell, Kevin. 2004. Contrastive focus reduplication in English (the SALAD-salad paper). *Natural Language & Linguistic Theory* 22: 307–357.

Harbour, Daniel. 2008. *Klivaj predika*, or predicate clefts in Haitian. *Lingua* 118: 853–871.

Hutchison, John Priestley. 1989. Copy nominals and the interpretation of predicate clefts in Haitian. Paper presented at the 3rd Niger-Congo syntax and semantics workshop, MIT.

Inkelas, Sharon & Zoll, Cheryl. 2005. *Reduplication*. Cambridge: CUP.

Jackendoff, Ray. 1997. *The Architecture of the Language Faculty*. Cambridge MA: The MIT Press.

Jackendoff, Ray. 2002. *Foundations of Language: Brain, Meaning, Grammar, Evolution*. Oxford: OUP.

Keenan, Edward & Comrie, Bernard. 1977. Noun phrase accessibility and universal grammar. *Linguistic Inquiry* 8(1): 63–99.

Kiparsky, Paul & Kiparsky, Carol. 1979. Fact. In *Progress in Linguistics,* Manfred Bierwisch & Karl Erich Heidolph (eds), 143–172. The Hague: Mouton.

Knittel, Marie-Laurence. 2005. Some remarks on adjective placement in the French NP. Probus 17: 185–226.

Koopman, Hilda. 1984. *The Syntax of Verbs: From Verb Movement Rules in the Kru Languages to Universal Grammar*. Dordrecht: Foris

Koopman, Hilda. 1997. Unifying predicate cleft constructions. Ms, UCLA.

Larson, Richard & Lefebvre, Claire. 1991. Predicate clefting in Haitian creole. In *Proceedings of the 21st Annual Meeting of the North Eastern Linguistics Society*, Tim D. Sherer (ed.), 247–62. Montreal: UQAM.

Lefebvre, Claire. 1989. Event, aspect and predicate cleft interpretation: The case of Haitian Creole. In *Lexicon Project Working Papers* 29, Carol Tenny (ed.), 17–33. Cambridge MA: The MIT Press.

Lefebvre, Claire. 1990. On the interpretation of predicate-clefts. *The Linguistic Review* 6: 169–194.

Lefebvre, Claire. 1998. *Creole Genesis and the Acquisition of Grammar*. Cambridge: CUP.

Lefebvre, Claire & Ritter, Elizabeth. 1993. Two types of predicate doubling adverbs in Haitian Creole. In *Focus and Grammatical Relations in Creole Languages* [Creole Language Library 12], Francis Byrne & Donald Winford (eds), 55–91. Amsterdam: John Benjamins.

Lumsden, John. 1990. The biclausal nature of Haitian clefts. *Linguistics* 28:741–759.

Lumsden, John & Lefebvre, Claire. 1990. Predicate-cleft constructions and why they aren't what you might think. *Linguistics* 28:783–807.

Manfredi, Victor. 1993. Verb focus and the typology of Kwa/Kru and Haitian. In *Focus and Grammatical Relations in Creole Languages* [Creole Language Library 12], Francis Byrne & Donald Winford (eds), 3–51. Amsterdam: John Benjamins.

Méry, Renaud. 1988. De la simplicité syntaxique et de son rendement dans la communication de l'information: Un créole à base lexicale française face à deux grandes langues standard. *Espaces créoles* 6:101–156.

Mufwene, Salikoko. 1987. An issue on predicate-clefting. Evidence from Atlantic Creoles and African languages. In *Varia Creolica*, Philip Maurer & Thomas Stolz (eds), 71–89. Bochum: Brockmeyer.

Mufwene, Salikoko. 1994. Genèse de population et genèse de langue. *Plurilinguismes* 8:95–113.

Parsafar, Parviz. 2008. Syntax, morphology and semantics of *ezafe*. ⟨linggraduate.unm.edu/conference/2008/HDLS%208%20ABS/Parsafar.doc⟩

Piou, Nanie. 1982a. Le clivage du prédicat. In *Syntaxe de l'haïtien*, Claire Lefebvre, Hélène Magloire-Holly & Nanie Piou (eds), 122–151. Ann Arbor MI: Karoma.

Piou, Nanie. 1982b. Le redoublement verbal. In *Syntaxe de l'haïtien*, Claire Lefebvre, Hélène Magloire-Holly & Nanie Piou (eds), 152–166. Ann Arbor MI: Karoma.

Reinhart, Tanya. & Siloni, Tal. 2005. The lexicon-syntax parameter: Reflexivization and other arity operations. *Linguistic Inquiry* 36:389–436.

Ross, John. 1967. On the nature of Island Constraints. Ph.D. dissertation, MIT.

Sylvain, Suzanne. 1936. *Le créole haïtien, morphologie et syntaxe*. Wetteren: Imprimerie De Meester/Port-au-Prince: By the author.

Veenstra, Tonjes. 2007. Information structure in Creoles. Talk presented at the 2nd Young Scholars' Workshop on Creole Languages. Paris: DILTEC, Université Paris-3.

Wittman, Henri. 1998. Les créolismes syntaxiques du français magoua parlé aux Trois-Rivières. In *Français d'Amérique: Variation, Créolisation, Normalisation*, Patrice Brasseur (ed.), 229–248. Avignon: Université d'Avignon, Centre d'Etudes Canadiennes.

Zribi-Hertz, Anne & Glaude, Herby. 2007. Bare NPs and deficient DPs in Haitian and French. In *Noun Phrases in Creole Languages* [Creole Language Library 31], Marlyse Baptista & Jacqueline Guéron (eds), 265–298. Amsterdam: John Benjamins.

Verb doubling in Breton and Gungbe

Obligatory exponence at the sentence level*

Mélanie Jouitteau
CNRS, UMR 7110 Université Paris Diderot

Breton tensed verbs show an synthetic/analytic structure alternation (*I.know vs. to.know I.do*), that is not conditioned by their semantic or aspectual structure but by their syntactic environment, namely word order. Such a paradigm of verb-doubling poses a strong case against iconicity, because knowing where a verb can double requires full information about the entire derivation of the sentence. The sentence is correct if and only if the tensed element is not at the left-edge of the sentence. The infinitive form of the analytic construction prevents the tensed element from occurring in the most left-edge position. This paper proposes that the analytic structure (*to.know I.do*) responds to the same trigger as expletive insertion (*expl I.know*). I claim that analytic tense formation is a last-resort strategy that forms the equivalent of an expletive by excorporation of the verbal root out of the complex tensed head. The excorporated lexical verb appears fronted as an infinitive form by default. The tensed auxiliary is either realized as a dummy 'do' auxiliary (*to.know I.do*), or, for an idiosyncratic list of verbs, as the tensed reiteration of the excorporated verb itself (doubling; *to. know I.know*).

---

* This paper has benefited from presentations at FACL 2009 (U. Arizona), and the workshop on verbal reiteration (Paris). I thank Leston Buell, Anne Zribi-Hertz and Enoch Aboh for their useful comments. Concerning the data in the paper, I have to thank three Breton native speakers: DL from Quimperlé, H.G. from Scaër and SB from Callac. Thanks also to Herve ar Bihan (U. Rennes II). Corpus data from Bijer, ar C'hog and Skragn come from the database constructed by Milan Rezac during his post-doc at the U. of Nantes, and to which he kindly provided me access. New Gungbe data comes from my pestering of Enoch Aboh. Any errors or misrepresentations are my responsibility alone.

   Abbreviations: R marks the preverbal particle, the '*rannig-verb*' that appears (syntactically at least) before all inflected verbs (Fin head in the left periphery, cf. Jouitteau 2005/2010). In the examples translations, small caps signal informational salience. Obl = oblique ; poss = possessive, PRT=particle.

1.   Introduction

Breton, the modern Continental Celtic language, allows for two types of analytic constructions. In the most common case (1a), an infinitive verb precedes a semantically dummy auxiliary that bears the tense and subject agreement markers. Though this auxiliary means 'to do' in isolation, its semantic import in the construction is null, and the sentence as a whole is fully equivalent to the synthetic constructions in (2a). Verb doubling as illustrated in (1b) is an alternative and rarer case of analytic construction, where the infinitive verb precedes its own inflected form. Though the auxiliary repeats the lexical content of the verb, the semantic import of the repetition in the construction is null, and the sentence as a whole is fully equivalent to the synthetic construction in (2b).[1]

ANALYTIC STRUCTURES:

(1) a. *Debriñ a ran avaloù.*   (Standard Breton)
         eat   R   do.1SG apples
         'I eat apples.'

     b. *Mont a yan   d' ar jardin.*   (Quimperlé Breton)
         go   R   go.1SG at the garden
         'I am going into the garden.'

SYNTHETIC STRUCTURES:

(2) a. *Bez' e tebran avaloù.*   (Western Breton)
         EXPL   R   eat.1SG apples
         'I eat apples.'

     b. *Bez' ez an   d' ar jardin.*   (Standard Breton)
         EXPL   R   go.1SG at the garden
         'I am going into the garden.'

Breton is a 'linear verb-second' language (Borsley & Kathol 2000; Jouitteau 2009), in the sense that the element that bears both tense and agreement morphemes cannot stand as the left-most element in a sentence (3). For clarity, I use in this paper the term 'Tense-second' instead of 'verb-second'.

(3) **E tebran avaloù.*   (Standard Breton)
      R   go.1SG apples
      'I eat apples.'

---

1.   The Breton data comes from a corpus of different dialects, and fieldwork in Quimperlé. The verbal particle, the *rannig*, noted 'R', is a realization of the Fin Head into which the tensed element incorporates (Jouitteau 2005/2010).

The goal of this article is to provide an account of the under-documented analytic constructions in (1). I propose that the two analytic constructions in (1), both with 'do' and with doubling, represent an expletive strategy alternative to the [expletive + synthetic Tense] groups in (2). I will show that analytic constructions in (1) appear, like the *bez* expletive, if and only if they serve as a last resort operation in order to meet obligatory exponence in the pre-tense position. The analysis will derive the odd facts of (1): first, in both cases of analytic constructions in (1), there is at least one element that fails to be interpreted. In (1a), the auxiliary doesn't seem to do more than providing morphological support, and in (1b), the lexical verb has two occurrences, only one of which seems to be interpreted, because it does not require two subjects, in apparent violation of the theta-criterion. Second, in both analytic constructions, the two verbal/auxiliary occurrences are phonologically distinct, and obligatorily appear in the relative [Infinitive – Tense] order: in analytic constructions, the infinitive lexical verb never appears to the right of the tensed element. In (4), the pre-Tense position has been filled with a focalized element. Despite satisfaction of the canonical 'Tense-second' order, the lexical verb cannot appear to the right of the tensed element.

(4)   a.   *Avaloù   a   ran   debriñ.
           apples   R   do.1SG   eat
           'I eat APPLES.'

      b.   *D' ar   jardin   a   yan   mont.
           at the   garden   R   go.1SG   go
           'I am going INTO THE GARDEN.'

This distributional restriction of analytic tenses is even more strict than strictly left-edge, because infinitive verbs of analytic constructions can never appear in a sentence where another element fills in the pre-tense position. In (5), an object and a prepositional phrase have been fronted by focus, and still the lexical verb cannot appear outside the tensed complex. Only synthetic tenses are allowed (6), showing that analytic tenses have a last-resort dimension.

(5)   a.   *Avaloù   debriñ   a   ran
           apples   eat   R   do.1SG
           'I eat APPLES.'

      b.   *D' ar   jardin   mont   a   yan.
           at the   garden   go   R   go.1SG
           'I am going INTO THE GARDEN.'

(6)   a.   Avaloù   a   zebran.
           apples   R   eat.1SG
           'I eat APPLES.'

    b. *D' ar jardin e yan.*
       at the garden R go.1SG
       'I am going INTO THE GARDEN.'

This striking distribution recalls the distribution of the Breton expletive *bez'* as illustrated in (2). Like infinitives of analytic constructions, the expletive *bez'* occurs only to the left of tensed elements, as a last resort strategy to avoid Tense-first orders as in (3). In formal terms, this means that there is some kind of a trigger in the grammar of the language that requires at least one element, head or XP, to precede the inflected element (Jouitteau 2005/2010, 2007). LEIT, as defined in (7), is the unique motivation for expletive insertion in (2).

(7)   *Late Expletive Insertion Trigger*
      LEIT is a morphological operation that operates at the level of the sentence
      and bans (Tense)-first orders.
      As a last resort, it either merges an expletive or attracts the closest
      postverbal element into the preverbal position.
      LEIT effects are invisible to the interpretative module.

In this paper, I will show that both analytic constructions (1a) and b pattern like expletives and show evidence for the LEIT. I therefore propose that the Breton analytic paradigms illustrate the creation of an expletive by means of a morphological excorporation operation (8). The dummy verb 'do' *ober* is not included in the numeration. Instead, it is generated as a last-resort default as in (8a) illustrated in (1a). An idiosyncratic alternative to this last-resort insertion is to pronounce the lower copy of the excorporated verb, leading to doubling structures as in (8b), illustrated in (1b).

(8)   a. V [FINP R [(V)do.T.AGR] [$_{vP}$ S V PP]   analytic tense in 'do'

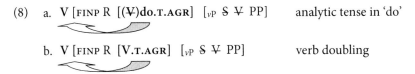

      b. V [FINP R [V.T.AGR] [$_{vP}$ S V PP]   verb doubling

I will start in Section 2 by investigating the syntactic properties of the analytic construction in 'do', and show that all these properties follow from the last-resort aspect of what is basically an expletive strategy. In the third section, I will contrast these properties with those of the doubling construction (1b). I will propose that despite their differences, verb doubling is a subcase of the 'do' auxiliation case. In a fourth section, I will focus on the main contrast between the two analytic constructions: their productivity. The analytic construction in (1a) is fully productive, whereas (1b) is clearly idiosyncratic. Only certain verbs can double. The list of the doubling verbs varies across dialects, and even from speaker to speaker. The list of doubling verbs always fails to form a homogeneous syntactic class. In Section 5,

I discuss several theoretical consequences of the idiosyncratic restriction of doubling in (1b), and propose that LEIT operates in a post-syntactic morphological module. I mention comparative evidence from Yimas and Basque verbal morphology, and propose an interpretation of V2 in terms of obligatory exponence. Section 6 provides a comparative exploration of verbal reduplication in Gungbe, opening the discussion to non sentence-initial environments.

2. Analytic construction with *ober*, 'do'

2.1 Syntactic properties of verbal head fronting

The analytic construction (henceforth AC) with *ober*, 'do' is very productive in Standard Breton and in all dialects, as briefly illustrated here below.

(9)   ***Eva***   *a*   *rafe*   *eur*   *werennad*   *lêz.*
       drink   R   would.do.3SG   DET   glass   milk
       'He would (like to) drink a glass of milk.'   (Kerne Breton, Trépos 2001: 438)

(10)   ***Ober***   *a*   *ray*   *glao*   *a-raog*   *an*   *noz.*
       do   R   do.FUT.3SG   rain   before   DET   night
       'It will rain before night.'   (Kerne Breton, Trépos 2001: 438)

(11)   ***Koéh***   *e*   *hras*   *ar*   *benneu*   *hé*   *deuhlin* (…)
       fall   R   did.PAST.3SG   on   ends   POSS   dual.knee
       'She fell on her knees.'   (Gwened Breton, Guillevic et Le Goff 1986: 161)

(12)   ***Tremen***   *a*   *reont*   *evit*   *tud*   *vad.*   (Quéré 1906: 230)
       pass   R   do.PRES.3PL   for   people   good
       'They pass for good people.'

Verbal head fronting with 'do' has the syntactic properties listed below.

(13)   *Verbal head fronting properties*
     i.   it is restricted to root tensed clauses.
     ii.   it is neutral in terms of information packaging.
     iii.   it is fully productive (except for some compounds of 'be').
     iv.   verb fronting is local.
     v.   the infinitive head is moved alone.
     vi.   movement violates the syntactic ban on excorporation.
     vii.   it is restricted to [VINF-do] order.
     viii. it (sometimes) has a doubling counterpart (1).

All these properties, except **(viii)**, directly follow from verb head fronting being a LEIT last-resort operation preventing tense-initial orders. I briefly review them here.

Verb fronting with auxiliary *ober* 'do' occurs only in environments where Tense-second is the canonical word order, hence the restriction to matrices of tensed domains, because embedded domains are canonically Tense-first (C-VSO, with complementizers that can be phonologically null).

(14)   Standard Breton
   a.   *Larout a ran   ø (*debriñ a ran   /e tebran) avaloù.*
         say   R do.1SG C   eat   R do.1SG /R eat.1SG apples
         'I say that I eat apples.'
   b.   *Un azen   hag (*debriñ a ra   /a zebr)   avaloù.*
         A donkey C   eat   R do.3SG R eat.3SG apples
         'a donkey that eats apples.'

Verb head fronting with 'do' is also banned from the imperative mood (Ernault 1888:247). The imperative mood is canonically tense-initial.

(15)   Standard Breton
         (* *Debriñ a (g)ra   / Debr)   avaloù!*
            eat   R do.IMP   eat.IMP apples
         'Eat apples!'

We already saw in (5) that analytic tense is not possible when focalized material occupies the pre-Tense position, that is, in minimalist terms, when preverbal A-bar material is brought into the left-periphery for independent reasons, and accidentally satisfies LEIT by providing pre-Tense material. In terms of information packaging, Stephens (1982:114) qualifies verb head-initial structures as 'neutral', which is also Schafer (1997)'s conclusion from a Modern Breton corpus study. Following Vallduví's (1995) terminology, Shafer states that verb head fronting appears in 'all-focus' and 'focus-tail' sentences (ii). In grammars from the first half of the 20th century, analytic structures are often said to create emphasis, without providing further details on the type of emphasis produced (see for example Leclerc 1986:63, 2⁰; Kervella 1995: §1997). To my knowledge, contemporary speakers of Breton do not use analytic structures in 'do' for emphasis at all. All readings brought by an analytic constructions can be brought by the synthetic ones. The reverse is not true, because of the last-resort dimension of analytic constructions: whenever an element is informationally salient in Breton (topic, focus), it must occupy a place in the clause's left periphery. This element thus automatically satisfies LEIT and cancels the trigger for an analytic construction. Only very high elements in the left periphery that never interfere with V2 orders, like hanging topics (inducing *as for* readings), scene-setting adverbs, question particles, pragmatic connectors (such as 'but'), and all conjunctions associated with prototypical cases of parataxis (*la* in Central Breton, *kar*, 'because' in all dialects, sometimes *ha...*) can precede analytic constructions in 'do'.[2] The last-resort character of infinitive fronting in analytic constructions is further revealed by its mutual exclusiveness with any other element brought into the preverbal area. Such a case is illustrated here by the negation C head in (16). Any other expletive strategy also logically blocks verb head fronting (17).

(16) Treger Breton, (Stephens 1982: 113)
  *_Koll_ **ne** **reas** _ket ar martolod _ e gasketenn._
  Lose NEG did.3SG NEG DET sailor   his cap
  'The sailor didn't lose his cap.'

(17) *_Bez_ **koll** _a_ **reas** _ar martolod _ e gasketenn._
  EXPL lose R did.3SG DET sailor   his cap
  'The sailor did lose/lost his cap.'

LEIT last-resort verb head fronting is fully productive, except for the verb 'be' and its compounds (iii). The verb _bezañ/bout_, 'to be', is uniformly rejected, as well as the synthetic verb _kaout_, 'to have', a compound of the verb _bezañ/bout_, 'to be' (Kervella 1995: §245[(bis)]; Jouitteau & Rezac 2006, 2008, 2009) as shown in (18).[3,4]

(18) D.L Quimperlé, S.B Callac
  *_Kaout_ _a_ **ran** _un oto._
  have R do.1SG a car
  'I have a car.'

Ploneis (1983) reports from Berrien another verb that fails to be auxiliated with _ober_ 'do', that also contains the stem of _bezañ/bout_ 'to be': the verb _gouzout_ 'to know'. For de Rostrenen (1795: 97) and Trépos (2001: 438), the restriction extends to all stative verbs. However, ACs are readily found with verbs like _seblantout_ 'to seem'; _chom_ 'to stay'; _dont da vezañ_ 'to become', or _tremen evit_ 'to pass for', as in (12). The semantic properties of the dummy auxiliary may have evolved over time, leading to these variations.

---

2. See Jouitteau (2005/2010: Chapter 2) for a detailed analysis of the Breton left periphery.

3. Le Roux (1957: 413) cites two cases in Middle Breton, but they can be analyzed as preverbal expletives before an impersonal form of 'to do'.

4. Auxiliations in 'do' appear only in the Gwened dialect that has kept an analytic variety of the verb 'have'. Ernault (1890: 473) mentions an AC with the analytic form of the verb 'have' (x). This Gwened variety of the verb 'have' in Breton is composed of a proclitic oblique argument on the verb 'to be', _bezañ_ (cf. Jouitteau et Rezac 2006, 2008, 2009). The 'infinitive' compound is presumably not the verb 'to be', but a small clause.

(x) **_hur bout_** _e ramb,_ [1PL.OBL be R do.1PL]; 'we have',
  hou poud _a ra,_ [2PL.OBL be R do.3SG]; 'you have'.

Another LEIT symptom is the locality of verb head movement (Holmberg 2000; Jouitteau 2005, 2010, 2007). No long-distance verb fronting is ever found (19).

(19)   *Livañ   [_FinP a   soñj   da   Anna [_FinP e   lare   Paol
       paint.INF   R   think to   Anna   R   say   Paul

       [_FinP 'raio   Nina an   daol.
               R do.FUT.3SG   Nina the table

       'Anna thinks that Paol said that Nina will paint the table.'

In (8), I propose that the site of extraction for the non-tensed verb head is the complex tensed head itself. A competing proposal would be to consider that the infinitive originates from the closest post-Tense position. If this were the case, we should observe all types of intervention effects. Indeed, verb head fronting is for example over-represented in sentences with a pronominal subject. This is noted by Le Roux (1957:408) for Middle Breton and by Le Gléau (1973:45) for Modern Breton. This conclusion however is not very strong, if one considers a larger body of Modern Breton data. First, Le Gléau (1973) draws conclusions from a written corpus study whose sources are not all native. Second, Le Gléau, does not claim that the [Infinitive-*do*-Subject…] order is ungrammatical: verb head fronting with null pronouns is merely a *statistical preference*. Moreover, the occurrence of a given construction with a null subject should be declared 'preferred' only if it could be proved that null subjects would not be preferred anyway for discourse reasons independent of the construction. Finally, testing this prediction on the basis of a correlation with null/incorporated subjects is a rather delicate move, since the respective order of the infinitive head and the subject after tense is unknown: recall that an infinitive verb is never found after the tensed auxiliary in this construction (4).

The excorporation scenario in (8), contrasting with the hypothesis of an ultra-local movement from the closest post-Tense position, offers a simple solution for the absence of the ['AUX do'-INF] order in ACs (**vii**). ACs are never found in the [… AUX – V…] order because the infinitive head never occupies a post-tense position during the derivation: the verb head moves up to the Tense and Fin heads. Excorporation of the lexical verb head in the pre-tense position occurs as a last-resort for LEIT to be satisfied. The surface order [… AUX – V…], though licit in Breton, reveals another 'do' auxiliary that is not dummy tense-Agr support, but a causative semi-auxiliary selecting a small clause as in (20).

(20)   Kerne Breton,   Trépos (2001:249)
       a.   Me   a   **ray**   **sevel** eun ti
            1SG R   do.FUT.3SG   build   a   house
            *'I will build a house.'   *vs.*
            'I will have a house built.'

b. ***Sevel** a **rin*** _ *eun ti.*
build R do.FUT.1SG a house.
'I will build a house.'
*'I will have a house built.'

One might note that this restriction is not universal, since some cases of [Aux V] order are documented for earlier stages of Breton, as well as in closely related languages. In Middle Breton, the auxiliary 'do' could precede its infinitive together with a cliticized object (cf. Hemon 2000: 238 Note 1). In Cornish, the language closest to Breton, […V-AUX…] is the canonical order, but the infinitive can also be found preceding 'do' (Le Roux 1957: 409; Fleuriot 2001: 21). In Northern Welsh, where the tensed element can be clause-initial, [AUX-V…] order is canonical. These cases could not be derived by (8).

There is syntactic evidence that the fronted non-tensed verb is merely a syntactic head (**v**). Prototypically, verbs move into the first position of the sentence, leaving their DP arguments stranded as in (9) and (10). Oblique arguments also remain IP-internal as in (11) and (12). The lexical verb can however be more important than a unique and simple head. In (21), it hosts a reflexive clitic, and in (22), a proclitic object.

(21) Leon Breton,   Le Bozec (1933: 53)
[***En em*** **blijout**] *a ra o henti al lec'hiou distro.*
REFLEXIVE please R do at haunt DET places solitary
'She likes to haunt the deserted places.'

(22) Gwened Breton,   Grégoire de Rostrenen (1795: 179)
a. [***Daz*** **caret**] *a rañ* _.
2SG.OBL love R do.1SG
'I love you.'

b. [***Da*** **garet**] *a rañ* _.
2SG.OBL love R do.1SG
'I love you.'

Depending on the analysis of clitics that one has, this could be evidence that what fronts is minimally a VP. I disregard this possibility here, and I consider that the fronted elements in (21) and (22) are complex syntactic heads originating from the tensed complex. Excorporation out of a morphologically complex head is not allowed in syntax, and I take it as evidence that the formation of analytic tenses is indeed not performed in syntax (**vi**).

2.2 Setting aside vP focalisation

We are now equipped with a reasonable set of syntactic tests in order to set aside another construction that also makes use a dummy auxiliary 'do': the *v*P focalization construction, as illustrated in (23), where an entire extended *v*P structure has been raised to a preverbal focus position in the left periphery ('anaphoric 'do' in Stephens 1982: 99).

(23)   Treger Breton,   Le Lay 1925, cited in Le Gléau (1973: 45)
       [$_{FOC}$ [$_{vP}$ PRO$_i$ **Dimeziñ gant ma merc'h**]   *ne*   *ri*$_i$ *ket* t_{vP}.
                    marry   with my daughter NEG do.FUT.2SG NEG
       'You won't MARRY MY DAUGHTER.'

This focalization construction has characteristic syntactic properties that sharply distinguish it from verb head fronting in (1a).[5]

(24)   *vP focalization properties*
       i.   it is not restricted to the root tensed clauses (26).
       ii.   it is strictly restricted to focalization readings (sometimes contrastive).
       iii. it is fully productive for all *v*Ps.
       iv.   movement is not local (23), (25).
       v.   the infinitive head is moved inside a large constituent (23).
       vi.   no violation of the head movement constraint is involved.
       vii. it is not restricted to [VINF-*do*] order (26).
       viii. No instances of verb-doubling.

(25)   Treger Breton,   Gros (1984: 113)
       [$_{vP}$ PRO$_i$ **Bale**]   *ne*   *gredan*   *ket*   *a rafe* t_{vP} *ken.*
                    walk   NEG believe.1 SG NEG R do.COND   plus
       'I don't think he will WALK anymore.'

(26)   Standard Breton,   Dupuy (2007: 16)
       An   eskob$_i$ *n'*   *en*   *deveze d'ober, a lavare an   teodoù*
       DET bishop NEG R.3SG had   to do   R said   DET tongues

       flemmus, nemet [$_{vP}$ PRO$_I$ **lakaat** *ur   vennigadenn da*
       caustic   only   put   DET benediction to

       zivizoù B].
       words   B.

       'According to slanderous rumors, all the bishop had to do was to GIVE HIS BENEDICTION TO B's WORDS.'

The two [VINF-*do*] constructions are distinguished by the size of the displaced element (i.e. head versus phrase), and consequently by the type of movement they undergo (ultra-local LEIT movement vs. XP movement). The motivation for movement is also different: *v*P fronting involves focalization of the fronted element. Such an A-bar movement, which can be understood as feature checking

---

5.   See also Stephens (1982) and Borsley, Rivero & Stephens (1996) for a study of the different 'do' auxiliaries.

under Chomsky's minimalism approach, automatically satisfies LEIT. As a consequence, *v*P focalization is mutually exclusive with verb head fronting, because the former satisfies a rule for which the latter is a last-resort strategy. Finally, because head-fronting resorts to excorporation, and *v*P fronting to XP movement, the latter is found in compound tenses and the former is ungrammatical in such contexts. In (27), the auxiliary 'have' does not contain the lexical verb 'to write' at any point in the derivation, therefore excorporation cannot lead to the fronting of the infinitive of *skrivañ*, 'to write'.

> (27) Treger Breton,   Leclerc (1986: 80)
>   *Skrivañ*   (*d' am breur*)   *am*   *eus*   *graet*   (**d'   am   breur.*)
>   write.INF   to my brother   R.1SG   have   done   to   my   brother
>   'I have written to my brother.'

I have shown that AC constructions in 'do' result from a last-resort strategy to satisfy LEIT. This hypothesis accounts for the syntactic properties of verb head fronting (**i–vi**), and for the contrasts between *v*P focalization movement and last-resort verb head fronting. The assumption that verb head fronting originates from the Fin site (that is the site where the tensed head itself stands) vs. a post-tense IP internal site is justified by the fact that the infinitive head is never found with this auxiliary 'do' after the tensed head (**vii**). There is a stronger argument in favor of excorporation: the fact that the AC with 'do' has a doubling counterpart (**viii**).

3. Analytic construction with doubling

3.1 Verb doubling as a subcase of analytic construction

Unlike analytic constructions with the auxiliary 'do', which is already found productively in Middle Breton, analytic constructions with doubling emerged at a later stage in the language (during the 17th century, see Le Roux 1957:416), and appear to be restricted to certain verbs only. The following examples illustrates verb than can double. They are: *ober* 'do', *bezañ* 'be', *rankout* and *dleout* 'must', *gallout* 'can', *dont* 'come', *mont* 'go', *gouzout* 'know', *kerzhout* 'walk', *redek* 'run', and *lenn* 'read'.

> (28) Quimperlé Breton,   (D.L 03/2009)
>   a. ***Rencout***   *a*   *rencan*   *da*   *vont.*
>   must.INF   R   must.1SG   to   go
>   'I have to go.'
>
>   b. ***Dleout***   *a*   ***zlean***   *ober*   *ma*   *gwele.*
>   must.INF   R   must.1SG   do   my   bed
>   'I have to make my bed.'

    c.   *Gallout a c'hallfen* lako ma avaloù   en   douar.
        can.INF R can   put my apple/potato in.DET soil
        'I can plant my potatoes.'

Treger Breton,   Schafer (1997)
    d.   *Gellout a c'hell* goro ho   bugale   ar   saout.
        can.INF R can.3SG milk your children DET cow
        'Your children could milk the cow.'

Leon Breton,   Troude (1886: 54)
    e.   *Dont*   a *zeuio*   re   vraz ha   re   vihan...
        come.INF R come.FUT.3SG 3PL big   and 3PL small
        'The big ones and the small ones will come...'

Low-Tréguier,   collected by Gros and cited in Le Roux (1957: 417)
    f.   *Mont 'ch I*   d' ar   gêr!
        go.INF R go.2SG at DET hous
        'Will you go home!'

Kerne Breton,   Bijer (2007: 138)
    g.   *Met gouzout* a *ouzont*   kavout   an   dud
        but know.INF R know.3PL find.INF DET people

        en-dro goude-se (...)
        again   after-that

        'But they know how to find people after that...'

Quimperlé,   (D.L 03/2009)
    h.   *Redek* a *redan*   bemdez.
        run.INF R run.1SG every.day
        'I run every day.'

Verb doubling is exceptional in corpora, and not all verbs are found with the same frequency in spontaneous speech. *Gouzout* 'know' is by far the most commonly heard in Modern Breton, whereas *redek* 'run', or *lenn* 'read', are fairly rare.

    I analyze doubling constructions as a subclass of the analytic constructions. Verb doubling exhibits most of the syntactic properties of *do*-ACs. The contrast lies in their different productivity and their effects on information packaging (italics).

(29)   *Verbal head doubling properties*
    i.   it is restricted to root tensed clauses.
    ii. *it is not neutral in terms of information packaging.*
    iii. *it is lexically restricted*
    iv. verbal movement is ultra-local.
    v.   the infinitive head is moved alone.
    vi. movement violates the syntactic ban on excorporation
    vii. it is restricted to the [VINF-*Tense*] order.
    viii. *It (always) has a 'do' counterpart.*

Doubling cases are found exclusively in canonical Tense-second environments. No case of doubling in infinitives or imperatives ever arises (i). Verb head doubling is ultra-local (iv), is hence incompatible with long distance extraction (30).

(30) *gouzout* ne   gredan   ket a *ouzez*   ken.
       know   NEG   know.1SG   NEG   R know.2SG anymore

Doubling does not allow intervening elements like those of clefts (31).

(31) *gouzout* 'ni eo   a *ouzon*.
       know   N   COP   R know.1SG

Doubling can be preceded only by elements following which Tense-second orders are not found anyway. I illustrate in (32) with a case of preceding conjunctions *ha*, 'and', *met/hogen*, 'but', in (33) (or Bijer 2007: 136). Examples in multi-clausal sentences boil down to cases of parataxis such as (34).

(32) (Testamant Nevez: lizher Jakez 3, Gwilh Ar C'hoad 1893)[6]
       ur   wezenn-fiez, ha **gallout** a **c'hell** reiñ olivez, pe ur   winieg fiez?
       DET   tree-fig   Q   can   R can   give olives   or DET   vine   fig
       'Can a fig tree give olives, or a grapevine figs?'

(33) Koatilouri, Barzig
       Hogen **goud'** **ouzon**   ne   'teus   ket   klasket laza...
       but   know   R know.1SG NEG   has.2SG NEG   tried   kill
       'But I know you didn't mean to kill...'

(34) Breton Kerne,   Bijer (2007: 156)
       rak   **gouzout** e **ouie** n' eo ket   mont a   dont (...) nemetken
       because   know   R knew   NEG is NEG   go   and come   only

       eo a rafe   e   genitervez.
       is R do.COND   his cousin

       '... Because he knew that his cousin would not only go back and forth.'

Verb doubling concerns syntactic heads (v) and never targets accompanying arguments (35), except incorporated ones (36).

(35) *[gouzout an   doare   da   vont] a *ouzez*.
        know   DET   reason for go   R know.2SG

(36) Quimperlé, D.L.
       [hen   **gouzout**] a *ouzon*.   / [E   **lenn**] a *lennan*
       CL.3SG   know   R know.1SG   CL.3SG   read   R read
       'I know it (well).'   'I do read it.'

---

6. This translation of the New Testament was written by Gwilh Ar C'hoad in the nineteenth century, with subsequent corrections in Modern Breton by Lukaz Bernikod.

These facts follow in the excorporation scenario: only elements that can ever be part of the synthetic morphologically complex head (clitics) can be excorporated from it.

The sentence in (37) would be a strong counterexample if it could mean: *He will come home walking*, which it can not, as confirmed by the ungrammaticality of 'tomorrow'. This is a case of accidental co-occurrence of two unrelated instances of the verb 'come', rather than copying. A goal argument is topicalized in the pre-tense area: *He will **come** walking* [$_{PP}$(*in order to*) ***come** home*].[7] Presence of the silent preposition is independently revealed by the *e* variant of the rannig noted R, providing a contrast with examples of doubling which tend to use the *a* variant.

(37)   Quimperlé Breton D.L., Callac S.B.
       [$_{PP}$ *Don't d' ar gêr*]   *e teuio*   war droad / **warc'hoazh.*
       P   come to DET house R come.FUT on   feet   / tomorrow
       '(In order to) come home, he will come (walking/*tomorrow).'

The doubling phenomena is strictly restricted to [VINF-do] orders **(vii)**. No doubling is ever found with the infinitive form following the inflected one. The relevant contrast between analytic constructions in *do* and with doubling thus seems to be due to information packaging.

3.2   Information packaging

Verb doubling triggers a saliency effect on information packaging, which fails to arise with analytic constructions in *do*. This effect is rather delicate to formalize, and even describe. Grammars are at best vague, at worst contradictory, about it. Ernault (1890: 470) proposes a gradation in emphasis: the doubling of *rankout*, 'must', would be a "more energetic synonym" of the *do*-AC, itself more emphatic than the synthetic strategy. This rare note is at odds with Le Gléau (1973: 46), for whom focalized *do*-ACs with semi-auxiliaries like *rankout* are ungrammatical. The pragmatic development of (38) that Herve ar Bihan comments on for a sentence by his father points toward a *verum focus* effect, a focalization on the truth value of the sentence, suggesting that doubling may even induce different types of readings on the sentence.

(38)   Guy ar Bihan, collected by H. ar Bihan
       Lenn a lennan!
       read   R   read.1SG
       'You see well that I am reading!'
       Pragmatic development: 'You see that I know how to read.'

---

7.   Thanks to Denis Pruel for drawing my attention on these structures.

In order to test focus effects in verb doubling ACs, I presented two speakers, D.L and S.B., with the corpus example (39), which seemed to me a good candidate for a neutral reading. The doubling of the verb 'to know' turned out to be grammatical for both speakers. The discourse context ensures that all information in the sentence is new, and pragmatically disfavors a *verum focus* reading. Both speakers, however, noted an emphasis effect (without further comment on what that consisted of). Emphasis in (39) could bear on (i) the lexical content of the verb, (ii) the sentence as a whole, or (iii) the internal argument of the doubled verb.[8]

(39)   Kerne Breton,   Bijer (2007: 165)
   a.   *Goude bezañ kimiadet diouzh an daou grennard ha danvez*
        after to.be separated from DET 2   adolescent C material

        beleg anezho, e kavas d' ar c'harretour en doa gounezet
        priest P.3PL R found to DET carter   3SG had won

        e   verenn.
        his lunch

        'After he left the two adolescent priests-to-be, the carter found he had won his lunch.'

   b.   **Gouzout** a **ouie** e oa e bourk ar Pont un   ostaleri ma
        to.know R knew R was in bourg DET Pont DET hostel   C

        veze selvichet enni   sklipoù eus ar c'hentañ. Ha Lorañs
        was served   in.3SGF tripe of the first   & Lorañs

        mont e-barzh.
        enter in

        'He KNEW there was in the town of Pont a hostel that served first class tripes. Lorañs went in.'

I leave for now the question open of the impact of doubling on information packaging. I just take note that verb-doubling *can* have an impact on information packaging and most probably has to, with possible readings beyond *verum focus*. The focus effect probably comes from doubling itself, and not from excorporation.

Breton indeed can use doubling for intensification, as it independently does in the domain of adjectives (*tomm-tomm*, 'very hot' (lit. 'hot-hot')). However, this can't be the entire story, because Breton reduplication does not always have this particular semantic effect. In (40), the infinitive verb 'to live' is reduplicated, and its second occurrence bears a diminutive marker. The interpretation of the

---

8.   Thanks to Alain Rouveret for pointing out this possibility.

construction is clearly not intensive. In (41), a nominal head or an entire DP has been reduplicated over a deictic marker. The obtained reading is specific-unknown or specific-uncited (Jouitteau 2011). More of the same morphology doesn't have to mean more of the same meaning.[9]

(40)   Standard,   Denez (1993:17)
       Bevañ-bevaik a   rae...
       live-live.DIM R   did.3SG
       'He was struggling along.'

(41)   *C'hoand am   euz   da gaoud ar   marc'h-mañ (ar)   marc'h.*
       wish   R.1SG   have to have   the horse-here (the) horse
       'I want to have such and such a horse.'

A much more extensive study, with carefully controlled questionnaires that would take variation into account would be necessary. For the sake of this paper, the important question is to see if doubling constructions are, as I propose, last-resort operations used to avoid Tense-first word orders, or if they are just triggered by a particular semantico-pragmatic effect. In the latter case, the doubling constructions could not be considered to be a subcase of analytic constructions.

The two hypotheses make diverging predictions as to the distribution of verb-doubling: an expletive operation prototypical of analytic constructions would appear only as a last resort in order to avoid Tense-first orders, whereas an operation driven by information packaging would appear in correlation with the salience reading. The distribution of verb doubling shows all prototypical last-resort properties that we already saw in the analytic constructions in *do*. Not only does verb doubling appear only in canonical tense-second contexts (i), but any independent satisfaction of LEIT renders doubling ungrammatical. Doubling is forbidden with an embedded C head (42a), a matrix negation C head (42b), or a preverbal expletive (42c). This is also the case for any A or A-bar preverbal XP.

(42)   a.   **Na   larez   ket din   ma gouzout a oar...*
            NEG.IMP tell.2SG NEG P.1SG if know   R know.3SG

       b.   *(*n') gouzout (*n') ouzon   ket.*
            NEG   know   NEG   know.1SG NEG

       c.   *(*bez') gouzout (*bez') 'ouzon.*
            EXPL   know   EXPL   R know.1SG

The distribution of doubling has to be considered in comparison with another Breton expletive strategy that also can bear on information packaging: the merge

---

9.   See http://arbres.iker.univ-pau.fr/index.php/Reduplication for extensive evidence and crossdialectal examples of intensive reduplication.

of expletive *bez*. In (43a), the preverbal expletive *bez* is neutral in an 'out of the blue' sentence, and in (43b), it can bear *verum focus*. *Bez* can be found in Western Brittany before all sorts of verbs, but its paradigm overlaps with verb doubling based on the 'be' stem.[10]

(43) a. *Bez' omp* *digemeret en eur zal*
          EXPL are.1PL welcomed in DET room

          vraz spontuz.   (Miossec 1981:7)
          big terrible

          'We are welcomed in a very big room.'

      b. *Bez' he-deus* *da vihanna, tri-ugent metr hed ha tregont*
          EXPL R.3SGF has at least 3–20 meter long and 30

          metr lehed.
          meter large

          '(Indeed) It is at least 60m long and 30 meter large.'

Despite its impact on information packaging, verb-doubling thus shows the last-resort properties prototypical of analytic constructions in *do*. The final contrast that remains between *do*-ACs and doubling ACs is the question of productivity. I will show in the next section that doubling is fully idiosyncratic and cannot be reduced to a syntactic operation.

4. Idiosyncracy of verb reiteration

This section is dedicated to showing that Breton verb doubling is idiosyncrati-cally restricted, and involves a list of verbs that fail to form a class at the syntactic level. No syntactic account of the limits of the paradigm is possible. This will pave the way to proposing that doubling is triggered at the Late Syntax/Morphology Interface and realized in a morphological post-syntactic module. I will proceed by exploring different alternatives for syntactic accounts and point out where they fail to explain the data.

4.1 Variation in doubling verbs

We saw that for Le Roux (1957:416), the emergence of verb doubling dates back to the 17th century. Kervella (1995: §274) proposes that all Middle Breton verbs

---

10. The expletive *bez'* is used with all verbs in Standard Breton. Eastern dialects restrict its usage to co-occurrence with the inflected verb 'be', and thus to verb doubling (cf. see documentation on http://arbres.iker.univ-pau.fr/index.php/Bezan and references therein).

could be inflected by taking their own root as an auxiliary. Ernault (1888: 247) argues on the contrary that the doubling analytic construction was found "only for a small number of verbs, in Modern and Middle Breton". Ernault illustrates this with some corpus data, and produces examples that are quite similar to those later produced by Hemon (2000: 239 Note 4) and Le Roux (1957: 416).

Breton grammars vary with respect to the verbs they claim can double. *Gouzout*, 'to know' is the only doubling verb noted by Kervella (1995: §197), though he dedicates an entire section to conjugations with semi-auxiliaries (§247–253). Gros (1984: 94), an expert on the Treger dialect, has a very detailed chapter on emphasis by doubling but also cites only 'to know' as a doubling verb. However, as reported in Le Roux (1957), Gros had reported a doubling structure with *mont* 'to go' in 1911, in Trédrez. Le Roux (1957: 414), also a Treger Breton speaker, mentions *gouzout* 'to know', but also *gallout* 'can', as does Ernault (1888), which he has consulted. He further mentions that there are « some others » and cites the data collected by J. Gros with *mont* 'to go'. Eugène Chalm, from Cap-Sizun (Kerne diaclect), signals verb doubling with *gouzout* 'to know', *gallout* 'can' and *rankout* 'must' (Chalm 2008: 45). This structure is absent from 38 hours of spontaneous speech recorded from Gwened Breton (*Lorient,* Cheveau 2007). I developed a questionnaire for two native speakers of Breton, D.L from Quimperlé, and S.B. from Callac. The list of verbs they can double is summarized in the table below. The rightmost column summarizes the doubled cases reported in the descriptive literature, found in a corpus, or reported to me as used by native speakers.

(44)

			D.L Quimperlé	S.B Callac	*reported in the literature*
AUXILIARIES	'be' 'do'	*bez(añ)* *ober*	√ √	√ √	(10)
	'have'	*kaout*	*	*	(18)
SEMI-AUXILIARIES	'know' 'can'	*gouzout* *gallout*	√ √	√ √	(28)
	'must'	*rankout*	√	*	(28)
	'must'	*dleout*	√	*11	(28)
	'look for'	*klask,*	*	*	-

---

11. The speaker hesitates because she thinks she had heard it, but insists she would not use it herself.

LEXICAL VERBS with homophonous semi-auxiliary	'know'	*gouzout*	√	√	(28)
	'come'	*dont*	√	√	
	'go'	*mont*	√	*	(28)
	'look for'	*klask,*	*	*	-
LEXICAL VERBS	'run' 'walk' 'read'	*redek* *kerzhout* *lenn*	√ - -	* - -	[12] Guy ar Bihan (28)
	'laugh' 'walk' 'danse' 'cry' 'cry'	*c'hoarzhiñ* *bale* *dañsal* *leñvañ* *oueleiñ*	* * * * *	* * * * *	- - - - -

The distribution of doubling verbs resists any attempt at syntactic reduction to a homogeneous class of verbs.

Let us first examine carefully the flexibility in ranking possibilities for auxiliaries because some ranking decisions are analysis-dependent. The verb *ober* 'to do' can either resort to doubling or to a *do*-AC (10). The analysis of *bezañ* 'to be', can also vary between verb doubling and expletive insertion (43a). Doubling of *kaout* 'have', partly depends on the analysis of 'to be'. The paradigm of *kaout* is visibly formed from a morphological compound including 'to be', with a more or less synthetic result depending on the dialect (cf. Jouitteau & Rezac 2006, 2008, 2009 and references therein). Though doubling is not grammatical with the *kaout* form of the infinitive (45), some dialects would allow *bez* insertion equally with *kaout* 'have' and *bezañ* 'to be' (43). These cases thus could equally 'count' as verb doubling or expletive insertion. The generalization on auxiliary-doubling is virtually analysis dependent. I take this into account in the coming discussion.

(45)   **Kaout   em   eus   un oto/gwelet/riv.*
        have.INF R.1SG have.√ a   car/seen/cold
        'I have a car/I have seen/I am cold.'   D.L., S.B.

Some of the semi-auxiliaries can be doubled. But not all of them (46). The list of doubling verbs also includes some lexical verbs. Herve ar Bihan reports his

---

12.   I found *redek a redan*, 'to run I run' for the first time in a written source, which I no longer recall. I am unsure if it was Modern or Middle Breton. This is what gave me the idea of testing this with DL and SB in Quimperlé.

father used to double the verbs *kerzhout* 'to walk' and *lenn*, 'to read' (38). S.B and D.L both double *gouzout* 'to know' and *dont*, 'to come' in their special and thus lexical interpretation. However, verb doubling is far from extending to all lexical verbs: neither of the two speakers can double lexical verbs like *bale*, 'to walk', *c'hoarzhiñ*, 'to laugh', *dañsal*, 'to danse', or finally *leñvañ (dourek)/oueleiñ*, 'to cry':

(46)   **Klask   a   glasko...*
         look.for.INF   R   look.for.3SG
         'She will try to...'

(47)   **Bale   a   vale.*
         walk.INF   R   walked.3SG.
         'He was walking/He walked.'

(48)   **Choarzhiñ (brav)   a   c'hoarzhes*
         laugh.INF   beautiful   R   laughs.
         'You are laughing (a lot)!'

(49)   **Dañsal   a   zansan   ar   jabadao.*
         danse.INF   R   danse.1SG   DET   jabadao
         'I am dancing the jabadao.'

(50)   **Leñvañ (dourek)   a   leñve   (dourek).*
         cry.INF   (water.ADJ)   R   cried.3SG   (water.ADJ)
         'He was crying a lot.'

(51)   **Oueleiñ a ouelent gant glac'har.*
         cry.INF   R   cry.3SG   by   pain
         'They cried with pain.'

Variation is dialectal or even idiolectal: D.L from Quimperlé can double the two auxiliaries *rankout* (28b) and *dleout* 'must', and the two lexical verbs *mont* and *redek*, which are ungrammatical to S.B from Callac (80 minutes driving distance away). Reduction to the verb structure seems a hard task: verbs that are semantically similar may still differ in doubling properties for the same speaker: D.L doubles *redek* 'to run', but not *bale*, 'to walk' (47); and S.B doubles *dont* 'to come', but not *mont* 'to go'. Idiolectal variation is a serious obstacle to any attempt at reducing verb doubling to a homogeneous syntactic class.

     No morphological particularity emerges either, that would set doubling verbs apart from other verbs. At most, we can note that an infinitival ending such as *-al*, is never present on doubling verbs, but so few verbs do double that it is hardly conclusive. The case of verbs ending in *-out* like *gouzout* 'to know', must however be discussed. *Gouzout* 'to know' is by far the verb that doubles the most frequently in modern Breton. When one wonders about the link between *gouzout* 'to know' and semi-auxiliaries, one can notice it is a compound containing the verb 'to be' (in its older form *-bout*). No reduction of the data is however possible. In Treger Breton as in Léon, the independent form of 'to be' is not *-bout*, like it is in Gwened Breton and Kerne Breton: it evolved into *bezañ* (Hémon 2000: §139,14). In these dialects, the verb 'to know' is arguably not a compound of 'to be' anymore.

Similarly, no correlation emerges between doubling verbs and those before which the expletive *bez'* can be found. Gros (1984: 110) notes that *bez'* is restricted in Treger Breton to the preverbal area of *bezañ* 'to be', *gouzout* 'to know' and *kaoud* 'to have'. The first two can double in this dialect, but *kaout* 'have' fails to. This hypothesis also would not hold for Standard Breton or Western varieties, where *bez'* can be used before any lexical verb.

I conclude that the difference between doubling verbs and non-doubling verbs is purely idiosyncratic. Knowing the language requires knowing, for each verb, if it is used in doubling constructions or not, pretty much in the same way gender is assigned to inanimate nouns. Dialects and speakers vary in the list of verbs they treat as doubling verbs.

4.2   A typologically unique situation

Verb doubling at the sentence level is well-documented in a large set of languages (see Gouget 2008; Kandybowicz 2008 and references therein). Some languages show cases of verb-doubling with two phonologically identical instantiations, as in Nupe, Fongbe, Mandarin Chinese, Haitian (Glaude and Zribi-Hertz this volume) or Gungbe (52). In Yoruba (53), an additional reduplication process takes place and distinguishes the instantiation in focus position from the lower one.

(52) Gungbe,   Aboh & Dyakonova (2009)
      Dù   wè   Sèná   dù   blèdì   lɔ́
      eat   FOC   Sena   eat   bread   DET
      'Sena has EATEN bread.'

(53) Yoruba,   Tamburri Watt (2003)
      Rírà   ni   mo   ra   ìwé.
      buy   FOC   1SG   buy   books
      'I BOUGHT the books.'

Finally, another set of languages resemble Breton more, with one of the two instantiations appearing with a tense marker, as in Portuguese, Spanish (54), Russian (55), Basque (56), Yiddish (Cable 2003), Classical or Modern Hebrew (57) and (58) (see also 1b in Cohen this volume).

(54)   Spanish,   Vicente (2007)
       Comprar, Juan ha comprador un libro!
       buy,   J.   has bought   a   book
       'Juan has bought a book!'

(55)   Russian,   Abels (2001)
       Citat, Ivan ee citaet.
       read Ivan it read
       'Ivan has read it.'

(56)   Basque,   Hualde & Ortiz de Urbina (2003)
       Hartu ere har-tzen dut erabakia
       take also take-IMPF AUX decision
       'As for taking, I TAKE my decision.'

(57)   Classical Hebrew,   Jeremiah 23: 17 cited in Harbour (2007)
       'omr- im   'aamoor li- mna' ṣay.
       say.benoni-3PL say   to-despisers.1SG
       'They say still unto them that despise me'

(58)   Modern Hebrew,   Landau (2007)
       Liknot et   ha-praxim, hi kanta
       buy   ACC DET-flowers, she bought
       'She bought the flowers.'

Doubling may be associated with different readings across languages. Kandybowicz (2008: Chapter 3) distinguishes (i) *contrast of topic/focus* in Russian, Hungarian, Korean, Kabiye and Brazilian Sign language, (ii) *emphasis of the 'really V' type* in Haitian and English, and (iii) *polarity effects*, that is, emphasis, contrastive or not, on the veracity of the sentence in Mandarin Chinese, Nupe and European Portuguese. The environment for doubling can be either pragmatic or syntactic (a restriction to negative contexts in Portuguese, a restriction to the perfect in Nupe). They can also be restricted to a given syntactic construction. In French, doubling requires a preposition (and also doubling of the arguments of the verb).

(59)   French
       Je peux te dire que pour l' avoir lu, elle l' a lu!
       I can 2SG tell that for 3SG have.INF read, she 3SG has read
       'I can tell you that she DID read it!'
       litt. : '... that as for reading it, she did indeed read it.'
       > pragmatic implication: she showed extensive evidence for this action.

In all the above languages, doubling is fully productive inside the pragmatic and syntactic environment that triggers doubling. The outstanding character of Breton verb doubling is its idiosyncrasy. In Breton, in a doubling configuration, not all verbs can double.

This generalization is of immediate interest to the question of iconicity addressed in this volume. If Breton verb-doubling had anything to do with iconicity, one should expect this iconic doubling principle to be fully productive, or at least reducible to a semantic class of verbs. The idiosyncrasy of verb-doubling shows that in the Breton case at least, the iconic dimension of doubling is null.

4.3   Theoretical analyses for syntactic doubling

Due to some major shifts of theory, doubling has received a number of different formal analyses in the generativist paradigm during the last few decades. The passage from the trace theory of movement, which was dominant in the 80–90's, to copy theory, has opened up a mass of analyses of doubling effects in syntax.[13]

Under Chomsky's trace theory (1973), an item moved in syntax exists under one and only one exemplary, because movement creates new elements in the derivation: phonologically null pronominal traces. The operation of verb doubling in the syntactic component is difficult because each occurrence should then require its own arguments to pass the theta-criterion, contrary to typological evidence. In a trace theory T model, doubling can only be viewed as a post-syntactic (morpho(phono)logic) operation. Copy theory (Chomsky 1955, 1993), reverses the perspective: every position in a movement chain is occupied by the same item (except their (un)interpretable features). At the syntactic level, the presence of multiple copies is no exception, but is merely the symptom of movement, as sometimes revealed by pronunciation of multiple copies by the sensorimotor system. The sensorimotor system generally compels pronunciation of the highest copy, and doubling can be obtained to the extent that one can predict where the sensorimotor interface will be in a situation to send two copies to spell-out. Gouget (2008) for example proposes that the complex movement of the verb copy in Mandarin Chinese is peculiar in that it always results in two copies that count as the highest in the chain. Depending on the respective ordering of movement and cyclic transfer of the derivation to the interface, reduplication or simple movement is obtained. For verb doubling in Nupe, Kandybowicz (2008) proposes that a tonal factitive morpheme calls for a realizational basis, with the result that the realization of multiple verb copies is associated with the factitive reading. Typological evidence for morphophonologically distinct instantiations can also easily be handled: two copies in the same chain are already distinct at the syntactic level thanks to the encoding of the motivation for movement into (the interpretability of) feature specification.

---

13.   For a clear an detailed presentation of the analysis of doubling verbs/structures, see Gouget (2008: Chapter 3).

Finally, in multidominance theory, two occurrences of the same chain are one and the same syntactic element and can only be differentiated when sent to the interfaces. Pronunciation of a copy/instantiation can be taken care of by a morphological operation such as Morphological Fusion (see Nunes 2004 & Kandybowicz 2006a, b).

The paradigm of verb doubling in Breton has key importance in the debate. This paradigm has no equivalent in the doubling literature because of the lexical restriction imposed on it: only an arbitrary list of verbs can be doubled, irreducible to a homogeneous syntactic class, or to a syntactic operation. This means that whatever mechanism is called upon to account for verb doubling in *gouzout a ouzon*, 'to know I know', this mechanism must be set such as to apply to an arbitrary list of verbs. Idiosyncrasy, however, is a prototypical symptom of lexical or morphological operations, crucially not of syntactic operations.

5.   A postsyntactic morphological level

This section investigates and discusses the question of the module of grammar where doubling operates: syntax or morpho(phono)logical interface.

5.1   Not in syntax

Doubling can be obtained inside the syntactic component (by means of copying or double instantiations), if and only if, inside the syntactic level, doubling verbs (A) can be distinguished from non-doubling ones (B) (±auxiliaries/modals/semi-auxiliaries? particular derivation?). If so, and for each derivation, the syntactic output can provide the interface with either verbal type A or B couples leading to different spell-outs. Basque provides the relevant contrast with Breton. Basque verb doubling is restricted to a list of verbs strangely reminiscent of those of Breton: 'to know', 'to take' (56), 'to walk' 'to come', and 'to go' (60).

(60)   Biscayan Basque,   Zuazo (1998:207)
    Juen   doie,   ala etorri   dator,   ba?
    go.INF go.3SG or   come.INF come.3SG then
    'Well, is he leaving (right now) or coming?'

Basque doubling verbs happen to also be the only verbs in the language that can show synthetic agreement, which means that doubling can be associated with a particular syntactic derivation leading to synthetic agreement. Verbs that can double are already distinguishable from non-doubling ones at the syntactic level. In Breton however, both doubling verbs and non-doubling ones appear in the same syntactic location and seem undistinguishable at the syntactic level.

Another attempt to locate the doubling operation internally to the syntactic level would be to set a morphological filter after syntax. In this scenario, all verbs are doubling verbs at the syntactic level, but some postsyntactic morphological filter avoids it for most verbs and realizes the AC in 'do' instead. Considering that we already rejected the hypothesis that only certain roots would have an independent spell-out, I can't see what this filter could consist of.

Another argument that ACs are not internal to the syntactic module is that its trigger, LEIT, resists encoding under feature-checking systems. LEIT, under different EPP-related names, has been proposed under different types of uninterpretable features: the phonological [P-] in Holmberg (2000) for Icelandic, the [δ] feature in Rezac (2004) or categorial [*u* CAT] in Jouitteau (2005, 2010) for Breton, the empty φ sets mentioned by Grohmann, Drury and Castillo (2000), the [−Foc] in Holmberg and Nikanne (2002) for Finnish, etc. The advantages of these feature-driven scenarios are that they accurately derive unselective locality (via Relativized Minimality), and blindness to the X/XP distinction. However, LEIT is an operation that does not exactly coincide with what we know about feature checking: **(A)** LEIT satisfaction does not ever seem to be possible at a distance. Instead, it is characterized by an ultralocal domain of impact, **(B)** LEIT effects are characterized by 'the far-sighted effect': in order to obtain unselective locality, feature checking accounts of LEIT need to postulate uninterpretable features that are present on the head itself. Feature-checking scenarios cannot avoid the stipulation that the uninterpretable feature is blind to the interpretable features of its own head (consisting of the inflected head itself or even the potential clitics that crosslinguistically fail to satisfy LEIT); **(C)** Lasnik's (2001) states that EPP cannot be seen as a strong feature, and his argument holds for LEIT: provided that features can be checked by erasure of their satisfier inside an ellipsis (of VP or IP), VP ellipsis should allow for Tense-first orders in V2 languages, which is not the case. The merge of expletives is also a problem **(D)**: Rezac (2004: 481) notes that it would be "the (unique) feature whose Agree results in the Merge component of the Move operation, and in expletive base-generation".

Finally, another argument that LEIT does not operate in syntax is its recurrent violation of the Head Movement Constraint (Stylistic Fronting in Icelandic, Long Head Movement in Breton, excorporation in Breton ACs). If LEIT operates outside of the syntactic component, no such filter as the Head Movement Constraint or any syntactic ban on excorporation is predicted to apply.

5.2 Pre-Tense vs. post-Tense infinitives: Not in the lexicon

There seems to be morphological evidence that preverbal infinitives should be set apart from post-Tense ones. In several dialects, their phonological spell-out may indeed differ. Ernault points out an asymmetry in Little Tréguier, where the verbal ending is optional in analytic constructions, but obligatory in post-Tense position. Indeed, all the infinitives that Favereau (1997:§347) notes to lack infinitive endings in Treger and Gwened Breton appear in a position preceding a 'do' auxiliary. Similarly, in the Low Kerne dialect, post-Tense infinitives bear the -*o* suffix (62), whereas the infinitive in AC shows up with -*ek* (63a).

(61) a. *gwel(-et) / zell(-ed) ë rañ*
          see   look   R do.1SG
          'I see/I am looking.'

      b. *red   e   gwel*(-et) /zell*(-ed)*
          obligatory COP see   /look
          'One must see/look.'

(62) Plélanff, Goarec Breton[14]
      kāno   ğwerho hœjò
      'to wash', 'to sell', 'to shake'

(63) Saint Mayeux;   Ernault (1888: 247)
      a. *c'hoarzhek a ra*
          laugh   R do.3SG
          'He laughs.'

      b. *labourek a zo   red _.*
          work   R COP.3SG obligatory
          'One must work.'

One could try to push the idea that the above data suggest an asymmetry in Breton between verb roots (preverbal) and regular infinitives (prototypically post-Tense). However, in (63b), the verb *labourek* is not part of an AC, but an XP moved across an auxiliary in a preverbal focused position. The prototypically preverbal ending -*ek* appears. The asymmetry thus seems to lie between the preverbal and post-Tense positions, rather than between the roots and infinitives.

This absence of root/infinitive asymmetry is important because it shows that the Breton verb-doubling idiosyncrasy does not originate in the lexicon. One could propose that verb heads are specified in the lexicon as having, or not having, independent spell-outs for their roots. Syntax thus derives an analytic construction composed of sets of abstract features of the sort [… verbal root+tense+AGR], before which the verbal root appears as a LEIT effect in linear order. This assumption would predict that only verbs that do have an independent spell-out for their

---

14. Leroux (1924–1953) *Atlas Linguistique de Basse Bretagne* point 60, maps 286, 295, 311 – diacritics have been omitted.

root would be found with doubling, and others not. However, such a hypothesis would have to assume an intrinsic distinction between roots and infinitives, despite the fact they 'happen' to have the same spell-out in Breton, giving rise to a global picture in the language where all verbs do have a spell-out for their infinitives, but not all of them can use this same bundle of morphophonological features in order to spell out the independent root of the verb. I consider such a scenario unlikely, and I stand by the idea that all verbal roots are, uniformly, and by default, spelled-out as infinitives in Breton. In fact, if there is a syntactic location where the spell-out of the infinitive seems to matter less than anywhere, it is the preverbal area.

The key to the preverbal/postverbal asymmetry in the spell-out of verbs is most likely to be found in Breton accentuation rules, and in the fact that preverbal items always have a following vowel available for syllabification: the *rannig* (R).

5.3   Not in phonology

The level where doubling arises can be shown to be sensitive to the [± nominal] distinction. In literary standard Breton and in the Léon dialect, the preverbal particle noted here 'R' in glosses, agrees in category with the ± nominal preverbal element (Rezac 2004; Jouitteau 2005, 2010). This particle is thus sensitive to the categorial identity of the fronted constituent, including LEIT-fronted constituents. The causality chain of LEIT effects is schematized in (64). LEIT triggers last-resort strategies at the end of the derivation, when a tensed head fronts first to fuse with the Fin head, and calls for any head or larger constituent to be Merged or Moved. The ± nominal category of this pre-tense element will decide for the particular spell-out of the Fin head: *a* follows [+ nominal] elements, and *e* follows [– nominal] elements. It is not unusual for the rannig *a/e* itself not to be spelled out, but its syntactic presence is discernable from the consonant mutation it triggers on the following right-adjoined tensed element.

(64)

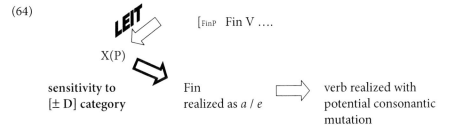

In doubling cases (as in ACs in general), the *rannig* appears under its *a* form that signals a [+nominal] preceding element, which is logical in a language where untensed verb structures show extensive nominal properties. The important point is that the LEIT last-resort operation is sensitive to the categorial identity of the element serving as an expletive.[15]

5.4   A morphological operation: Obligatory exponence in morphology

I assume a T model of grammar (65), and propose that LEIT is located in a post-syntactic morphological structure. As such, LEIT effects are predicted to be blind to phonological properties, but sensitive to the output of syntax (word order).

(65)

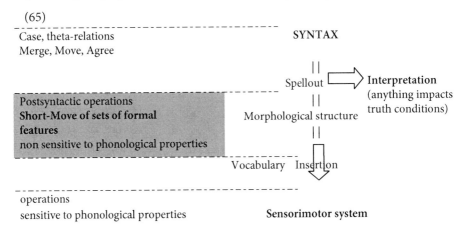

The absence of any impact by analytic structures on the interpretative component, as well as deviant syntactic behavior automatically follows. Sensitivity to categorial features is also easily accounted for: categorial features have independently to be visible in morphological structure. This proposal bears a surprising implication for our theory of Information Packaging. It implies that some discourse effects are never interpreted semantically. If I am right in locating verb doubling in a module of grammar that is independent from the interpretative component, there is a part of information structure manipulation that is separated from Interpretation proper. These effects should never impact on truth-conditions, as is verified for verb-doubling.

The idea suggested here that LEIT effects could be crosslinguistically tied to morphology finds independent cross-linguistic support in some well-documented morphological paradigms that strongly recall the LEIT effects. I will briefly present the case of obligatory exponence in the Basque morphology, where a second position phenomenon is identified at the level of a morphologically complex word.

---

15.   This argument is convincing, but could not hold in all dialects. All dialects show the *a* variant of the rannig in doubling, but not all dialects follow the [± nominal] distinction for the *rannig*.

Laka (1993) treats a case of obligatory exponence in the Basque verb morphological complex. The obligatory exponent location precedes the agreement complex, and is canonically realized by the absolutive marker, *g-* in (66a) and b. The absolutive argument controls the preceding exponent as long as it is first or second person. In cases where the absolutive argument is third person, a Tense-Mood conditioned morphology fills in the gap as in (66c). These prefixes, *d* (present), *z/Ø* (past), and *l* (irrealis), are last-resort defaults, meaning that they are strictly restricted to contexts lacking any absolutive controller for the prefix.

In certain tenses, however, no prefix is available, and the morphological complex shows ultralocal movement of the ergative marker into the prefix position as in (66d), referred to as 'ergative displacement'. Finally, in these critical contexts where the prefix morphology is exceptionally controlled by the ergative argument, some dialects show doubling of the ergative marker in (two) different locations in the complex as in (66e).

(66)

a. *Berak$_i$ gu$_j$*
   He.ERG us.ABS
   'He has us.'

?	-TM	SG/PL	√have	ERG 1/2	-past
g$_j$	-a	-it$_j$	-u		
1'		-PL			

ABS = 1/2 > ABS control

b. *Berak$_i$ gu$_j$*
   He.ERG us.ABS
   'He had us.'

?	-TM	SG/PL	√have	ERG 1/2	-past
g$_j$	-in	-t$_j$	-u		-en
1'		-PL			

ABS = 1/2 > ABS control

c. *Guk$_i$ hura/haiek$_j$*
   we.ERG it/them.ABS
   'We have it/them.'

?	-TM	SG/PL	√have	ERG 1/2	-past
d		-Ø/it$_j$	-u	-gu$_i$	
				–1'	

No 1/2 ABS > Tense/ Mood-conditioned morphology

d. *Guk$_i$ hura/haiek$_j$*
   we.ERG it/them.ABS
   'We had it/them.'

?	-TM	SG/PL	√have	ERG 1/2	-past
g$_i$	-en	-Ø/it$_j$	-u		-en
1'					

In some tenses..... ABS = 3 > ERG 1/2 control ("displacement")

e. *Guk$_i$ hura/haiek$_j$*
   we.ERG it/them.ABS
   'We had it/them.'

?	-TM	SG/PL	√have	ERG 1/2	-past
g$_i$	-en	-Ø/it$_j$	-u	-gu$_i$	-n
1'				–1'	

In these tenses in some dialects.... ABS = 3 > ERG 1/2 doubling

The parallel with Breton LEIT effect is striking. Breton preverbal position is canonically filled in by some XP, in a manner prototypical of V2. LEIT last-resort dimension is evidenced when no such XP is fronted. Merge of the Basque Tense-Mood conditioned prefixes strongly recalls the Breton *bez/bet* expletive strategy, where the expletive used is prototypically verbal (it is realized as a morphological shortening of the verb 'to be', and contains a [± past] encoding). Ergative displacement mimics LEIT ultralocal movement, and ergative doubling seems to recall verb-doubling.

The surprising, but, unavoidable conclusion from Breton is that an edge-sensitive morphological process, similar to the second position phenomena exemplified above in Basque, is active at the level of the sentence, and leads to a generalization concerning word order (linear V2).[16]

The remaining section provides a cross-linguistic comparison. Breton is not alone in presenting a paradigm of verb-doubling that reflects obligatory exponence. I present an identical pattern in a genetically unrelated language: Gungbe. The Gungbe paradigm provides an interesting contrast with Breton because obligatory exponence is not relative to the tensed element of the sentence. A comparison suggests therefore that there is no cross-linguistic rule that would intrinsically avoid the left-edge appearance of Tense morphology. The Gungbe obligatory exponence paradigm is also located at the left-edge of an IP-internal aspectual structure, which suggests that the left-edge position of the sentence is not intrinsically responsible for these obligatory exponence effects themselves.

6.   LEIT-reduplication in Gungbe

Gungbe provides a case of an obligatorily exponence in the preverbal position, inside a nominalized small clause structure. This small clause is selected by an aspectual control verb (e.g. *refuse*, *begin*) and could be headed by a purpose marker (in purpose constructions) or a final low-tone (in the case of the progressive) noted 'NR'. In (67b), I present the derivation proposed by Aboh (2009) for these structures, with the internal argument of the purpose marker that fronts into its specifier. The position of obligatory exponence is at the left edge of this moved constituent. The element canonically in preverbal position is the internal

---

16.   See also Foley (1991) and Phillips (1994) for a similar ABS displacement paradigm showing morphological obligatory exponence in Yimas (Papua New Guinea).

argument (here in bold), whose preverbal movement is neither case-related (Aboh 2005: 158), nor related to information packaging (Aboh p.c.).[17]

(67)   a.   Àsíbá wá   [A_{SPP} *lέsì ɖù*] gbé _.   (Gungbe, Aboh 2009: 14–15)
              Asiba come   rice eat PRT
              'Asiba came in order to eat rice.'

       b.   [AspP *wá* [FP   [F *gbé* t_{AspP}

              [A_{SPP} *lέsì* [Asp *ɖù* [vP t_{Àsíbá} [v_{EXT} t_{ɖù} [vP [VP t_{ɖù} t_{lέsì}]]]]]]]]]

LEIT signature is a full battery of last-resort strategies, some of which syntactically bad behaved, with mutual exclusive distribution of heads and XPs. Indeed, when the verb is intransitive, or when the object is absent, being either a pronominalized clitic or A′-extracted, another element has to 'take its place' and front preverbally. This element can be a locative PP (68), a reduplicated adverb like *dέdέ*, 'slowly' (69), a goal argument of a double object constructions (70).

(68)   Àsíbá tò   [*àxì   mὲ yì*]`.   (Gungbe, Aboh 2005: 157)
       Asiba PROG market in go-NR
       'Asiba is going to the market.'

(69)   Àsíbá tò   [*dὲdέ   zɔ̀n*]`.
       Asiba PROG slowly walk.PRT
       'Asiba is walking slowly.'

(70)   Été   wὲ à   tò   [*Kòfí kpl   ɔ́n*]`?   (Gungbe, Aboh 2009: 12)
       What FOC 2SG PROG Kofi teach. PRT
       'What are you teaching Kofi?'

A reduplication process of the verb is also a last-resort strategy (71). This means that like the verb excorporation process in Breton, sub-extraction of the verbal root is an available option that obeys the same trigger as a full preverbal XP does. Moreover, as in Breton, the presence of a preverbal functional head, the prospective marker *ná*, satisfies LEIT as illustrated in (72). When the numeration conforms to LEIT in this way, no fronting operation is required and the sentence is licit.

---

17.   In Aboh's terms, FP which embeds the AspP and VP is a predicate, and [spec AspP] functions as the subject of that predicate. He labels the preverbal position the 'subject position' (Aboh 2005), but the term is merely induced by his analysis that preverbal movement is EPP-triggered. Aboh (2009) clearly shows that no subject ever stops in AspP where it would fail to receive Case. The Tense marker, when realized, is the [+future] morpheme *ná*. It distributes Direct Case and is located higher in the structure (Aboh 2005: Example 11). The fully developed structure can be found in Aboh and Smith this volume.

(71) a. *Été   wè   Àsíbá   wá*
          what FOC Asiba come

          [*t*_{wh} *dùdù*] *gbé?*   (Gungbe, Aboh 2009: 14–15)
          eat.eat PRT

          'What did Asiba come to eat (it)?'

      b. *Kòfí ná   ná   tò   [*dùdù-ì*]* `.   (Gungbe, Aboh 2005: 158)
          Kofi FUT HAB PROG eat.eat-3SG NR
          'Kofi will be habitually eating it.'

(72) *Kòfí ná   nò   tò   [*ná   dù-ì*]* `.   (Gungbe, Aboh 2005: 158)
      Kofi FUT HAB PROG PROSP eat-3SG NR
      'Kofi will be habitually about to eat it.'

Contrary to the generalization that I propose above, Aboh (2005) and Aboh &
Smith (this volume) assume that neither the reduplicated verb nor the prospective
marker fill in the preverbal gap itself. They propose instead that both heads license
a null expletive *via* the Spec/head relation. The problem I can see with an expletive
hypothesis is that a phonologically null placeholder would easily vanish under XP
fronting. On the contrary, as we will see in the next section, *ná* in (72) blocks any
further XP movement or reduplication process.

6.1   Last-resort

As both the XP object and the prospective *ná* are imposed by the numeration, they
can both appear preverbally (73). In contrast, preverbal movement for LEIT satisfaction is a last-resort operation. As such, any independent satisfaction of LEIT
renders it ungrammatical. Consequently, the prospective aspect marker blocks
reduplication in all contexts (74) (see also Aboh 2005: 158–159).

(73) *Dáwè lò   tò   [*kèké   nà   xò*]* `.   (Gungbe, Aboh 2005: 143)
      man DET PROG bicycle PROSP buy-NR
      'The man is about to buy a bicycle.'

(74) a. *Jíkù tò   ná   (*jì)jàn* `.   (Gungbe, Aboh 2009: 13)
          rain PROG PROSP   fall.PRT
          'It is just about to rain.'

      b. *Súrù tò   ná   (*sì)sà è   ná   mìn* `.
          Suru PROG PROSP   sell 3SG PREP me.PRT
          'Suru is just about to sell it for/to me.'

      c. *Été*_i *wè   Súrù tò   ná   (*sì)sà t*_i *ná   mìn* `.?
          what FOC Suru PROG PROSP   sell   PREP me. PRT
          'What is Suru just about to sell for/to me?'

Adverb movement in itself is not banned, as illustrated by the extraposed adverb
dédé 'slowly' in (75). However, preverbal adverb fronting is ungrammatical

with either reduplication (77), PP fronting (78), or the prospective marker *ná* (75), (76).

(75) *Été wè Àsíbá wá (??dèdɛ́) ná (*dèdɛ́) ḍù (?dèdɛ́)*
      What FOC Asiba come slowly PROSP slowly eat slowly

      gbé (,dèdɛ́)?
      PRT slowly

      'What did Asiba come to be about to eat (slowly)?'

(76) *Kòfí ná nɔ̀ tò (*dèdɛ́) ná (*dèdɛ́) ḍù-ì (dèdɛ́)) `.*
      Kofi FUT HAB PROG slowly PROSP slowly eat-3SG slowly NR
      'Kofi will be habitually about to eat it (slowly).'

(77) *Été wè Àsíbá wá (*dèdɛ́) ḍùḍù*
      What FOC Asiba come slowly eat.eat

      (?dèdɛ) gbé?   (Gungbe, Aboh p.c.)
      slowly PRT

      'What did Asiba come to eat (it) (slowly)?'

(78) *Àsíbá tò (*dèdɛ́) àxì mè (*dèdɛ́) yì (dèdɛ́) `.*
      Asiba PROG slowly market in slowly go- slowly NR
      'Asiba is (slowly) going to the market.'

Not all elements are eligible targets for LEIT fronting. As is the case with Icelandic Stylistic Fronting paradigms, and in Breton as well, phonologically null elements seem invisible to this operation (Holmberg 2000; Jouitteau 2005, 2010). Traces or intermediate copies also are unavailable targets. We can deduce likewise that A-bar traces of object extraction are invisible for LEIT, because they never block further LEIT effects. The A-trace of the subject also never satisfies LEIT by accident, on its way to SpecTP. Aboh (2009) proposes that EPP positions are 'frozen' in the sense of Rizzi and Shlonsky (2007). As such, "the extracted constituent cannot check the EPP feature under Asp on its way to the left periphery because Spec, AspP is a freezing position." If I am right about LEIT effects being at the Late Syntax/Morphology Interface, this just follows from the invisibility of traces/copies in this component. The subject itself is never LEIT-attracted because it needs Case higher up in the sentence (Aboh 2009: 13).

6.2 Hierarchical scale

The ultralocality of LEIT last-resort effects suggests a hierarchical scale as illustrated in (79) for LEIT satisfying strategies.

(79) Object fronting > reduplication > reduplicated adverb fronting / (except non reduplicated elements)

Object fronting is always chosen over reduplication. Speakers vary as to allowing for verb reduplication to take place with a postverbal object (Aboh 2005: Footnote 12). An object also fronts over the adverb (80). We also find data showing that reduplication can take place over the fronting of some PPs (81) (to be compared with (68)).

(80)   *Kòfí tò lɛ́sì   ɖù dɛ̀dɛ́.*   (Gungbe, Aboh 2005: 147)
        *Kofi tò dɛ̀dɛ̀ ɖù lɛ́sì
        'Kofi is eating rice slowly.'

(81)   a.   *Súrù tò   [sìsà   ɛ̀   ná   mì]`.*   (Gungbe, Aboh 2009: 12)
              Suru PROG sell.sell 3SG PREP me.PRT
              'Suru is selling it for/to me.'

        b.   *Étɛ́ᵢ   wɛ̀   Súrù tò   [sìsà   tᵢ ná   mì]`.?*
              what FOC Suru PROG sell.sell   PREP me.PRT
              'What is Suru selling for/to me?'

In Gungbe, it is likely that the reduplication option takes place before the fronting of some postverbal elements, hence creating unavailable postverbal targets. A sharp contrast between the Breton and Icelandic paradigms emerges: any closest postverbal element is an eligible target for preverbal last-resort movement in Icelandic or Breton. However, Gungbe has a class of elements that can show up postverbally, but still are not selected for LEIT fronting. For example, low non-reduplicated adverbs like *bléún,* 'quickly' can appear post-verbally but not fronted to satisfy LEIT.

(82)   a.   *Àsíbá tò (*bléún) lɛ́sì ɖù (bléún).*   (Gungbe, Aboh p.c)
        b.   *Àsíbá tò lɛ́sì (*bléún) ná (*bléún) ɖù (bléún)*
              'Asiba is (about to) eat rice *quickly.*'

The respective postverbal order of indirect object, non-reduplicated adverb and adverbial PPs is [IO-PP-ADV] or [IO-ADV-PP] (83). The assumption that ultra-local movement applies as a last resort predicts that in (84), the indirect object, and only the indirect object, being the closest target for fronting, will front. But it doesn't (84).

(83)   a.   *Métrù lɔ́ tò   wémà lɔ́ ná   zé   [xlán ví   lɛ́] [tò*
              teacher DET PROG book DET PROSP take P   child PL P
              flɛ̀n] [hàɖòkpólɔ́]`.
              there immediately

        b.   *Métrù lɔ́ tò wémà lɔ́ ná zé [xlán ví lɛ́ hàɖòkpólɔ́]   [tò flɛ̀n].*
                                                    Immediately P there
              'The teacher was about to immediately send the book to the children right there.'

(84) a. *Métrù   lɔ́   tò   **xlán ví**   lέ   zé   ὲ   _   tò
               teacher DET PROG P   child PL take 3SG   P

               flὲn   hàɖòkpólɔ́.
               there immediately

    b. *Métrù   lɔ́   tò   **tò flέn**   zé   ὲ   xlán   ví
               teacher DET PROG P   there take 3SG P   child

               lε   _   hàɖòkpólɔ́.
               PL   immediately

    c. *Métrù   lɔ́   tò   hàɖòkpólɔ́   zé   ὲ   xlán   ví   lέ   _
               teacher DET PROG immediately take 3SG P   child PL

               tò   flὲn.
               P   there

               'The teacher was sending it immediately to the children right there.'

In view of this resistance to fronting, it is rather unclear what postverbal redupli-cated adverbs have that make them eligible targets for LEIT fronting over verb reduplication. I also note, following Aboh, that VP and *v*P are never eligible targets either, and leave these mysteries for further investigation. For the purposes of this article, it is sufficient that I remark that in (79), like in the Breton cases, obligatory exponence is satisfied by mixed strategies that vary from XP-fronting to morpho-logical doubling operations, characteristic of LEIT effects.

The Gungbe syntactic environment for LEIT effects is also interesting because of its differences from the Breton context: first, the obligatorily filled position is not sentence initial. Gungbe LEIT effects arguably arise at the left edge of an aspectual verb structure. The obligatorily filled gap, as is the case in Breton, can be preverbal, but this parallel is not clear cut: LEIT effects in Breton are relative to the head that bears both tense and subject agreement markers. In Gungbe, no V-to-I movement takes place and the verb lands lower, in an internal IP position (V-to-AsP).

7. Conclusions

Breton analytic structures obey LEIT
The choice between synthetic structures and analytic structures in Breton depends on the need for an expletive insertion trigger to be satisfied. This *Late Expletive Insertion Trigger* that leads to verb-second orders is responsible for all sorts of last-resort strategies, one of them being excorporation of the verbal root, and the consequent pronunciation of the lexical content of the verb in the preverbal area. The default spell-out of the excorporated verb is an infinitive, with the mor-phological properties attached to all verbs in the pre-tense area. The mysterious restriction of analytic structures to the relative [...V-Aux...] order follows.

The tensed auxiliary is either realized as a dummy 'do' auxiliary, or, for an idiosyncratic list of verbs, as the tensed reiteration of the excorporated verb itself (doubling).

Breton analytic structures result from a morphological operation
The very existence of doubling structures is one of the arguments that excorporation happens in a post-syntactic morphological component. The list of doubling verbs is an arbitrary set and does not form a homogeneous syntactic class or classes: nothing distinguishes doubling verbs from non-doubling ones at the syntactic level. Non-doubling verbs resort uniformly to the AC in 'do'.

It follows that no scenario involing doubling in syntax is possible for Breton. Theoretically, the hypothesis that doubling arises in a post-syntactic morphological component implies strongly that it exists cross-linguistically, independently of either the copy theory of movement or multidominance.

The rule leading to V2 orders operates in a morphophonological module
On the one hand, we know of obligatory exponence cases in morphology (cf. Basque ergative displacement, Yimas morphological EPP), and on the other hand, we know of second position phenomena at the level of the sentence, for example V2 languages (Old Irish, Middle Welsh, Cornic, Breton, Medieval dialects of Northern Italian, Old French, Old Spanish, Rhaetoromance, Sorbian, Estonian, Kashmiri, Karitiana, Hebrew, Papago and almost all Germanic languages), but also clitic-second languages (Warlpiri, Tagalog, most Slavic languages, etc.). The present analysis of the Breton analytic structures and Gungbe reduplication structures leads to the major conclusion that mixed systems exist, in which obligatory exponence operates at a level where a subject or an object with a potentially long relative embedded structure 'counts' the same as the excorporated subcomponent of a head for word order. This of course opens interesting perspectives for a unified understanding of second position effects across languages. Among other things, the cross-linguistic violations of the Head Movement Constraint in these languages (Stylistic Fronting, Long Head Movement, verb fronting, etc.) would follow if word order is indeed finalized in a post-syntactic component.

Information Packaging and iconicity
The Breton paradigm of analytic tenses is of great interest for the study of the limits of iconicity in doubling. At first sight, In modern Breton varieties, verb-doubling structures obtain some sort of salience effect on the verb. Doubling thus intuitively seems to iconically obtain 'more of the same', here a salience effect on the doubled item. However, the Breton data presents two major challenges for an

I think that iconicity is a distinct issue from variation and idiosyncrasy and productivity.

iconicity theory of doubling: variation and idiosyncrasy. First, iconicity cannot explain the variation of the salience effect in either synchrony or diachrony. In modern Breton, a rare doubling case like *lenn*, 'to read', induces a clear contrastive focus reading, whereas the commonly doubled verb *gouzout*, 'to know', can have a rather mild salience effect, not restricted to a contrastive reading. It is more likely that salience results from a new/known contrast. Likewise, the analytic construction with 'do' is reported in Breton Grammars, to have been used for a salience effect on the verb for varieties at the beginning of the 20th century. This salience effect has completely disappeared from the modern varieties, suggesting a probable erosion of the effect over time. My analysis is that *LEIT* last-resort strategies are invisible to the grammar because they arise in a post-syntactic component. Indeed, LEIT operations never impact the truth-conditions of the sentence. My proposal implies that some discourse effects are interpreted in a pragmatic component, distinct from semantic interpretation proper. Finally, the idiosyncratic restriction of Breton verb-doubling presents the greatest challenge for an iconicity scenario: an iconicity dimension of doubling should indeed trigger full productivity, contrary to facts. I conclude that if the iconic dimension of doubling at the sentence level plays a role in how one language creates strategies to express salience, as a sort of free tool available for a speaker's creativity, the iconic dimension disappears as soon as the construction is installed in the language. In that sense, the iconic dimension is fully disconnected from the language's grammar.

References

Abels, Klaus. 2001. The predicate cleft construction in Russian. In *Formal Approaches to Slavic Linguistics,* Steven Franks, Tracy Holloway King & Michael Yadroff (eds), 1–19. Ann Arbor MI: Michigan Slavic Publications.

Aboh, Enoch. 2005. Object-shift, verb-movement and verb reduplication. In *The Oxford Handbook in Comparative Syntax*, Ch. 4, Guglielmo Cinque & Richard S. Kayne (eds), Oxford: OUP.

Aboh, Enoch. 2009. Clause structure and verb series. *Linguistic Inquiry* 40(1): 1–33.

Aboh, Enoch & Dyakonova, Marina. 2008. Predicate doubling and parallel chains. *Lingua* 119: 1035–1065.

ARBRES, research website on the syntax of Breton dialects: ⟨http://arbres.iker.univ-pau.fr/index.php/Grammaire_du_breton⟩

Al Lay, Fañch. 1925. *Bilzig*. Quimper: Buhez Breiz.

Ar C'hoad, Gwilh [= Guillaume Le Coat] 1893, *Testamant nevez, Lizher Jakez 3*, Société Biblique Trinitaire pour la Bretagne. Manuscrit révisé, mis en langue bretonne moderne par Luc Bernicot, en 2004 (Société Biblique d'Anjou éd.). version KOAD 21.

Ar C'hog, Y.V. 1983. Notennoù gramadeg a-ziwar skridoù Ivon Krog. *Hor Yezh* 148–149: 3–14.

Barzig, Ernest, *Koatilouri*. ⟨http://embann.an.hirwaz.online.fr/⟩

Bijer, Yann. 2007. *Avel gornôg*. Brest: Al Liamm.

Borsley, Robert. D. & Kathol, Andreas. 2000. Breton as a V2 language. *Linguistics* 38: 665–710.

Borsley, Robert. D, Rivero, Maria Luisa & Stephens, Janig. 1996. Long head movement in Breton. In *The Syntax of the Celtic Languages: A Comparative Perspective*, Robert D. Borsley & Ian Roberts (eds), 53–74. Cambridge: CUP.

Cable, Seth. 2003. The Yiddish predicate cleft: A base-generation analysis. Ms, MIT.

Chalm, Eugène. 2008. *La Grammaire bretonne pour tous*. An Alac'h embannadurioù.

Cheveau, Loig. 2007. Approche phonologique, morphologique et syntaxique du breton du grand Lorient, Ph.D. dissertation, MIT.

Chomsky, Noam. 1955. *The Logical Structure of Linguistic Theory*. Ms, MIT/Harvard University. (Partly published in 1975, New York NY: Plenum).

Chomsky, Noam. 1973. Conditions on transformations. In *A Festschrift for Morris Halle*. Stephen R. Anderson & Paul Kiparsky (eds), 232–286. New York NY: Holt, Rinehart and Winston.

Chomsky, Noam. 1993. A minimalist program for linguistic theory. *The View from Building 20. Essays in Linguistics in honor of Sylvain Bromberger,* Kenneth Hale & Samuel J. Keyser (eds), 1–52. Cambridge MA: The MIT Press.

Denez, Per. 1993. rakskrid Kervella, F. 1993. *Skridoù Frañcez Kervella, dastumet ha kinniget gant Per Denez*. Brest: Al Liamm.

Dupuy, Yann Fulub. 2007. *Ar gariadez vaen*. An Alarc'h Embannadurioù.

Ernault, Emile. 1890. Etudes bretonnes, VII. Sur l'analogie dans la conjugaison. *Revue Celtique* XIL: 458–487.

Ernault, Emile. 1888. Etudes bretonnes. VI. La conjugaison personnelle et le verbe avoir. *Revue Celtique* IX: 245–266.

Etxepare, Ricardo & Ortiz de Urbina, Jon. 2003. Event focalization. In *A Grammar of Basque,* Jose Ignacio Hualde & Jon Ortiz de Urbina (eds), 459–516. Berlin: Mouton de Gruyter.

Favereau, Francis. 1997. *Grammaire du breton contemporain*. Morlaix: Skol Vreizh.

Fleuriot, Léon. 2001. Skoueriou emdroaduriou e morfologiezh hag ereadur ar brezhoneg, class Léon Fleuriot translated by Herve Bihan in *Hor Yezh* 228.

Foley, William A. 1991. *The Yimas language of New Guinea*. Standford CA: Stanford University Press.

Gouget, Jules. 2008. La réduplication syntaxique et la structure du groupe verbal en mandarin, en anglais et en d'autres langues. Manuscrit de thèse, Paris 7.

Grégoire de Rostrenen, 1795. *Grammaire française-celtique ou française-bretonne,* An III; nouvelle édition. Brest: Alain Le Fournier.

Grohmann, Kleanthes K., John Drury & Juan Carlos Castillo. 2000. 'No More EPP', In Roger Billerey & Brook Danielle Lillehaugen, eds. *Proceedings of the Nineteenth West Coast Conference on Formal Linguistics*. Somerville, MA: Cascadilla Press, 153–166.

Gros, Jules. 1984. *Le trésor du breton parlé III. Le style populaire*. Brest: Emgleo Breiz–Nevez: Brud.

Guillevic, A.; Le Goff, P. 1986. *Grammaire Bretonne du Dialecte de Vannes*, Brest: Ar Skol Vrezhoneg- Emgleo Breiz.

Harbour, Daniel. 2007. Against PersonP. *Syntax* 10(3): 223–242.

Harbour, Daniel. 2008. Klivaj predik, or predicate clefts in Haitian. *Lingua* 118: 853–871.

Hemon, Roparzh. 2000. *Yezhadur istorel ar brezhoneg*. Translation A. Dipode. *Hor Yezh* 227.

Holmberg, Anders. 2000. Scandinavian stylistic fronting: How any category can become an expletive. *Linguistic Inquiry* 31(3): 445–483.

Holmberg, Anders & Nikanne, Urpo. 2002. Expletives, subjects and topics in Finnish. In *Subjects, Expletives and the EPP*, Peter Svenonius (ed.), 71–105. Oxford: OUP.

Jouitteau, Mélanie. 2005[2010]. *La syntaxe comparée du Breton: Une enquête sur la périphérie gauche de la phrase bretonne*. Thesis published by Éditions universitaires européennes.

Jouitteau, Mélanie. 2007. The Brythonic reconciliation: From V1 to generalized V2. *Linguistic Variation Yearbook* 7:163–200.

Jouitteau, Mélanie. 2009. A typology of V2 with regard to V1 and second position phenomena: An introduction to the V1/V2 volume. *Lingua* 120(2): 197–209 (Special issue: *Verb-First, Verb-Second*).

Jouitteau, Mélanie. 2011. Doing the work of free choice determiners without 'any'. Presentation at *Workshop on Languages With(out) Articles*, Paris, March 3–4.

Jouitteau, Mélanie & Rezac, Milan. 2006. Deriving the complementarity effect: Relativized minimality in Breton agreement. *Lingua* 116:1915–1945. (Special issue: Celtic Languages).

Jouitteau, Mélanie & Rezac, Milan. 2008. From mihi est to have across Breton dialects. In *Proceedings of the 34th Incontro di Grammatica Generativa*, Paola Benincà, Federico Damonte & Nicoletta Penello (eds). *Rivista di Grammatica Generativa* 32:161–178.

Jouitteau, Mélanie & Rezac, Milan. 2009. Le verbe 'avoir' à travers les dialectes du breton. *La Bretagne Linguistique* 14. Brest: CRBC.

Kandybowicz, Jason. 2008. *The Grammar of Repetition. Nupe Grammar at the Syntax-Phonology Interface* [Linguistik Aktuell/Linguistics Today 136]. Amsterdam: John Benjamins.

Kandybowicz, Jason. 2006a. Conditions on Multiple Copy Spell-Out and the Syntax-Phonology Interface. Ph.D. dissertation, UCLA.

Kandybowicz, Jason. 2006b. On fusion and multiple copy spell-out: The case of verbal repetition. In *The Copy Theory of Movement* [Linguistik Aktuell/Linguistics Today 107], Norbert Corver & Jairo Nunes (eds), 119–150. Amsterdam: John Benjamins.

Kervella, Frañsez. 1995 1947.*Yezhadur bras ar brezhoneg*, 1947 éd. Skridoù Breizh, La Baule; 1995 (éd.), Al Liamm, Brest.

Konan, Jakez. 1981. *Ur marc'hadour a Vontroulez*. Brest: Al Liamm.

Krog, Ivon. 1924. *Ur zac'had marvailhou*. Quimper: Ur Buhez Breiz.

Inizan, Lan. 1879 1902. *Emgann Kergidu*, new edn. Brest: Lefournier.

Landau, Ilan. 2007. Partial VP-fronting. *Syntax* 10(2): 127–164.

Lasnik, Howard. 2001. A note on the EPP. *Linguistic Inquiry* 3(2): 2.

Le Bozec. 1933. Le français par le breton, méthode bilingue, cours préparatoire. Guingamp: Thomas edition.

Leclerc, Louis. 1986. *Grammaire bretonne du dialecte de Tréguier*. Nevez: Brud. (Réédition de 1908 et 1911, Saint-Brieuc: Prud'homme).

Le Roux, Pierre. 1924–1953. *Atlas linguistique de la Basse-Bretagne*, 6 vols. grouping 100 maps each, Rennes/Paris. Reprinted 1977, Brest: Éditions Armoricaines; last edition Nevez: Brud.

Le Roux, Pierre. 1957. *Le Verbe breton (morphologie, syntaxe)*. Rennes: Librairie Plihon/Paris: Librairie Champion.

Maï-Ewen, 2004. *Hanvezhioù*. Laz: Keit Vimp Bev.

Miossec, Yves. 1981. *Dreist ar mor bras*. Nevez: Brud.

Nunes, Jairo. 2004. *Linearization of Chains and Sideward Movement*. Cambridge MA: The MIT Press.

Phillips, Colin. 1994. On the nature of polysynthetic inflection. In *Proceedings of CONSOLE 2*. Leiden: SOLE.

Ploneis, Jean-Marie. 1983. Au carrefour des dialectes bretons – Le parler de Berrien: Essai de description phonématique et morphologique. Paris: Société d'études linguistiques et anthropologiques de France (SELAF).

Quéré, Jean. 1906. *Sarmoniou an Aotrou Quere*, Christophe Jézégou (ed.), ⟨http://www.gutenberg.org/files/23685/23685-8.txt⟩

Red an Amzer 11.01.2009. France 3 programme text. ⟨http://ouest.france3.fr/emissions/2367205-fr.php⟩ (unavailable).

Rezac, M. 2004. 'The EPP in Breton: An unvalued categorial feature', *Triggers*, Studies in Generative Grammar, A. Breitbarth & H. V. Riemsdijk, Mouton de Gruyter, 451–492.

Rezac, Milan. 2008. Building and interpreting a non-thematic A-position: A-resumption in English and Breton. In *Resumptive Pronouns at the Interfaces* [Language Faculty and Beyond 5], Alain Rouveret (ed.), Amsterdam: John Benjamins.

Schafer, Robin. 1997. Long head movement and information packaging in Breton. *Canadian Journal of Linguistics* 42(1–2): 169–203.

Skragn, Jan-Mari. 2002. *Ma buhez e Kêr ar Vinaoued*. Brest: Emgleo Breiz.

Stephens, Janig. 1982. Word Order in Breton. Ph.D. dissertation, School of Oriental and African Studies, University of London.

Tamburri Watt, Linda. 2003. What marks Squamish focus? In *Actes: Interfaces Prosodiques*, Amina Mettouchi & Gaëlle Ferré (eds), Nantes. ⟨http://www.lling.fr/ip2003/actes-ip2003.pdf⟩

Taraldsen, Tarald. 2002. The 'Que/Qui' alternation and the distribution of expletives. In *Subjects, Expletives, and the EPP*, Peter Svenonius (ed.), Oxford: OUP.

Trépos, Pierre. 2001 [1968, 1980, 1996]. *Grammaire bretonne*. Brest: Brud Nevez. (1968 édition Simon, Rennes; 1980 édition Ouest France, Rennes; 1996, 2001 édition Brud Nevez, Brest).

Troude, Amable-Emmanuel. 1886. *Nouveau dictionnaire pratique Français et Breton du dialecte de Leon*, 3 (éd.), Brest: Lefournier.

Vallduvi, Enric. 1995. Structural properties of information packaging in Catalan. In *Discourse Configurational Languages*, É. Katalin Kiss (ed.), 122–152. Oxford: OUP.

Vicente, Luis. 2007. *The Syntax of Heads and Phrases. A Study of Verb-(phrase) Fronting*. Utrecht: LOT.

Zuazo, Koldo. 1998. Euskalkiak gaur. *Fontes Linguae Vasconum* 30: 191–233.

NN constructions in Modern Hebrew*

Dana Cohen
University of Paris 8

This paper proposes structural analyses for several nominal reiteration constructions (NN) in Modern Hebrew which function as adverbials. The properties and distribution of these patterns indicate an interaction of nominal distinctions (number and mass/count denotation) with Aktionsart, suggesting that reiteration is derived through the insertion of the same lexical element twice into a regular syntactic structure, rather than involving specialized morphological derivation. Although all three constructions share a pluralizing semantic effect, it is argued that the notion of iconicity does not capture the intricacy of their interpretive properties. The proposed analysis ties these Hebrew constructions to related phenomena attested cross-linguistically, both reiterative and non-reiterative.

1. Introduction

Reduplicative phenomena can be found in many typologically distinct languages of diverse families (for discussion of the cross-linguistic range of such phenomena, see Aboh, Smith & Zribi-Hertz (this volume)). And yet, all too frequently, reduplication is considered particularly characteristic of Creole languages, or as somehow more inherent to the Creole stage of a language, a simple enrichment method in a young language that lacks more complex mechanisms (see Bakker 2003; Kouwenberg 2003b; a.o.). Hebrew can be seen as a prime counter-example to this approach. Reduplicative phenomena are varied and productive in Hebrew; only a few of the available constructions are mentioned in this article. Examination of

---

* Particular thanks are due to Enoch Aboh and Anne Zribi-Hertz for their insights and suggestions on earlier versions of this paper. The study described in this article also benefited from discussions with Bridget Copley, Abdelkader Fassi Fehri, Elena Soare, and Il-Il Yatziv-Malibert. Versions of this study were presented at the Workshop on Nominal and Verbal Plurality (Paris, Nov. 2009) and at the Grammar of Reiteration Workshop (Amsterdam, Dec. 2009). I would like to thank the participants in both events for their fruitful comments and discussion.

diachronic data shows that many, if not all, of the constructions mentioned below were robust in Biblical Hebrew,[1] remained in use during intermediate stages, and are productive to this day. This very fact is a strong argument against the view of reiteration as a simple strategy replacing complex mechanisms. Hebrew, in all its stages, exhibits a rich morphological system and complex syntactic structures. Thus, reduplicative and reiterative constructions do not replace such complex tools, but exist alongside them and necessarily interact with them. The diversity, complexity, and productivity of these constructions are further evidence against their classification as a simple enrichment method. Rather, reiteration, to the extent that it is a unified phenomenon, emerges as one of the many linguistic tools available universally, regardless of the typological associations or linguistic complexity of a given language.

This paper examines several nominal reiteration constructions in Hebrew that involve two adjacent occurrences of the same nominal form (NN). The first aim of the paper is to distinguish between several NN constructions and characterize them. Four patterns are distinguished based on distribution and interpretation, one of which carries a scalar contrastive meaning and is also available with other categories, whereas the other three are limited to nouns and exhibit various pluralizing readings. The second aim is to propose an analysis of the pluralizing NN patterns, correlating the various properties they exhibit. Thus, the reiteration of singular nouns (NNsg) marks dynamic events as pluractional, signaling a plurality of sub-events; plural noun reiteration (NNpl) modifies states and signals the existence of multiple sub-components of a property; the third NN pattern (NNpred) contains an internal predication, which modifies a collective or mass participant of an event and marks a distinguishing property among sub-components of this

---

1. As illustrated below, many of these constructions are already productive in Biblical Hebrew: morphophonological reduplication: *ptaltol* 'twisted/crooked' (Deut. 32:5, from the root p.t.l 'twist/wind'), *adamdam* 'reddish', *yerakrak* 'greenish' (Ps. 38:10, from *adom* 'red' and *yarok* 'green' respectively); cognate objects (somewhat different from the Modern Hebrew constructions): *ele ha.dvarim ašer tedaber el bnei israel* (Exod. 19:6, "these are the words that you shall speak to the sons of Israel", these DF.utterances that utter.FUT.2SG P(to) son.PL.CS yisrael); verbal reiteration (somewhat different from the Modern Hebrew constructions): *gareš yegareš etxem mi.ze*, (Exod. 11:1, "he shall thrust you out hence", banish.PRT banish.FUT3SG, you.PL P(from).here); contrastive reiteration: *me'at me'at agaršenu mi.panexa*, (Exod. 23:30, "little by little I will drive them out from before thee", lit. 'little little'); NNsg: *mi.kol ha.behema ha.tehora tikax lexa šiv'a šiv'a, ha.iš ve.išhto*, (Gen. 7:2, "Of every clean beast thou shalt take to thee by sevens, the male and his female", lit. 'seven seven'); NNpl: *gam hem ma'aser* [...] *hevi'u vayitnu aremot aremot*, (II Chron. 31:6, "they also brought in the tithe. [...] and laid them by heaps", lit. 'heap.PL heap.PL'); NNpred: *ve.itxem yihyu iš le.mate*, (Num. 1:4, "and with you there shall be a man of every tribe", lit. 'man man P(to).tribe').

participant. The structural analysis proposed has implications for broader issues with respect to reiteration phenomena cross-linguistically, particularly regarding the place of iconicity in the analysis of these phenomena.

The next section presents central distributional factors regarding dual lexical reiteration (LL) in Hebrew (§2.1) and draws a distinction between contrastive NN and pluralizing NN patterns (§2.2). Pluralizing patterns are discussed in detail in Sections 3–4, outlining the characteristic properties of each, and offering an appropriate structural analysis. The concluding section summarizes the proposed analysis, and considers the relevance of these constructions to the broader question of iconicity in reiteration. The analysis is based on attested data collected from a wide range of Hebrew sources in a variety of styles and registers (written and oral, formal and informal).

2. Reiteration in Modern Hebrew

Hebrew exhibits a range of reiterative phenomena that can be found on all linguistic levels. Word formation strategies involving word-internal reduplication have been studied from morphophonological and semantic perspectives (e.g. Graf 2002; Bat-El 2006; Greenberg 2010; and references therein). Several syntactic constructions involve the reiteration of the same word-stem/root in various forms (e.g. Landau 2006 on verbal reiteration; Mittwoch 1998 on cognate objects; Pereltsvaig 2002 on both).[2] Constructions involving complete word reiteration – the identical repetition of full words – have received little attention in the literature. Word reiteration can operate on bare stems, inflected stems, and stems with various affixes and clitics. Several distinct patterns of complete, contiguous reiteration are attested in Modern Hebrew, each with specific distributional and prosodic characteristics. Complete word reiteration may involve the contiguous occurrence of two identical full words (henceforth dual reiteration), contiguous multiple reiteration

---

2. Verbal reiteration (known as predicate clefting or VP-fronting) involves an infinitival or other non-finite V or VP in the left periphery, paired in the same clause with a finite V form of the same root: *liknot et ha.praxim hi* **kanta** (buy.INF OM DF.flowers, 'buy the flowers she bought'). Cognate object constructions are predicates that involve verbs and modifying nouns derived from the same root: *rakadnu šnei rikudim* (danced.1PL two dances, 'we danced two dances'), *hu* **nifca pci'a** *kaša* (he injured.PASS injury serious, 'he was injured a serious injury'), *hu* **axrai axrayut** *elyona* (he responsible responsibility ultimate, 'he holds the ultimate responsibility'). Pereltsvaig (2002) distinguishes cognate objects that function as regular arguments from what she terms adverbial cognate objects, which function as secondary predicates. She includes biblical predicate clefting in the latter pattern.

of full words (that is, where the number of repetitions is structurally unlimited), and the reiteration of sequences larger than words (for discussion of the latter two, see, Yatziv 2002; Yatziv & Livnat 2007).[3] Complete word reiteration constructions of all these types are evident both in spoken informal registers and in higher registers (both written and oral), and so cannot be regarded as merely colloquial phenomena.

2.1   Dual lexical reiteration in Modern Hebrew

Dual lexical reiteration (LL) refers here to a set of complete reiteration patterns which consist of two occurrences of a word, forming a contiguous sequence that cannot be separated by another element or by a pause. The term dual reiteration is intended to distinguish LL constructions from other types of reiteration, stressing that no more than two items are involved, and that these must be identical and adjacent. LL constructions are productively available for all lexical categories in Hebrew (1), including nouns, verbs, adjectives and adverbs; cliticized prepositions are allowed as well (small caps indicate prosodic prominence within the reiterated pair).[4]

(1)   a.   *kaninu   lo   matana   MATANA.*   [N/N]
              bought.1PL   P(to)M3SG   gift   gift
              'We bought him a really good/real gift.'

       b.   *racti   RACTI   ad   kav ha.siyum.*   [V/V]
              ran.1SG   ran.1SG   P(until)   line   DF.end
              'I really ran/ran well until the finish line.'

---

3.   Multiple word reiteration in Modern Hebrew (e.g. *xol xol xol* (lit. 'sand sand sand'); *le'at le'at le'at le'at* (lit. 'slowly slowly slowly slowly'), *holex holex holex holex* (lit. 'walk walk walk walk' (forms in PRS.MSG)) has been analyzed as indicating a so-called 'iconic' extension of the spatio-temporal domain (Yatziv & Livnat 2007). The reiteration of sequences larger than a word in Modern Hebrew has been analyzed as a rhetorical and cohesive device (see Yatziv 2002; Yatziv & Livnat 2007).

4.   Abbreviations in the glosses: CS = construct state; DF = definite; F = fem.; FUT = future; INF = infinitive; M = masc.; OM = object marker; P = preposition (meaning in parentheses); PASS = passive; PL = plural; POSS = possessive; PRS = present ('*benoni*'); PRT = participle; PST = past; SG = singular; 1,2,3 = first, second, third person.

Hebrew displays a rich agreement system, which includes number and gender marking on nouns, verbs, adjectives and on inflected prepositions; pronouns and verbs also show person features. Since much of this marking is irrelevant for the present topic, I leave agreement information out of the gloss when possible, to enhance expository simplicity. When necessary, F or M will be used to mark gender.

c. *hu lavaš xalifa yafa   YAFA.* [ADJ/ADJ]
   he wore.M3SG suit beautiful.F beautiful.F
   'He wore a really beautiful suit.'

d. *hem racu maher MAHER.* [ADV/ADV]
   they ran.3PL quickly quickly
   'They ran very quickly.'

e. *kamnu BA.BOKER   ba.boker.* [PP/PP]
   got-up.1PL DFP(in).morning DFP(in).morning
   'We got up very early in the morning.'

Similar reduplicative patterns have been identified in a variety of languages, such as English, Italian, Spanish, Russian, Persian, Haitian, Mauritian, and São Tomense (cf. Horn 1993; Ghomeshi et al. 2004; Hurch 2005; Glaude & Zribi-Hertz this volume; Henri this volume; Schang this volume). The English pattern is characterized by contrastive stress on the first element of the pair, and is productive with various lexical categories as well as with phrases. Horn (1993:48) characterizes its function as singling out a member or subset of the extension of the N "that represents a true, real, default or prototype instance". According to Ghomeshi et al. (2004), the phenomenon (prototypical/contrastive focus reduplication (CR) in their terms) serves to focus the denotation of the reduplicated element, signaling that one meaning of the word is being contrasted with other possible meanings; "the use of a word or phrase often leaves open some vagueness, lack of precision, or ambiguity. CR is used as one way to clarify such situations, by specifying a prototypical denotation of the lexical item in contrast to potentially looser or more specialized reading" (p. 311).

The function of Hebrew contrastive NN (1a above) can be characterized along similar lines. As evident in the glosses above, we can distinguish a prototypical interpretation (the 'real' N) and an intensive interpretation (the 'super' N).

a. *The prototypical ('real') option* marks an entity as a prototypical token of a type, compared to other, less-prototypical alternatives. Thus, the NN sequence is interpreted as a 'real/prototypical' token of N. In (1a), *matana MATANA* 'gift gift' indicates a real gift, as opposed to alternatives that the speaker considers too insignificant or insufficient to count as 'proper' gifts (e.g. chocolates or a card). This interpretation is equivalent to the non-reduplicated sequences *mamaš matana/matana be'emet* ('really gift'/'gift in truth').

b. *The intensive option* marks an entity as a token with particularly good properties, higher on a scale of some relevant property compared to alternatives of the type. Thus, the NN sequence is interpreted as an enhanced, 'super' token of N. Under this reading, *matana MATANA* in (1a) indicates a special or particularly good gift in some way (e.g. particularly desired, rare or expensive).

Doubled nouns of this pattern are interchangeable with nominal phrases that include explicit modification indicating the intended property: *matana me'ula/matana mamaš yekara* ('gift excellent'/'gift really expensive').

 Although such reiteration can be taken to encode "more of the same", i.e. having some additive meaning, it is important to realize that the pattern actually involves restrictive modification (the modified token excludes other alternatives, that is, 'gift gift' excludes other types of gifts), and therefore does not really follow an iconic pattern.

Similarly to the English construction noted above, the Hebrew contrastive NN sequence is accompanied by prosodic accentuation of one of the elements. However, in this case, it is the second element that is accentuated, paralleling the standard prosodic pattern of noun modification in Hebrew (evident in the non-reiterative equivalents as well, with the exception of the intensifier *mamaš*, which is always prosodically accentuated, whether it is a pre- or post-modifier). This prosodic pattern marks the second N of the pair as a modifier of the first.[5] The same prosodic property holds regardless of the specific interpretative effect (prototypical or intensive).

Do these interpretations involve distinct NN constructions? Probably not. There are no distributional differences to distinguish the two. Both interpretations are fairly close, and share the end-of-scale evaluation of the N referent, while the difference in interpretation can be attributed to different contextual factors leading to comparison against different sets of alternatives. It should be noted, however, that the accentuation in the intensive option seems to be systematically stronger than with the prototypical option, at least for some speakers.

As shown above, this pattern of contrastive LL is available for other lexical categories (1a–e). However, in other categories it is harder to separate the prototypical from the intensive interpretations. Non-nominal contrastive LL can be interpreted as 'really L', 'very L' or 'more L', producing an intensified token, where L itself marks the property of the scale. This can be seen as the realization of either the prototypical or the intensive interpretation in the relevant non-nominal domain, or as highlighting their convergence. Prosodic cues are also less helpful. The VV pair exhibits the same prosodic patterns found with contrastive NN. However, reiteration with adjectives, adverbs and PPs (1c–e) can also display accentuation of the first element of the pair, while maintaining the same 'very' reading. All of these follow the standard prosody appropriate for

---

5.   A similar prosodic pattern is reported by Henri (this volume) with respect to CR in Mauritian.

[handwritten margin note: which suggests that new words are not being formed]

modification in each specific category. The equivalent non-reiterated sequences involve modification by intensifiers (e.g. *mamaš* 'really' in *racti mamaš maher* 'ran.1SG (really) fast'), or elaboration with more specific content (*mukdam* 'early' in *mukdam ba.boker* 'early in.morning'), suggesting a fluidity between the two interpretations.

A detailed structural analysis of contrastive LL constructions requires examination of the various cross-categorial patterns and comparison with non-dual reiteration; it is therefore beyond the scope of the present study (cf. the extensive discussion on the structural analysis of Haitian verbal CR in Glaude & Zribi-Hertz this volume). It should be noted, however, that this LL pattern operates not on stems or uninflected forms, but on syntactic units: cliticized PPs (1e) and fully-inflected forms (most evident in the inflected verb in (1b), and the gender-marked adjective in (1c)). This factor indicates that these constructions are derived in syntax rather than in morphology. The semantic and prosodic facts noted above suggest a standard modification structure (as in *salat tuna* 'tuna salad', *salat yarok* 'green salad' for the NN sequence).

2.2 Pluralizing NN patterns

Unlike contrastive LL, pluralizing patterns are only available with nouns. Three pluralizing NN constructions are distinguished below, as illustrated in (2).

(2) a. *naʾamis   (et   ha.mitʾan) mizvada   mizvada.*   [NNsg]
         load.FUT1PL   OM   DF.cargo   suitcase   suitcase
         'We will load (the cargo) suitcase by suitcase.'

     b. *kol ha.bayit   mizvadot   mizvadot.*   [NNpl]
         all DF.house   suitcases   suitcases
         'The whole house (is full of) suitcases upon suitcases.'

     c. *kol   ha.mitʾan   yišalax,   mizvada$_i$*
         all   DF.cargo   send.PASS.FUT3SG,   suitcase

         mizvada$_i$ le.yaʾada$_i$.   [NNpred]
         suitcase   P(to).destination.POSS.FSG
         'All cargo will be sent, each suitcase to its destination.'

Several properties distinguish these NN patterns from the contrastive LL constructions discussed above. Prosodically, all three pluralizing NNs display a similar pattern wherein both nouns are evenly stressed. This contrasts with the asymmetric prosodic patterns associated with contrastive LL, mentioned above. These NN constructions seem to have a balanced, parallel internal structure, with no indication of internal hierarchy (that is, there is no sense of one of the items modifying the other in some way); this observation correlates with the prosodic pattern.

The distribution of NN constructions is much more limited compared to that of simple nouns (this is true for both pluralizing and contrastive NNs). Unlike typical nouns (3), NNs remain bare, and cannot occur with the cliticized definite determiner *ha-* or the object marker *et*, nor can they be directly modified by an adjective or quantifier, or form a construct state with another modifying noun, as illustrated with pluralizing NNs in (4–5).

(3)   a.   *na'amis*   *et*   *ha.mizvada*   *(ha.gdola).*
            load.FUT1PL   OM   DF.suitcase   (DF.big.FSG)
            'We will load the (big) suitcase.'

        b.   *na'amis*   *et*   *ha.mizvadot*   *(ha.gdolot).*
            load.FUT1PL   OM   DF.suitcases   (DF.big.FPL)
            'We will load the (big) suitcases.'

        c.   *na'amis*   *kol*   *mizvada*   *(gdola).*
            load.FUT1PL   *every*   suitcase   (big.FSG)
            'We will load every (big) suitcase.'

        d.   *na'amis*   *[harbe/arba]*   *mizvadot (gdolot).*
            load.FUT1PL   [many/four]   suitcases (big.FPL)
            'We will load [many/four] (big) suitcases.'

        e.   *na'amis*   *mizvadat*   *or*   *(gdola).*
            load.FUT1PL   suitcase.CS   leather   (big.FSG)
            'We will load a (big) leather suitcase.'

(4)   a.   *na'amis*   *(et ha.mit'an)*   *mizvada*   *mizvada.*   [=2a]
            load.FUT1PL   OM DF.cargo   suitcase   suitcase
            'We will load (the cargo) suitcase by suitcase.'

        b.   **na'amis*   *(et)*   *[ha.mizvada ha.mizvada/ha.mizvada mizvada].*
            load.FUT1PL   (OM)   [DF.suitcase   DF.suitcase/DF.suitcase   suitcase]

        c.   **na'amis*   *[mizvada gdola*   *mizvada gdola/mizvada*
            load.FUT1PL   [suitcase   big.FSG   suitcase   big.FSG/suitcase
            mizvada gdola/gdolot].
            suitcase   big.FSG/big.FPL]

        d.   **na'amis*   *[kol/arba]*   *mizvada*   *mizvada.*
            load.FUT1PL   [every/four]   suitcase   suitcase

        e.   **na'amis*   *mizvadat*   *or*   *mizvadat*   *or.*
            load.FUT1PL   suitcase.CS   leather   suitcase.CS   leather

(5)   a.   *hictabru*   *mizvadot mizvadot.*
            accumulated.PASS.3PL   suitcases   suitcases
            '(There were) accumulated suitcases upon suitcases.'

        b.   **hictabru*   *[ha.mizvadot*
            accumulated.PASS.3PL   [DF.suitcases
            ha.mizvadot/ha.mizvadot   mizvadot].
            DF.suitcases/DF.suitcases   suitcases]

    c.   *hictabru   et
           accumulated.PASS.3PL   OM

           [ha.mizvadot ha.mizvadot/ha.mizvadot mizvadot].
           [DF.suitcases DF.suitcases/DF.suitcases suitcases]

    d.   *hictabru   [mizvadot gdolot mizvadot
           accumulated.PASS.3PL [suitcases big.FPL suitcases

           gdolot/mizvadot mizvadot gdolot].
           big.FPL/suitcases suitcases big.FPL]

    e.   *hictabru   [harbe/arba] mizvadot mizvadot.
           accumulated.PASS.3PL [many/four] suitcases suitcases

    f.   *hictabru   mizvadot or   mizvadot or.
           accumulated.PASS.3PL suitcases.CS leather suitcases.CS leather

However, despite these distributional restrictions on the NN sequence, contrastive NNs function as arguments, whereas pluralizing NNs do not. Thus, contrastive NNs are interchangeable with simple N objects in the syntactic string, allow coordination with other nouns (6a), establish referents available for zero anaphora (6b), and can serve as a reply to a referential *wh* question (6c).

(6)   a.   *kaninu   lo   matana MATANA ve.uga.*
           bought.1PL P(to)M3SG gift   gift   and.cake
           'We bought him a really good/real gift and a cake.'

     b.   *kaninu   lo   matana matana$_i$.*
           bought.1PL P(to)M3SG gift   gift

           Ø$_i$ *haxi yafa še.kibel   ba.xayim.*
           Ø$_i$ most pretty that.gotM3SG DFP(in).life
           'We bought him a really good/real gift. The best (gift) he ever got.'

     c.   A: *as ma   kanitem   lo?*   B: *matana MATANA.*
           A: so what bought.2PL P(to)M3SG   B: gift   gift
           A: 'So what did you buy him?'   B: 'A really good/real gift'

In contrast, pluralizing NNs typically function as adverbial or predicative. As illustrated in the following examples, coordination with pluralizing NNs is only possible with predicative or adverbial elements, but not with a DP (7a–c), suggesting that the entire NN construction is not nominal but adverbial in its function within the clause.

(7)   a.   *na'amis   mizvada mizvada*
           load.FUT1PL suitcase suitcase

           [ve.bi.zrizut   / *ve.argaz].   [NNsg]
           [and.P(in).speed / *and.box]
           'We will load suitcase by suitcase [and quickly/ *and a box].'

b. *kol ha.bayit   mizvadot mizvadot* [*ve.metunaf/* *ve.argaz*]. [NNpl]
   all DF.house   suitcases suitcases [and.filthy/ *and.box]
   'The whole house (is) suitcases upon suitcases [and filthy/ *and a box].'

c. *kol ha.mit'an yišalax,   mizvada_i mizvada_i*   [NNpred]
   all DF.cargo send.PASS.FUT3SG, suitcase   suitcase

   le.ya'ada_i   [*ve.bi.zrizut/*   *ve.argaz*].
   P(to).destination.POSS.FSG [and.P(in).speed/ *and.box]

   'All cargo will be sent, each suitcase to its destination [and quickly/*and a box].'

The sub-components triggered by pluralizing NNs, although individuated as distinct elements, remain non-referential and do not designate specific referents, as indicated by the inappropriateness of singular pronominal reference (8a–b). Similarly, they cannot serve as answers to referential *wh* questions, only to manner questions (8d–c).

However, pluralizing NNs bring up a collective set of entities into the discourse model, so later reference can be made to the set or parts of it (9a–c), using cardinals and ordinals, quantified nominals, and other referring expressions, including plural pronouns for some speakers.

(8) a. *gilgalnu   kadur kadur.*
       roll.PST1PL ball   ball
       'We rolled (the balls) ball by ball.'

       #*hu hitgalgel   pnima./ ?hem hitgalgelu   pnima.*
       he roll.PST3SG inside/   they roll.PST3PL inside
       'It/they rolled inside.'

    b. #*gilgalnu   kadurim, kadur kadur be.zavit   axeret.*
       roll.PST1PL ball.PL,   ball   ball   P(in).angle different
       'We rolled balls, every ball in a different angle.'

    c. A: *ma   na'amis?*   B: # *mizvada mizvada.*
       A: what load.FUT1PL   B: # suitcase suitcase
       A; 'What will we load?'   B: # 'Suitcase by suitcase'

    d. A: *eyx   na'amis?*   B: *mizvada   mizvada.*
       A: how load.FUT1PL   B: suitcase suitcase
       A; 'How will we load?'   B: 'Suitcase by suitcase'

(9) *gilgalnu   kadur kadur.*
    roll.PST1PL ball   ball
    'We rolled (the balls) ball by ball.'

    a. [*ha.rišon/ha.revi'i/ha.axaron*] *hitgalgel   pnima.*
       [DF.first/DF.fourth/DF.last]   roll.PST3SG inside
       '[The first/the fourth/the last] rolled inside.'

b. [*šnayim/rov   ha.kadurim*] *hitgalgelu   pnima.*
   [two/most   DF.balls]   roll.PST3PL inside
   '[Two/most of the balls] rolled inside.'

c. [*kulam/hem/ha.kadurim (ha.yerukim)*] *hitgalgelu   pnima.*
   [All.3PL/they/DF.balls   (DF.green.MPL)] roll.PST3PL inside
   '[All of them/they/the (green) balls] rolled inside.'

Although the object of a transitive verb is frequently left out in the presence of the pluralizing NN construction (e.g. 2a, 8, 9 above), the discussion above indicates that the NN sequence does not function as an object itself (a phenomenon which is not unique to Hebrew, cf. Fr. *Ils vont peser (les bagages) valise par valise* 'they will weigh (the luggage) suitcase by suitcase').

Semantically, contrastive NN signals prototypicality and intensification, as shown above. The other NN constructions intuitively indicate a sense of multiplication (the specific characterization in each case is discussed in detail below). In the literature, the only discussion of these pluralizing constructions concerns the typological-semantic perspective, wherein they have been classified as pluralizing/distributive, with particular focus given to reiterated cardinal numerals (Gil 1995 and references therein; Hurch 2005). However, while the labels of plurality and distributivity are indeed appropriate for many NN examples, numerals being a prototypical case, the examination of naturally-occurring data reveals a complex distribution that merits more fine-grained distinctions. This issue will be addressed in the following sections.

One central issue is the status of these constructions, whether reiteration in the NN sequences under discussion arises from a special morphological mechanism, or from the application of independently motivated syntactic operations. Several relevant factors support the latter assumption. One important fact is that reiteration in these constructions involves items inflected for number. And yet, the internal predicate in an NNpred, which is connected via coordination or a preposition, shows agreement with the individual N component rather than with the entire NN as a plural unit (see §4). These facts suggest that the Ns are still accessible for syntactic operations as separate units, whether we assume that this internal predicate operates on only one of the Ns, or that it modifies the unit composed of the NN pair, which inherits the agreement features of its components. The latter assumption is more consistent with the symmetry noted above.

Another significant factor is that the three pluralizing NN patterns are freely productive and their interpretations are systematically compositional. Evidence supporting this arises from NN sequences that are (or are becoming) lexicalized: most notably *yom yom* (lit. 'day day'), *exad exad* ('one one') and *ca'ad ca'ad* ('step step'). In a subset of their uses, these NNs seem to show a looser or more idiomatic reading that is no longer as transparently derived from their NNsg use nor carrying the expected distributive meaning (i.e. lexicalized/idiomatic *exad exad* means 'each and every one of' rather than 'one by one' like its compositional counterpart; *ca'ad ca'ad* is interpreted as 'slowly' rather than as indicating a sequence of steps like its compositional counterpart). As a result of this change of meaning, these idiomatic NNs can be used in constructions not available to the NNsg and are not interchangeable with the compositional NNsg (e.g. lexicalized *exad exad* is not interchangeable with the compositional *šnayim šnayim* 'two two', cf. (13c) below, where the compositional NNsg shows such interchangeability).

(10) a. *hem   yeladim   tovim   exad exad.*
          They children good.PL one   one
          'They (are) good children, each and every one.'

   b. **hem   yeladim   tovim   šnayim šnayim.*
          They children good.PL two   two
          'They (are) good children, two by two.'

   This doesn't make sense pragmatically

   c. *nikax   et   ze ca'ad ca'ad.*
          Take.FUT1PL OM it step step
          'We'll take it step by step.'

   d. #*nikax   et   ze šalav šalav.*
          Take.FUT1PL OM it stage stage
          'We'll take it stage by stage.'

A further illustration of the lexicalization of these forms is the adjective *yomyomi* ('daily/mundane') that is derived from *yom yom*. This isolated example attests to the unique, fully lexicalized status of *yom yom*, and underlines the fact that the systematic, productive NN constructions in Modern Hebrew are not freely available as input to derivational processes. The combination of these factors suggests that Hebrew NN constructions are not complex words but syntactic constructions. They shall be treated as such in the analysis below.

3. Singular NN (NNsg) vs. plural NN (NNpl)

3.1 Distribution and structure

The examples in (11–12) illustrate the NNsg and the NNpl patterns respectively.

NNsg

(11) a. *hu bana   et   ha.bayit levena levena.*
          He built.PST3MSG OM DF.house brick   brick
          'He built the house brick by brick.'

b. *tafru   et   ze ba.yad   xaruz xaruz.*
sewn.3PL OM it DFP(with).hand bead   bead
'They sewed it by hand, bead by bead.'

c. *nitkadem   šalav šalav.*
progress.FUT1PL stage stage
'We will progress step by step.'

d. *badaknu   laxem   et   ha.mizvadot axat axat.*
checked1PL   P(to)M2PL OM DF.suitcases one one
'We checked the suitcases$_i$ for you one$_i$ by one$_i$.'

NNpl

(12) a. *ha.kir   banui   levenim levenim.*
DF.wall built.PRS bricks   bricks
'The wall is built(PASS) bricks upon bricks.'

b. *ha.simla mekušetet xaruzim xaruzim.*
DF.dress decorated beads   beads
'The dress is decorated with beads upon beads.'

c. *hu hišlim   et   ha.proyekt šlavim šlavim.*
He completed.3MSG OM DF.project stages stages
'He completed the project in stages (upon stages).'

Several properties distinguish the two patterns:

– As evident from Examples (11–12) above, NN with singular count nouns is interpreted as distributive over the predicate. NN with plural nouns indicates the existence of a quantity of entities, typically a large quantity forming a regular or extensive pattern.

– The distributive, sequential reading associated with the NNsg pattern excludes both plurals and mass denotations (13a). The exclusion of mass denotations suggests that discreteness or individuation is necessary for this pattern. The exclusion of both mass and plurals suggests that the acceptable nouns in this pattern are indeed singular (–pl) nouns. Reiteration of collective count Ns in their singular form produces the same distributive interpretation (13b). In contrast, the spatial quantity reading associated with the NNpl pattern is only acceptable with plural nouns, including collective Ns in their plural form (14b), but excluding both singulars and mass denotations (14a). This suggests that (+pl) itself plays a role in the construction. Interestingly, cardinals are possible with both readings (13c, 14b).

(13) a. *hišxalnu   [xaruz xaruz/ *xaruzim xaruzim/ *meši meši].*
threaded.1PL [bead bead/ *beads   beads/ *silk silk]
'We threaded [bead after bead/ *beads after beads/ *silk after silk].'

b.   *ha.yeladim   avru   [zug   zug/kvuca   kvuca].*
DF.children   passed   [pair   pair/group   group]
'The children passed [one pair at a time/one group at a time].'

c.   *nivdok   laxem   et   ha.mizvadot   [štayim*
check.FUT1PL   P(to)M2PL   OM   DF.suitcases   [two

štayim/arba   arba].
two/four   four]
'We will check the suitcases for you [two/four at a time].'

(14)   a.   *ha.tik   asuy   [xaruzim   xaruzim/   *xaruz   xaruz/   *meši   meši].*
DF.bag   made   [beads   beads/   *bead   bead/   *silk   silk]
'The bag is made (of) [(lots of) beads/*bead after bead/ *(lots of) silk].'

b.   *ha.yeladim   yašvu   [zugot   zugot/kvucot   kvucot/arbaʿa   arbaʿa].*
DF.children   sat.PL   [pairs   pairs/groups   groups/four   four]
'The children sat down [in pairs/in groups/in fours].'

These NN constructions bring to mind strings with equivalent interpretations in which the two Ns are mediated by a preposition (15).

(15)   a.   *hišxalnu   xaruz   axrei   xaruz.*
threaded.1PL   bead   P(after)   bead
'We threaded bead after bead.'

b.   *ha.kir   banui   levenim   al-gabei   levenim.*
DF.wall   built.PRS   bricks   P(upon)   bricks
'The wall is built(PASS) bricks upon bricks.'

These [N P N] constructions not only have the same interpretations, but show the same restrictions with respect to quantifiers, determiners, and modification on the N.[6] Reiterative [N P N] constructions such as these are evident cross-linguistically, e.g. in Russian, English and French (see Beck & von Stechow 2006, and references therein, on pluractional adverbials, such as *piece by piece* and *dog after dog*; Braginsky & Rothstein 2008 on Russian incremental constructions [N *za* N] (N *by* N); cf. Fr. adverbial constructions like *valise par valise, joue contre joue*). All these constructions show an explicit linking element mediating between the two reiterated (or semantically related) nouns. In all these languages, as in Hebrew, the

---

6.   A related set of examples are [N P N] constructions in which the two nouns are not reiterated, but semantically related (*exad axrei ha.šeni*, lit. 'one after the second'; *akev be.cad agudal*, lit. 'heel beside toe'). Another related construction involves two prepositions, one before each N [P N P N], typically indicating a path (*mi.exad la.šeni*, lit. 'from one to the second'; *mi.cad le.cad*, 'from side to side'). Such constructions in English have been examined as examples of syntactic reduplication (see, Travis 2003; Zwarts 2009, and references therein).

nouns in adverbial [N P N] constructions cannot take determiners, quantifiers, or any type of modification, suggesting that they involve less structure than a full DP. An additional point supporting this argument is that the Ns in these constructions are not referential (e.g. *piece by piece* which evokes an indeterminate set of pieces, but the N does not refer to any specific piece vs. *(put) one piece by another piece* which involves two specific pieces).

Returning to the NN constructions under discussion, given the crucial significance of number, specifically (±pl), in these constructions, these NN structures must minimally include the number domain, assuming a compositional structure for DP/NP (cf. Borer 2005a; Cohen & Zribi-Hertz 2011). However, the impossibility of standard nominal definite marking or direct modification within the NN constructions (see 4–5 above) suggests that these constructions do not project a DP. In light of the prepositional counterparts of these constructions, I assume a functional linker (F⁰) connecting the reiterated items, similar to a preposition or a coordination marker. The combination of factors above leads me to propose the following structure.

(16)

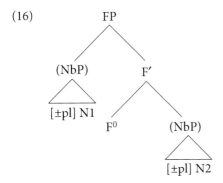

I assume the same structure for both NNsg and NNpl, wherein the two linked components must be identical, thereby ensuring the same features in both. The distinctions in interpretation are not due to the internal configuration of the NN sequence itself, and will be the topic of the next section.[7]

---

7.   Schang (this volume) proposes a similar structure for reiterated sequences in São Tomense, which he analyzes as exhibiting coordination with a silent coordinator. Although this structure is also similar to the structures proposed for contrastive reiteration in Haitian (Glaude & Zribi-Hertz, this volume) and São Tomense (Schang, this volume), it must be recalled that contrastive reiteration involves modification of one reiterated item by another, therefore the relation is inherently asymmetrical, whereas the reiterated NNs in the Hebrew patterns under discussion are balanced, indicating a symmetrical relationship comparable to coordination.

The incorporation of cardinals into this structure is an interesting issue. In the NN constructions, cardinals are as limited as any other N, and cannot occur with definite *ha-* or any other modifier, nor can they quantify another N in the reiterated structure. Consequently, cardinals too must reiterate at a level lower than NP. The only difference in behavior between cardinals and other NNs is their compatibility with both NNsg and NNpl interpretations (including the singular *exad* ('one')). Given the crucial importance of number specification (±pl) in these constructions, this is a significant difference. At this stage, this issue must remain an open question.

3.2   Number, pluractionality and Aktionsart

A significant difference in the distribution of NNsg and NNpl is the type of predicates they combine with.

– The NNsg occurs with both telic and atelic predicates (11a, 11c above), but cannot occur with non-dynamic predicates, as illustrated by the ungrammatical (14a, 17a).
– In contrast, the NNpl does not get a dynamic reading. As the examples above show, it is most frequently found with statives and can combine with a dynamic predicate only as a resultative, or as a property of one of the participants. The incompatibility of the NNpl with dynamic predicates is illustrated by the ungrammatical (13a, 17b).

(17)   a.   *ha.kir   banui   levena   levena.
             DF.wall   built.PRS   brick   brick
             'The wall is built brick by brick.' (stative)

       b.   *nivdok   laxem   mizvadot   mizvadot.
             check.FUT1PL   P(to)M2PL   suitcases   suitcases
             'We will check suitcases upon suitcases for you.'

This distinction is highlighted in (18–19). The dynamic predicate in (18) can be combined with both NNsg and NNpl, but their interpretation is crucially different. The NNsg in (18a) modifies the process of cutting ('circle by circle'), while the NNpl in (18b) is resultative, indicating the state of the carrot after cutting.

(18)   a.   lekalef   et   ha.gezer   ve.laxtox   oto   igul   igul.
             peel.INF   OM   DF.carrot   and.cut.INF   OM.3MSG   circle   circle
             'To peel the carrot and cut it circle by circle.'

       b.   lekalef   et   ha.gezer   ve.laxtox   oto   igulim   igulim.
             peel.INF   OM   DF.carrot   and.cut.INF   OM.3MSG   circles   circles
             'To peel the carrot and cut it into circles.'

The predicate in (19a) is ambiguous between a dynamic and a stative reading. However, the NNsg renders it unambiguous, and the sentence in (19b) can only have the dynamic reading. The NNpl version in (19c) is equally unambiguous, this time forcing the stative reading.

(19)   a.   *ha.sefer   meturgam.*
            DF.book   translated.PRS
            'The book is translated/is being translated.'

       b.   *ha.sefer   meturgam   perek   perek.*
            DF.book   translated.PRS   chapter   chapter
            'The book is (being) translated chapter by chapter.'

       c.   *ha.sefer   meturgam   prakim   prakim.*
            DF.book   translated.PRS   chapters   chapters
            'The book is translated(PASS) in chapters.'

It should be noted that for some speakers, this correlation is not as clear-cut. These speakers accept a dynamic interpretation with the NNpl, particularly in resultative examples such as (17b, 18b, 19c), possibly affected by the presence of both dynamic and stative elements in the predicate. In rarer cases, a stative reading of an NNsg is accepted (e.g. 14a). This appears to stem from the inherent ambiguity of present *benoni* forms between the dynamic and passive readings (as noted in the discussion on Example 19). While passive forms such as *banui* in (17a) are not typically interpreted as ambiguous, they seem to marginally get a dynamic reading for some speakers. However, even speakers who accept the NNsg in constructions such as (17a), find it unacceptable in a non-verbal construction that enhances the stative reading, as in (20).

(20)   **ha.kir   kulo   levena   levena*
        DF.wall   all.POSS   brick   brick
        'The wall is all (made of) brick by brick.'

The incompatibility of the NNsg with the unambiguously stative non-verbal construction in (20) suggests that it is only acceptable in (17a) if interpreted as dynamic rather than as a stative. Thus, both constructions which allow a convergence of NNsg and NNpl are constructions in which the dynamic/stative distinction is less clear to begin with.

As shown in (18, 19) above, the NNsg provides a dynamic distributive reading that is directly triggered by the addition of the NNsg. This process conforms with the definition of a pluractional marker (in Newman's 1990 terminology and henceforth). While it is not, of course, a morphological marking of the verb, NNsg modifies the predicate in a similar way, dividing a process into multiple sub-phases indicated by the reiterated noun. As shown above, the NNsg can occur with both atelic and telic predicates, but in the latter, it systematically modifies only the process phase, and never the culmination or the combined sequence.

Newman (1990) argues that pluractionality distributes over times, places, or participants. NNsg shows temporal distribution, giving a sequential reading (as in 21a, 11); this is by far the most predominant use of the NNsg. Distribution over participants is exemplified in (21b). Locative distribution is evident in (21c), but, significantly, co-occurs with the temporal dimension. Spatial distribution does not appear to occur in isolation with this construction.

(21)   a.   *tizreku*   *kadur kadur.*
              throw.FUT.2PL ball   ball
              'Throw one ball at a time.'

        b.   *ha.yeladim$_i$ banu*   *ohalim* [*šnayim$_i$ šnayim$_i$/exad$_i$ exad$_j$*].
              DF.children   built.3PL tents   [two   two/one   one]
              'The children built tents [two by two/one by one].' (=tents or children per tent)

        c.   *nesader*   *xeder xeder.*
              tidy.FUT.1PL room   room
              'We will tidy room by room.'

The NNpl indicates a stative cumulative property of a participant in an event, typically a theme, specifying that it consists of, or is characterized by, multiple subparts of the same type, which form a pattern. I suggest that the NNpl modifies stative phases of an event (whether this is the sole phase or a result/culmination phase as in accomplishments).

The nature of the correlation of singular nouns with processes and plural nouns with states raises an interesting question.[8] All these elements, singulars and plurals, processes and states, have been extensively discussed in the linguistic literature, particularly from a semantic perspective (e.g. Landman 2000; Rothstein 2004, 2010, and references therein). An interesting line of inquiry in explaining the correlation evident in Hebrew NN constructions is the notion of divisibility, which is an essential prerequisite for distributivity. The NNsg is divisible into individual components (atomized, in the sense of Rothstein 2004), and

---

8.   The correlation between distributivity and number is not unique to Hebrew, of course. Gil (1995: 328) notes a similar cross-linguistic correlation with respect to universal quantifiers. He notes that if a distributive universal quantifier and its simple counterpart are associated, in a certain construction, with different number morphology (whether marked on a head noun, a verb, or on the quantifier itself, if it shows agreement), then the distributive universal quantifier is associated with singular morphology and the non-distributive universal quantifier with plural morphology.

therefore naturally denotes a quantity of individual elements. A plural NN, on the other hand, is inherently divisible into plural components, but specific individuals within this collective set are not directly accessible (although their existence within this set is evident). Processes and activities have been defined as containing internal phases or stages; states, on the other hand, are homogeneous and do not have stages. A state does not have distinguishable phases in the temporal domain, whereas a process progresses in the temporal domain.

The combination of these properties may provide the answer to the NN correlation (summarized in Table 1). The divisible, atomized NNsg is incompatible with the atemporal, non-atomized state, and easily complements the individuatable phases of a process. The same properties of the process render it incompatible with the cumulative, non-atomized NNpl, which complements the atemporal, non-atomized state.

Table 1. Number correlation with predicates based on divisibility (atomization)

	+atomized	–atomized
Noun	singulars	plural
Predicate	process	state

The existence or absence of distinguishable phases in the temporal domain of the predicate highlights the differences in temporal/locative distributivity with reiterated nouns – the tendency of the NNsg to distribute over the temporal domain (the sequential reading), while the NNpl lacks the temporal distribution entirely and predominantly tends to display locative distributivity (the pattern reading), showing multiple sub-components in space.

A similar distinction between dynamic and stative readings is needed for non-reiterative adverbials, as in *the books were stacked quickly/elegantly*. Consequently, I propose that in both NN types, the reiteration unit FP (see 16) combines with the predicate on par with other adverbial structures, as illustrated in (22).

(22)

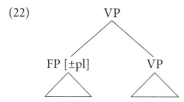

The semantic interpretations of the NNsg and NNpl, that is, the signaling of distributivity (sequential or over individuals) or cumulativity respectively, are consistent even when they are used in isolation without a predicate. This consistency indicates that the difference is indeed encoded in the internal structure of the NN construction and does not stem solely from its realization in a specific predicate. Consequently, the resultant interpretation in a sentence does not stem from the properties of the predicate in itself, but from an interaction of the number properties of the NN construction with the predicative properties. To capture this fact, I will assume that the (number) features of the N component percolate up to the FP.

4. Predicative NN (NNpred)

The third pattern to be distinguished here consists of an NN sequence which includes further predication or modification (and is therefore provisionally labelled 'Predicative NN'), as illustrated in (23–25). The predication is non-verbal, and may be joined with a preposition (e.g. *bi.mkoma* 'in its place' in 23a; see also 23c, 24a, 25a) or coordination[9] (e.g. *ve.kšayav* 'and its difficulties' in 23b; see also 25b), but may also be asyndetic, showing no explicit connector (e.g. *šaxor ve.lavan* 'black and white' in 24b). The predicate typically shows agreement in number and gender with the N component, and is frequently marked as possessive, indexed with the N component.

(23) a. *ha.bniya   mukpedet,   levena$_i$ levena$_i$ bi.mkoma$_i$.*
          DF.construction   meticulous,   brick.F   brick.F   P(in).place.POSS.FSG
          'The construction is meticulous, every brick in its place.'

      b. *hitkadamnu   le'at,   šalav$_i$ šalav$_i$ ve.kšayav$_i$.*
          progressed.1PL slowly,   stage.M   stage.M   and.difficulties.POSS.MSG
          'We progressed slowly, each step and its difficulties.'

      c. *ha.cevet   hitpazer   ba.zira,   iš$_i$ iš$_i$ le.mesimato$_i$.*
          DF.team   dispersed   DFP(in).arena,   man   man   P(to).task.POSS.MSG
          'The team dispersed in the arena, each to his task.'

(24) a. *ha.vilon   asuy   xaruzim   xaruzim   mi.sugim   šonim.*
          DF.curtain   made   beads   beads   P(of).kinds   different.MPL
          'The curtain is made of (many) beads of different kinds.'

---

9. The Hebrew coordination marker *ve-* appears in various non-prototypical coordination constructions, connecting non-parallel elements, such as conjoining a predicative or attributive element to a nominal or to a clause, e.g. *kol adam* **ve.pxadav** ('every man **and his own fears**'); *haya corex le-kabel haxlatot goraliyot,* **ve.maher** ('It was necessary to make crucial decisions, **and quickly**'); for discussion of the latter type, see Meir (2008).

b. *zebrot   ba.teva,   pasim   pasim,   šaxor ve.lavan.*
zebras DEP(in).nature, stripes stripes, black and.white
'Zebras in nature, stripe upon stripe, black and white.'

c. *ha.sefer   meturgam   garu'a,   prakim   prakim*
DF.book translated.PRS badly,   chapters chapters

be.signonot šonim.
P(in).styles different.MPL
'The book is badly translated, every chapter in a different style.'

(25) a. *ha.xavilot   muxanot   le.mišlo'ax,*
DF.parcels ready.FPL P(for).delivery

kafe$_i$ kafe$_i$ be.arizato$_i$ ha.mekorit.
coffee coffee P(in).packaging.POSS.MSG DF.original
'The parcels are ready for delivery, each coffee in its original packaging.'

b. *baxanu   et   ha.mivxar   be.sakranut,*
checked.1PL OM DF.selection P(with).curiosity,

orez$_i$ orez$_i$ ve.nixoxo$_i$.
rice   rice   and.scent.POSS.MSG
'We examined the selection curiously, each rice and its own scent.'

The internal predicate in these constructions can be found as the sole predicate of a standard DP argument in an independent clause (given that Hebrew allows non-verbal clauses, e.g. *kol šalav$_i$ ve.kšayav$_i$* 'every stage coord. difficulties.POSS'). However, the NN sequence cannot function as a subject of such a predication in an independent clause. This aspect certainly requires further investigation.

Aside from the secondary predication issue, the NNpred is not subject to the same restrictions as the NNpl and NNsg, and differs from them in three respects: the nouns it takes, its distribution, and its interpretation.

– NNpred is open to both singular and plural nouns, and is also possible with mass denotations.
– NNpred is acceptable with both dynamic predicates (23b, 23c) and stative predicates (24).
– NNpred does not have a pluractional effect on the predicate of the clause comparable to that of NNsg, as illustrated in (26a, 26b (cf. 11, 23)).

(26) a. **hu bana   et   ha.bayit levena$_i$*
He built.3MSG OM DF.house brick.F

levena$_i$ umekoma$_i$.   [cf. 11a, 23a]
brick.F and.place.POSS.FSG

    b.   *hitkadamnu   šalav_i   šalav_i   ve.kšayav_i.   [cf. 11c, 23b]
        progressed.1PL stage.M stage.M and.difficulties.POSS.MSG

The NNpred distributes over a collective, individuating similar sub-components and specifying the existence of a differentiating factor (progress as a collection of steps (of varying difficulties), the team as a collection of people (with distinct tasks), a translated book as a collection of chapters (differing in styles)). As shown in (23–25), this pattern may be distributing over participants, or indicating internal phases in the event itself. The internal predicate specifies the distinguishing factor. The individuating effect of the internal predicate licenses the use of mass denotations in this construction (as in 25), which is unacceptable in the other two patterns.

This combination of properties leads to the conclusion that NNpred does not modify the predicate of the clause directly. Rather, it operates on the clause level, adjoining to TP and adding a secondary predication (see (28) below). NN stands as an argument for the internal predication, thereby allowing further specification on a participant of the clause to which it adjoins (such as the progress, the book or the team in the examples above).

As noted above, the NNpred, like the other NN patterns, differs from simple nouns in not allowing the cliticized definite marker *ha-* or the object marker *et*, nor can it be directly modified by an adjective, quantifier or noun (thus it cannot form the construct state).

(27)   *kol ha.mit'an yišalax,*
       all DF.cargo send.PASS.FUT3SG,

    a.   *mizvada_i   mizvada_i le.ya'ada_i,*   [=2c]
       suitcase suitcase P(to).destination.POSS.FSG
       'all cargo will be sent, each suitcase to its destination.'

    b.   *(*ha.)mizvada (*ha.)mizvada le.ya'ada*
       DF.suitcase   DF.suitcase   P(to).destination.POSS.FSG

    c.   *mizvada (*gdola) mizvada (*gdola) le.ya'ada.*
       suitcase   big.FSG suitcase   big.FSG P(to).destination.POSS.FSG

    d.   *(*kol/ *arba) mizvada mizvada le.ya'ada.*
       every/four suitcase suitcase P(to).destination.POSS.FSG

    e.   **mizvadat   or   mizvadat   or   le.ya'ada*
       suitcase.CS leather suitcase.CS leather P(to).destination.POSS.FSG

These distributional facts suggest that the NNpred neither projects a DP nor an NP. Given the internal agreement between the internal predicate and the reiterated N, I propose a structure for the reiterated sequence itself that is essentially similar to the structure proposed above for the other two patterns (16). The NN FP projection is headed by a covert functional element and assumed to still retain the properties of the individual reiterated components, like in a coordinated structure,[10] thereby accounting for the internal agreement.[11] The FP and its predicate are linked in turn by another functional element, which can be overt, as in the case of the coordinated and prepositional predicates (23, 24a, 24c, 25), or covert (as in 24b). The NNpred adjoins to TP and serves as a secondary predication in the clause.

(28)

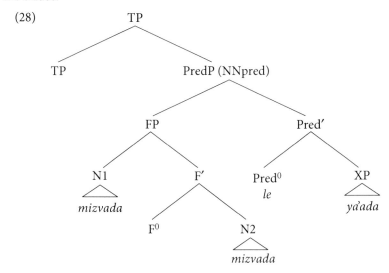

5. Conclusion

The primary goal of this paper was to examine the behavior of NN constructions, a group of phenomena in Modern Hebrew that has received little attention in the linguistic literature. I have shown that NN sequences instantiate several different

---

10.   The comparison here is with attributive or predicative coordination where the conjuncts do not refer individually, but designate properties of the same referent, such as the [DP+DP] *every man and his own fears* or the [N+N] *friend and brother*, in *you have been a friend and brother to me*. This should be distinguished from referential coordination, where each DP denotes a distinct referent, and the entire coordination denotes a sum of the referents mentioned.

11.   Here, too, we find related constructions that involve an explicit linker. Hebrew exhibits a distributive quantified subject that involves non-adjacent reiterated Ns, linked by an overt coordinator (*kol iš ve.iš*, lit. 'every man and man'). Gil (1995: 355) briefly compares this construction with a similar construction in Ga wherein the universal quantifier itself is positioned between the two occurrences of the noun (*nūù fɛ́ɛ́ nūù.* 'man Q man').

syntactic constructions, each triggering distinct interpretations. Contrastive NN reiteration has been distinguished from pluralizing NN reiteration.

- *Contrastive NN* can function as an argument, and indicates a prototypical or intensive token; the contrastive LL pattern is available with other categories (see 1 above).
- *Pluralizing NN* patterns function as adverbial or as secondary predicates, and indicate various types of multiplication and distributivity, that is, the division of a whole into an unspecified quantity of sub-components of the same type. Pluralizing LL is available only to nouns. In the proposed analysis, these sequences are argued to be derived in syntax rather than in morphology.

Three pluralizing NN patterns have been distinguished: NNsg, NNpl, and NNpred.

- *NNsg – distributive/pluractional*: this construction functions as an adverbial and modifies dynamic predicates. It marks an event as pluractional, indicating that the event consists of multiple sub-events distributed over a set of individuated elements, indicated by the N.
- *NNpl – cumulative*: this construction functions as an adverbial and modifies states. It marks a property of a participant of an event, indicating the participant contains or displays a (large) quantity of sub-elements, indicated by the N. Depending on the predicate, the property may be a state or a result state.

Both constructions were given a syntactic analysis that correlates the two Ns through a covert functional linking element, on par with a coordinated construction or a [N P N] construction. The resultant FP is then analyzed as an aspectual adverbial of the predicate, and the semantic effects are obtained through an interaction of the Aktionsart of the predicate and the internal features of the component nouns, particularly number.

- *NNpred – distributive*: this construction divides a collective or mass into sub-components, indicated by the N, which are distinguished through the internal predicate. This pattern is open to nouns of all types, by virtue of the individuating force of the predicate. Structurally, the NN sequence is headed by a covert functional element, like the previous patterns; the internal predicate is linked through a functional element, which can be overt, and realized as a coordination marker (see nn. 9–10) or as a preposition. The entire construction operates on the clause level, adjoining to TP and serving as a secondary predicate.

The data and the analysis proposed here shed light on some of the reiterative constructions in Modern Hebrew and contribute to our understanding of these phenomena. This topic merits further detailed study, and various issues remain open for further exploration as noted above, such as the status of cardinals, or the nature of the relation between NNpred and the main predicate it is adjoined to. Further research is also necessary to examine the structure of the various [N P N] and their relation to the NN patterns discussed here. The constructions examined above, in particular NNpred, raise another interesting question – the nature of the connection between coordination and prepositional constructions, both in predicated constructions (as in the NNpred and the constructions in nn. 9–10) and in balanced constructions (as in the [N X N] constructions cross-linguistically).

Contrastive reiteration and pluralizing NNs have been shown to have distinct properties in both distribution and function. Their reiterative nature is therefore only a spell-out property without any structural significance. This conclusion is strengthened when taking into account the variety of characteristics exhibited by other reiterative constructions mentioned above (see §2 and nn. 1–3). This range suggests that reiteration in general should not be regarded as a single linguistic phenomenon but as a spell-out property correlating distinct constructions with diverse morpho-phonological, syntactic, semantic and discursive properties.

Finally, the notion of iconicity has long been associated with reduplication, reducing reiterative phenomena to simple strategies, the semantic effects of which are taken as self-evident (see, a.o., Sapir 1921; Kouwenberg 2003), and this despite the variety of semantic and structural patterns exhibited cross-linguistically (for discussion see, Aboh, Smith & Zribi-Hertz, this volume). As the iconicity perspective highlights specific semantic effects, it may obscure finer distinctions between constructions showing such effects, or intricacies within a specific reiterative construction. Furthermore, this approach overlooks parallels between reiterative (so-called iconic) and non-reiterative (non-iconic) constructions. The structures presented here demonstrate such complexity. Although seemingly iconic, they exhibit a much more elaborate set of characteristics, the interactions of which are far from self-evident and not unique to reiteration. The constructions under discussion have been shown to involve complex interactions of specific number-features with the Aktionsart of the predicate they modify, producing aspectual effects as part of their interpretation. This complex interaction between number, Aktionsart, and pluractionality can be derived from syntax, using structures that are independently motivated and are not unique to reiteration.

References

Aboh, Enoch O. & Smith, Norval. 2012. The morphosyntax of non-iconic reduplications. A study in Eastern Gbe and the Surinam creoles. This volume: 27–75.

Alleesaib, Muhsina. 2008. A look at reduplicated lexemes in Mauritian Creole. Paper presented at the International Workshop on Nominal and Verbal Plurality, Paris, November, 2008.

Alleesaib, Muhsina & Zribi-Hertz, Anne. 2008. Lexical reduplication in Mauritian Creole. Paper presented at the Grammar of Reiteration Workshop, Paris, December 15, 2008.

Bakker, Peter. 2003. The absence of reduplication in Pidgins. In *Twice as Meaningful. Reduplication in Pidgins, Creoles and Other Contact Languages* [Westminster Creolistic Series 8], S. Kouwenberg (ed.), 37–46. London: Battlebridge.

Bat-El, Outi. 2006. Consonant copying and consonant identity: The segmental and prosodic structure of Hebrew reduplication. *Linguistic Inquiry* 37(2):179–210.

Beck, Sigrid & von Stechow, Arnim. 2006. Dog after dog revisited. *ZAS Papers in Linguistics* 44. ⟨http://www.zas.gwz-berlin.de/fileadmin/material/ZASPiL_Volltexte/zp44/zaspil44-beck-stechow.pdf⟩

Borer, Hagit. 2005a. *Structuring Sense*, Vol. I: *In Name Only*. Oxford: OUP.

Borer, Hagit. 2005b. *Structuring Sense*, Vol. II: *The Normal Course of Events*. Oxford: OUP.

Braginsky, Pavel & Rothstein, Susan. 2008. Vendlerian classes and the Russian aspectual system. *Journal of Slavic Linguistics* 16(1):3–55.

Cohen, Dana & Zribi-Hertz, Anne. 2008. The singular indefinite article with mass nouns: Sorting out a paradox via language comparison. Ms, University of Paris 8.

Cohen, Dana & Zribi-Hertz, Anne. 2011. On the compositional nature of the 'mass/count' distinction: Fresh evidence from language comparison. Ms, University of Paris 8.

Filip, Hana & Carlson, Gregory N. 2001. Distributivity strengthens reciprocity, collectivity weakens it. *Linguistics & Philosophy* 24(4):417–466.

Ghomeshi, Jila, Jackendoff, Ray, Rosen, Nicole & Russel, Kevin. 2004. Contrastive focus reduplication in English (The salad-salad paper). *Natural Language and Linguistic Theory* 22:307–357.

Gil, David. 1995. Universal quantifiers and distributivity. In *Quantification in Natural Language*, Emmon Bach, Eloise Jelinek, Angelika Kratzer & Barbara Partee (eds), 321–362. Dordrecht: Kluwer.

Glaude, Herby & Anne Zribi-Hertz. 2012. Verb Focus in Haitian: From lexical reiteration to Predicate Cleft. This volume: 77–134.

Graf, Dafna. 2002. A study of nominal reduplication in Modern Hebrew. *Proceedings of the 18th Meeting of the Israeli Association of Theoretical Linguistics.*

Greenberg, Yael. 2010. Event internal pluractionality in Modern Hebrew: A semantic analysis of one verbal reduplication pattern. *Brill's Annual of Afroasiatic Languages and Linguistics* 2(1):119–164.

Henri, Fabiola. 2012. Atenuative verbal reduplication in Mauritian: A morpho-semantic approach. This volume: 203–233.

Horn, Laurence R. 1993. Economy and redundancy in a dualistic model of natural language. *Yearbook of the Linguistic Association of Finland*, 33–72.

Hurch, Bernhard. 2005. *Graz Database on Reduplication*. ⟨http://reduplication.uni-graz.at./redup⟩

Inkelas, Sharon & Zoll, Cheryl. 2005. *Reduplication: Doubling in Morphology* [Cambridge Studies in Linguistics 106]. Cambridge: CUP.

Kouwenberg, Silvia (ed.). 2003a. *Twice as Meaningful: Reduplication in Pidgins, Creoles and Other Contact Languages* [Westminster Creolistic Series 8]. London: Battlebridge.

Kouwenberg, Silvia. 2003b. Introduction. In *Twice as Meaningful. Reduplication in Pidgins, Creoles and Other Contact Languages*, S. Kouwenberg (ed.), 1–6. London: Battlebridge.

Kouwenberg, Silvia & LaCharité, Darlene. 2003. The meanings of 'more of the same'. Iconicity in reduplication and the evidence for substrate transfer in the genesis of Caribbean Creole languages. In *Twice as Meaningful, Reduplication in Pidgins, Creoles and Other Contact Languages* [Westminster Creolistic Series 8], S. Kouwenberg (ed.), 7–18. London: Battlebridge.

Landau, Idan. 2006. Chain resolution in Hebrew V(P)-fronting. *Syntax* 9(1): 32–66.

Landman, Fred. 2000. *Events and Plurality: The Jerusalem Lectures*. Dordrecht: Kluwer.

Lasersohn, Peter. 1995. *Plurality, Conjunction and Events*. Dordrecht: Kluwer.

Meir, Irit. 2008. Sentence-phrase coordination in Hebrew and the syntax–pragmatics interface. *Studies in Language* 32(1): 1–21.

Mittwoch, Anita. 1998. Cognate objects as reflections of Davidsonian event arguments. In *Events and Grammar*, Susan Rothstein (ed.), 309–332. Dordrecht: Kluwer.

Newman, Paul. 1990. *Nominal and Verbal Plurality in Chadic*. Dordrecht: Foris.

Pereltsvaig, Asya. 2002. Cognate objects in Modern and Biblical Hebrew. In *Themes and Issues in Arabic and Hebrew Syntax*, Jamal Ouhalla & Ur Shlonsky (eds), 107–136. Dordrecht: Kluwer.

Rothstein, Susan. 2004. *Structuring Events: A Study in the Semantics of Lexical Aspect*. Oxford: Blackwell.

Rothstein, Susan. 2010. Counting and the mass count distinction. *Journal of Semantics* 27(3): 343–397.

Sapir, Boaz. 1921. *Language. An Introduction to the Study of Speech*. New York NY: Dover.

Schang, Emmanuel. 2012. Reduplication in São Tomense: Issues at the syntax-semantics interface. This volume: 235–250.

Tovena, Lucia & Kihm, Alain. 2008. Event internal pluractional verbs in some romance languages. In *Recherches Linguistiques de Vincennes* 37: 9–30. In *Aspect et pluralité d'événements*, Tovena Lucia (ed.).

Travis, Lisa. 2003. Reduplication feeding syntactic movement. *2003 CLA Proceedings*, 236–247.

Yatziv, Il-Il & Livnat, Zohar. 2007. Self repetition in spoken monologue discourse. *Proceedings of the 20–22 Meetings of the Israeli Linguistic Society*, Vol. 16. ⟨http://www.biu.ac.il/JS/hb/ils/yatziv_livnat2007.pdf⟩

Yatziv-Malibert, Il-Il. 2002. Méthodologies pour la description de quelques phénomènes syntaxiques de langue parlée: Application à l'hébreu moderne. Ph.D. dissertation, École Pratique des Hautes Études Sciences historiques et philologiques, Paris.

Zwarts, Joost. 2009. Plurality and reduplication in the from-N-to-N construction(s). Paper presented at the Grammar of Reiteration workshop, Amsterdam, December 17, 2009.

Attenuative verbal reduplication in Mauritian

A morpho-semantic approach

Fabiola Henri
Université Sorbonne Nouvelle, Paris 3 & LLF, UMR 7110

This paper presents an aspect of the grammar of Mauritian, a French-based Creole, called 'Attenuative Reduplication' (AR). AR is not specific to Mauritian since it can be found in other Creoles, and in languages like Mandarin Chinese, Setswana and Malagasy to cite but a few. The properties of reduplicated constructions has been the topic of extensive research and have for the most been characterized as iconic (Sapir 1921). *No!* Kouwenberg & LaCharité argue that the Iconicity principle can somehow be extended to AR although they do not seem, at first glance, to fit the generalization. However, data from Mauritian show that AR is not necessarily *who says it must be?* iconic nor pluractional. I argue that AR is a lexical formation process and that the interpretations available with AR are dependent on the aspectual properties of the predicate. The analysis, couched within a constraint-based grammar, can be extended not only to other lexical categories but also to other languages where the phenomenon is available.

1. Introduction

Research in theoretical linguistics has often focused on linguistic doubling which covers various sub-phenomena including iteration, triplication, predicate doubling, and so forth. As illustrated by the following Mauritian examples linguistic doubling is fascinating in many respects. Structurally, it may involve different modules of grammar: phonology, where the reduplicant satisfies a templatic requirement (1), morphology, where lexeme formation processes provide compounds (2) and syntax, where words or phrases may be duplicated (3)–(5).

(1)   *dodo,   titit/sisit,   nana.*
        'sleep', 'sit',   'eat'

(2)   *Zan   pe   sant-sant   sega.*[1]   (AR)
      John PROG sing-sing.SF sega
      'John is humming the sega.'

(3)   *Pa   tigit marse   li   'nn   marse!*   (predicate doubling)
      NEG bit   walk.LF 3SG PERF walk.LF
      'It's not a little walk that she made!'

(4)   *Zan   sante,   sante   mem.*   (iterative)
      John sing.LF   sing.LF still
      'John keeps singing.'

(5)   a.   *Mari inn   sante   pou so   mariaz.*
           Mary PERF sing.LF for POSS.3SG wedding
           'Mary has sung at her wedding.

      b.   *Li   'nn   sante   SANTE? Ou bien li   'nn   fer*
           3SG PERF sing.LF sing.LF? Or else 3SG PERF make.SF

           enn ler?   (prototype/contrastive)
           IND hour

           'She has SUNG sung? (Or was she just KILLING TIME?)'
           (= 'Has she REALLY sung?')

Crosslinguistically, the meanings expressed by reduplication cover an array of semantic spheres contrary to what has most of the time been advocated. In fact, since Sapir (1921), "reduplication" has been analyzed as expressing *iconicity*. Iconicity, which refers to repeated occurrences such as distribution, plurality, repetition and habitual activity. Under this approach, it seems that the diminution effect expressed by 'attenuative reduplication' (Baker 2003) (AR) does not fit the bill. However, Kouwenberg & LaCharité (2003) show that the attenuative/dispersive effect available with reduplication in some languages could also be derived from an iconic reading. They argue that "more of the same content" can both be interpreted as continuous and discontinuous; the latter interpretation being a cover term for augmentative and distributive readings as well as the dispersive reading. Their analysis is actually very similar to the notion of 'pluractionality' as described by Tovena & Kihm (2008). The latter argue that Italian and French verbs like *fumacchiare* and *mordiller* are plural events occurring at the internal level.

[handwritten: We say that diminutivity could derive from iconic disper readings, not that they are iconic]

---

1.   Abbreviations used in the Mauritian glosses: COMP = complementizer; DEF = definite determiner; DEM = demonstrative; IND = indefinite determiner; IRR = irrealis; PROG = progressive marker; LF = long form (verbs); NEG = negation; PERF = perfective; PL = plural; POSS = possessive; PST = past (tense); SF = short form (verbs); SG = singular; STR = strong form (pronouns); WF = weak form (pronouns); 1, 2, 3: first, second, third person.

Based on data from Mauritian, I show that AR, which will be argued to be a morphological process, provides complex semantic interpretations correlated with the event type of the predicate. The assumption that AR is a morphological phenomenon is supported by the fact that its morphosyntactic properties differ from those of iteration or contrastive reduplication (Ghomeshi et al. 2004) and do not show any templatic constraints. The paper focuses on Mauritian reduplicated verbs but the analysis may be extended to other lexical categories. I also argue that although the extended definition of iconicity (Kouwenberg & LaCharité 2003) can account for most readings of Mauritian reduplicated forms, it does not fully account for the data. The analysis proposed here, couched within a non-derivational signed-based framework, SBCG (Sag 2010), has the advantage of providing a unified morphophonological analysis of Mauritian simplex verbs together with their reduplicative forms. And because it exhibits complex morphology despite its tiny paradigms, Mauritian inflection provides interesting evidence supporting an abstractive ('word-based') view of morphology.

2. Empirical background

2.1 Paradigm structure

Mauritian verbs show an interesting verb form alternation which probably stems from the convergence of factors such as SLA and the recognition of prominent verb forms from the French inflectional system, in particular from the 1st conjugation group. Veenstra (2004) argues that they derive, historically, from the French infinitive or past participle, and the present singular. However, the French variety spoken at the creolization period suggests that they more probably were infinitival loans (Bonami et al. 2011). On this assumption, Mauritian has innovated in distinguishing between two forms: the long and short forms (henceforth LF and SF). This is illustrated by the sample of verbal patterns available in the language (Bonami & Henri 2010).

Table 1. Sample of Mauritian verbal patterns

LF	brize	brije	vɑ̃de	amɑ̃de	kɔ̃siste	egziste	fini	vini	print	debute
SF	briz	brij	van	amɑ̃d	kɔ̃siste	egzis	fini	vin	print	debut
INF.	brize	brije	vɑ̃dʁ	amɑ̃de	kɔ̃siste	ɛgziste	finiʁ	vɔniʁ	*eng.*	*adj.*
PPE.	brize	brije	vɑ̃dy	amɑ̃de	kɔ̃siste	ɛgziste	fini	vɔny	*eng.*	*adj.*
TRANS.	'break'	'glow'	'sell'	'amend'	'consist'	'exist'	'finish'	'come'	'print'	'stand'

(6) a. *Zan   manze   toulezour.*
John   eat.ʟꜰ   every.day
'John eats every day.'

   b. *Zan manz kari.*
      John eat.SF curry
      'John eats curry.'

However, unlike French, Mauritian does not show inflection with respect to Tense, Mode and Aspect, or to number, gender and person.

(7) a. *Mo/to/li/nou/zot   manz kari.*
       1SG.WF/2SG.WF/3SG/1PL/2-3PL eat.SF curry
       'I/you/he/she/they eat(s) curry.'

     b. *Mari/Zan manz kari.*
       Mary/John eat.SF curry
       'Mary/John eats curry.'

     c. *Mo ti manz kari.*
       1SG PST eat.SF curry
       'I ate curry.'

     d. *Mo pou manz kari.*
       1SG IRR eat.SF curry
       'I will eat curry.'

Corne (1982) and Seuren (1990) argue that the LF/SF alternation is a phonological phenomenon. Corne (1982)'s system, for instance, is concerned with two major issues: the phonological patterning, and the LF/SF alternation, excluding non-alternating verbs. He argues that for a given LF pattern, the SF is derivable. As shown in Henri (2010), Corne's (1982) phonological rules do not properly account for 'undecidables' such as *briye* or *demande* vs *amande* the SF is not always predictable. This unpredictability supports the idea that the distinction between LF and SF is not a phonological but rather a morphological phenomenon. As illustrated in Table 2, neither form is predictable from the other (Henri 2010; Bonami & Henri 2010).

Table 2. Orientation and predictability

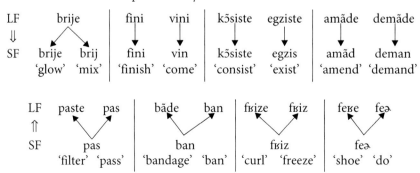

While verbs with a LF ending in -*e* tend to drop the final vowel when it is preceded by a single consonant, -*e* never drops after a branching onset. However, both situations are found when the penultimate syllable of the verb has a non-empty coda (*konsiste* vs. *egziste*), or when the single consonant is a glide (*briye* 'mix' vs. *briye* 'glow'). Almost all verbs with a LF ending in -*i* are syncretic, but there are two exceptions (*sorti* and *vini*), which are not phonologically distinguishable from syncretic verbs (*parti* and *fini*). Only verbs with a final consonant in the LF are uniformly syncretic. On the other hand, verbs with a vowel-final SF are always syncretic. Verbs with a consonant-final SF may have a syncretic LF, a LF in -*e* or a LF in -*i*: *brize* vs *friz*, *arete* vs *aparet*, *mine* vs *vini*, *porte* vs *sorti*. As will be shown, the phenomenon of AR together with the distribution of the two forms further supports a morphological analysis of verb form alternation in Mauritian.

2.2 Distribution

If the verb form is not correlated with inflection as is the case with French verbs, the question is what is it correlated with? It seems that the status of the complements of the verb determines the alternation. But more interestingly, the two forms show a morphomic distribution (Aronoff 1994), viz. they appear in contexts that do not form a natural class (Henri & Abeillé 2008; Henri et al. 2008; Henri 2010).

2.2.1 Syntax

Zribi-Hertz & Li Pook Tan (1987) and Henri & Abeillé (2008), among others, discuss the syntactic distribution of LF and SF. Verb form is sensitive to argument structure: The SF is used only when the verb is immediately followed by a non-clausal complement (8).

(8) a. *Mo ti manz/*manze kari.*
1SG PST eat.SF/LF curry
'I ate curry.'

b. *Sa stati la dat/*date depi lepok lager.*
DEM statue DEF date.SF/LF from period war
'This statue dates from the war period.'

Predicative APs (9a) and locative goals (9b) as well as postverbal arguments of unaccusative verbs count as complements (10), thus triggering the SF of the verb.

(9) a. *Nou res/*reste malad.*
1PL stay.SF/LF sick
'We remain sick.'

b. *Li pe mars lor disab.*
3SG PROG walk.SF on sand
'He is walking towards the sand.'

(10)   *Inn   ariv/*arrive   enn   aksidan.*
       PERF arrive.SF/LF IND accident
       'There has been an accident.'

Verbs with a clausal complement surface as SF, only if another non-clausal complement precedes them (11).

(11)   *Mari   inn   demann/*demande* [*ar   tou   dimounn*] [*kiler   la*]
       Mary PERF ask.SF/LF   with all people   what.time DEF
       'Mari asked everyone what time it was.'

Conversely, LF occurs if the verb is clause final (12a). It also occurs with an extracted complement (12b), with a clausal complement (12c), or when followed by an adjunct (13).

(12)   a.   *Mo   ti   manze/*manz.*
            1SG PST eat.LF/SF
            'I ate.'

       b.   *Tibaba   ki   mo   mama   ti   veye/*vey   toule   zour.*
            little.baby COMP POSS.1SG mother PST look.after.LF/SF every day
            'It's little babies that my mother looked after every day.'

       c.   *Mari   inn   demande/*demann* [*kiler   la*]   [*ar   tou   dimounn*]
            Mary PERF ask.LF/SF   what.time DEF   with all people
            'Mari asked everyone what time it was.'

(13)   *Li   pe   marse   lor disab.*
       3SG PROG walk.LF on sand
       'He is walking on the sand.'

One could argue that the occurrence of the SF is linked to object-drop, which could support the assumption that the LF/SF alternation is phonologically conditioned. However, a complement that is not adjacent to the verb still triggers the SF (14), and, as shown in the next section, the LF may occur with an *in situ* object in specific dialogical contexts.

(14)   *Nou   res/*reste   toultan   malad.*
       1PL stay.SF/LF always sick
       'We always remain sick.'

2.2.2   *Discourse*
Interestingly, the LF may appear with a nonclausal complement under certain discursive conditions, precisely in counter-oriented moves (deferments, counter- implicative and counter-propositional moves) (9b). In such contexts, the LF may be analyzed as an exponent of Verum Focus (Henri et al. 2008; Henri 2010).

(15) *Mo ti krwar Mari pa MANZE/*MANZ kari poul!*
       1SG PST think Mary NEG eat.LF/SF   curry chicken
       'I thought Mary DIDN'T eat chicken curry!'

And as shown in Section 3.2.1 despite this tiny paradigm, Mauritian makes use of both forms in morphological processes in an unexpected way but which typologically is interesting.

3. Identifying morphological reduplication

The forms introduced in the previous sections are both used in reduplicated constructions, morphological or syntactic. A first claim of this paper is that the example illustrated in (2) above, repeated here for ease of reading, is a case of lexeme formation, and must be derived in morphology rather than in syntax. Although the constraints on verb form alternation mentioned above suggest that in such constructions the form of the reduplicant could be syntactically motivated, I will argue that reiteration in (16) shows morphological properties rather than syntactic properties.

(16) *Zan pe   sant-sant   sega.*
       John PROG sing-sing.SF sega
       'John is humming the sega.'

A clear contrast between two types of syntactic reduplication and AR is provided in order to support this analysis. Mauritian shows indeed two types of syntactic iteration, namely repetition and contrastive reduplication which have properties differing from those of AR.

3.1 Syntactic reduplication

Iteration is probably a cross-linguistic phenomenon where predicative elements such as verbs, adjectives or nouns are repeated. In such cases, a durative (17b), a cumulative (17c), or a pluractional (17a) reading may arise.

(17) a. *Zan nek sant   sega, sant   sega enn lazourne.*
          John just sing.SF sega sing.SF sega IND day
          'John just keeps singing the sega all day.'

      b. *Mo 'nn get   sa po fler   la tonbe, tonbe, tonbe*
          1SG PERF watch.SF DEM pot flower DEF fall.LF fall.LF fall.LF

          depi lao.
          from upstairs
          'I have watched this flower pot fall, fall, fall from upstairs.'

c. *Mari anvi dormi, dormi, dormi.*
Mary want.SF sleep.LF sleep.LF sleep.LF
'Mary wants to sleep, sleep and sleep.'

The syntactic nature of such iterations is supported by the fact that they exhibit properties of simple verbs. For instance both the copy and its base can be coordinated (18). When clause final, they surface as LF (17b), and when followed by a non-clausal complement, as SF (17a).

(18) *Li sante (ek) sante (ek) sante.*
3SG sing.LF (and) sing.LF (and) sing.LF
Lit. 'He keeps singing (and) singing (and) singing.'

But more importantly, the copy and its base always surface in the same form. If the base is SF, the copy is also SF and if the base is LF then the copy is obligatorily LF. Moreover iteration is not limited to duplication (17c).

Contrastive reduplication (CR), on the other hand, is restricted to a prototypical or an intensive reading (19). As Ghomeshi et al. (2004: 311) observe, CR is used as one way to clarify possibly ambiguous or vague interpretations by specifying a prototypical denotation of the lexical item. This is possible due to the set of denotations paired with the prototypical element.

(19) *Zan kontan sante SANTE.*
John like.SF sing.LF sing.LF
'John likes to REALLY sing.'

CR is similar to contrastive focus, which signals that a word is being contrasted with a set of alternatives. But in the case of CR, one meaning of a word is contrasted with other possible meanings. CR in Mauritian contrasts with its English homologue in two respects (see also Cohen on Modern Hebrew and Glaude & Zribi-Hertz on Haitian this volume). First, while in English it is the first copy which triggers the prototypical effect, in Mauritian, it is the second. This is shown by the fact that stress falls on the second copy in Mauritian. And second, similar to Persian, CR in Mauritian is undoubtedly syntactic while in English the non-homogeneity of domain of copying does not allow us to settle the issue (cf. Ghomeshi et al. 2004: 320, who finally settle for a syntactic analysis, as do Glaude & Zribi-Hertz this volume). Unlike English, where verbs can reduplicate without their inflectional exponent, Mauritian does not allow such modifications in a CR. In fact with CR, verb form is restricted to LF even when the verb is followed by a complement. CR is thus similar to Verum Focus since the focused verb is always LF, with or without a complement. And lastly, the syntactic nature of CR is also shown by the fact that an adversative conjunct may be inserted between the two verbs (20).

(20)   *Sa   boug la   sante   me   SANTE!*
     DEM   man   DEF   sing.LF   but   sing.LF
     Lit. 'This man sings but SINGS!' (= 'He sings soooo well.')

With respect to event types, verbal CR does not seems to show any restrictions.[2]

(21)   a.   *Ou   touse   TOUSE?   Ou bien ou   'nn   TRANGLE?*
         2SG   cough.LF   cough.LF?   or   else   2SG   PERF   choke.LF
         'Did you COUGH cough? Or did you CHOKE?'

      b.   *Zan   deteste   DETESTE   pwason?   Ou bien li   kapav   manze*
         John   hate.LF   hate.LF   fish?   or   else   3SG   can.SF   eat.LF

         dan   bouyon?
         In   broth
         'Does John (really) HATE fish? Or can he eat it in broth?'

      c.   *Minis   la   inn   mor?   Li   'nn   mor   MOR   ou bien*
         minister   DEF   PERF   die.LF?   3SG   PERF   die.LF   die.LF   or   else

         li   fatige?
         3SG   tired
         'Has the Minister died? Is he DEAD dead or is he just tired?'

Iteration, on the other hand, is only possible with activity or accomplishment predicates. It is however expected, as in the case of AR, that coercion should be possible if an appropriate scale is provided. Since iteration is not the focus of this paper, I propose to leave it on the agenda for future research.

(22)   a.   **Zan   deteste,   deteste,   deteste kan   to   fer   sa*
         John   hate.LF   hate.LF   hate.LF   when   2SG.WK   do.SF   this

      b.   **Minis   la   inn   mor,   mor,   mor.*
         Minister   DEF   PERF   die.LF   die.LF   die.LF

Table 3. Basic properties of iteration and prototypical reduplication

	Conj.	N of copies	Base form	Reduplicant	Event type
Iteration	*ek* 'and'	n	SF/LF	SF/LF	activities /accomplishment
Contrastive Red.	*me* 'but'	1	LF	LF	any

---

2.   CR is also possible with other grammatical categories such as nouns (common and proper), adverbs, adjectives and prepositions with a semantic content. Like English, Mauritian does not allow functional categories in CR constructions.

3.2   Morphological reduplication

3.2.1   *Identifying the base*

Before discussing the characteristic properties of AR, it is crucial to identify the base and the reduplicant. Haspelmath (2002:24) distinguishes between pre-reduplication and post-reduplication depending on whether the reduplicant precedes or follows the base. According to this author, "the base is the element to which a morpho-phonological operation applies". Mauritian AR makes use of both the SF and the LF: the SF of a reduplicated verb is the concatenation of two tokens of the SF (23b), whereas the LF of a reduplicated verb is the concatenation of the SF with the LF (23a).

(23) a. *Zan   nek   manz-manze.*
          John   only eat-eat.LF
          'John only sort of eats.'

      b. *Zan   nek   manz-manz   gonaz.*
          John   only eat-eat.SF   junk
          'John only sort of eats junk food.'

In sum, a reduplicated verb behaves like a simplex verb with respect to SF/LF alternation and their function respectively, but only the first part of the reduplicated verb undergoes a morpho-phonological operation in the derivational process. Furthermore, for simplex verbs, LF is the form which is generally involved in lexeme formation processes: An instance of this are deverbal adjectives which are derived from the LF. Moreover, the LF is the citation form and as shown in Section 2.1, the SF may be predicted from the LF in many cases, but the reverse is not true. I therefore conclude that the base in AR is the second occurrence of the verb, i.e. the element whose form is sensitive to the syntactic context.

3.3   A lexeme formation process?

It could therefore be argued that the reduplicant surfaces as SF because it treats the base as a complement (cf. Section 2.2). However, the base cannot be analyzed as a syntactic complement of the reduplicant: It cannot be a VP complement, since reduplication is also allowed by verbs which do not take VP complements. For instance, verbs like *manze* or *sante* are neither raising nor control verbs but can both undergo AR (Henri 2010). If they are not restructuring verbs, the base cannot be a complement. A second argument is provided by the behavior of modal verbs, which are analyzed as special types of raising verbs. These verbs their VP complement to be marked by aspectual markers *pe* and *inn* (24a) or to be modified by adverbs (24b). But in the case of AR, the base can neither be marked by aspectual markers nor modified by adverbs (25a–c).

(24) a. *Zan   ti   paret   pe   sante.*
           John PST seem.SF PROG sing.LF
           'John seemed to be singing.'

      b. *Zan   ti   paret   touzour pe   sante.*
           John PST seem.SF always   PROG sing.LF
           'John seemed to be always singing.'

(25) a. **Zan   sant   toultan sante.*
           John sing.SF always sing.LF

      b. **Zan   sant   souvan sante.*
           John sing.SF often   sing.LF

      c. **Pol   ti   manz pe   manz poul.*
           Paul PST eat.SF PROG eat.SF chicken

Moreover, the base and the reduplicant cannot be coordinated as witnessed by the following example.

(26) **Mari manz ek   manze.*
        Mary eat.SF and eat.LF

Reduplication occurring in languages like Sanskrit can be explained phonologically. However, in the case of Mauritian AR, the reduplicant is not phonologically predictable, but is always the SF. And as illustrated in Table 4, there are no restrictions with respect to syllable structure.

Table 4. Syllable structure of reduplicated verbs

Regular verb	Reduplicated verb	Syllable structure
Reste	res-reste	CVC-CVCCV
Manze	manz-manze	CVC-CVCV
Balie	balie-balie	CVCVV-CVCVV
amene	amenn-amene	VCVC-VCVCV
Pak	pak-pak	CVC-CVC
zwe-zwe	zwe-zwe	CCV-CCV

Another property, which distinguishes syntactic reduplication, i.e. iteration and CR, from morphological reduplication, is stress. With syntactic reduplication every occurrence of the verb is stressed on its last syllable. Contrastively, AR shows word stress only on the last syllable of the base. This means that AR behaves like simplex verbs or generally as morphological words with respect to stress.

(27) a. *Li   nek sant-santé.*
          '(S)he only sort of sings.'

    b.   *Li   santé,   santé,   santé.*
        '(S)he is singing, singing, singing.'

    c.   **Li nek sánt-santé.*

3.4   Basic properties

Reduplicated verbs behave like simplex verbs with respect to iteration or coordination. But more importantly, they exhibit the LF/SF alternation with respect to argument structure. They surface as SF when followed by a non-clausal complement (23b), and as LF with no complement (23a), an extracted (29a) or clausal complement (29b), or when followed by an adjunct (30b).

(28) a. *Mari pas   so   letan manz-manze, manz-manze mem.*
           Mary pass.SF POSS.3SG time eat-eat.LF   eat-eat.LF   still
           Lit. 'Mary spends her time only sort of eating, sort of eating.'

      b. *Zan sant-sante   (ek) sant-sante   (ek) sant-sante.*
           John sing-sing.LF and sing-sing.LF and sing-sing.LF
           'John is humming, humming, humming.'

(29) a. *Ki   sa   bann madam la   inn   koup-koupe?*
           what DEM PL   woman DEF PERF cut-cut.LF
           'What have these women sort of cut?'

      b. *Mo   'nn   atann-atann ki   li   vini   pou mo   ale.*
           1SG.WF PERF wait-wait.LF that 3SG come.LF for 1SG.WF go.LF
           Lit. 'I have sort of waited that he come for me to go.'

(30) a. *Li   pe   mars-marse   lor laplaz.*
           3SG PROG walk-walk.LF on beach
           'He is sort of walking on the beach.'

      b. *Li   pe   mars-mars   lor laplaz.*
           3SG PROG walk-walk.SF on beach
           'He is sort of walking on the beach.'

As with simplex verbs, reduplicated verbs are still SF even when they are non-adjacent to their complements (31).

(31) *Sa   lisyen la   mord-mord toultan sa   sofa la   so   lipye.*
      DEM dog   DEF   bite-bite.SF always DEM sofa DEF POSS.3SG leg
      'This dog always sort of eats this sofa's legs.'

Unlike with simplex verbs, however, AR is disallowed both in Verum Focus and in passives. That reduplication is not possible in Verum Focus contexts can be explained in terms of conflicting pragmatic effects. Verum Focus necessarily implies that the speaker is confident about what he believes. Reduplicated verbs, on the contrary, suggest that the event is uncertain as regards time, frequency and so on. Hence, the speaker cannot consider as true an event, which he himself cannot precisely ascertain. In a way, LF with nonclausal complements are exponents of Verum just as reduplicated forms are exponents of uncertainty. Notice here the difference between (32b) and (32c). Reduplication *is* possible in a contrastive expression but not in its LF as expected in Verum Focus contexts.

(32) a. Zan nek manz-manz poul. ('John just sort of eats chicken.')

b. *Be non. Zan pa MANZ-MANZE poul,   li   BOURE!
    but no. John NEG eat-eat.LF   chicken 3SG fill-up.LF
    'No, John doesn't SORT OF EAT chicken, he STUFFS HIMSELF.'

c. Be non. Zan pa manz-manz poul,   li   boure!
    but no. John NEG eat-eat.SF chicken 3SG fill-up.LF
    'No, John doesn't SORT OF EAT CHICKEN, he STUFFS HIMSELF.'

The impossibility of AR in passives is quite mysterious and further research should be carried out on the topic. AR is possible with only few *gagn*-passives (*get*- passives) (33a–c) and is totally ungrammatical with *ar*-passives (*by*-passives) (34a–c).

(33) a. *Tibaba la   inn   gagn   pik-pike   ar moustik.*
          baby   DEF PERF get.SF bite-bite.LF by mosquito
          'The baby got sort of bitten by mosquitoes.'

b. *?Pol inn   gagn   mord-morde ar li.*
    Paul PERF get.SF bite-bite.LF by 3SG
    'Paul got sort of bitten by him.'

c. *Pol inn   gagn   bat-bate   ar mwa.*
    Paul PERF get.SF beat-beat.LF by 1SG.STR
    'Paul got sort of beaten by me.'

(34) a. *Enn kontrater   inn   ranz-ranz   lakaz la.*
          IND contractor PERF build-build.LF house DEF
          'A contractor has sort of built the house.'

b. *Lakaz la   inn   ranz-ranze   par enn kontrakter.*
    house DEF PERF build-build.LF by IND contractor

c. *Lakaz la   inn   ranz-ranze.*
    house DEF PERF build-build.LF

3.5 A case of compounding

A compound word is defined as "a type of word structure made up of two constituents, each belonging to a lexical category" (Selkirk 1982) or as "a word which consists of two or more words" (Fabb 2001). I argue that AR is a compounding process, because each part of the resulting word corresponds to an independently attested word. AR is however a peculiar type of compounding where there is no change in category, and where recursivity is not possible. This is also true in Pichi (cf. Yakpo this volume) where true compounds differ from reduplication only by the fact that the "first component is a copy of the root". In the next section, I examine the aspectual verb types which are compatible with AR. As will be shown, AR is possible only with so-called scalar predicates (Section 4.2).

Table 5. Basic properties of iteration and constrastive reduplication

	Conj.	N of copies	Base form	Reduplicant	Event type
Iteration	*ek* 'and'	n	SF/LF	SF/LF	Activities/ accomplishment
Contrastive Red.	*me* 'but'	1	LF	LF	any(?)
Attenuative Red.		1	SF/LF	SF	scalar predicates

4. The semantics of AR

As has often been assumed with reduplicated predicates, AR may be iconic, but can have other interpretations associated with a weakening effect. These different interpretations are directly correlated to the event type of the verb. Kouwenberg & LaCharité (2003) argue that the attenuative effect observed with reduplicated constructions such as AR still instantiate iconicity. Their claim bears a strong resemblance to Tovena & Kihm's (2008) account of internal plurality, available with diminutive verbs like *mordiller* (French) and *mordicchiare* (Italian) 'nibble'. Internal plurality or pluractionality is described as a particular type of redistribution within an event. The pluractional verb *mordiller* denotes an event which can be decomposed into a plurality of phases where each phase constitutes an iteration of the event. The operation of decomposition operates on at least one participant, which as a result is also decomposed into parts. Phases are thus considered as internal events acting upon the parts of the decomposed argument, thus exhibiting the range of readings available with pluractional verbs, viz. distributivity, diminution, iteration. In the same spirit, Kouwenberg & LaCharité (2003) define the discontinuous and the dispersive readings available with reduplication in Jamaican as (a) several occurrences of the same event or object, and (b) scattered occurrences of the predicate. The diminutive reading available with such predicates can be explained by the scattered distribution, or the decomposition in Tovena & Kihm's (2008) sense. Under this view, the discontinuous and dispersive readings both meet the iconicity criterion whereby "more of the same form stands for more of the same content." (Kouwenberg & LaCharité 2003: 536).

Although, these two analyses seem very attractive, they both miss one crucial fact about AR. If we assume that we have internal phases corresponding to internal iteration or external multiplication of the simplex event, then how do we account for the fact that AR triggers, with some predicates, unaccomplished effects? Consider for instance the verb *manze* 'eat'. Reduplicated *manz-manze* in a sentence like (35a) means that 'John has not finished the chicken' as opposed to (35b) where it is understood that the chicken has been completely eaten. This is confirmed by the ungrammaticality of (35c).

(35)   a.   *Zan   ti   manz-manz enn poul.*
            John PST eat-eat.SF   IND   chicken
            'John sort of ate a chicken.'

      b.   *Zan   ti   manz enn poul.*
            John PST eat.SF IND   chicken
            'John ate a chicken.'

      c.   **Zan   inn   manz-manz enn poul   net.*
            John PERF eat-eat.SF   IND   chicken completely
            Lit. 'John sort of ate a chicken completely.'

If we had several occurrences of the same event, then we would expect the same final result as in (35b) but this is not the case. Moreover, AR does not always trigger internal plurality. Attenuation can also mean that the event is weakened but nevertheless singular (cf. Section 4.3). The meaning of AR is in fact closely linked to the aspectual properties of the predicate. In the next section, I provide a classification of event types based on traditional classifications of verbs. The classification is also meant to distinguish classes which allow for AR from those that do not.

4.1   Event types

Following Vendler (1967)'s and Moens & Steedman's (1988) classification of verbs with respect to lexical aspect (Table 6), the following generalizations can be drawn: Activity/accomplishment and semelfactive predicates reduplicate, while States and Achievements, at first glance, do not.

Table 6. Event types

	Events		States
	Atomic	Extended	
+*conseq*	ACHIEVEMENT	ACCOMPLISHMENT	*ete* 'be', *resanble* 'ressemble', *paret* 'seem', *konsiste* 'consist', *konpran* 'understand', *kontan* 'love', *kone* 'know', *reste* 'stay/ remain', …
	rekonet 'recognise', *gagn lekours* 'win a race', *arive* 'arrive/happen', *perdi* 'lose', *vini* 'come', *ale* 'go', *deboute* 'stand', …	*ranz enn lakaz* 'build a house', *manz enn samousa* 'eat a samosa', *rod enn travay* 'look for a job', *sant enn sante* 'sing a song', *zwe monopoli* 'play monopoly', …	
−*conseq*	SEMELFACTIVE	ACTIVITY	
	tape 'hit/knock', *mase* 'chew', *terne* 'sneeze', …	*manze* 'eat', *galoupe* 'run', *dormi* 'sleep', *zwe piano* 'play piano', *naze* 'swim', *koze* 'talk', …	

(36) a. *Zan   kontan   sant-sante.*
          John   like.SF   sing-sing.LF
          'John likes to sort of sing.'

      b. *Zan   kontan   sant-sant   sega.*
          John   like.SF   sing-sing.SF   sega
          'John likes to sort of sing the sega.'

      c. *Mo   'nn   dormi-dormi.*
          1SG.WF   PERF   sleep-sleep.LF
          'I have slept sporadically.'

(37) a. *#Mari   konn-kone.*
          Mary   know-know.LF

      b. **Mo   mama   res   deteste-deteste   gato   sokola.*
          POSS.1SG   mum   remain.SF   hate-hate.LF   cake   chocolate
          Intended: 'My mum keeps sporadically hating chocolate cake.'

      c. **Enn   aksidan   inn   ariv-arive.*
          IND   accident   PERF   occur-occur.LF

But the situation is far from simple. In fact, states and achievement verbs can reduplicate if, and only if, they can somehow be coerced into scalar readings. Looking back at the event types which are inherently reduplicable from those that can be coerced, and those that cannot reduplicate at all, it becomes obvious that reduplicable predicates are scalar predicates. AR, which triggers a weakened construal of the predicate, can thus be represented in terms of scales in the spirit of Kennedy & McNally's (2005) work on adjectives. The relevant scales can be of two types: (1) inherent to the predicate or (2) triggered by aspectual markers. It is the scalar nature of the predicate which triggers the different readings available with AR.

4.2   Scales

According to Kennedy & McNally (2005), a predicate can be described as in Figure 1. They argue that gradable predicates are associated with scales. Basically, gradable predicates are associated with abstract representations of measurements (degrees) formalized as points partially ordered along a dimension. Expressions like *pandan enn period* 'for a while' or *depi enn moman* 'since a while ago' provide a time scale within which a punctual event can be iterated. Scalar predicates can be of two types: Relative or absolute. Relative predicates need a contextually given standard to be evaluated. Absolute predicates come with their own conventionally fixed standard. Absolute predicates can be either *partial* or *total*. Partial predicates hold as long as a minimal degree of the property is possessed by the argument of the predicate. Total predicates hold only if the argument of the predicate possesses the highest degree of the property.

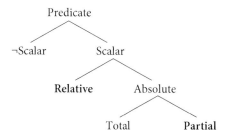

Figure 1. Predicate hierarchy

Scales are further analyzed as either closed or open. Closed scales (e.g. *full, invisible, closed*) have a minimal and a maximal element. On the other hand, open scales (e.g. *long, expensive, old, wet, pure*) lack a minimal element, a maximal element or both. Closed scalar predicates are those that can be modified by proportional modifiers. With respect to such a distinction, we expect closed scalar predicates not to reduplicate. This prediction is borne out for verbs like *deteste* 'hate' and *kontan* 'love' since they lack a minimum value. That is 'hate' and 'love' only have maximum values.

(38) *Mo   deteste-deteste   sa   tifi   la.*
      1SG hate-hate.LF   DEM girl DEF

Relative predicates can be reduplicated no matter what, whereas absolute predicates can be reduplicated only if they are partial predicates.

(39) a. *Mo   'nn   mouy-mouy latab la.*
          1SG.WF PERF wet-wet.SF   table DEF
          'I've somewhat wet the table.'

      b. #*Mo   'nn   ferm-ferm   laport la.*
          1SG.WF PERF close-close.SF door   DEF
          'I've somewhat closed the door'.

In sum, AR signals that the predicate holds of its subject to a degree inferior to the usual standard.

4.3   The meanings of 'attenuative reduplication'

With gradable predicates, AR triggers a weak-intensity effect (40a, b).

(40) a. *Mo   'nn   ennjoy-ennjoy konser la   apr   mo*
          1SG.WF PERF enjoy-enjoy.SF concert DEF then 1SG.WF

          'nn   ale.
          PERF go.LF

          'I somewhat enjoyed the concert then I left.'

    b. *Avan mo bien dekouver so zwe mo ti*
        before 1SG.WF well discover.SF POSS.3SG game 1SG.WF PST

       pe krwar-krwar li.
       PROG believe-believe.SF 3SG

       Lit. 'Until I discovered his game (= found out who he really was), I somewhat believed him.'

In (40b) the stative verb *krwar* is coerced into an activity verb by the aspectual marker *pe* and a time scale provided by the initial clause. Scales, viz. quantity scales, intensity scales, frequency scales and so forth, can be provided by aspectual markers such as the perfective *inn* or the progressive *pe*, degree modifiers or time adverbials.

    With punctual predicates, AR triggers low frequency (41a), iterative (41b) or even distributive (42) readings. In these examples, aspectual coercion is achieved by an aspectual marker in (41b) and by a time scale in (41a). In the case of (42), distributivity is allowed by the plural subject.

(41)   a. *Mari perdi-perdi pasians enafwa.*
        Mary lose-lose.SF patience now.and.then
        'Mary loses her temper once in a while.'

     b. *Mo zip pe tom-tonbe.*
        POSS.1SG skirt PROG fall-fall.LF
        'My skirt keeps sort of falling.'

(42) *Bann aksidan ariv-arive.*
      PL accident happen-happen.LF
      'Accidents sort of happen.'

With incremental themes, AR may trigger pluractionality or unaccomplished effects. Similar readings with similar predicates are triggered in French and Italian by special derivational affixes, e.g. French *-ot-* in *tournicoter* (cf. Tovena & Kihm 2008).

(43)   a. *Zan inn ranz-ranz so lakaz.*
        John PERF build-build.SF POSS.3SG house
        'John has sort of built his house.'

     b. *Mari ti pe manz-manz enn banann talerla.*
        Mary PST PROG eat-eat.SF IND banana earlier
        'Mary was sort of eating a banana earlier.'

As argued by Tovena & Kihm (2008), with similar French and Italian forms, a pluractional reading is always available. However as witnessed by the above examples and by (44) below, it is not always the case that reduplication gives rise to a pluractional effect in Mauritian. Sometimes, the pluractional interpretation is impossible (45).

(44) *Lisien la   inn   mord-mord Zan.*
      dog   DEF PERF bite-bite.SF Zan
      'The dog sort of bit John.'
      'The dog nibbled at John.'

(45) *Fouzer la   inn   pous-pouse.*
      fern   DEF PERF grow-grow.LF
      'The fern sort of grew. '
      *'The fern grew bit by bit.'

Finally, with verbs like those in (45) or (46b), AR triggers a brevity or a cumulative effect. The cumulative effect should not be confused with the iterative reading. In the case of (45), the fern has not grown the way one would have expected – it is a lame plant. This interpretation is supported by the fact that the proposition in (46a) is felicitous.

(46) a. *Fouzer la   inn   pous-pouse   apre li   'nn   seti.*
          fern   DEF PERF grow-grow.LF then 3SG PERF stunted
          'The fern sort of grew then got stunted.'

      b. *Sima   la   inn   dirsi-dirsi.*
          cement DEF PERF harden-harden.LF
          'The cement sort of hardened.'

Sometimes no scale is available. Reduplication is then impossible. Such is the case with stative verbs like *deteste* 'hate' (47b) or *kontan* 'love' (47a) and punctual verbs like *ne* 'be born'.

(47) a. **Zan pa   tro   kontan-kontan sorbe   lavani.*
          John NEG much like-like.SF   ice-cream vanilla
          Lit. 'John doesn't much sort of like vanilla ice-cream.'

      b. **Mo   deteste-deteste enn tigit sorbe   lavani.*
          1SG.WF hate-hate.SF   IND bit   ice-cream vanilla
          Lit. 'I sort of hate a bit of vanilla ice-cream.'

      c. **Tibaba la   inn   ne-ne   depi   yer.*
          baby   DEF PERF born-born.LF since yesterday
          Lit. 'The baby was sort of born yesterday.'

5. Areal patterns of AR

While it is clear that morphological reduplication such as that described above does not seem to have ever been typical of the superstrate, it is less clear whether AR arose in earlier Bantu-Austronesian contact, or during the Indo-Aryan immigration period, or if it is in fact a convergence of both. Let us first have a look at the lexifier. French verbs showing similar semantic effects are those which have allomorphic suffixes (-ouil-, -ot-, etc.). As shown by (Tovena & Kihm 2008), pluractional verbs in French cannot be analyzed as a derivational process.

Table 7. Pluractional verbs in French (Tovena & Kihm 2008, p. 8)

V-PL	Simple V	V-PL	No simple V
chantonner 'to hum'	*chanter* 'to sing'	*barbouiller* 'to daub'	*barber* 'to bore'
crachouiller/crachoter	*cracker* 'to spit'	*bavasser* 'to chat idly'	*baver* 'to slobber' but *bavard* ' talkative
Souffloter…	*souffler* 'to blow'		

They show that the suffixes involved in pluractional verbs cannot be analyzed as derivational suffixes because (i) they are non-productive, (ii) some verbs containing different suffixes exhibit no differences in meaning and (iii) more importantly, some pluractional verbs fail to have simplex (non-suffixed) counterparts.[3] The authors also argue that simple verbs can belong to a conjugation class which differs from that of their pluractional counterparts. Hence, French pluractional verbs are analyzed as 'autonomous word-forms realizing simple stems'. However, the non-productivity of pluractional suffixes argued for by Tovena & Kihm (2008) does not explain speakers' behaviors. There is in fact room for nonexisting pluractional forms for simple verbs, e.g. *manger* (> *mangeouiller*) or *bavarder* (> *ban vardasser*). Although, the pluractional counterparts of these verbs do not exist, French speakers do understand their (*derived*) meaning. It therefore seems that, although pluractional verbs are autonomous word-forms, they (at least some of them) are intrinsically linked (*derivationally*) to their simple counterpart, since this is how speakers interpret them. Coming back to the language at stake here, it seems that none of these pluractional verbs have been adopted from French except maybe for *tiraye* (from *tirailler*) but which in Mauritian does not have the meaning 'to pull'; It seems then that French pluractional verbs have not been inherited in Mauritian at all, and more generally in many French-based Creoles. In the Caribbean, a diminutive pluractional meaning of a predicate is made available by prefixing *ti* to it. Isle de France Creoles on the other hand use attenuative reduplication. That French pluractional verbs are nonexistent in French-based Creoles can be either due to the fact that they instantiate derivational processes, which have rarely been taken over in Creoles, or to the fact that they have emerged recently and thus were not part of the settlers' vocabulary. Further investigation is needed to support either hypothesis.

---

3. Editors' note: The theoretical framework of this article does not employ the normal meaning given to the term *derivation(al)*. For her usage of the term see Tovena & Kihm (2008).

But that reduplication can be found in Isle de France Creoles, and not in the Caribbean, can alternatively be explained by the fact that similar types of compounding are quite predominant in Bantu and Malagasy, languages spoken by the Africans that were brought to these islands, but not in Gbe languages where reduplication rather derives new lexical categories from verbs. AR is certainly found in Bantu languages such as Makua and Makonde, and in Malagasy, all of which are possible substrates for Mauritian.

Table 8. AR in substratic languages

Language	Simple V	Trans.	Reduplicative form	Trans.
Malagasy	*ló*	rotten	*lòló*	somewhat rotten
	máimbo	stinky	*máimbomáimbo*	somewhat stinky
	hadíno	forget	*hadìnodiíno*	forget a bit
Makonde	*tóngólá*	speaking	*tóngólátóngólá*	to keep on speaking
	kúlyá	eating	*kúlyáúlyá*	to keep on eating
Makua	*kóhá*	ask	*kóhá-koh*	ask repeatedly
Bhojpuri	*thor*	little	*thor thor*	little by little

Reduplication is also found in Bhojpuri, an Indo-Aryan language mainly spoken by the population of Indian descent. So obviously, this could also have played an important role in strengthening the use of AR, which according to old texts dates back to the 1880's (Baissac 1880).

6. SBCG analysis

6.1 A SBCG primer

The analysis proposed below is phrased within a non-derivational-based framework, SBCG (Sign-Based Construction Grammar) (Sag 2010). It is a model-theoretic syntactic framework in the sense that it only states constraints ensuring well-formed features, i.e. it defines the conditions that well-formed features must satisfy. It is composed of two major linguistic components: utterances which are modelled by a mathematical object *sign*, and rules which capture another mathematical object *construct*. The *sign* formally represents linguistic objects such as *words* and *phrases*. *Constructs*, on the other hand, are formal representations of grammar rules or schema that are used to license *signs*.

Like HPSG, SBCG considers language as "an infinite set of signs" modelled as feature structures. *Signs* are classified into two immediate subtypes, *expressions* and *lexical-signs*. *Expressions* are further classified into *phrases* and *words*, and *lexical-signs* (*lex-sign*) into *words* and *lexemes*. (cf. Figure 2).

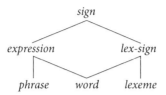

Figure 2. A hierarchical classification of the *sign's* subtypes

Words and *phrases* are also modelled as feature structures specifying the phonological, morphological, syntactic, semantic and contextual values of each particular sign. The sign can hence be said to be a 'polymorphic' function which maps the features in (48) onto their appropriate values. The sign is the most basic kind of feature structure, and illustrates De Saussure's idea of the sign. It includes a lot of linguistic information. As can be seen from (48), linguistic objects are assigned a type. Hence *phonological-object, morphological-object* and the like are types which are organized into a (type) hierarchy. Types are used to classify feature structures in allowing precise constraints. They also allow constraints in respect of smaller or larger classes of feature structures.

(48)
$$
\begin{bmatrix}
sign \\
\text{PHON} & \text{list}(phonological\text{-}object) \\
\text{FORM} & \text{list}(morphological\ object) \\
\text{SYN} & syntactic\text{-}object \\
\text{SEM} & linguistic\text{-}meaning \\
\text{CTXT} & context\text{-}object
\end{bmatrix}
$$

Feature structures, usually described as Added Value Matrices (AVMs), are mathematical objects which can either be atoms, or functions mapping a feature to an appropriate value. This value can be atomic (a type), a feature structure of a particular type, a list of feature structures or a set of feature structures.[4]

---

4.   Lists are represented by ordered elements (zero or more) within angled brackets whereas sets are represented by elements within curly brackets.

In (48), the appropriate value for the feature SYN is a value which must be a *syntactic object*. Features are used to specify constraints that well-formed structures should satisfy. Often, though, precise values of different features are left open, but are still required to be identified. Examples of identification using tags will be provided shortly. In addition, a *sign* is constrained by the following principle of well-formedness (Sag 2010: p.23):

(49) **Sign Principle**:
       Every sign must be lexically or constructionally licensed:
       A sign is lexically licensed only if it satisfies some entry in the lexicon, and
       A sign is constructionally licensed only if it is the mother of some
       construct.

Words are determined partly by their lexical entry, and partly by morphological constructions (inflectional or derivational constructions). Hence, *lexemes* or *words* can be formed by other lexemes via derivational constructions and words by lexemes via inflectional constructions. Examples of *lexeme-to-lexeme* are *barmaid*, *singer* and so on; examples of *lexeme-to-word* are *bars* and *sings*, from *bar* and *sing*, respectively. *Lexeme-to-lexeme* or *lexeme-to-word* are types modelled as feature structures as well, and are referred to as *constructs*. Constructs can be defined by the feature structure in (50), where the mother (MTR) value specifies the constructed sign, and the daughters (DTRS) value specifies the sign that is (or must be) licensed to give rise to the MTR.

(50) $$\begin{bmatrix} construct \\ \text{MTR} \quad sign \\ \text{DTRS} \quad nelist(sign) \end{bmatrix}$$

*Construct*s also have subtypes (Figure 3): lexical-constructs (*lex-cxt*) and phrasal constructs (*phr-cxt*). Lexical constructs are meant for the constructions described and we will mainly be concerned here with derivational and inflectional constructions.

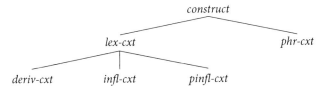

Figure 3. A hierarchical classification of the subtypes of *construct*

Lexical constructs are constrained to have DTRS of type *lex-sign*, i.e. words or lexemes, and *infl-cxt* are constrained by the type declarations (as opposed to constraints defined in terms of operations on objects). Type declarations are perspicuously abbreviated in labelled AVMs and specify which features are appropriate for which types of feature structure. This means that a grammar is seen as a system of constraints both unique and inherited on types of linguistic objects.

(51)   *lex-cxt* $\Rightarrow$ $\left[\text{DTRS} \quad \textit{list(lex-sign)}\right]$

With this basic background of the framework, we can account for the morphological aspects of Mauritian verbs. I will first account for simplex verbs, and will then propose a reduplication construction which should be able to pick a scale associated with the reduplicated predicate. A device interfacing with aspectual coercion still needs to be handled (cf. Bonami 2002), and will be proposed in future work.

6.2   Analysis of SF and LF

Recall that Mauritian verbs have a two-cell paradigm distinguishing the LF and the SF. Verbs in SBCG are categories which are also encoded within a feature structure with an attribute VFORM (verb form). The value of this attribute obviously depends on the language we are dealing with. In English, VFORM is a *cat* value, an appropriate feature structure for not only verbs, but also complementizers, and is used to specify their inflectional category. Its values are finite (*fin*), infinitive (*inf*), base, present-participle (*prp*), past-participle (*psp*), and passive-participle (*pas*). To account for Mauritian inflectional forms, I redefine VFORM as being appropriate for verbs only since the Mauritian complementizer *pou*, unlike the English complementizer *to* does not have selectional constraints.[5] The values of VFORM are further reduced to two values relevant for Mauritian, *long* and *short*.

(52)

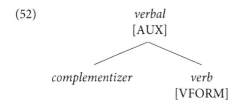

___

(53)

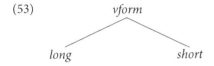

In addition to constraints on lexical constructs discussed in the previous section, inflectional constructs *infl-cxt* have properties specified as in (54). It says that the mother and the only daughter of an inflectional construct is of type *word*.[6] Following Blevins (2006), I assume here an abstractive view of morphology, where stems, roots, and exponents are abstractions over a set of words. The reason behind this choice lies in the fact that verb form alternation in Mauritian does *not* result from simply truncating the final vowel (Henri 2010). It is in most cases but, for instance, verbs like *reste* or *deteste* display two different patterns. In the former the last syllable is truncated, while in the latter truncation is not possible, i.e. the LF and the SF show a syncretic form. The non-predictibility of forms, together (Bonami & Henri 2010) with the allomorphy of exponents resulting from segmentation in a morph-based approach, obviously hinders productivity. Moreover, it is an obvious fact that speakers compare words in order to deduce the shape of novel forms.

(54)
$$
\textit{infl-cxt} \Rightarrow \begin{bmatrix} \text{MTR} & \textit{word} \\ \text{DTRS} & \textit{list(word)} \end{bmatrix}
$$

Furthermore, SBCG expresses the list of formatives or morphological objects associated with a lexeme as the value of the feature FORM. These morphological objects describe "lexical processes" such as derivation and inflection. The FORM value of the mother in a construct is provided by a morphological function associated with the lexeme's FORM, the domain and a set of values returned by the morphological function corresponding to the construction, and which belong to the co-domain. The lexeme DTRS, has a FORM value which is a singleton list, and which is the mirror image of the first element of FORM of the MTR. Hence, the morphological function of shortening $F_{shorten}$ (x) in Mauritian is a function that returns short forms of verbal lexemes when applied to the corresponding verbal base. The intuition behind this type of function is that speakers are able to predict the LF by looking at the SF.

---

6. In Sag (2010), inflectional constructs have a daughter which is of type lexeme. The intuition behind this assumption is that inflectional constructions are meant to derive words from lexemes. However, the author leaves open the possibility of having words in the daughters list.

x	$F_{Shorten}(x)$	x	$F_{Shorten}(x)$
reste	res	tranble	tranm
demande	demann	...	
briye	briye		
sorti	sort		
vini	vin		

The lexical construct accounting for verb forms can thus be stated as in (55). The verb alternation construct *vb-alt-cxt* is a type of word which specifies a FORM, syntactic information, where the verb is categorially specified for its VFORM, its Lexical-Identifier (LID), the value for BASIC and so forth. The attribute LID al- lows one to distinguish lexical items semantically. I will not go into detail here but basically, the value of LID is a frame that specifies the meaning of a lexeme. It, for instance, allows the distinction of two noun-words *bank* in English or the two LF *briye* in Mauritian, which do not have the same meaning. The feature BASIC has a Boolean value and is introduced to distinguish between simplex and redu- plicated forms.

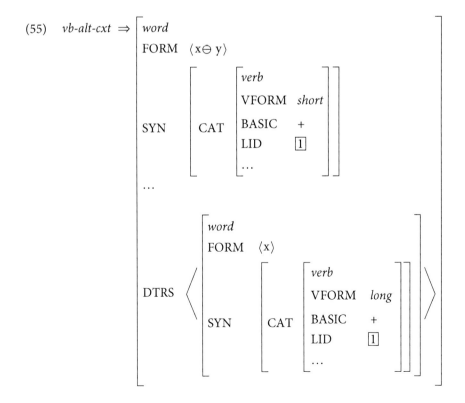

(55)   *vb-alt-cxt* ⇒

The construct is a *word-to-word* construct. This means that the DTRS list has only one element. It is simply meant to derive the SF from the LF. The DTR's LID is identical to that of the MTR meaning that they are semantically identical. It is the same word, which has undergone a morphological alteration. Note finally that both the MTR and the DTR are specified as being BASIC +. BASIC + words are simplex words, viz. they can be DTRS in derivational constructions such as the reduplication construction. But if words are specified as BASIC –, they are already reduplicated, and thus cannot be selected as DTRS in a reduplication construction.

6.2.1   *The reduplicated construct*

We are now in a position to account for AR in Mauritian. Since reduplication is a particular type of compounding, it is expected that the construct licensing such forms be a type of derivational construct. I propose a new subtype for derivational constructs (*deriv-cxt*) : the reduplicated construct which has as immediate subtypes the kinds of reduplicated forms available in Mauritian, viz. verbal reduplication (*reduplicated-vb-cxt*), adjectival reduplication (*reduplicated-adj-cxt*), and adverbial reduplication (*reduplicated-adv-cxt*). This is structured as in (56).

(56)

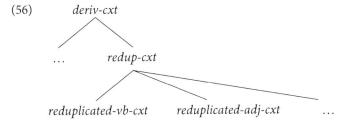

A derivational construct is defined as in (57). As can be noted, the construct is again modified with respect to the type of forms it can select. In this setting, both the MTR and the DTRs of a derivational construction are *words*. Again I assume that affixes in derivational morphology are abstractions over full forms, and that the output derivational constructs can feed other derivational constructs such as *re-vb-cxt* (*remanz, remanze, remanz-manze*).

(57) $deriv\text{-}cxt$: $\begin{bmatrix} \text{MTR} & word \\ \text{DTRS} & nelist(word) \end{bmatrix}$

The selection of *words* in the DTRS list also ensures that the verb form alternation construct proposed above can feed derivational constructs like *redup-vb-cxt*. Since, verbs are not the only categories that undergo reduplication, reduplicated verb constructs are a subtype of *deriv-cxt* and *redup-vb-cxt* are a subtype of *redup-cxt*, which also includes cases of adjectival reduplication, adverbial reduplication, nominal reduplication and so on. The reduplication verb construct is stated as in the AVM in (58).

(58) *rexm-tedup-vb-cxt* ⇒

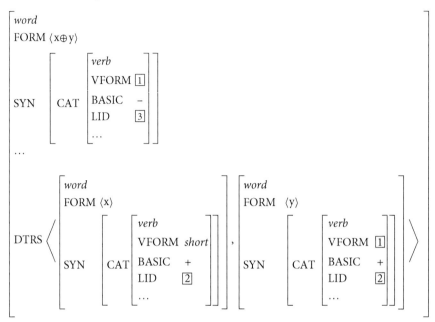

An illustration is given in (59). The value of BASIC is crucial here. It allows us to select the appropriate non-reduplicated form as DTRS.

(59) *redup-vb-cxt* ⇒

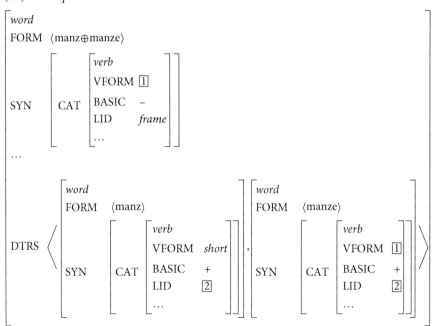

And finally note that the LID value of the DTRS differs from that of the MTR since a reduplicated predicate does not share the meaning of its non-reduplicated form. The value of LID should look like something in (60).

(60)

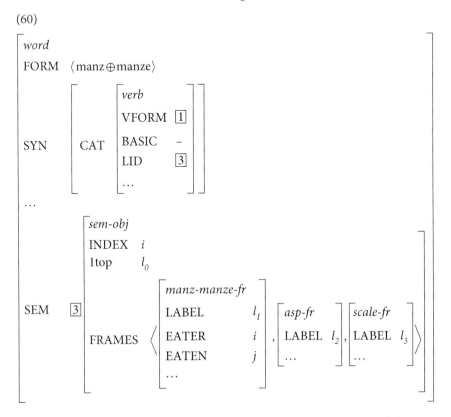

With respect to the semantics interface, we assume that the DTRS are of the appropriate types, viz. scalar (relative or partial), and that the value of the mother is appropriately coerced into an activity type whenever this is required.

7.   Conclusion

In this paper, I have shown that there are different types of reduplication in Mauritian. Focusing on verbal reduplication, I distinguished between syntactic and morphological reduplication. I further argued that the phenomenon studied here can best be accounted for under a word-based view of morphology. I have proposed a unified account for both inflectional and derivational morphology, both present in the language. Furthermore, we saw that the morphological derivation of reduplicated verbs is crucially dependent on the lexical aspect of the verb. Typically, achievement and state verbs are not allowed in AR but a scalar reading of the event description may overcome this constraint. I further showed that reduplicated verbs are semantically attenuative in a particular way. The attenuative effect boils down to the reduplicated event being lower on a scale than some standard. Different interpretations arise depending on the aspectual type of the verb. With punctual verbs, an iteration effect obtains, whereas with incremental theme predicates, as well as with gradable and durative predicates, a cumulative effect arises. Interestingly, the semantic complexity of AR provides strong evidence against the assumption that (morphological) reduplication is iconic, at least in Mauritian. As has been shown, a pluractional reading is not always available. Finally, I devoted a section to the emergence of the AR pattern in Mauritian, which must clearly result from substrate influence, since it fails to be attested in French-based Creoles spoken in the Caribbean for instance. Moreover, I showed that these patterns are not found in the lexifier language. Some remaining problems have been left unsolved such as the impossibility of reduplicated verb forms appearing in Verum Focus contexts and passive constructions. Coercion is another issue which needs further investigation.

References

Aronoff, Mark. 1994. *Morphology by itself*. Cambridge, MA: The MIT Press.

Baissac, Charles. 1880. Étude sur le patois créole mauricien. Nancy: Berger Levrault.

Baker, Philip. 2003. Reduplication in Mauritian Creole, with notes on reduplication in Reunion Creole. In *Twice as Meaningful. Reduplication in Pidgins, Creoles and Other Contact Languages* [Westminster Creolistic Series 8], Silvia Kouwenberg (ed.), 211–218. London: Battlebridge.

Blevins, James P. 2006. Word-based morphology. *Journal of Linguistics* 42:531–573.

Bonami, Olivier. 2002. A syntax-semantics interface for tense and aspect in French. In *The Proceedings of the HPSG '01 Conference*, Frank Van Eynde, Lars Hellan & Dorothee Beerman (eds). Stanford CA: CSLI.

Bonami, Olivier & Henri, Fabiola. 2010. How complex is creole inflectional morphology? Paper presented at the International Meeting of Morphology, Budapest.

Bonami, Olivier, Henri, Fabiola & Luís, Ana R. 2011. The emergence of morphomic structure in Romance-based Creoles. Paper presented at the GRGC Workshop, Paris.

Corne, Chris. 1982. Final vowel truncation in Indian Ocean Creole French. *In Isle de France Creole: Affinities and Origins*, 49–63. Ann Arbor MI: Karoma.

Fabb, Nigel. 2001. Compounding. In *The Handbook of Morphology*, Andrew Spencer & Arnold Zwicky (eds), 339–361. Oxford: Blackwell.

Ghomeshi, Jila, Jackendoff, Ray, Rosen, Nicole & Rusell, Kevin. 2004. Contrastive focus reduplication in English (the salad-salad paper). *Natural Language & Linguistic Theory* 22:307–357.

Haspelmath, Martin. 2002. *Understanding Morphology*. London: Arnold.

Henri, Fabiola. 2010. A Constraint-based Approach to Verbal Constructions in Mauritian: Morphological, Syntactic and Discourse-based Aspects. Ph.D. dissertation, University Paris-Diderot, Paris 7 & University of Mauritius.

Henri, Fabiola & Abeillé, Anne. 2008. Verb forms alternation in Mauritian. In *The Proceedings of the 15th International Conference on Head-Driven Phrase Structure Grammar*, Stefan Müller (ed.). Stanford CA: CSLI. ⟨http://csli-publications.stanford.edu/HPSG/9/⟩

Henri, Fabiola & Laurens Frédéric. 2011. The complementation of raising and control verbs in Mauritian. In *Empirical Issues in Formal Syntax and Semantics*, Vol. 7., Olivier Bonami & Patricia Cabredo Hofherr (eds). ⟨http://www.cssp.cnrs.fr/eiss7/index_en.html⟩

Henri, Fabiola, Marandin, Jean-Marie & Abeillé, Anne. 2008. Information structure coding in mauritian: Verum focus expressed by long forms of verbs. Paper presented at the workshop on Predicate focus, verum focus, verb focus: Similarities and differences, University of Potsdam, Germany.

Kennedy, Christopher & McNally, Louise. 2005. Scale structure, degree modification, and the semantics of gradable predicates. *Language* 81(2): 345–381.

Kouwenberg, Silvia & LaCharité, Darlene. 2003. Less is more: Evidence from diminutive reduplication in Caribbean creole languages. In *Twice as Meaningful. Reduplication in Pidgins, Creoles and Other Contact Languages* [Westminster Creolistic Series 8], Silvia Kouwenberg (ed.), 533–545. London: Battlebridge.

Moens, Marc & Steedman, Mark. 1988. Temporal ontology and temporal reference. *Computational Linguistics* 14(2): 15–28.

Pollard, Carl & Sag, Ivan. 1994. *Head-driven Phrase Structure Grammar*. Stanford CA: CSLI.

Sag, Ivan. 2010. Sign-Based Construction Grammar: An informal Synopsis. In *Sign-based Construction Grammar*. Stanford CA: CSLI.

Sapir, Edward. 1921. *Language: An Introduction to the Study of Speech*. Mineola NY: Dover.

Selkirk, Elizabeth. 1982. *The Syntax of Words* [Linguistic Inquiry Monograph 7]. Cambridge MA: The MIT Press.

Seuren, Pieter. 1990. Verb syncopation and predicate raising in Mauritian Creole. *Theoretical Linguistics* 1(13): 804–844.

Tovena, Lucia & Kihm, Alain. 2008. Nibbling is not many bitings in Italian and French: A morphosemantic analysis of event internal plurality. *Proceedings of the 34th Annual Meeting of the Berkeley Linguistics Society*.

Veenstra, Tonjes. 2004. What verbal morphology can tell us about creole genesis: The case of French-related creoles. In *Phonology and Morphology of Creole Languages* [Linguistische Arbeiten 478], Ingo Plag (ed.), Tübingen: Max Niemeyer.

Vendler, Zeno. 1967. *Linguistics in Philosophy*. Ithaca NY: Cornell University Press.

Zribi-Hertz, Anne & Li Pook Tan, Louis-Jacques. 1987. Gouvernement et syntagme verbal: A propos de la troncation verbale en créole mauricien. *Documents de travail. Université Paris 8* 1: 57–8.

Reduplication in São Tomense

Issues at the syntax-semantics interface

Emmanuel Schang
Université d'Orléans, LLL, UMR-7270

This paper studies lexical reduplication in São Tomense, a Portuguese-based Creole language. Its central claim is that lexical reduplication in São Tomense results from the external merge of the same lexical item in two structural slots available in independently-motivated syntactic structures: the modification structure and the coordination structure.

1. Introduction

In his book on São Tomense creole, Ferraz (1979:49) analyses reduplication as a derivational compounding process:

> In São Tomense, compounding is primarily a morphological process whereby the repetition of a word yields a single lexical item, or one meaning. This lexical item is one word phonologically; in ST [São Tomense] each compounded element retains its stress pattern, the stress on the last element being the stronger.

At first sight, this claim seems plausible. But since no study of stress in São Tomense is available, it is a priori questionable. Moreover, where there is a repetition of five identical entities, let alone entities larger than words, we should wonder if this is still a morphological process. As a starting point, I will take for granted that reduplication differs from accidental coocurrence of identical entities (stammer, etc.) in that the latter (called a *disfluency*) does not trigger any semantic effect. Contrastively, reduplication associates a meaning and a form.

With these preliminaries in mind, this paper will address the nature of reduplication in São Tomense.[1] My central claim is that what may be called 'reduplication'

---

1.   I would like to thank warmly Joseth Dos Santos, her family and friends, and Gabriel Pires Dos Santos and his family who provided many examples and sound comments on São Tomense language. I would also like to express my gratitude to the editors for their precious comments and patience.

in São Tomense covers two different syntactic patterns that are not dedicated to the particular meanings that are usually associated with reduplication. The data in this paper come from documented sources (Ladhams et al. (2003) (from now on LHMP); Ferraz (1979)) as well as from fieldwork carried out by myself in São Tomense since 1995. Section 2 deals with the first syntactic reduplication pattern, i.e. the modification pattern, and Section 3 deals with the coordination pattern.

2.   Modification structures, intensity and contrast

Many studies dedicated to reduplication focus on its intensive effect, regarded as iconic (cf. Kouwenberg (2003); Michaud & Morgenstern (2007)). Kouwenberg & LaCharité (2001:7) illustrate this view: "Where an adjective stands for a property, more of the adjective stands for more of the property."

São Tomense presents many such cases of intensive reduplication with nouns (1) and adjectives (2).[2]

(1) *sôdê   sôdê   na   te   medu   fa.*
    soldier soldier NEG1 have fear   NEG2
    'The real soldier doesn't have fear (for anything).'

(2) *Mese   kafe   **kentxi kentxi.***
    I.want coffee hot   hot
    'I want very hot coffee' (F).

This last example can also be translated by 'I want HOT hot coffee' with a contrastive meaning, depending on the context.

While the discussion of such reduplication in the literature often bears on lexical items, São Tomense also displays reduplication of functional items such as pronouns (3) and locative adpositions (4):

(3) *non non; inen   inen.*
    Us   us; them them
    'Just us, just them' (LHMP).

(4) *e   sa   **nome   nome**   d(i)   omali.*
    3s be   middle middle of   sea
    'He's right in the middle of the sea' (LHMP).

---

2. Examples from Ladhams et al. (2003) are indicated as LHMP, examples from Ferraz (1979) are indicated as F, the other examples come from my own consultants.

A problem in (4) is the categorial status of the repeated material. Indeed *mê* is a noun meaning 'middle' (Rougé (2004:203)), while *no* is a preposition borrowed from Portuguese *no* 'in, into'. The complex *nome* can therefore be seen as a complex preposition comparable to English 'in the middle of' as suggested by the translation. Given this description, the reduplication in (4) targets two arguably independent elements fused into one. This description is compatible with the analyses I propose below in §2.3. The reduplication pattern in (4) also exists in (colloquial) Portuguese *no meio no meio está São Tomense e Príncipe* (literally: 'in the middle in the middle is STP').³ This example is to be considered as a direct borrowing from Portuguese since this construction is not allowed with other prepositions: **liba liba* ('on top of'); **nglentu nglentu* ('into') nor in sequences such as **ni basu ni basu* ('in bottom'). It is not a productive reduplication in ST and therefore does not deserve further investigation here.

The point I wish to study is the structure underlying ST reduplications. We should determine whether the grammar of ST involves special mechanisms accounting for reduplicative strings, or whether such strings result from the application of independently-motivated operations. For instance, is there a particular syntactic structure behind *sôdê sôdê* in (1) or is this string licensed by the same structure as *sôdê kubanu* ('Cuban soldier')?

Ghomeshi et al. (2004) answer these questions in their study of contrastive reduplication (CR) in English. In particular, they claim that CR is a construction "which involves movement into a focus-like position with both the head and the tail of the resulting chain spelled out".

Before discussing their assumptions, I briefly summarise Ghomeshi et al. (2004)'s analysis.

2.1   The CR hypothesis

Ghomeshi et al. (2004) make a clear distinction in English between Intensive Reduplication and what they call Contrastive Reduplication. Intensive Reduplication (IR) may involve three or more identical items (*You are sick sick sick*) and exhibits a special prosodic contour. CR differs from IR because its scope can be larger than a single word (as in *Oh, we're not LIVING-TOGETHER-living together*). The semantic function of CR is to restrict the meaning of an item to its central or prototypical meaning. Evidence supporting this claim is the fact that CR doesn't occur with functional items (since they lack the appropriate sort of semantic content).

---

3.   A quick Google search hit many examples. The variant *no meio do meio* is also very frequent.

"[...] CR rules out not denotations that are truth-conditionally false (not FALSE-false), but rather denotations that are less prototypical: many things are salads but not SALAD-salads".

In syntax:

the CR morpheme consists of the features [P/E/S, +contrast], but no phonology. Akin to a modifier of category A (adjective or adverb), it heads a CR phrase that can take any lexical phrase (NP, VP, AP, etc.) as its complement. Assuming that the features of the CR morpheme are strong, they must be associated with a syntactic head that is lexically filled. These features trigger head-movement of the adjacent X.   (Ghomeshi et al. (2004: 347))

The result is the following structure:

(5)

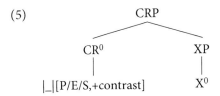

$\lfloor\_\rfloor$ stands for the head of the chain, whose phonological content comes from its complement X. In CR both the head and the tail of the chain are pronounced. This issue is discussed elsewhere in this volume (cf. Glaude & Zribi-Hertz: Section 3.5.2) so I will not go into details here, but this analysis is not compatible with the data I present below. As for the scope of CR, Ghomeshi et al. (2004: 332) make the following claims:

(6)   a.   The scope of CR is either X or XP
      b.   The scope of CR must include a full lexical item, to whose meaning the semantic effect of CR is applied.
      c.   In addition to a single contentful lexical item, the scope of CR may include only noncontrastive functional/grammatical morphemes.

2.2   Contrast in ST

Ghomeshi et al. (2004) thus make some strong claims on the nature of this type of reduplication (CR). They claim that CR can also be found in other languages (Italian, Persian, Spanish, Russian...) with a similar structure, except that some languages restrict their uses (Persian only allows this type of copying with adjectives).

The contrastive reduplication data in São Tomense differ from those reported for English. ST allows it with nouns (even if it is unusual in the basilectal creole):

(7a) *sôdê   sôdê   na   te   medu fa.*
     soldier soldier NEG1 have fear   NEG2
     'The SOLDIER soldier has no fear' (= 'a REAL soldier').

(b) *Zé sa **sôdê**   sôdê.*
     Zé be soldier soldier
     'Zé is a SOLDIER soldier' (= 'a REAL soldier').

This construction may involve pronouns, as shown in (3) and adjectives (but it is stylistically disfavored, as I will explain below):

(8) *mwala   se   sa **glavi**   glavi   o   e*
     woman this be beautiful beautiful or she

     sa glavi   mo basu   mpo nganha?
     be beautiful like under roost chicken

     'Is this woman BEAUTIFUL beautiful or is she beautiful like the ground of a chicken house' (literally: like under the chickens' roost)?'

The modifier *me* 'real, very' is preferred by my consultants to convey the intended contrastive effect:

(9) *mwala   se   sa **glavi**   me   o   e*
     woman this be beautiful really or she

     sa glavi   mo basu   mpo nganha?
     be beautiful like under roost chicken

     'Is this woman really beautiful or is she beautiful like the ground of a chicken house'.

Unlike English, São Tomense doesn't allow a contrastive reading with verbs:

(10a) *piskado   nda nda.*
      fisherman go   go
      'The fisherman kept on walking' (LHMP) (continuative reading only).

(b) **piskado*   nda nda (ba ke).*
     fisherman go   go   (to house)
     '*The fisherman really walked home' (no contrastive interpretation available even in a context where other participants in the story don't really go home)

All the examples that allow a contrastive reading also allow an intensive reading in contexts which do not provide any alternative for contrast. For instance, example (2) can be understood as intensive (as noticed in Ferraz (1979)) in a context where there is no other coffee to be distinguished.

In absence of any clear difference in stress between intensive reduplication and contrastive reduplication, I assume that the context is the relevant factor providing the correct interpretation in São Tomense. Thus, there is no need to distinguish contrastive from intensive reduplication at the syntactic level.[4]

2.3   Modification structures in ST

2.3.1   *NN reduplication as a type of attributive modification*
Example (7a) apparently contains an NN string. Note however that the categories N and A are not unconnected. Schang (2002: 123), proposes various examples of lexemes which may occur either as N heads or as adnominal modifiers, as in:

(11)   *mosu   konki.*
      boy   hump
      'the (or a) humpbacked boy'.

In (11), *konki* occurs as the modifier of the N and as such, is merged in a position where one can also find postnominal adjectives. ST has three series of adjectives:

– strictly prenominal adjectives (rare), such as *meme* 'big':

(12)   *e   te   meme   kabisa.*
      he   have   big   head
      'He has a big head'.

– prenominal adjectives that can also be postnominal: such as *bō* 'good'. As in many languages, these adjectives have different meanings when prenominal or postnominal.
– postnominal adjectives (and other postnominal modifiers). Noun modifiers such as *konki* can only be postnominal.

---

4.   In (i), my consultants put a stress on the second *kentxi* for both contrastive and intensive readings:

(i)   kafe kentxi 'kentxi.

On the other hand, stress is clearly on the first element with intensive ideophones (cf. Footnote 6):

(ii)   'kentxi   zuzuzu
      hot   ideophone
      'very hot'.

This is probably consistent with Ferraz(1979)'s comment on the stress pattern of reduplication (see Section 1 of this paper). But an accurate description of stress/pitch/tone in São Tomense is yet to be done and whether Gulf of Guinea Creoles are stress or tone languages is still a debated issue (see Schang 2002).

As suggested for other languages (see for instance Knittel (2005), Cinque (2010)), and in particular for Romance, postnominal adjectives are merged higher than N, and the surface order results from an internal merge of N to a higher position.

I assume then, that (7a) is the result of external merge of *sôdê* (N) as the head of the NP and the merge of a second *sôdê* in a FP higher than the NP:

(13a)   *sôdê sôdê*
  (b) $[_{ZP} [sodê_z] [_{Z^0} [_{FP} [sodê] [_{F^0} [_{NP} t_z]]]]$

Under this analysis, the NP raises past its modifier. It may even raise to a higher position, above the specificity marker, as witnessed by (14):

(14)   *sôdê   se   sôdê.*
        soldier   SPECIFIC   soldier
        'This SOLDIER soldier'.
        (meaning: this soldier, who is a real soldier)

The contrastive reduplication of pronouns, as in (3) is consistent with this general description. These cases involve situations where the pronoun 'we' refers to a subset which is contrasted to the rest of the group.[5] I therefore propose that the structure assumed in (13) also holds for reduplicated pronouns.

2.3.2   *AA reduplication*

Example (2) repeated in (15) shows a slightly different syntactic pattern.

(15)   *Mese   kafe   kentxi   kentxi.*
        I.want   coffee   hot   hot
        'I want very hot coffee'.

Here, two syntactic patterns are a priori available:

Recursive modification. As above, the NP raises beyond the FPs which host the adjectives. The upstairs adjective has its scope over the lower structure:

(16) $[_{ZP1} [kafe_z] [_{Z^0} [_{FP1} kentxi] [_{F^0} [_{ZP2} [t_z] [_{FP2} [kentxi] [_{F^0} [_{NP} t_z]]]]]]]$

The following examples are further evidence that the NP raises while the adjectives remain *in situ*:

(17a)   *kafe   se   kentxi   kentxi.*
         coffee   SPECIFIC   hot   hot
         'This very hot coffee'.

---

5.   Perhaps clumsily translated by 'just us, just they' in LHMP, even though I have no better translation to propose.

(b)   *kafe kentxi se kentxi.

(c)   *kafe kentxi kentxi se.

Adjective-on-adjective modification. An alternate view is the modification of *kentxi* only (and not *kafe kentxi*) by another adjective *kentxi*, as in *a pale blue shirt*. Glaude & Zribi-Hertz (this volume, §3.5.2) defend this approach for Haitian Creole and propose to derive the 'contrastive reduplication' of verbs (e.g. Haitian *malad malad*, English *sick sick*) from the external merge of the same lexical root in the Spec and L positions. This structure (18) is independently supported by languages where the F^0 head is filled by an overt morpheme (e.g. Farsi).

(18)

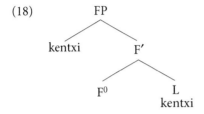

This structure is not limited to reduplication since it corresponds to the cases of ideophonic modification.[6] Both structures can trigger the contrastive reading and it is hard to find semantic clues in ST to rule out one or the other.

2.3.3   *QQ reduplication*

LHMP (after Ferraz (1979)) propose an example of intensifying adjective reduplication:

(19)   *n   sebe   **mina   mina**   kwa.*
       1s. know   small   small   thing
       'I know a tiny little bit'.

---

6.   Some adjectives have a specialized ideophone, e.g. *blanku fenene* 'white as snow'; *fio kokoko* 'freezing cold', *vleme bababa* 'bright red', *pletu lululu* 'pitch black', *lizu kankankan*, 'smooth as silk', *limpu pyênêpyênê* 'clean as a whistle', etc. These modifiers usually signal intensity and may be used to translate the English contrastive reduplication in a relevant context:

(i)   Is it COLD cold?

(ii) *E   sa   fio   kokoko?*
      it   be   cold   ideophone
      'Is it COLD cold?' (or just cool).

These ideophones have no existence as notional words and are not segmentable: **ko, *koko, *pyênê, ...*They apply to a (sometimes extended) meaning. For instance, both *blanku* 'white' and *klalu* 'clear' have *fenene* as their ideophone.

This translation is probably misleading. The appropriate translation should have been 'I know a few things'. The meaning of *mina* here can be more easily captured in (20a) where it contrasts with (20b). Here, *mina* is clearly a quantifier:

(20a) *m te   mina djêlu.*
     1s have little money
     'I have got a little money'.

(b) *m te   jo   djêlu.*
     1s have much money
     'I have got much money'.

Turning back to (19) allows us to revise LHMP's analysis. We are facing the same problem as in AA modification where two different structures may be assumed, viz. (leaving aside functional details):

(21) $[_{QP}$ mina $[_{QP}$ mina $[_{NP}$ kwa]]]
(22) $[[_{QP}$ mina $[_{QP}$ mina]] $[_{NP}$ kwa]]

Once again, neither structure is specific to reduplication, since both are independently motivated for non-reiterative modification.

3.   Coordinated structures

3.1   Intensity, iteration, continuation and the VP

Under the same line of reasoning, it might be possible to identify one basic structure with different but related context-dependent interpretations for the VV strings with intensive, iterative and continuative meanings. For instance, the reduplication of *uanga* 'to spread' has an iterative meaning in (23).

(23) *nge   maxi tame ka pega kume se   ku   mon (PRO) ka*
     person more old   ASP take food DEM with hand PRO   ASP

     uanga, uanga, uanga.
     spread spread spread
     'The oldest one takes the food with his hand and spreads it, spreads it, spreads it.'

This example contrasts with (24) where reduplication doesn't trigger an iterative reading but a continuative reading:

(24) *Tataluga   ka   gwada gwada gwada...*
     Mr.Turtle TMA wait   wait   wait
     'Mr. Turtle is waiting, waiting, waiting...'

These effects are present in coordinated structures. It has often been noticed in the literature on conjunction (e.g. Bassac (2010)) that coordination can involve continuative, iterative and distributive meanings. As for São Tomense, Hagemeijer (2007:65) convincingly claims that:

- ST is not a pro-drop language
- ST has a covert conjunction for coordination at VP level or higher
- There are instances of discourse-bound topic drop (a discourse-bound empty pronoun (*pro*) referring to a participant disjoint from both speaker and addressee), as in (23). This fact is also noted in Ferraz (1979:65).

In many cases, sequences of reduplicated Vs, e.g. VVV in (23) are equivalent to coordinated structures with the overt conjunction *i* 'and':

(25)   *Tataluga   ka   gwada gwada i   gwada...*
        Mr.Turtle   TMA   wait   wait   and   wait
        'Mr. Turtle is waiting, waiting and waiting...'

In (25), the conjunction is overt and appears before the last conjunct. A third piece of information comes from speech analysis (see Figure 1) which shows that a pause occurs between the reduplicated verbs. This pause is similar to that observed with silent coordination, as in (23) between *mon* and *ka*.

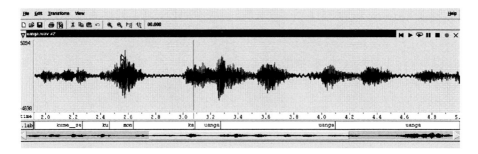

Figure 1. Waveform of... *ka uanga, uanga, uanga*

I therefore assume that the iterative interpretation of VV(V) arises from the silent coordination of verbs satisfying some Aktionsart requirements. Iterative effects are favoured by achievements and accomplishments (26) while continuative or intensive effects are favoured by states or activities (24).

(26)   *e   fe   ke,   fe   ke,   fe   ke...*
        he   make   house   make   house   make   house
        'He built several houses.' (iterative effect)

Hence, 'reduplication' in such cases as (23) boils down to regular coordination. Example (23) may thus be represented as in (27), where *e* stands for the silent conjunction (see Hagemeijer (2007:65)).

(27)

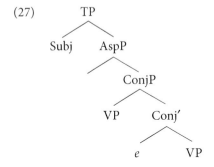

Under this analysis, the only difference between (23) and (28) below is the fact that the coordinated VPs are phonologically identical. This is a stylistic contrast, I claim, not a syntactic contrast.

(28) *e   bêbê vin,   kume ua bon   kume, ua bon   kitxiba*
      3PS drink wine eat   a   good meal   a   good banana
      'He drank a good wine, (he) ate a good meal, a good banana'

I assume that reduplicated VV strings have no remarkable grammatical properties, since the silent-coordination pattern is also available for larger repeated units (complete IPs for instance), as witnessed by (29) and its wave form in Figure 2.

(29) *a   pega nai   zuga   naie,   a   pega nai   zuga   naie*
      one take here throw there, one take here throw there
      'one takes here to throw there...'

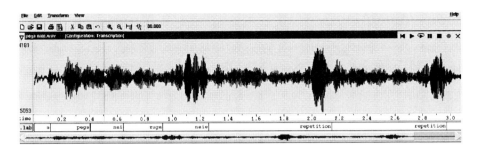

Figure 2. Waveform of (29)

3.2 Distributivity

I have so far left aside the distributive interpretation of the iterated strings which arise with adjectives (30), nouns (31) and quantifiers (32). I claimed that two syntactic structures suffice to account for lexical reduplication. I will extend the silent coordination analysis to distributive interpretations.[7,8]

As recalled in LHMP (p.168), Post (1998:96) analyses NN reduplication in Fa d'Ambu to which she ascribes the function of "marking a closed class of objects, rather than any number of occurrences of the objects described". LHMP consider that theses cases illustrate plural distributive effects. I agree with them and believe that this analysis holds for such examples as (30), (31) and (32):

(30)   *inen ploko se   sa godo godo.*
       PL. pig DEM be fat fat
       'These pigs are fat.' (LHMP)

(31)   *inen ska nda matu matu.*
       3PL ASP go bush bush
       'They are walking from bush to bush.'

(32)   *tufu inen nge   se   pe karu xinku xinku.*
       put 3P person DEM in car five five
       'Put these people in the car(s) five by five (five at a time).' (LHMP)

There is no need to have a precise count of the pigs or bushes to interpret (30) and (31). The silent-coordination assumption allows us to derive the correct interpretation. In example (33), *mon* 'hand' is repeated five times rather than ten times (while crabs have ten legs), the sentence does not mean that five legs only get cut:

(33)   *e   pega anka se,   kota mon mon mon mon mon de.*
       he take crab DEM cut hand hand hand hand hand of-it
       'He took that crab and cut off all its legs.' (F)

---

7.   LHMP claim that partial reduplication may occur with the cardinals 'two' and 'three', (*do-dosu* and *tle-tlexi*) but I found the same pattern for other numerals (*xi-xinku* 'five-five', see example (34)). Apocope is frequent in ST (see Ferraz (1979), Schang (2002)) and the pairs *dosu dosu/do-dosu* and *xinku xinku/xi-xinku* show that the usage with two morphemes is always available. I assume that this is a stylistic device and that nothing differentiates these pairs except apocope.

8.   Ferraz also gives the following example to illustrate the iterative effect (which he calls *repetitiveness*):

(i)   *ūa   ūa   ja.*
     one one day
     'Now and then, on some days.'

Since the same meaning is conveyed by *ūa dosu* 'one two' ('on some days') the iterative effect cannot result from reduplication.

A similar remark holds for distributive effects with iterated quantifiers. The example in (32) does not mean that ten people are split into two groups. The sentence is true for any multiple of five. The sum reading is not the only available reading.

The example in (34) below in effect shows that reduplicated quantifiers may contextually trigger a sum reading.

(34) *xi-xinku kontu,*   *xinku be, xinku bi,*
      five-five thousand.dobras five   go five   come

      sa dexi kontu   ku nga   paga tudu dja.
      be ten   thousand that 1SG-ASP pay every day
      'five-five thousand dobras, five to go, five to come back, it's ten thousand dobras that I pay everyday.'

In this example, it is impossible to understand *xi-xinku* as meaning 'any multiple of five'. It can only mean 'ten'.

3.3 The structural representation of coordinated structures

There are three coordinators in São Tomense: Ø (asyndeton or zero), *i* 'and' and *ku* 'with' (comitative). *ku* is restricted to the comitative use. *i* is very frequent in sentence coordination. Zero marking is frequent:

(35) *e   bêbê   vin,   kume ua   bon   kume, ua   bon   kitxiba.*
      3PS drink wine eat   one good meal   one good banana
      'he drank wine, ate a good meal, (and) a good banana.'

So far, I haven't proposed any structure for coordination and I have accepted without discussion the structure proposed in Hagemeijer (2007: 67). However, this representation based on Kayne (1994) is far from being universally accepted.

Kayne (1994: 58) proposes an analysis of coordination that has become popular under the name of *ConjP*:

(36a) [DP$_i$ [and DP$_j$]

(b)
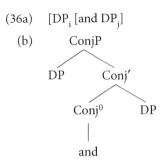

In this model, the entire phrase (ConjP) is a projection of *and*, and coordination of heads is ill-formed. Nevertheless, a series of objections have been put forward by Borsley (2005a, 2005b) and Abeillé (2006) amongst others. Borsley (2005b) observes that coordinate structures are analysed differently in frameworks such as HPSG (Pollard & Sag 1994) or LFG (Bresnan 2001). In these frameworks, it is usually admitted that coordinations are exocentric (headless) structures and that the coordinators (conjunctions) are some kinds of 'markers'.

Borsley (2005b) provides a range of arguments against the ConjP hypothesis. He shows that the ConjP analysis overgenerates and that it misanalyses coordinate structures which have more than two conjuncts but only one overt connective (as in *Hobbs, Rhodes and Barnes*).

As regards São Tomense, the analysis presented in Munn (1993) meets the expectations presented in the previous sections. Instead of making the conjunction the head of a phrase that contains the conjuncts, Munn (1993) proposes that the conjunction phrase consisting of the conjunction and the second conjunct is adjoined to the first conjunct. Conjoined NPs, for instance, have the following structure:

(37)

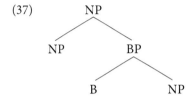

BP stands for Boolean Phrase and B hosts the conjunction.

The advantage of substituting the adjoined BP analysis for the ConjP analysis lies in the fact that the category of the coordinated structure is similar to the category of a non-coordinated element. For instance, the coordination of two VPs is a VP, not a ConjP. Adjunction can apply recursively at various levels. I assume that (37) is the structure that holds for VP reduplications (triggering intensive, iterative and continuative effects) and also for reduplications with a distributive meaning.

4.   Conclusion

The leading assumption put forward in this study is that no specific morphosyntax is needed to account for the lexical reduplication patterns attested in São Tomense (contra Ferraz (1979), see §1). I argued that lexical reduplication results from the external merge of the same lexical item in two structural slots available in independently-motivated syntactic structures: the modification structure and the coordination structure. It contradicts the claim (Schang 2002: 184) that reduplication is the main morphological process in São Tomense.

The above proposals are consistent with the analyses proposed for Haitian (Glaude & Zribi-Hertz this volume) and Hebrew (Cohen this volume). However, São Tomense does not present the Verb Fronting with Doubling constructions (VFD) that are attested in Haitian.

The syntactic structures proposed here are universally available (Cinque (2010), Glaude & Zribi-Hertz this volume). As such, this paper does not lend weight to the idea of Creole Exceptionalism with regards to reduplication. Moreover, the above results do not bring support to the iconicity theory (as advocated in Kouwenberg & LaCharité (2001)). Finally, there is nothing more 'iconic' in XX sequences involving modification or coordination than in any similar XY sequences involving no reduplication.

References

Abeillé, Anne. 2006. In defense of lexical coordination. *Empirical Issues in Syntax and Semantics* 6: 7–36.

Bassac, Christian. 2010. Sémantique de la coordination: Une brève introduction. *Revue de Sémantique et Pragmatique,* numéro thématique *Sémantique de la coordination*, 7–23.

Borsley, Robert. 2005a. Against ConjP. *Lingua* 115(4): 461–482.

Borsley, Robert. 2005b. Les coordinations relèvent-elles de la syntaxe X-barre? *Langages* 2005(4): 25–41.

Bresnan, Joan. 2001. *Lexical-functional Syntax*. Malden MA: Blackwell.

Cinque, Guglielmo. 2010. *The Syntax of Adjectives: A Comparative Study* [Linguistic Inquiry Monographs]. Cambridge MA: The MIT Press.

Ferraz, Luis.I. 1979. *The Creole of São Tomense*. Johannesburg: Witwatersrand University Press.

Ghomeshi, Jila, Jackendoff, Ray, Rosen, Nicole & Russell, Kevin. 2004. Contrastive focus reduplication in English (The salad-salad paper). *Natural Language & Linguistic Theory* 22(2): 307–357.

Hagemeijer, Tjerk. 2007. Clause structure in Santome. Ph.D. dissertation, University of Lisbon.

Kayne, Richard. 1994. *The Antisymmetry of Syntax*. Cambridge MA: The MIT Press.

Knittel, Marie. 2005. Some remarks on adjective placement in the French NP. *Probus* 17(2): 185–226.

Kouwenberg, Sylvia (ed.). 2003. *Twice as Meaningful: Reduplication in Pidgins, Creoles and Other Contact Languages* [Westminster Creolistic Series 8]. London: Battlebridge.

Kouwenberg, Sylvia & LaCharité, Darlène. 2001. The iconic interpretations of reduplication: Issues in the study of reduplication in Caribbean Creole languages. *European Journal of English Studies* 5(1): 59–80.

Ladhams, John, Hagemeijer, Tjerk, Maurer, Philippe & Post, Marieke. 2003. Reduplication in the Gulf of Guinea Creoles. In *Twice as Meaningful: Reduplication in Pidgins, Creoles and Other Contact Languages* [Westminster Creolistic Series 8], Silvia Kouwenberg (ed.), 165–74. London: Battlebridge.

Michaud, Arnaud & Morgenstern, Aliyah. 2007. *La reduplication*. Paris: Ophrys.

Munn, Alan. 1993. Topics in the Syntax and Semantics of Coordinate Structures. Ph.D. dissertation, The University of Maryland.

Pollard, Carl & Sag, Ivan. 1994. *Head-driven Phrase Structure Grammar*. Chicago IL: University of Chicago Press.

Post, Marieke. 1998. La situacion lingüistica del Fa d'Ambó. In *Sociolingüística: Lenguas en contacto*, Pieter C. Muysken (ed.), Amsterdam: Rodopi.

Rougé, Jean-Louis. 2004. *Dictionnaire étymologique des créoles portugais d'Afrique*. Paris: Karthala.

Schang, Emmanuel. 2002. *L'émergence des créoles portugais du Golfe de Guinée*. Villeneuve d'Ascq: Presses Universitaires du Septentrion.

Reiteration in Pichi

Forms, functions and areal-typological perspectives[*]

Kofi Yakpo
Radboud University Nijmegen

Pichi, an Afro-Caribbean English-lexifier Creole spoken on the island of Bioko, Equatorial Guinea, features four types of reiteration. Amongst them, reduplication and repetition can be distinguished on formal and semantic grounds. Reduplication is a derivational operation consisting of self-compounding and tone deletion. It is restricted to dynamic verbs and yields iterative, dispersive and attenuative meanings. Repetition occurs with all major word classes, renders more iconic meanings and is analyzed as semi-morphological in nature. A comparison with verbal reiteration in a cross-section of West African languages and two of its sister languages in the Caribbean allows the conclusion that Pichi reduplication reflects an areal pattern. I conclude further that Pichi reduplication is not exceptionally iconic nor specifically "creole" in nature.

1. Introduction

Pichi is a member of the vast family of Afro-Caribbean English-lexifier Creoles (henceforth AECs) and is spoken on the island of Bioko, Equatorial Guinea by at least 100,000 speakers. The language is an offshoot of Krio and arrived with African settlers from Freetown, Sierra Leone in 1827 (Fyfe 1962: 165). Pichi belongs to the African branch of the AECs and shares many characteristics with its sister languages Nigerian, Cameroonian and Ghanaian Pidgin, as well as Aku (Gambia) (cf. Yakpo 2009b for a detailed grammatical description of the language). At the same time, one and a half centuries of extensive language contact with Spanish have given the language a distinct character of its own. Pichi features a mixed prosodic system with the majority of words specified for pitch-accent and a minority for tone. Pichi has a largely isolating morphology with a limited use of inflectional and derivational morphology in

---

[*] This paper was written with the support of the ERC grant no. 230310 "Traces of Contact".

which tonal and non-tonal affixes, as well as suppletive forms are made use of. The language is aspect and mood-prominent and employs particles for the expression of tense, mood and aspect. Pichi exhibits an SV(O) word order and a nominative-accusative alignment. The language also makes use of various types of multiverb constructions.

The objective of this study is to provide a detailed description of reiteration in Pichi, and of reduplication in particular. The latter process stands out as a morphologized operation amongst the other types of reiteration. In doing, so I focus on the understudied prosodic aspects of reiteration. I will show that in Pichi, as in the entire family of AECs, prosody is central to an understanding of the formal and functional properties of reiteration, and by extension, the question of iconicity and the relation between morphology and syntax. I show that in form and function, reduplication in Pichi (and in the other African AECs) shares deep-rooted typological affinities with the languages of the entire linguistic area of "West Africa". These affinities can also be observed, albeit to a lesser degree, in the AECs of the Caribbean branch. An in-depth investigation of the prosodic characteristics of reiteration (and verbal reduplication in particular) in the languages of West Africa can help us advance our understanding of reiteration in the entire family of Afro-Caribbean English-lexifier Creoles. In this way, an approach grounded in areal typology can help provide answers to the issues raised by Aboh et al. in the introduction to this volume.

Section 2 presents an overview of the four types of reiteration in Pichi. Section 3 briefly addresses patterns of lexicalized reiteration. Sections 4 and 5 take a detailed look at morpho-phonological and semantic aspects of reduplication and repetition. The sections focus on verbal reiteration and also provide phonetic evidence for the tonal processes that accompany these two types of reiteration. Section 6 places reduplication within the areal context. Section 7 concludes the chapter. All unreferenced examples stem from field data, i.e. a corpus of approximately 50,000 words gathered on Bioko island between 2003 and 2007.

2.   Overview of reiteration

Pichi features four distinct types of productive processes involving the reiteration of words: (1) reduplication, (2) repetition, (3) the use of cognate objects, and (4) predicate doubling. The four types may be distinguished in terms of the word classes they apply to, the morphosyntactic process involved in their formation, the number of possible iterations, the morphosyntactic domain or structural level at which formation takes place, and the resulting meanings.

Reduplication involves reiteration and the simultaneous operation of tone deletion, as shown in (1).[1] Reduplication is only productive with dynamic verbs. In contrast, repetition involves duplication without a tonal change, as in (2), and is found with members of all major word classes. The repetition of larger constituents, i.e. phrases and entire clauses is also attested, and I will show in §5 that the distinction between morphological and syntactic repetition is not easily made:

(1) *Wetin yù dè* **chènch-chench** *nɔmba dèn so?*
     what 2SG IPFV RED.CPD-change number PL like.that
     'Why are you constantly changing (telephone) numbers like that?'

(2) *À dè si* **big big** *faya.*
     1SG.SBJ IPFV see big big fire
     'I was seeing a huge fire.'

Pichi cognate objects are deverbal nouns derived from themselves. Cognate objects occur with a few particular verbs in a non-emphatic, non-specific context and contribute little if nothing at all to the meaning denoted by the verb. For example, one of the few objects with which the intransitive verb *day* 'die' is attested is a cognate object as in the following example:

(3) *Ey, dan kayn spétìkul, à* **day day.**
     INTJ that kind glasses 1SG.SBJ die die
     'Hey, that kind of glasses, (if I had it) I would die.'

Aside from that, the use of cognate objects provides an important means of expressing emphasis. When used in this way, cognate objects are very frequently preceded by the indefinite determiner *wan* 'one, a'. The presence of the indefinite determiner in (4) also provides evidence for analyzing the cognate object as nominal in nature. In this, the Pichi structure patterns with analogous structures in other Creoles discussed in this volume, e.g. Matinikè (cf. Glaude & Zribi-Hertz this volume, Section 3.2, Bernabé 1983):

(4) *Dan tòrí bìn dè* **swit** *mi* **wan swit.**
     that story PST IPFV be.tasty 1SG.EMP one tastiness
     'I ENJOYED that story.'

---

1. Tones in Pichi are graphicized in the following way: monosyllables and penultimate syllables always bear a high tone if they bear no tone accent. Low-toned mono- or penultimate syllables always bear a grave accent, as in /ò/ When a high tone occurs elsewhere in the word it is marked so by an acute accent, hence /ó/. Syllables not covered by these notation rules are always low and remain unmarked. Words of other languages are fully marked for tone. A mid-tone is indicated by a horizontal line, as in /ō/.

In constructions involving verb doubling, the focused verb appears twice in the sentence: fronted in the initial focus position directly after the focus marker *nà*, and at the same time in its original syntactic position in the out-of-focus part of the sentence. Compare the following example featuring the dynamic verb *go* 'go':

(5) *Nà   go   à   dè   go   ò.*
     FOC go   1SG.SBJ   IPFV go   EMP
     '(Mind you) I'm GOING.'

The construction in (5) is also known as "predicate clefting" (cf. Koopman 1984; Larson & Lefebvre 1991). But the analysis by Glaude & Zribi-Hertz (this volume) shows that the evidence for seeing this construction as involving fronting of the predicate, rather than the verb(al root) alone is rather tenuous. And in fact, in Pichi structures involving verb doubling, predicate constituents such as TMA particles may not be fronted together with the verb, thence the ungrammaticality of the option in parentheses in (6):

(6) *Nà   (*bìn   dè)   waka   wì   bìn   dè   waka   go   de.*
     FOC   PST   IPFV walk   1PL PST   IPFV walk   go   there
     'We WALKED there.'

Verb doubling signals presentational or contrastive focus of the predicate and produces intensifying, emphatic meanings. Neither temporal or causal adverbial meanings, nor factive clauses are expressed through predicate doubling, as is the case in Haitian Creole (cf. Glaude & Zribi-Hertz this volume).

The following table summarizes the features of the four types of reiteration in Pichi.

Table 1. Features of reiteration

Feature/Type	Reduplication	Repetition	Cognate objects	Predicate doubling
Word classes	Dynamic verbs	Dynamic verbs, numerals, adverbs, attributive property items, nouns	Verbs	Verbs
Formation	Derivation	Inflection, adjunction	Selection	Fronting
Domains	Word	Word, phrase, clause	Phrase	Clause
Number of iterations	Duplication	Duplication and triplication	Duplication	Duplication
Meanings	Iterative, dispersive, attenuative	Iterative (verbs), distributive (numerals), augmentative (property items, nouns)	Augmentative (emphasis)	Augmentative (emphasis)

In view of the large range of forms and functions of reiteration in Pichi, I will limit the following discussion to the two first types of reiteration in the table above – reduplication and repetition. As we will see, these two processes can be interpreted as not exclusively syntactic, albeit in varying degrees. Secondly, they do not chiefly serve the pragmatic, discourse-related functions of emphasis and intensification, as is the case with the use of cognate objects and predicate doubling. In addition, we will have a closer look at verbs, the word class that can undergo both types of reiteration. In the further course of this paper, the crucial issue of iconicity will also be discussed – and in particular, whether the two productive types of reiteration in Pichi can be ranked with respect to their degree of inherent iconicity.

3. Lexicalized reiteration

In the following sections, I only discuss productive reiteration in Pichi in more detail. Yet, a brief overview of non-productive, lexicalized reiteration is in order to clearly demarcate it from productive types of reiteration. The language features a modest number of words consisting of at least two identical components that cannot be separated and used on their own. I suggest that lexicalized iterations are for their largest part carry-overs from African substrate and adstrate languages. The prosodic pattern of one portion of such lexicalized iterations is suggestive of reduplication, the other features a pattern that points towards repetition.

All words involving lexicalized repetition in the corpus are ideophones. Hence, the following ideophonic adverb *gbogbògbo* in (7), which expresses haste has no attested simplex form **gbò*. The ideophone only occurs as a duplicated or triplicated reiteration, as in this example:

(7) *Tokòbé dɔn wɛr klos   gbogbògbo.*
     NAME PRF wear clothing IDEO
     'Tokòbé had put on (her) clothes in haste.'

The same holds for the ideophone *kamúkàmú*, which depicts the countermovement of the individual halves of a pair of buttocks as their owner strides along:

(8) *Yù si lɛk haw in   bàta   dɛn dè sek kamúkàmú?*
     2SG see like how 3SG.POSS buttock PL IPFV shake IDEO
     'Do you see her buttocks moving to-and-fro (as she walks along)?'

When we turn to lexicalized reduplication, it is noteworthy that the corpus only contains two instances of this type of reiteration involving a dynamic verb – hence the only category that can normally be subjected to productive reduplication. The reduplication *hàyd.háyd*, which could be analyzed as [RED.CPD-hide] if it were a derived reduplication, is an adverb meaning 'secretly', while *chùk.chúk* [RED.CPD-pierce] means 'thorn':

(9)   *Chico, yù   dɔn chɔp=àn   hàydháyd.*
      boy   2SG PRF eat=3SG.OBJ secretly
      'Man, you've eaten it secretly.'

All other lexicalized reduplications belong to other syntactic (sub-)categories. For example, we find nouns like *pɔtɔpɔtɔ́* in (10) and the (attributively used) property item *katakatá*, a fossilized reduplication of *kata* 'scatter' in (11):

(10) *Dan say   gɛt bɔ̀kú   pɔtɔpɔtɔ́.*
      that side get much   mud
      'That place is very muddy.'

(11) *Nà   wan kàta-kata   man.*
      FOC one RED.CPD-scatter man
      'He's a hectic man.'

The existence of lexicalized reduplications of categories other than dynamic verbs may be indicative of the existence of a less constrained productivity of reduplication in earlier stages of the language. This may be seen as supportive evidence for viewing reduplication as an expansive morphosyntactic strategy in emerging creole languages; one that makes up for the "lack" of (other types of) bound morphology. However, certain phonological cues (e.g. the presence of the labiovelar consonants /gb/ and /kp/, unattested in other word classes, as well as syllable structure) suggest that the vast majority of Pichi ideophones are not the fossilized outcomes of productive reiteration. Rather they are more or less established loans from African substrate and adstrate languages. Hence *pɔtɔpɔtɔ́* 'mud(dy) substance' has cognates in Akan *pɔtɔ* 'to mash', *mpɔtɔmpɔtɔ* 'a type of meal consisting of a mashed substance' (Ofori 2006: 50, no tonal notation provided) and in Niger-Congo languages further afield, e.g. Lingala *pɔtɔ* 'squash', *pɔtɔpɔtɔ́* 'mud', Van Everbroeck 1985: 167–68). I therefore assume that lexicalized reduplications consisting of English cognates like *hayd* (< 'hide') are "one-shots", i.e. creative neologisms based on substrate patterns (cf. e.g. Ibibio *dípé* 'hide', *Ǹdípé-Ǹdípé* 'secretly'; Kaufman 1968: 141). It should also be pointed out that lexicalized reiterations are common in languages not generally considered to be creoles, amongst others Pichi's lexifier language English (cf. Aboh et al. this volume, Section 1).

4.   Reduplication

Reduplication in Pichi involves a complex morphological operation consisting of the two distinct and simultaneous processes of self-compounding and tone deletion. In the process, the verb is reduplicated and the high tone over the first, reduplicated component is deleted and replaced by a default low tone. The tonal process inherent to reduplication is formally no different from compounding, except that the first component is a copy of the root. Words that have been subjected to reduplication can therefore be analyzed as special types of compounds. The application of the morphological process of tone deletion to the first component of the reduplicated verb suggests that Pichi reduplication is right-headed and involves preposing of the reduplicant to the base. As a productive derivational process, reduplication is only predicative in nature and solely attested with dynamic verbs. In the following, I first present the morpho-phonological characteristics of reduplication and the distribution of reduplicated forms. I then look at semantic aspects of reduplication.

Reduplicated verbs have virtually the same tonal configuration as compound nouns. Figure 1 presents the pitch trace of the compound noun *wàch-man* 'watchman', consisting of two monosyllabic components, namely the verb *wach* 'watch' and the noun *man* 'man'. As in all compounds, the lexical H-tone over the initial component (*wach*) has been deleted and replaced by a default L-tone (henceforth indicated by an X in the gloss). In contrast, the H-tone over the final component (*man*) remains unchanged. The resulting compound noun therefore features an X.H pitch configuration, which is pronounced as L.H. Note that the compound in Figure 1 is in sentence-medial position. Hence, *man* 'man' does not exhibit a fall, as it would if it were in sentence-final position:

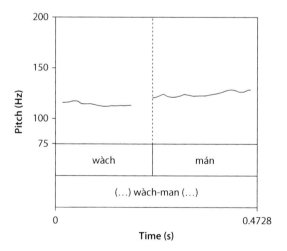

Wàch-man
L-H
watch.CPD-man
'Guard'

Figure 1. Monosyllabic components

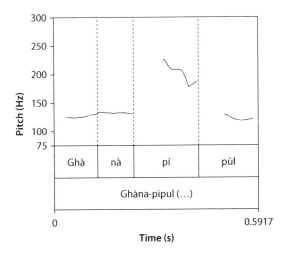

Ghàna-pipul
L.L-H.L
PLACE.CPD-people
'Ghanaians'

Figure 2. Bisyllabic components

Figure 2 above exemplifies the formation of a compound with two bisyllabic components, namely the place noun *Ghana* 'Ghana' and the common noun *pipul* 'people'. *Ghana* is a pitch-accented word with an H.X pitch configuration. Hence it bears a lexical H-tone over the first syllable. The second syllable of *Ghana* is toneless, hence bears a phonetic L-tone. Once more, the process of compounding involves the deletion of the H-tone over *Ghana*, the initial component of the compound. Conversely, the noun *pipul* retains its original H.X pitch configuration. The pitch contour graphically shows the rise over the first syllable of *pipul* by more than a 100 Hz above the level of the L-toned syllables of the compound. As expected, the second syllable of *pipul* retains its default low tone as well. It remains at roughly the same pitch level as the two L-toned syllables of *Ghana*.

Reduplicated verbs exhibit virtually the same pitch configuration as the two compound nouns in Figure 1 and Figure 2. The pitch trace of the reduplicated (and sentence-medial) monosyllabic *rɔn* 'run' in Figure 3 shows the X.H pitch configuration over the two identical components (even if the contour is relatively flat). This parallels the pitch trace over the compound *wàch-man* 'watchman' above. We must therefore assume that reduplication involves the same process as compounding: the lexical H-tone over the first component is deleted and replaced by an X, a default low tone:

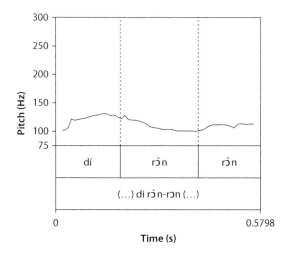

Dí   ròn-rɔn (...)
H   L-H
this RED.CPD-run
'This running around (...)'

Figure 3. Monosyllabic reduplicated verb

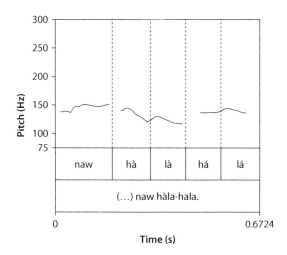

Naw   hàla-hala.
H   L.L-H.H
now   RED.CPD-shout
'Now (it was) constant shouting.'

Figure 4. Bisyllabic reduplicated verb

Likewise, the pitch contour over the bisyllabic reduplicated verb *hala* 'shout' in Figure 4 parallels that of the compound noun *Ghàna-pipul* 'Ghanaians' in Figure 2, even if the differences between the H and L tones are less pronounced in Figure 4. Here too, the H-tone over the first component of the reduplicative compound is erased and replaced by a default L-tone (hence an (X). At the same time, the pitch contour over the second component of the reduplicative compound in Figure 4 differs slightly from the pitch contour over the second component of the compound in Figure 2. Although the base is in sentence-final position in Figure 4, the toneless (hence L-toned) second syllable of the base does not exhibit the characteristic utterance-final fall. Instead, the sentence-final syllable stands at approximately the same pitch level as the preceding H-toned syllable of *hala*. As a result, we have a sequence of two phonetic L-tones over the reduplicant followed by a sequence of two phonetic H-tones over the base. Such a configuration over bisyllabic reduplicated verbs with an H.X configuration is the more common alternative. The less common alternative is for the second syllable of the bisyllabic base to feature a phonetic L-tone (realized as a falling tone) like the second syllable of *pipul* 'people' in Figure 2 above. This fact speaks to the conventionalized operation of H-tone spreading during reduplication; the H-tone of the first syllable of the base spreads to the second syllable due to emphatic stress. The succession of two identical tones over each component creates a segmentally and supra-segmentally symmetrical structure, which is in prosodic terms, no different from simplex XH words or XH compounds consisting of two monosyllables.

Reduplication is applied to the verb root. The reduplicated verb may appear in any syntactic position that a simplex form may be found in. This includes uses in which the verb does not function as the predicative nucleus of a clause. Sentence (12) features a reduplicated *rɔn* 'run' in a noun slot preceded by the demonstrative *di* 'this'. In (13), a reduplicated *waka* 'walk' appears as the second predicate of a serial verb construction:

(12)   *Pero di   rɔ̀n-rɔn   no dè gi   no natin   de.*
       but this RED.CPD-run NEG IPFV give NEG nothing there
       'But this running about aimlessly does not lead anywhere there.'

(13)   *Yéstàdé wì   kan go wàka-waka   mɔ.*
       yesterday 1PL PFV go RED.CPD-walk more
       'Yesterday we went strolling about again.'

The meanings engendered by reduplication are iterative-dispersive and may therefore be seen to express either temporal and/or spatial disaggregation (cf. Huber 2003:146 on the preference of "dispersive" over "distributive" as a function label for this kind of verbal reiteration). Pichi reduplication is "event-internal" (Cusic 1981:238); it denotes the reiteration of a single event on a single occasion, consisting of repeated internal phases. Therefore reduplication does not express habitual aspect and is only found with dynamic verbs. I argue that reduplication is a derivational process, but one that may be functionally akin to inflection when used with a purely iterative sense. The following sentence exemplifies such a primarily temporal interpretation of reduplication. Compare the meaning of the reduplicated verb *chench* 'change' in (14).

(14) *Wetin yù dè **chènch-chench** nɔmba dèn so?*
      what 2SG IPFV RED.CPD-change number PL like.that
      'Why are you constantly changing (telephone) numbers like that?'

The iterative notion expressed by reduplication harmonizes with the meanings expressed by imperfective aspect. In fact, the data reveals a much stronger tendency for reduplicated predicates to co-occur with the imperfective aspect marker *dè* 'IPFV' than with any other TMA marker. Compare the reduplicated verb *rɔb* 'rub' in (13) which expresses iterative aspect in combination with the imperfective marker *dè* 'IPFV':

(15) *Nà us=kayn tin mek yù dè rɔb-rɔb yù sɛf*
      FOC Q=kind thing make 2SG IPFV RED.CPD-rub 2SG self

      nia mi bìfó mì fambul?
      next.to 1SG.EMP before 1SG.POSS family
      'Why are you rubbing yourself up to me [getting all cozy with me] in front of my family?'

Nevertheless, reduplicated verbs may co-occur with any TMA marker that simplex forms may appear with. In (16), the reduplicated verb *tayt* 'be tight, tighten' appears with the potential mood marker *gò* 'POT':

(16) *À no want no natin we gò tàyt-tayt*
      1SG.SBJ NEG want NEG nothing SUB POT RED.CPD-tighten

      mì skin.
      1SG.POSS body
      'I don't want [to wear] anything that would pinch me (in various places).'

The example above also shows that the temporal-iterative sense of reduplication may subsume a spatial-dispersive sense. Beyond that, reduplication may acquire the attenuative nuances of low intensity and casualty of the action denoted by the verb. The data suggests that an attenuative sense is likely to arise when the reduplicated verb is intransitive or a transitive verb is employed in an intransitive clause. In each case it is the cumulative meaning of the various elements of the clause that tilts the balance towards a particular reading of the reduplicated verb. Hence in (17), the intransitive use of the reduplicated verb *tɔn* 'turn', in concert with the singular subject *è* '3SG.SBJ' (rather than a plural subject) favours a reading of low intensity. Further examples that involve attenuative nuances of low intensity or casualty are (12), (13), (15) and (16) above, as well as (20) below:

(17) *È   se   è   want kan   tòn-tòn   fò   Guinea.*
     3SG.SBJ QUOT 3SG.SBJ want come RED.CPD-turn PREP PLACE
     'He said he wanted to come travel around (a bit) in Equatorial Guinea.'

The distribution of verbal reduplication in my corpus also suggests that it principally occurs in contexts of low transitivity, even if reduplication does not categorically function as a detransitivizing device. Preceding examples featuring reduplication for one part involve low transitivity locomotion verbs (i.e. *rɔn* 'run' in (12) and *waka* 'walk' in (13)) and other verbs denoting body movement (i.e. *rɔb* 'rub (oneself) (15), *tɔn* 'turn' in (17) and *jump* 'jump' in (28) below). Further, where reduplicated verbs (irrespective of their semantic class) do appear in transitive clauses, these clauses involve less prototypical transitivity. Hence they may feature reflexive and reciprocal constructions (i.e. (16) above and (19) below), more or less lexicalized verb-noun collocations (i.e. *chench nɔmba* 'change one's telephone number' (14) above) or verbs followed by quantifier phrases like *ɔl say* 'all place' = 'everywhere'. The latter type of phrase functions as an adverbial indefinite pronoun and is therefore not a prototypical undergoer object either:

(18) *Dèn   dè   lɔk-lɔk   ɔl   say.*
     3PL   IPFV RED.CPD-lock all side
     'They're constantly closing every place.'

(19) *Dèn   kìn   dè   chàp-chap   dèn sɛf kɔtlas   ò.*
     3PL   HAB IPFV RED.CPD-chop 3PL self cutlass SP
     '(Mind you) they have the habit of chopping each other up with cutlasses [referring to political violence in northern Nigeria].'

Where reduplicated verbs with a higher degree of prototypical transitivity do occur, they are found in intransitive clauses, i.e. they are not followed by an object. In the following sentence, the reduplicated Spanish-origin verb *pica* 'snip, cut up' appears without a patient object:

(20) *À   bigín dè   pica-pica,   wì fray patata, wì*
     1SG.SBJ begin IPFV RED.CPD-cut.up 1PL fry potato 1PL

     fray plàntí.
     fry plantain
     'I began to (casually) snip (the trimmings), we fried potatoes, we fried plantain.'

A question to be addressed is whether Pichi reduplication should be seen as derivational or inflectional. Traditionally, a morphological process is classified as
derivational if it either has a category-changing effect, i.e. creates a new lexeme, or
in the absence of a category change, induces a substantial meaning change in the
lexeme (cf. Bauer 1988: 77ff). An inflectional process, on the other hand, should be
characterized by lexical generality, i.e. produce a new form of the same lexeme and
involve a minimal semantic modification (cf. e.g. Bybee 1985: 83ff). The iterative
sense produced by reduplication in examples like (14) and (15) above renders an
iconic "more of the same" meaning (Lakoff & Johnson 1980: 128; Kouwenberg &
LaCharité 2003). Hence in such instances reduplication could be argued to possess sufficient lexical generality to warrant being seen as inflectional. However, we
have also seen that such iterative uses also acquire non-predictable, non-iconic
attenuative meanings. These are thus diametrically opposed to "more of the same",
iterative meanings.

   An argument in favour of derivation in addition to lack of generality and predictability in meaning is the distribution of reduplication. The process appears to
be limited in productivity to dynamic verbs in Pichi. It is therefore not attested
with stative and inchoative (resultative) verbs. A final feature that speaks for derivation is the lack of obligatoriness of reduplication for the expression of iterative
aspect. The iterative sense can be expressed by the TMA marker *kin* alone. The
focal function of *kin* is the expression of habitual aspect, but in a small number
of cases in my data, this marker also expresses iterative aspect by itself without
additional reduplication. The speaker in the two consecutive sentences in (21),
explains how she repeatedly feels the temperature of her sick grandchild:

(21)   *We   à   **kin   mek** so,   à   no   dè   fil   hɔt,*
       SUB 1SG.SBJ HAB make like.that 1SG.SBJ NEG IPFV feel heat

       *pero we   à   **kin   tɔch** ìn   fut,   ìn   han   de,*
       but SUB 1SG.SBJ HAB touch 3SG.POSS foot 3SG.POSS hand there

       nà   so   dèn   [ko:::l].
       FOC like.that 3PL be.cold.EMP

       'When I would do like this, I wouldn't feel heat, but when I would touch his
       leg, his hand there, that's how terribly cold they were.'

At this point, it is important to underline the fundamental differences between
Pichi verbal reduplication and the type of verbal reiteration described in the non-
AEC creoles in this volume. For one part, Schang (this volume) convincingly
shows that São Tomense verbal reiteration can be analyzed in terms of syntactic
concatenation alone, hence without recourse to a morphological process. We will
see in the following section that Pichi also has a largely syntactic type of verbal
reiteration whose functional properties are distinct from reduplication. Hence, the

various functions of verbal iteration are only realized by a single non-derivational process in São Tomense while Pichi features a neat formal-functional differenciation of verbal reiteration.

Secondly, Pichi reduplication also differs from verbal reiteration in the French-lexifier creole Morisyen. Henri (this volume) demonstrates for Morisyen that the central meaning engendered by verbal reiteration is an attenuative one while the presence of secondary senses such as iterative and cumulative is conditioned by the lexical aspect of the verb. In Pichi, the reverse holds: Reduplication has been shown to typically produce an iterative sense, a meaning that has been interpreted as iconic by Kouwenberg & LaCharité (2003), Aboh et al. (this volume) and Aboh & Smith (this volume). An attenuative sense arises in contexts of syntactic intransitivity in Pichi and this reading may therefore be seen as a by-product of a lack of clausal telicity. The Pichi and Morisyen data therefore show an interesting parallel. Where Morisyen interpretations of reduplication hinge on lexical aspect, Pichi appears to show similar effects as a result of clausal aspect. An important difference between Morisyen and Pichi reduplication is, however, that the latter is more restricted in its distribution. It is only attested with dynamic verbs, even if this lexical aspect class encompasses the vast majority of Pichi verbs (including the large class of labile verbs that alternate between dynamic and resultative readings). In contrast, Morisyen verbal reiteration may also be applied to stative verbs (e.g. *krwar* 'believe') as long as they may be interpreted as gradable.

The differences between Pichi, São Tomense and Morisyen suggest that the individual contact trajectory of the creole and the family it belongs to is largely responsible for the emergence of the various types of reiteration and their characteristics in these languages. I will show further below that Pichi verbal reduplication patterns with that found in its West African sister languages and related Caribbean AECs. I argue in Section 6 that these family-wide similarities can be accounted for by substrate and adstrate influence rather than by a phylogenetic peculiarity common to creole languages.

5.   Repetition

Repetition in Pichi is a semi-morphological operation during which an item is duplicated or triplicated (more repetitions are not attested in the data). Although a pause or boundary tone is not normally inserted between the repeated elements, repetition does not involve the tonal process that characterizes compounding and reduplication. Hence every repeated constituent retains its lexically determined tone pattern. I argue further below that the process may be called inflectional, but do so with reluctance: there appears to be a fuzzy boundary between repetition as a morphological, word-level process and the pragmatically determined reiteration of phrases, even whole clauses by asyndetic adjunction.

The pitch trace in Figure 5 exemplifies repetition. It contains the triplicated manner adverbial *sen* '(in the) same (way) (pronounced [sjén]). As can be seen, the first and second occurrences of *sen* do not bear a lower pitch than each following one. In fact, the opposite is the case: each reiteration is slightly higher in pitch than the following one, and lower than the preceding one. The tonal declination in repetitions is caused by downstep, a phenomenon that we encounter in all successions of adjacent H tones in Pichi (cf. Yakpo 2009b: 92–93). This shows that repetition does not involve any special tonal process at the word or phrase-level, but rather a regular clause-level tonal process encountered with other, non-reiterated constituents as well:

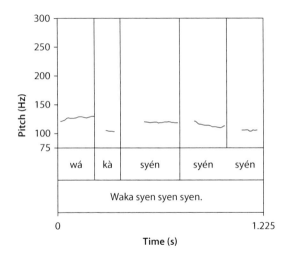

Waka	*sen*	*sen*	*sen.*
H.X	H	H	H
walk	same	same	same

'Walk exactly in one line.'

Figure 5. Repetition

I suggest that the core meaning of repetition is augmentative, hence an iconic "more of the same". Repetition therefore produces a range of mostly emphatic, intensifying nuances, whose exact meanings vary with the word class of the item repeated. The expression of plural number does not lie within the functional range of repetition. Repetition is much wider in its application than reduplication. My data features the repetition of nouns, verbs, property items functioning as prenominal modifiers, adverbs and ideophones. Very often, the word in question is triplicated rather than duplicated for increased emphasis or dramatic effect. The following three sentences exemplify the use of intensifying repetition for emphasis with the temporal adverb *naw* 'now' (22), the locative adverbial *dɔn* 'down' (23), the common noun *fambul* 'family' and the attributively used property item *bɔkú* '(be) much' (24). Note the triplication of *dɔn* 'down' in (23) and *fambul* 'family' in (24):

(22)   À   dè   kɔmɔt   nà   tɔn   **naw naw.**
       1SG.SBJ IPFV come.out   LOC town   now   now
       'I coming from town right now.'

(23)   Bɔt   in   sìdɔn dɔn   dɔn   dɔn   yàndá.
       but   3SG.EMP stay   down down   down   yonder
       'But he lives far down over there.'

(24)   Fɔ   mì   **fambul fambul fambul** à   no   sàbí
       PREP 1SG.POSS family   family family 1SG.SBJ NEG   know

       bɔkú   bɔkú pɔsin   dèn.
       much   much   person   PL
       'Within my immediate family I don't know really know a lot of people.'

Another type of repetition that may be seen as iconic involves numerals and renders a distributive sense. In (25), the repeated numeral *tu* 'two' functions as a depictive modifier to the clause and is oriented towards the plural object pronoun *dɛn* '3PL.EMP'. In Pichi, numbers higher than five are normally expressed through the corresponding Spanish numeral. Sentence (26) features the triplicated Spanish numeral *quinientos* 'five hundred':

(25)   Yù   fit   kyɛr   dɛn   **tu   tu.**
       2SG   can   carry 3PL.EMP   two   two
       'You can carry them in pairs.'

(26)   À   bay=àn   **quinientos   quinientos   quinientos.**
       1SG.SBJ buy=3SG.OBJ five.hundred five.hundred five.hundred
       'I bought them for five hundred (Francs) each.'

Examples (22)–(26) show the large variety of syntactic categories that may be subjected to repetition. Nevertheless, nouns as in (24) above are very rarely found to be repeated while repeated property items functioning as prenominal attributive modifiers like *bɔkú* in (24) above, numerals like *tu* 'two' in (25) and time expressions like *naw* 'now' in (22) are found more frequently in the corpus. This distribution points towards the fact that repetition is strongly associated with gradable, hence quantity and quality denoting lexical items. In this context, the distributive sense yielded by the repetition of numerals is interesting since an augmentative sense could conceivably produce intensive-augmentative meanings like 'just two' and 'exactly five hundred' in the two examples above. Nevertheless, a distributive sense appears to be equally natural to the construction in as far as the quantification expressed by the numeral is scattered over each referent. This view is supported by the meaning of a reduplicated non-numeral quantifier like *smɔl* 'a bit, few' in the following example. Here both partitive, hence quantity-gradable, as well as distributive interpretations are possible with duplications and more repetitions. In that, Pichi differs from São Tomense. In the latter language, a contrastive (hence intensive-augmentative) reading of a quantifier like *mina* 'little' is only possible in the event of duplication, while triplication only renders a distributive sense (cf. Schang this volume, Section 2.5)

(27)　*Yù　fit　kyɛr　dɛn　**smɔl smɔl (smɔl).***
　　　2SG　can　carry　3PL.EMP　few　few　few
　　　'You can carry them little by little/one after the other.'

A further distributional characteristic of repetition is of interest. There is not a single instance in my corpus of a repeated property item that functions as a predicate, e.g. *ʔè big big* 'it is very big'. Instead predicatively used property items are emphasized through various other means at the disposal of the language. One common way of emphasizing quantity and quality denoting predicates is by the use of suprasegmental modification, as with the property item *kol* 'be cold' in (21) above: the vowel is lengthened and receives an extra-high pitch, which indicates a larger amount of intensity or dimension of the property specified for the referent. This distribution of repetition is peculiar, since we should assume that dimension and other quantity-denoting predicates should be susceptible to augmentative reduplication. Yet this apparent contradiction may be explained. Just like reduplication, the corpus only contains instances of repetition applied to dynamic verbs, to the exclusion of non-dynamic property concepts. Dynamic verbs denote situations that lack relatively time-stable qualities, so "more of the same" implies that repetition produces non-time stable quantity-related meanings. Like reduplication, verbal repetition is therefore only iterative, not augmentative. With prototypically dynamic verbs, repetition therefore produces a focus on inherent temporal boundaries. There is thus no restriction on the concurrence of reduplication and verbal repetition. In (28), reduplication and the simultaneous repetition of the reduplicated sequence collude to give an emphatic iterative and dispersive sense to the clause:

(28)　*Sɔ̀ntén　è　　bìn　dè　**jùmp-jump　　jùmp-jump,***
　　　perhaps　3SG.SBJ　PST　IPFV　RED.CPD-jump　RED.CPD-jump

　　　pero　è　　stret　　naw.
　　　but　3SG.SBJ　be.straight　now

　　　'Let's assume she was constantly jumping around but she's upright now.'

Finally, it should be noted that there is a fuzzy boundary between what we have so far interpreted as the morphological repetition of single words and the syntactic repetition of phrases and even entire clauses by simple adjunction for purely pragmatic ends. One way of differentiating the former from the latter type of repetition is the presence of an intonation break – either a pause or a declarative boundary tone (an utterance-final L-tone) between the repeated elements, as in (29):

(29)   *Nɔ,   ìn   estómago,   ìn   estómago,   ìn   estómago.*
      NEG   3SG.POSS   stomach   3SG.POSS   stomach   3SG.POSS   stomach
      '[She would repeatedly say] no, (it's) her stomach, her stomach, her
      stomach.'

The borderline between the asyndetic concatenation of phrases and inflectional repetition is far more brittle once there is no prosodic boundary-marking. The three-fold repetition of a verb phrase consisting of the dynamic verb *kɔt* and its clitic object pronoun *=àn* in (30), yields an iterative sense that is virtually indistinguishable from the one engendered by reduplication in examples like (14) and (18) above. Yet, each reiteration could theoretically be separated from the following one by a pause or boundary tone if the speaker chose to do so.

(30)   *Dì   de   yù   bwɛl   jakato,   yù   kɔt=àn   kɔt=àn*
      DEF   day   2SG   boil   bitter.tomato   2SG   cut=3SG.OBJ   cut=3SG.OBJ

      kɔt=àn   yù   bay   wan   sardina.
      cut=3SG.OBJ   2SG   buy   one   sardine.
      'The day you boil bitter tomato, you cut it up into small bits (and) you buy
      a sardine.'

Ultimately, repetition should be seen as a continuum ranging from relatively morphologized to largely syntactic processes. The latter would encompass the pragmatically-oriented kind of phrasal reiteration contained in (29) above. The former would include, in particular, the repetition of numerals and property items. For example, the highly conventionalized repetition of the dimension-denoting property items *big* '(be) big' and *smɔl* '(be) small' renders the regular meanings of 'huge' and 'tiny', as in the two following examples:

(31)   *À   dè   si   **big big**   faya.*
      1SG.SBJ   IPFV   see   big big   fire
      'I was seeing a huge fire.'

(32)   *È   dè   sɛl   è   dè   put   **smɔl   smɔl**   wan   fɔ   kɔna.*
      3SG.SBJ   IPFV   sell   3SG.SBJ   IPFV   put   small   small   one   PREP   corner
      'She's selling (and) she's saving tiny amounts (of money)'

Rather than being particularly common to "creoles" as a presumed typological class of languages (e.g. Bakker 2003b, 2011), repetition with an iconic, augmentative sense of the kind described in this section appears be cross-linguistically common. It is, for example, also encountered in extensively documented languages like English and French, even if somewhat understudied (cf. Aboh et al. this volume, example 10(a)–(d), Ghomeshi et al. 2004; Cadiot & Nemo 1997). Nevertheless, even in such show-case examples of iconicity as in the sentences above, there appears to be enough leeway for the emergence of language-specific meanings of iconic reiteration. For example, the reiteration of the noun *fambul* 'family' in (24) renders more of the proto-typically same thing, rather than a plural sense, hence 'my real family' instead of 'my family members' (*fambul* can also mean 'family member' in Pichi) (cf. Cohen this volume, and Horn 1993 for a similar effect in Hebrew, as well as Ghomeshi et al. 2004 on "contrastive reduplication" in English). There is therefore a need for more studies of iconic reiteration in individual languages.

An open question is how much the form and functions of Pichi repetition reflect ad- and substratal patterns. The iconic nature of Pichi repetition, i.e. the full copying of the base without an additional morphological operation and the emphatic and iterative meanings that it produces make this a difficult question. The widespread existence of this kind of reiteration in other linguistic areas of the globe would require a careful assessment beyond the scope of this paper in order to distinguish between adstratal, areal and universal, iconicity-induced patterns.

6.   An areal view on Pichi reduplication

This section places Pichi reduplication within an areal and genetic context. I show that the reduplication of verbs in Pichi follows a morphophonemic template that is widespread in the linguistic area that the language belongs to and that Pichi reduplication also fits into an areal tendency with respect to its functions. I base this section on the hypothesis that Pichi reduplication with its tonal morphology is too distinct an operation to have arisen through internal development alone. I conclude that the form and functions of Pichi reduplication have been influenced to no small degree by adstrate (and substrate) patterns that can be found in a linguistic area that I define as "West Africa". I also suggest that adstratal pressure from English and the lack of a continuing African adstratal input has given Caribbean verbal reiteration a character distinct from that of Pichi.

I do not wish to exclude *a priori* the possibility of lexifier influences on the forms and functions of reiteration in Pichi. Thanks to comprehensive studies like

Ghomeshi et al. (2004) our understanding has broadened of seemingly "exotic" reduplication patterns in informal English (and in the non-normalized varieties of other European languages like French, cf. Aboh et al. this volume). There is no reason to assume that such patterns were not already in use when English was taking part in the creation of Pichi's ancestor. Yet the evidence is greatly in favour of a substrate and adstrate input into the present form and functions of reduplication in Pichi, rather than a lexifier input. One piece of evidence is formal: Verbal reduplication in English shows a stress pattern that is diametrically opposed to the prominence pattern found in Pichi reduplication (cf. Horn 1993:48). Additional evidence is functional: The meanings rendered by verbal reduplication in Pichi manifest a high degree of grammaticalization. English verbal reduplication is entirely syntactic in form and pragmatic in function.

I limit the analysis in this section to reduplication. We should expect this type of reiteration with its less iconic meanings to be expressed through processes that are correspondingly more grammaticalized and formally more complex than mere reiteration by itself. In the absence of a broader typological survey of the morphophonemics of reiteration in the linguistic area, the conclusions drawn from the data presented below can only be tentative and intuitive, and too weak to count as conclusive evidence. Aside from that, the comparison presented here must be seen as exploratory due to methodological shortcomings: Only a small number of languages, and only those that feature the relevant phenomena are included. Nevertheless, I consider it to be non-trivial that these phenomena are found in a cross-section, however small, of genealogically unrelated and distant languages of "West Africa". I therefore suggest that the forms and functions of Pichi reduplication probably fit into a wider areal pattern and that the question deserves a more detailed investigation.

The linguistic area which I henceforth refer to as "West Africa" is partially coterminous with the corresponding politico-geographical entity. The area is meant to encompass Africa south of the Sahara and north of the Bight of Biafra, and the region eastwards from Senegal as far as north-western Cameroon. The area includes the following major families of the Niger-Congo phylum (roughly from west to east): Mande, Kru, Gur, Kwa, Dogon, West and East Benue-Congo (excluding Narrow Bantu) and Adamawa. Likewise, the area includes languages of the Nilo-Saharan and Afro-Asiatic phyla, from which examples will also be drawn in the following. Not only did a large proportion of the population that created the Afro-Caribbean English-lexifier Creoles originate in this region (cf. e.g. Curtin 1969; Rodney 1975:79ff). This is also the region where the African AECs are presently spoken and which therefore constitutes the contact zone of the African AECs and languages from the families cited above. Beyond that, the areal-typological unity of a linguistic area corresponding in varying degrees to "West Africa" has long been proposed in the literature (cf. Güldemann 2008 for a recent discussion, also Westermann 1911; Wolff & Gerhard 1977; Jungraithmayer 1980).

Pichi reduplication fits into an areal pattern in two ways. First, in the following sample of (tonal) languages of "West Africa", a suprasegmental process of tone deletion and replacement similar to the one found in Pichi accompanies the formation of compounds. The tonal processes underlying compound formation are often highly complex and varied in individual languages. Yet a recurring pattern is for the first component of a compound to surface with a tone that is lower (irrespective of its lexically assigned tone) than that of the second component. In prosodic terms, this renders a nonprominence-prominence pattern over the resulting compound. This pattern can also be found in all related African AECs and has been described for Krio (Fyle & Jones 1980: xxxiv; Jones 1990: 119) Ghanaian Pidgin English (Huber 1999: 242–43, 2003: 148), and Nigerian Pidgin (Faraclas 1996: 251–52). I therefore suggest that Pichi reduplication is a feature inherited from Krio.

The examples in (33) illustrate the phonetic outcome of nominal compounding that we have already seen in Pichi: the lexical tone(s) of (the) first component(s) of the compound are lowered, while (a segment within) the second component bears a higher relative pitch. We find this pattern in Akan (Kwa; Marfo 2005: 73) and Bobo (Mande; Morse 1976: 151). In Jamsay (Dogon; Heath 2008: 187, 15) an analogous pattern includes compounds and larger constituents, such as common NPs. The pattern is also found in Gwari (West Benue-Congo; Hyman & Magaji 1970: 29) and Kanuri (Saharan; Hutchison 1981: 68). Still, this pattern is far from uniform and we find diverging patterns of compound formation in many major languages of the region (a notable exception being Yoruba, cf. Awoyale 1974: 356ff). But the examples in (33) indicate a pattern in which the second component features one or more syllables with a higher pitch than any found on the first component and thereby bears the prosodic peak of the construction.

(33)

Language	Components			Compound	
Akan	àbɔ́foɔ́, èdáí	'messengers, house'		àbɔ́fò-dáí	'guest house'
	sìká, kɔ̀kɔ́ɔ́	'money, red'		sìkà-kɔ̀kɔ́ɔ́	'gold'
Bobo	vàgàká, lāgā	'corn, fields'		vàgàkā-lágà	'corn fields'
	pī, zɔ̀gɔ̀	'to cover, cover'		pī-zɔ́gɔ̀	'blanket'
Jamsay	tɔ́rɔ́, ñĕ̌, -m	'mountain, woman, -PL		tɔ̀rɔ̀-ñĕ̌-m	'mountain women'
	úró, dáɣá, pírú	'house, small, white'		ùrò dàɣà pírú	'small white house'
Gwari	knú, ōnyá	'sell, thing'		nyà-knú	'selling'
	gyè, ōnyá	'sharpen, thing'		nyà-gyé	'sharpening'
Kanuri	cî, kùndúlì	'mouth, hair'		cì-kùndùlì	'moustache'
	dágɔ̀l, bùlóngú	'dog, type of tree'		dàgɔ̀l-bùlóngú	'baboon'

Pichi appears to conform to an areal pattern with respect to a second characteristic as well. In all the languages listed above verbal reduplication involves the same suprasegmental process as compounding, as shown in (34) below. Additional languages have a Pichi-type reduplication without featuring the corresponding process in compounding. Hence a prominent pattern of verbal reduplication in Kroumen Tépo (Kru; Thalmann 1987:25–26) involves polar tone sequences in which the high-toned second component retains its lexical tone, while the partial reduplicant acquires a tone one notch lower. The same holds for Akan (Kwa): in a subtype of reduplication, low-toned verbs acquire high tones while the preceding partial reduplicant bears a low tone (Christaller 1964 [1875]: 65ff). Reduplication accompanied by tone lowering over the first component appears to be particularly common in Kwa and is the regular pattern in Ewe (field notes) and Ga (Kropp Dakubu 1999: 33, 55). In Bobo (Morse 1976:146), a lexical high tone over the first component of a verbal reduplication surfaces with a mid tone, while the second component retains its high tones. In Jamsay (Heath 2008:356), the dominant pattern of verbal reduplication involves the prefixation of a low-toned reduplicant, as with the perfective reduplications below. A similar pattern can be observed in Kanuri (Hutchison 1981:74) where a high-toned suffix attaches to the second component, as well as in Ngie (East Benue-Congo; Umenjoh 1997:74) verbal reduplication, where the second component in a reduplication bears high tones over all syllables.

Yoruba (West Benue-Congo; Awoyale 1974:356ff) is once more an exception to this pattern, and so is Gwari (Hyman & Magaji 1970:31). Nevertheless, verbal reduplication in both languages conforms to the other languages cited with respect to its semantics. In virtually all of the genealogically disparate languages listed in (34), reduplication yields deverbal nouns, as can be seen by the translations provided:

(34)

Language	Simple		Reiterated	
Kroumen Tépo	lá	'kill'	lī-lá	'act of killing'
	hré	'exit'	hī-hré	'act of exiting'
Akan	pàm	'sew'	pè-pám	'sew (many things) repeatedly'
	sɔ̀rè	'pray'	sò-sɔ́ré	'pray repeatedly'
Ewe	kpɔ́	'see'	kpɔ̀-kpɔ́	'act of seeing, sight'
	dzó	'leave'	dzò-dzó	'departure'
Ga	bálà	'wrap'	bàlà-bàláí	'wrap up repeatedly'
	fútù	'mix'	fùtù-fútú	'act of mixing, mixture'
Bobo	sɔ̀	'cut'	sɔ̀-sɔ́	'chop up'
	tìgè	'jump'	tìgè-tīgē	'jump around'
Jamsay	cé:né	'be good'	cì-cé:nè	'(it) has been good'
	píné	'be shut'	pì-pínè	'(it is) kept shut'

Kanuri	kòm	'count'	kòm-kòmí	'calculations'
	sáp	'collect'	sàb-sàwí	'collection'
Ngie	sà	'(be) tall'	sài-sáy	'(be) very tall'
	dɔ̀tɔ̀	'(be) dirty'	dɔ̀tɔ̀i-dɔ́tɔ́	'(be) very dirty'
Yoruba	ṣè	'cook'	ṣí-ṣè	'act of cooking'
	lò	'go'	lí-lò	'act of going'
Gwari	knú	'sell'	knú-knŭ	'act of selling'
	gyè	'sharpen'	gyè-gyè	'act of sharpening'

In a good number of genetically diverse West African languages, deverbal nouns, whether derived through reduplication or through other means, also appear in progressive/imperfective constructions that represent the end-point of a location-to-aspect grammaticalization channel (cf. Anderson 1971:15ff; Heine et al. 1991: 36–37). The formation of deverbal nouns through reduplication is productive in the entire Gbe group of the Kwa family of languages. The process is found in Gungbe (cf. Aboh & Smith this volume, Section 1) and in Ewe, for example. In the latter language we not only find the typical nominalizing function of verbal reduplication involving the characteristic tone replacement in the reduplicant (cf. (34) above). The Ewe progressive construction also illustrates the use of the reduplicated deverbal noun in a grammaticalized progressive construction, as in the following example:

(35) Kòfí lè   sì-sí-ḿ.
      NAME be.at[PRS] RED-run-PROG
      'Kofi is running (away).'   (Ameka 1991:42; gloss adapted)

In (35) above, a verbal noun sì-sí, derived from the verb sí 'run (away)' co-occurs with the locative copula lè and the bound progressive morpheme ḿ in an aspectual auxiliary construction expressing progressive aspect. The morpheme ḿ is diachronically related to the Ewe postposition mé 'inside, inner part'. Hence a diachronically informed literal translation of the construction would give 'Kofi is located in running (away)'. During the derivational process, the verb is duplicated and the tone over the first component deleted and replaced by a low tone. The reduplicative pattern in Ewe parallels that found in Pichi structures like (18) above. There is some morphophonemic variation in the formation of deverbal nouns in Gbe, since Gungbe apparently does not feature a tone replacement over the first component (cf. the tonal notation of kúkú in Aboh & Smith this volume, Section 1). However, the LH pattern seems to be a majority pattern and is also found in Gengbe (cf. Aboh & Smith this volume, Footnote 12).

A question that comes to mind in this context is whether Pichi verbal reduplication also produces a kind of verbal noun, or at least features some nominal characteristics that set it apart from the non-reduplicated, simplex form. This question is not easily answered because Pichi makes use of conversion in order to derive deverbal nouns. A simplex verb can therefore appear in the syntactic position of a noun without undergoing an overtly expressed derivation (Yakpo 2009b: 128–29). However, one distributional characteristic nevertheless points to the possibility of a decreased verbiness of the form. My data reveals a stronger tendency for reduplicated verbs to appear in nominal slots than corresponding simplex forms. Thus verbs in argument positions are more likely to involve a reduplicated verb than not. In fact, my data does not contain a single instance of an underived simplex verb functioning as an action noun in an object position as does *jwèn-jwen* in (36) below. Hence the reduced clausal transitivity that seems to correlate with the use of reduplicated forms may also be taken to indicate reduced prototypical "verbiness" of the reduplicated verb:

(36) *Mi*   *wèt* *Rubi* *wì* **mek** **jwèn-jwɛn,**   *wì* *bay* *pia,*
      1SG.EMP with   NAME   1PL   make   RED.CPD-join   1PL   buy   avocado

      wì *bay* *sàdín,* *wì* *bay* *tomates,* *wì* *desayuna.*
      1PL   buy   sardine   1PL   buy   tomatoes   1PL   breakfast

      'Me and Rubi, we joined up, we bought avocados, we bought sardines, we bought tomatoes, we had breakfast.'

A second distributional aspect may also be adduced to argue for a decreased verbiness of the reduplicated form. In the vast majority of recorded instances, reduplicated forms with a predicative function co-occur with the imperfective aspect marker *dè* 'IPFV'. This means that a clause like (16) above is rare, in which a predicatively used reduplicated verb is specified for potential mood alone, without the additional appearance of the imperfective marker (verbs may be marked simultaneously for both categories). Obviously, the mutual attraction between imperfective marking and reduplication is intimately tied to the iterative meanings expressed by reduplication itself. But beyond that, we might speculate that the co-occurrence of reduplication and imperfective marking is also due to the possibility of a diachronic development of imperfective marking in Pichi via the same locative schema as in Ewe. Such a scenario has implicitly been proposed for Nigerian Pidgin by Faraclas (1996), in providing the literal translation of the following example involving imperfective aspect:

(37) *Fɔr*   *vilɛj*   *naw,* *à*   **dè**   *fam,* *à*   **dè**   *fish.*
      PREP   village   TOP   1SG.SBJ   IPFV   farm   1SG.SBJ   IPFV   fish

      Lit: 'while I am in my village, I am located (or existing) in the state of farming and in the state of fishing.'
                                    (Nigerian Pidgin; Faraclas 1996: 49; glosses adapted)

Such a trajectory is in fact plausible, for the low-toned imperfective marker *dè* 'IPFV' is segmentally identical to the high-toned AEC locative copula *de* 'BE. AT'. The tonal difference between the two forms may have developed via the grammaticalization of the copula into an aspect marker in very much the same way as that of the high-toned lexical verb *go* 'go' into the low-toned mood/tense marker *gò* 'POT'. In one possible scenario, the proto-language of Pichi and its sister languages could have had a progressive construction in which the use of a locative copula and a nominal reduplicated form was conventionalized, as in Gbe. With the increased grammaticalization of the construction, the simplex form might have come to replace the reduplicated form, with the latter retaining its semantically more specialized functions (cf. Migge 2003 for a similar proposal with respect to Eastern Maroon Creole, Surinam). One indication for the plausibility of such a scenario is the restriction of reduplication in Pichi to dynamic verbs.

The overall impression from the data presented above is that a nonprominence-prominence pattern in reduplicated verbs stands out as the only common cross-cutting feature in the areal diversity of (supra-)segmental processes associated with verbal reduplication. It therefore appears that Pichi and its African sister languages have retained and reinforced or acquired this type of reduplicative strategy through their continuing ad- and substratal contact with the languages of the region.

We would therefore assume *a priori* that the languages of the Caribbean branch of the AECs would only feature Pichi-style reduplication if it had been transferred from the substrates and maintained under superstrate pressure. In Jamaican Creole, the largest AEC of the insular Caribbean. Kouwenberg et al. (2003) and Gooden (2003b) suggest the existence of "inflectional" and "derivational" reiteration as the two formally and functionally distinct types of reiteration in Jamaican, as shown in (38) below.

(38)	Type	Simple		Reiterated	
	Inflectional	kata	'scatter'	kátá-kata	'scatter a lot'
		jala	'yellow'	jálá-jala	'very yellow'
		faya	'fire'	fáyá-faya	'scattered fires'
	Derivational	kata	'scatter'	kata-kata	'scattered'
		jala	'yellow'	jala-jala	'yellowish'
		faya	'fire'	faya-faya	'quick-tempered'

Both types of reiteration can be applied to verbs, adjectives and nouns alike. Inflectional reiteration produces "more of the same", hence augmentative meanings, while derivational reiteration renders diminutive-distributive meanings. We will not dwell further on the observation that the functions of both types of Jamaican reiteration cut across the two Pichi reiteration types of repetition and reduplication and also include additional ones not available to Pichi (e.g. the adjectivizing function of derivational reiteration). Relevant from the formal perspective is that the two Jamaican types can also be distinguished in prosodic terms. In inflectional iterations involving a monomorphemic base, the entire first component bears stress. The reiteration thus has a high-low pitch pattern. In contrast, the first component in derivational iterations lacks stress and the entire reduplication carries a level pitch on both components (Gooden 2003b: 94–95). This means that Jamaican Creole has no prosodic pattern that corresponds to the Pichi low-high configuration encountered in reduplication.

The loss of lexical and grammatical tone and the development of strict stress-accent (i.e. cumulative syllable weight plus high pitch) in Jamaican (cf. Devonish 1989) may have been responsible for the disappearance of the nonprominence-prominence pattern found in Pichi, the African AECs in general, and the adstrate/substrate languages. In Jamaican, light word-final syllables may not bear primary stress (Gooden 2007: 70). I assume that this is why verbal iterations like the ones presented above may not bear stress on the second component if the first component carries no stress at all.

Support for the proposal that the absence of a nonprominence-prominence pattern in Jamaican iterations is indeed contact-induced comes from the English-lexifier creole Sranan, spoken in Surinam. This language has also lost lexical and grammatical tone – disregarding a residual tonal phenomenon (cf. Adamson & Smith 1994: 221). However, and presumably so due to the lack of contact with its lexifier English, Sranan has not fully discarded the African-style nonprominence-prominence pattern described above. Sranan has retained an intermediate system in which the tonal pattern found in African AEC verbal reduplications has been translated into a stress-based one. In terms of distribution, the Sranan types of reiteration seem to match those found in Pichi more closely than the Jamaican ones. All three productive Sranan types listed here are applied to predicates and thus parallel the restriction of reduplication to verbs in Pichi. I retain the function labels used by the authors:

(39)   Function   Simple   Reiterated
       Diminutive/   férfi   'paint'   férfi-férfi   'paint (a bit)'
       imperfective   sríbi   'sleep'   sríbi-sríbi   'doze; sleep'
       Augmentative   férfi   'paint'   ferfi-férfi   'paint a lot/too much'
       Iterative   férfi   'paint'   férfi-ferfi   'paint several times'

When turning to form, we see that the language employs three prominence patterns: even stress on both components (diminutive/imperfective), stress on the second component (augmentative) and stress on the first component (iterative).

At the same time, there is no complete form-function overlap with Pichi reiteration. For example, the Pichi high-low pattern renders iterative-dispersive-attenuative meanings while the Sranan unstressed-stressed pattern yields the opposite, namely augmentative meanings. Nonetheless Sranan features a formal exponent of the nonprominence-prominence pattern. Further, Sranan is the only language of the three creoles treated that features a maximal system with all three possible prominence permutations.

I suggest that this peculiarity of Sranan is linked to its contact history. Pichi and the African AECs have maintained a typologically West African type of reduplication through adstrate reinforcement. In turn, Sranan appears to have expanded its formal repertoire in iterations. It has done so by, on the one hand, retaining an originally tonal low-high contour from the substrate and transforming into a stress-based one. The retention of this prosodically "un-English" pattern must have been facilitated through the lack of adstatal contact with English since the formative period of Sranan. On the other hand, Sranan used the leeway offered by the departure from a tone system (presumably also caused by contact with the stress-accent language Dutch) in order to make use of additional prominence patterns. Yet lest we forget, the lack of overlap in form and function between Jamaican Creole, Sranan and Pichi reiteration also indicates a healthy degree of separate development in these three languages since the split from their common ancestor. How the separate trajectories of reiteration in these languages have been determined beyond common genealogical inheritance by differing degrees of substrate retention, adstratal contact with African and European languages and internal development respectively can only be determined by further research. These differences also suggest that there may be more to the morphosyntax of reiteration than meets the eye. Detailed studies of the underlying structure of constructions involving verbal reduplication in creole and non-creole languages such as Aboh & Smith (this volume) are therefore still needed (cf. also Aboh 2005a).

We have seen that there is a substantial form-function overlap between the languages of "West Africa" and Pichi with respect to the suprasegmental characteristics of verbal reduplication. The picture is however different if the segmental level is included in the analysis. Reduplication patterns in about half the languages listed in (34) involve partial reiteration – via segment alternation (e.g. Yoruba), segment alternation plus truncation (e.g. Akan and Jamsay) as well as (additional) affixation (e.g. Ngie). Reduplication in Pichi and its AEC sister languages could therefore be seen as formally less marked, hence requiring less rule processing, and therefore formally more iconic (cf. Kouwenberg 2004) than the reduplication patterns found in a good number of the languages of the linguistic area. Full reduplication is, however still widespread in "West Africa". The evidence is therefore inconclusive as to whether "creolization" or substrate transfer is responsible for the existence of full rather than partial reduplication in Pichi.

7.   Conclusion

Pichi has been shown to possess four distinct types of reiteration. The formation of these types involves processes at different structural levels. Two processes were singled out for a more detailed analysis. Reduplication was analyzed as a complex morphological operation restricted to dynamic verbs involving reiteration and a simultaneous tone change. Repetition was analyzed as a semi-morphological operation that straddles the boundary between morphology and syntax. In view of its narrower distribution, higher morphological complexity, and potential to express non-iconic attenuative meanings, reduplication should be seen as typologically more marked than repetition (cf. also Kouwenberg & LaCharité 2003: 10ff).

The following figure represents the functions of reduplication and word-level repetition in Pichi. It shows that there is a functional overlap between the two types of reiteration with respect to dynamic verbs:

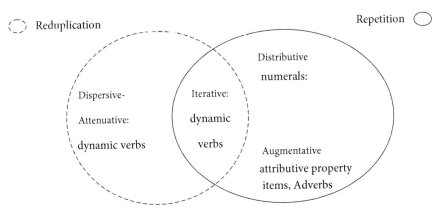

Figure 6.   Functions of reduplication and repetition in Pichi

A cursory glance at verbal reiteration in a cross-section of African languages of diverse genealogical affiliations, including potential substrate languages shows that in formal terms, Pichi reduplication falls squarely within a pattern that appears to be areal in nature. Further evidence for an areally induced patterning of Pichi reduplication through substrate and adstrate influence is provided by the comparison with two of its sister languages in the Caribbean. We can therefore conclude with some confidence, that Pichi reduplication, and by extension that of its African sister languages, appears to reflect a common, underlying areal current, both in terms of form and functions. It should be of interest to investigate how this pattern ties in with the distribution of headedness and the typology of word and constituent order across "West Africa". But an adequate treatment of this question would go well beyond the scope of this paper.

One question that still begs an answer is whether the pitch pattern found in the African AECs, the restriction to dynamic verbs, and its specific functions developed exclusively in contact with African adstrate languages in West Africa. Alternatively, these could be seen as substrate retentions from the formative period of the AEC proto-language. The West African type of reduplication would then have been reinforced and expanded in the African AECs through adstratal contact. The Caribbean AECs would have taken the opposite direction. The substrate features would have been progressively weakened through the isolation from West African languages, through contact with English and other non-African adstrates, and through independent development.

The close similarities between Pichi patterns of reduplication and the patterns found in the substrates and adstrates allow the conclusion that the emergence of this particular part of the grammar of the AECs was substrate-driven. Continuous contact with adstrate languages in the linguistic area of "West Africa" must have reinforced substrate patterns in the West African creoles. In the Caribbean creoles, the lack of adstrate contact and continuous contact with European superstrate languages has weakened the link with the linguistic area of "West Africa" and led to a partially idiosyncratic development of reduplication. I conclude that Pichi reduplication shows no signs of an exceptional iconicity, and that it is unsuitable for studying pristine features of the human language capacity. It appears then that reduplication and probably the entire functional domain of reiteration in the AECs reflects the contact trajectories of the individual languages. Due to various linguistic and non-linguistic factors, substrate features may dominate in one scenario as I have intended to show for Pichi reduplication. Sometimes the balance is more evenly distributed between substrates and a lexifier, as has been shown by Aboh & Smith (this volume) for reduplication in Saramaccan.

On a final note, I hope to have shown that the presence of genealogically related Afro-Caribbean English-lexifier Creoles on both sides of the Atlantic provides an ideal backdrop for studying individual features in very different contact settings. An approach informed by areal typology and language contact may allow us to disentangle genealogical inheritance, substrate retention, adstrate transfer and independent development in the AECs. Above all, it shows how regular language contact, more than anything else continues to shape the profiles of creole languages like Pichi, Jamaican Creole and Sranan.

Abbreviations

–	morpheme boundary	OBJ	object case
=	clitic morpheme boundary	PFV	perfective aspect marker
BE.AT/BE	existential-locative/identity copula	PL	plural
COP	copula	PLACE	place name
CPD	default low tone suprafix in compounds	POSS	possessive case
DEF	definite article	POT	potential mood marker
EMP	emphasis marker	PREP	associative preposition
FOC	focus marker	PRF	perfect marker
H	high tone	PROG	progressive aspect marker
HAB	habitual aspect marker	PST	past tense marker
INTJ	interjection	QUOT	quotative marker
IPFV	imperfective aspect marker	RED	reduplicant
L	low tone	SBJV	subjunctive marker
LOC	locative preposition	SG	singular
NAME	personal name	SP	sentence particle
NEG	negative particle	SUB	subordinator
NP	noun phrase	TMA	tense-mood-aspect
O	object	TOP	topic marker
ó	high tone	VP	verb phrase
ò	low tone	X	toneless syllable

References

Aboh, Enoch O. 2005a. Object shift, verb movement and verb reduplication. In *The Oxford Handbook of Comparative Syntax*, Guglielmo Cinque & Richard Kayne (eds), Oxford: OUP.

Adamson, Lilian & Smith, Norval. 1994. Sranan. In *Pidgins and Creoles. An Introduction* [Creole Language Library 15], Jacques Arends, Pieter Muysken & Norval Smith (eds), Amsterdam: John Benjamins.

Adamson, Lilian & Smith, Norval. 2003. Productive derivational predicate reduplication in Sranan. In *Twice as Meaningful: Reduplication in Pidgins, Creoles and Other Contact Languages* [Westminster Creolistic Series 8], Silvia Kouwenberg (ed.). London: Battlebridge.

Ameka, Felix K. 1991. Ewe: Its Grammatical Constructions and Illucutionary Devices. Ph.D. dissertation, Australian National University.

Anderson, John M. 1971. *An Essay Concerning Aspect: Some Considerations of a General Character Arising from the Abbé Darrigol's Analysis of the Basque Verb*. The Hague: Mouton.

Awoyale, James Oladuntoye Yiwola. 1974. Studies in the Syntax and Semantics of Yoruba Nominalizations. Ph.D. dissertation, University of Illinois at Urbana-Champaign.

Bakker, Peter, Daval-Markussen, Aymeric, Parkvall, Mikael & Plag, Ingo. 2011. Creoles are typologically distinct from non-creoles. *Journal of Pidgin and Creole Languages* 26: 5–42.

Bakker, Peter. 2003b. Pidgin inflectional morphology and its implications for creole morphology. In *The Morphology of Creole Languages*, Ingo Plag (ed.), 3–33. Dordrecht: Springer.

Bauer, Laurie. 1988. *Introducing Linguistic Morphology*. Edinburgh: EUP.

Bernabé, Jean. 1983. *Fondal-natal*. Paris: L'Harmattan.

den Besten, Hans & Veenstra, Tonjes. 1994. Fronting. In *Pidgins and Creoles. An Introduction* [Creole Language Library 15], Jacques Arends, Pieter Muysken & Norval Smith (eds.). Amsterdam: John Benjamins.

den Besten, Hans & Veenstra, Tonjes. 1994. Fronting. In *Pidgins and Creoles. An Introduction* [Creole Language Library 15], Jacques Arends, Pieter Muysken & Norval Smith (eds.), 303–315. Amsterdam: John Benjamins.

Bybee, Joan. 1985. *Morphology: A Study of the Relation between Meaning and Form* [Typological Studies in Language 9]. Amsterdam: John Benjamins.

Cadiot, Pierre & Nemo, François. 1997. Analytique des doubles caractérisations. *Sémiotiques* 13:123–145.

Christaller, Johann Gottlieb. 1964. *A Grammar of the Asante and Fante Language Called Tshi, Based on the Akuapem Dialect with Reference to the Other (Akan and Fante) dialects*. Reprint of 1875 edition. Farnborough: Gregg Press.

Curtin, Philip De Armind. 1969. *The Atlantic Slave Trade: A Census*. Madison WI: University of Wisconsin Press.

Cusic, David D. 1981. Verbal Plurality and Aspect. Ph.D. dissertation, Stanford University.

Devonish, Hubert. 1989. *Talking in Tones: A Study of Tone in Afro-European Creole Languages*. Kingston: Caribbean Academic Publications.

Faraclas, Nicholas G. 1987. Creolization and the tense-aspect-modality system of Nigerian Pidgin. *Journal of African Languages and Linguistics* 3(2):77–97.

Faraclas, Nicholas G. 1996. *Nigerian Pidgin*. London: Routledge.

Fyfe, Christopher. 1962. *A History of Sierra Leone*. Oxford: OUP.

Fyle, Clifford & Jones, Eldred Durosimi. 1980. *A Krio-English Dictionary*. Oxford: OUP.

Ghomeshi, Jila, Jackendoff, Ray, Rosen, Nicole & Russell, Kevin. 2004. Contrastive focus reduplication in English. *Natural Language & Linguistic Theory* 22:307–357.

Gooden, Shelome. 2003b. Reduplication in Jamaican Creole: Semantic functions and prosodic constraints. In *Twice as Meaningful: Reduplication in Pidgins, Creoles and Other Contact Languages* [Westminster Creolistic Series 8], Silvia Kouwenberg (ed.). London: Battlebridge.

Gooden, Shelome. 2007. Morphophonological properties of pitch accents in Jamaican Creole reduplication. In *Synchronic and Diachronic Perspectives on Contact Languages* [Creole Language Library 32], Magnus Huber & Viveka Velupillai (eds), 67–90. Amsterdam: John Benjamins.

Güldemann, Tom. 2008. The Macro-Sudan belt. In *A Linguistic Geography of Africa*, Bernd Heine & Derek Nurse (eds), Cambridge: CUP.

Heath, Jeffrey. 2008. *A Grammar of Jamsay*. Berlin: Mouton de Gruyter.

Heine, Bernd, Claudi, Ulrike & Hünnemeyer, Friederike (eds). 1991. *Grammaticalization: A Conceptual Framework*. Chicago IL: Chicago University Press.

Horn, Laurence R. 1993. Economy and redundancy in a dualistic model of natural language. *Yearbook of the Linguistic Association of Finland*, 33–72.

Huber, Magnus. 1999. *Ghanaian Pidgin English in its West African Context* [Varieties of English around the World G24]. Amsterdam: John Benjamins.

Huber, Magnus. 2003. Verbal reduplication in Ghanaian Pidgin English: Origins, forms and functions. In *Twice as Meaningful: Reduplication in Pidgins, Creoles and Other Contact Languages* [Westminster Creolistic Series 8], Silvia Kouwenberg (ed.), London: Battlebridge.

Hutchison, John P. 1981. *A Reference Grammar of the Kanuri Language*. Madison WI: African studies program, University of Wisconsin.

Hyman, Larry M. & Magaji, Daniel J. 1970. *Essentials of Gwari Grammar*. Ibadan: Institute of African Studies.

Jones, Frederick C.V. 1990. Reduplication and reiteration in Krio. In *Arbeiten zur deskriptiven und theoretischen Linguistik*, Manfred Kohrt & Klaus Robering (eds), 119–29. Berlin: Institut für Linguistik, TU Berlin.

Jungraithmayer, Herrmann. 1980. Kontake zwischen Adamawa-Ubangi- und Tschad-Sprachen: Zur Übertragung grammatischer Systeme. *Zeitschrift der Deutschen Morgenländischen Gesellschaft* 130: 70–85.

Kaufman, Elaine Marlowe. 1968. Ibibio Grammar. Ph.D. dissertation, University of California Berkeley.

Koopman, Hilda 1984. *The Syntax of Verbs: From Verb Movement Rules in the Kru Language to Universal Grammar*. Dordrecht: Foris.

Kouwenberg, Silvia & LaCharité, Darlene. 2003. The meanings of 'more of the same'. In *Twice as Meaningful: Reduplication in Pidgins, Creoles and Other Contact Languages* [Westminster Creolistic Series 8], Silvia Kouwenberg (ed.), London: Battlebridge.

Kouwenberg, Silvia & LaCharité, Darlene. 2004. Echoes of Africa: Reduplication in Caribbean creoles and Niger-Congo languages. *Journal of Pidgin and Creole Languages* 19(2): 285–331.

Kouwenberg, Silvia, LaCharité, Darlene & Gooden, Shelome. 2003. An overview of Jamaican reduplication. In *Twice as Meaningful: Reduplication in Pidgins, Creoles and Other Contact Languages* [Westminster Creolistic Series 8], Silvia Kouwenberg (ed.). London: Battlebridge.

Kropp Dakubu, M. Esther. (ed.). 1999. *Ga-English Dictionary*. Accra: Language Centre, University of Ghana.

Lakoff, George & Johnson, Mark. 1980. *Metaphors we Live by*. Chicago IL: University of Chicago Press.

Larson, R. & Lefebvre, Claire. 1991. Predicate clefting in Haitian Creole. *NELS* 21: 247–261.

Marfo, Charles Ofosu. 2005. Aspects of Akan Grammar and the Phonology-syntax Interface. Ph.D. dissertation, University of Hong Kong.

Migge, Bettina. 2003. The origin of predicate reduplication in Eastern Surinam Maroon Creole. In *Twice as Meaningful: Reduplication in Pidgins, Creoles and Other Contact Languages* [Westminster Creolistic Series 8], Silvia Kouwenberg (ed.), London: Battlebridge.

Morse, Mary Lynn Alice. 1976. A Sketch of the Phonology and Morphology of Bobo (Upper Volta). Ph.D. dissertation, New York University.

Ofori, Seth Antwi. 2006. Topics in Akan Grammar. Ph.D. dissertation, University of Bloomington.

Parkvall, Mikael. 2000. *Out of Africa. African influences in Atlantic Creoles*. London: Battlebridge.

Rodney, Walter. 1975. *Afrika, die Geschichte einer Unterwicklung*. Berlin: Klaus Wagenbach.

Thalmann, Peter. 1987. Eléments de grammaire Kroumen Tépo: Parler kru de la Côte d'Ivoire. Ph.D. dissertation, Université de Paris VII.

Tsunoda, Tasaku. 1985. Remarks on transitivity. *Journal of Linguistics* 21: 385–396.

Umenjoh Andoumbene, Florence. 1997. Reduplication in Ngie. MA thesis, University of Yaoundé.

Van Everbroeck, René. 1985. *Maloba ma lokóta: Lingála.*: Kinshasa: Epiphanie

Westermann, Diedrich. 1911. *Die Sudansprachen: Eine sprachvergleichende Studie* [Abhandlungen des Hamburgischen Kolonialinstituts 3]. Hamburg: L. Friederichsen.

Wolff, H. Ekkehard & Gerhardt, Ludwig. 1977. Interferenzen zwischen Benue-Kongo und Tschadsprachen. *Zeitschrift der Deutschen Morgenländischen Gesellschaft* 3:1518–43.

Yakpo, Kofi. 2009a. Complexity revisited: Pichi (Equatorial Guinea) and Spanish in contact. In *Simplicity and complexity in Creoles and Pidgins*, Nick Faraclas & Thomas Klein (eds) London: Battlebridge.

Yakpo, Kofi. 2009b. A grammar of Pichi. Ph.D. dissertation, Radboud University Nijmegen.

Subject index

Language index

.